PATHWAYS TO SOCIAL CLASS

# Pathways to Social Class

## A QUALITATIVE APPROACH TO SOCIAL MOBILITY

DANIEL BERTAUX

and

PAUL THOMPSON

*with contributions by*

RUDOLF ANDORKA
GIOVANNI CONTINI
MIKE SAVAGE

ISABELLE BERTAUX-WIAME
BRIAN ELLIOTT
DAVID VINCENT

CLARENDON PRESS · OXFORD
1997

Oxford University Press, Great Clarendon Street, Oxford OX2 6DP
Oxford New York
Athens Auckland Bangkok Bogota Bombay
Buenos Aires Calcutta Cape Town Dar es Salaam
Delhi Florence Hong Kong Istanbul Karachi
Kuala Lumpur Madras Madrid Melbourne
Mexico City Nairobi Paris Singapore
Taipei Tokyo Toronto
and associated companies in
Berlin Ibadan

Oxford is a trade mark of Oxford University Press

Published in the United States by
Oxford University Press Inc., New York

© The several contributors, 1997

All rights reserved. No part of this publication may be reproduced, stored in a retrieval system, or transmitted, in any form or by any means, without the prior permission in writing of Oxford University Press. Within the UK, exceptions are allowed in respect of any fair dealing for the purpose of research or private study, or criticism or review, as permitted under the Copyright, Designs and Patents Act, 1988, or in the case of reprographic reproduction in accordance with the terms of the licences issued by the Copyright Licensing Agency. Enquiries concerning reproduction outside these terms and in other countries should be sent to the Rights Department, Oxford University Press, at the address above

British Library Cataloguing in Publication Data
Data available

Library of Congress Cataloging in Publication Data
Bertaux, Daniel.
Pathways to social class: a qualitative approach to social mobility/Daniel Bertaux and Paul Thompson; with contributions by Rudolf Ankora ... [et al.].
Includes bibliographical references (p.   ) and index.
1. Social classes.  2. Social mobility.  I. Thompson, Paul Richard, 1935– .  II. Title.
HT611.B468  1996  305.5—dc20  96-26405
ISBN 0-19-827931-0

1 3 5 7 9 10 8 6 4 2

Typeset by Best-set Typesetter Ltd., Hong Kong
Printed in Great Britain by
Biddles Ltd, Guildford and King's Lynn

# CONTENTS

*List of Figures* vii
*Notes on the Contributors* viii

1. Introduction  
   DANIEL BERTAUX AND  
   PAUL THOMPSON  1

2. Women, Men, and Transgenerational Family  
   Influences in Social Mobility  
   PAUL THOMPSON  32

3. Heritage and its Lineage: A Case History of  
   Transmission and Social Mobility over  
   Five Generations  
   DANIEL BERTAUX AND  
   ISABELLE BERTAUX-WIAME  62

4. Shadow and Reality in Occupational History:  
   Britain in the First Half of the Twentieth Century  
   DAVID VINCENT  98

5. The Familial Meaning of Housing in Social  
   Rootedness and Mobility: Britain and France  
   ISABELLE BERTAUX-WIAME AND  
   PAUL THOMPSON  124

6. The Local World View: Social Change and Memory  
   in Three Tuscan Communes  
   GIOVANNI CONTINI  183

7. Migration, Mobility, and Social Process: Scottish  
   Migrants in Canada  
   BRIAN ELLIOTT  198

8. Transmission in Extreme Situations: Russian Families  
   Expropriated by the October Revolution  
   DANIEL BERTAUX  230

9. Social Mobility in Hungary since the Second
   World War: Interpretations through Surveys
   and through Families Histories                    259
   RUDOLF ANDORKA

10. Social Mobility and the Survey Method:
    A Critical Analysis                              299
    MIKE SAVAGE

*Index*                                              327

# LIST OF FIGURES

| | | |
|---|---|---|
| 3.1. | Social Genealogy of the Terrenoire Lineage | 68 |
| 9.1. | Social Genealogy of the Tiller Family | 265 |
| 9.2a. | Social Genealogy of the Smith Family | 271 |
| 9.2b. | Social Genealogy of the Smith Family | 272 |
| 9.3. | Social Genealogy of the Chester Family | 282 |
| 9.4a. | Social Genealogy of the Hawk Family | 287 |
| 9.4b. | Social Genealogy of the Hawk Family | 288 |

# NOTES ON THE CONTRIBUTORS

DANIEL BERTAUX is Directeur de recherche at the Centre d'Étude des Mouvements Sociaux of the CNRS and EHESS in Paris. His many publications on social mobility and on life stories include: *Destins personnels et structure de classe* and *Biography and Society*.

PAUL THOMPSON is Research Professor in Sociology at the University of Essex. His books include: *The Edwardians, The Voice of the Past, I Don't Feel Old*, and *The Myths We Live By*. He is co-editor with Daniel Bertaux of *Between Generations: Family Models, Myths and Memories*.

ISABELLE BERTAUX-WIAME is a researcher in sociology at Travail et Mobilités, University of Paris X, and has written especially on families, mobility, and housing.

DAVID VINCENT is Professor of Social History and Deputy Vice-Chancellor at Keele University. His many publications on life histories and popular culture include: *Bread, Knowledge and Freedom* and *Literacy and Popular Culture*. He is currently researching on the making of the modern career.

GIOVANNI CONTINI was formerly a research fellow at King's College, Cambridge, studying shop-floor bargaining, and is now responsible for the audio-visual archives of Tuscany. His publications include books on oral history and on the Galileo engineering factory in Florence.

BRIAN ELLIOTT is Professor of Sociology at the University of British Columbia. His main publications are: *The Petite Bourgeoisie, The City: Patterns of Domination and Conflict*, and *Property and Power in a City*. He is currently writing on migration and social mobility.

## Notes on the Contributors

RUDOLF ANDORKA researched and wrote on demography and social mobility and for many years was head of the Statistical Institute in Budapest. He then became Professor of Sociology at the University for Economic Sciences, where he is now Rector. His work in English includes: *Socio-occupational Mobility in Hungary and Poland* and *The Rich and Poor: Social Differentiation in Hungary*.

MIKE SAVAGE is Professor of Sociology at the University of Manchester. His research interests lie in social stratification and historical sociology. His books include: *Social Change and the Middle Classes, Property, Bureaucracy and Culture: Middle Class Formation in Contemporary Britain,* and *Gender, Careers and Organisations*.

# 1

# Introduction

DANIEL BERTAUX AND PAUL THOMPSON

Behind this book lies a dream, which we have shared for many years: a dream of a renewed study of social mobility rising to grapple with the astonishing diversity and complexity of its fundamental theme. We are convinced that such a renewal must depend upon a broadening of methodological and theoretical perspectives. The closely linked case studies which we present here are demonstrations of the richness of insights which new approaches to social mobility can bring.

Social mobility processes are integral to the very metabolism and core regulation of societies, both to their continuity and change over time. It is through such processes that basic social structures of class, status, and situs (branches of industry) are reproduced or transformed, emerge or disappear; that societies themselves move forward, consolidate or splinter, that institutions and enterprises recruit, that families launch their children, that individuals imagine and seek personal fulfilment in their lives. These processes are complex because they operate within unstable frameworks, and because they are intrinsically reflexive. All these levels interact between each other and none of them are constant. The incessant thrust of technological and economic change continually creates new types of work and opportunity in some places, while wiping out entire industries and ways of life in others. Just as marriages break and firms go bankrupt, so whole political societies may be recast or split through revolutions, wars, or the dissolution of empires. Individuals swim in waters now benign, now turbulent. Some may flourish in an inherited family niche, while others will starve in the same way. Against those who succeed or fail through transmission, we need to set those who choose to migrate in search of a better life, those who move to escape an economic trap, or those driven to adapt by the turmoil of revolution, fleeing from persecution or war, and death.

Change originates not only from above, but equally from below, through the initiatives of masses of people. Through having fewer children or more, or through moving, voting with their feet, they can transform the structures of social space or demography.[1] At any given moment the range of possibilities for a given social group, or family, or individual, are limited: shaped negatively by restrictions such as lack of economic or cultural resources but also by group prejudice and privilege, positively by the opportunities provided by the local and national economy, access to education, means of travel and social imagination. Most people take the structure they see as given and circulate within it, filling a space; but a sufficient minority contribute to the momentum of change by either creating new spaces within the old structures, or moving. The changing roles of women and men, the world-wide currents of emigration and immigration, are all witnesses to the widely dispersed human drive towards a better life. And in the development of this drive, the engine of social change and individual fulfilment—or disappointment—the primary location of generation and transmission lies within families, which provide the social and emotional launch pads for individual take-off.[2]

At all social levels—from politics and economics to local and family relationships—social competition and rivalry intertwine with mutuality and obligation. And because all these levels interlock and interact and yet are propelled by their own semi-independent logic, the outcomes must always be uncertain. Equally important, the strategies which succeed in a particular historical time and social context cannot be assured to work in another. Individuals, families, and organizations struggle after ways of surviving or succeeding in social worlds which are always evolving: to create limited spheres of order in the perpetual shadow of turbulence or even chaos. This fundamental instability of the human social universe means that laws of social mobility would themselves be timebound illusions. The understandings which we can reach of the social meanings and experiences of mobility, and the complexity of processes which underlie it, cannot pretend to universality: their validity depends upon how clearly they reflect their historical moment.

# Introduction

## THE CLASSICS OF SOCIOLOGY

If we look back to the classic texts of the founding fathers of sociology, it is immediately evident that within the broad canvasses which they drew, most of them saw the characterization of social mobility processes, whether of individuals or whole groups in competition, as crucial to understanding the evolution of societies.

Thus when de Tocqueville depicted early 19th-century American society, he highlighted its lack of an aristocratic tradition on the European model, and how its heavy emphasis on equality of opportunity and equity in reward made for a special dynamism, by allowing its most energetic citizens to win prosperity unchecked by entrenched privileges. For him individualism and the aspiration to upward mobility were at the centre of the American cultural model, which he rightly perceived as different from the European ones. In the same spirit, when de Tocqueville compared the fates of England and France at the end of the 18th century, he pointed to the openness of the English aristocracy, so that successful commoners could readily be co-opted to its ranks through ennoblement, thus greatly reducing the chances of social revolution, in contrast to the rigidity of the French aristocracy which prepared the ground for the French revolution.[3] For Pareto too the relative openness of the upper classes was a central issue. He devoted his main book to the battling for social power between élites and counter-élites, and concluded that a core process in European societies was the 'circulation of elites'.[4]

The same theme fascinated Sorokin, whose magnificently ambitious *Social Mobility* is the last and most explicitly titled of these classic texts. It centres on the recurrent competition between social groups, but again especially between élites and counter-élites. Sorokin draws up his interpretations through examining a remarkably wide range of historical cases, from the skill of India's Brahmins in holding on to their power through centuries to the less lucky fates of some of the European aristocracies, including that of Russia, whose catastrophic demise and fall he himself witnessed in 1917.[5]

Durkheim, whose social theory was dominated by a conservative sense of the need for social order and integration, tended to view social mobility as a disruptive rather than an adaptive process.[6]

Subsequently Parsons similarly focused on the social mechanisms of systemic integration, continuity and stability rather than change, and he also showed too little sense of the historical dimension. On the other hand, in terms of understanding the connections between different social levels, and especially the importance of the institution of the family, his contribution was important and far-sighted.[7]

The opposite view was of course taken by Marx, who saw social conflict as the principal dynamic of change. Yet when re-examined more closely, his perspective has more in common with the other founding sociologists than might be first assumed. For if there is a vital thread connecting these earlier classic pieces of sociological thinking, it is certainly not simply social mobility in the narrower sense of individual movement which the term is widely taken to imply today. The issue can be better characterized as the continual process of 'generalised social competition' through which individuals, families, and social groups all fight for their share of resources and their spot in the sun. For instance the proletarian revolution for which Marx called would have resulted in a clear and dramatic process of collective social mobility, upwards for the proletariat, downwards for the bourgeoisie: and it is the anticipation of such fates that fuelled the dynamic of class struggle—especially the constant struggle of the capitalist class against the formation of the proletariat into a class for itself.[8]

Seen in this way, Marx's thinking confronts many of the same issues. For instance he was well aware of the openness of American society, and indeed foresaw the possibility that through a combination of continuing immigration, followed by upward mobility often through small independent enterprise, the American working class, even if swelling in numbers, might fail to consolidate into a class on European lines, because too few families stayed in it for long enough. A working class with such a fluidity was inimical to solidarity.[9]

Driven by close observation to a reluctant admiration of the English bourgeoisie's entrepreneurial spirit and the French bourgeoisie's political courage, Marx found much less to admire in the German middle ranks which he found wanting in both economic initiative and political audacity. Weber, however, was much less pessimistic about them. His *The Protestant Ethic and the Spirit of Capitalism* is a brilliant case study of how cultural values contributed crucially to the historic upward mobility of Calvinists and other Protestant groups as economically successful entrepreneurs. Weber also shared with Simmel—in his *Philosophy of Money*—an understanding of the emergence of a modern urban society reshaped by markets, creating a free-for-all space in which individuals, bringing initially drastically unequal sets of resources and thus of life chances, nevertheless competed for goods and money, for social recognition and political power. Both Weber and Simmel sought to identify the games and rules of this generalized competition, whose outcome was and still is the sharply differentiated life trajectories which mark out mobility.[10]

Social mobility processes in the broader sense were thus a concern in one way or another of all the founding fathers of sociology. Most of them also showed a clear understanding of the importance of specific historical contexts. It is true that too many of them tried to push their interpretations into social equivalents of natural laws. But above all, for us their strength is the breadth and diversity of perspective within which they situated their discussions of social competition and mobility: and in this they exemplify the broader spirit in which social mobility can still be studied.

## THE SURVEY PARADIGM

Whereas the early classics of sociology set the social-historical processes of social mobility and social dynamics at the heart of their thinking, today social mobility research has become a highly specialized and technical field. Over the last forty years it has been entirely reshaped by the adoption and development of the survey as its almost exclusive method. Increasingly, as its methodological sophistication has intensified, social mobility research has narrowed its interests to hypotheses which a survey can test, at the price of cutting itself off from the observation of other dimensions of mobility processes and from the development of sociological and historical thinking as a whole.

The attraction of the survey for the study of social mobility is obvious. It is indeed an excellent tool for describing statistically the relative sizes of human flows between social classes or strata. The patterns of these intergenerational flows show the enormous impact of economic development (structural mobility) and the relatively low level of downward mobility flows. These patterns can also be tested against an ideal society of equal opportunity, to provide a mathematical measure of social justice.[11] They can also be compared across nations, as Goldthorpe and Erikson have done with great mastery in *The Constant Flux*.[12] It is also possible to test, across large numbers of individual cases, whether for example a mother's or father's occupation or education or a son's own education or first job are likely, *on average*, to weigh more or less in the son's main occupation.[13] Quantitative description and testing clearly has a crucial role in social mobility research.

The problems start when the survey, instead of being conceived as one way of looking at the flows of men and women in social space, comes to be regarded as the *only* scientific approach to the study of social mobility processes. For the technical requirements of the survey tend to dictate substantive choices and narrow down the range of observed phenomena—as for example in the repeated focus on men rather than women. There is far more to social mobility processes than is ever likely to catch the unaided survey eye, as we believe this book demonstrates. Indeed at their narrowest, statistical studies of social mobility resemble the observation of a carnival through a keyhole.

To some extent the limitations of the survey perspective are ascribable to a narrowness of theoretical perspective, for stratification has been the only major theoretical field with which mobility research normally interacts. But our belief is that the difficulty lies with the intrinsic logic of the method itself as much as with its theoretical orientation. Certainly, as Mike Savage argues in Chapter 10, the survey method can and should be modified in important respects; and there are very few aspects of human life which are absolutely out of range of the survey. But the survey method is best used to do what it can do most efficiently, rather than in aiming at reducing other methods, with different strengths, to its own ways of seeing. It is condemned to remain blind to core aspects of the very processes which it aims to investigate; which is why the approach of case study—which, conversely, also has its own built-in limits—is vital for the full development of the field.

The strength of the survey method derives from its ability to describe social phenomena in terms of numbers, and to generalize its empirical findings to the whole population which it investigates through the technique of the representative sample of individuals. From this sample each interviewee must answer to the same basic list of closed questions. The built-in limitations which ensue are characteristic weaknesses of the survey method: the obverse side of these same strengths.[14]

One basic corollary of analysing through numbers is that argument and description become dominated by the language of variables, and give little space to matters which cannot be adequately conveyed through that language. Thus life stories show the centrality of subjective perceptions and evaluations in shaping the life choices. They are redolent with descriptions of feeling and experience of relationships with significant others, with interpretations of turning-points, with influences which were rejected rather than followed, with dreams of lives that might have been. They also reveal the crucial importance of local contexts, local structures of opportunities, and local games of competition. The essential point is not whether or not some of these matters are quantifiable, but that they are much more clearly expressed in words. The language of words is infinitely vaster, richer, and more capable of subtler, particular variation; while the attraction of mathematics is precisely in its simplifying abstraction. The strength of one cannot be reduced to the strength of the other: they flourish best in their own ways, distinct but complementary.

Another weakness of the survey approach to social mobility research derives from the unit of observation: the randomly-chosen individual, whom the analysis tends to treat as an isolate. Yet individuals are embedded within family, occupational, and local contexts, and mobility is as much a matter of family praxis as individual agency, for it is families which produce and rear individuals with specific characteristics and social skills, endowing them with their original moral and psychic energy and with economic, cultural, and relational resources. Equally, as Schumpeter once remarked, social—as opposed to occupational—status is primarily carried by families rather than by individuals.[15]

It would of course be possible for surveys to base their samples on households or—as in our own Anglo-French research[16]—on the core kin of families. This has the immediate advantage of restoring women to full view, not only as workers but as sisters, spouses, mothers, aunts, and grandmothers shaping and influencing the lives of their kin. But in order fully to grasp the processes and relationships underlying the pathways of the individual members of each kinship group, it becomes necessary to build up an in-depth case history of each family: and this runs in direct contradiction with the survey's basic requirement to standardize the data.

On top of this, social mobility surveys are founded not only on individuals, but on individuals expected to have occupations, because occupations are readily classified numerically. Until very recently this meant men only: a severe limitation which we discuss at length in Chapter 2. But defining an individual's status by occupation alone has other equally serious consequences. It focuses the study on the lifetime career at work, which has been a predominantly male view of mobility, even if possibly less so today. And in terms of occupations alone, the social mobility survey is bound to find the positions of the self-employed, the unemployed, the housewife, and the retired, difficult to grasp. There is an additional difficulty with élites, that their numbers are impractically small to study as part of a general survey: although clearly the extent to which they are open or closed is crucial to understanding social mobility in any society. At the other end of the spectrum, because of falling interview response rates it is in any case increasingly difficult to register the poorest, whose lives have fallen apart, and the trajectories of those who die early are inevitably missing. So too are those of emigrants from the society; while immigrants can again often be only very crudely categorized in terms of origin. Effectively the demands of the random sample predicate as the basic unit of analysis a type of long-term employed man who, with the spread of unemployment and part-time casual work, seems increasingly a symbol of a passing historical era.[17]

In most social mobility research the complexity of social mobility patterns are also smothered over by focusing on the single comparison between father's main occupation in the past and son's occupation at the present. Both the time period and definition of the father's occupation are open to doubt, and it must also be uncertain whether the son has reached his main occupation, or will move upward or downward in the future. Work histories, by contrast, not only show that the patterns of movement are indeed more elaborate, but provide the material from which mobility processes can be analysed. Yet although this criticism has been recognized by the leading mobility survey researchers, the collection and analysis of sets of (standardized) work histories is only beginning.[18] Besides, as we shall see below in the example of Nicole-Drancourt's research, it seems that the necessity to standardize work histories prevents the identification of their contrasted inner logics. This unconscious pressure from the technical requirements of the sample to focus on an ideal type of mobility through long-term employment is further reinforced by the strait-jacket which the need for standardization imposes on the interview itself. The questions must be predetermined, so that there is no space for unexpected variety; and they have to be designed to apply as far as possible to every interviewee. Thus typically the same closed questions will be posed to an unskilled worker and a businessman, to a farmer, a civil servant, or a manager in private enterprise—to mention only male cases. Yet these different occupations do not share life chances or careers with the same kinds of logic: the path of a dependent employee on the secondary labour market is not shaped in the same way as that of the self-employed on the stepping-stones to economic accumulation; the manager in private enterprise does not advance through the same criteria as the civil servant in local or national government. The one feature which they all have in common is some initial educational achievement, which is readily measurable, and which influences their starting-place in the labour market: and hence the focus of surveys on education. But this in itself is hardly enough to explain the transition from education into work, and certainly not to grasp the other processes shaping achievement within given occupations. If we look, for example, at small business owners, we could hardly explain the chances of their success, survival, or failure through their earlier educational qualifications. We would need to know much more specifically what counts in their own world, especially if they are immigrants.

These dangers are made worse by the way in which the conversion of the words spoken in the questionnaire's interview into quantifiable formulae suppresses the interviewee's attempts at describing the complexities of her/his situation. While in-depth life historians have wrestled with the problems of the limitations, malleability, and subjectivity of memory which full interview texts present, social mobility researchers have swept such problems under the carpet.[19] In fact, even in terms of occupational level there are striking differences between contemporary statistics based on interviews with employees and employers for the same industries, with employees reporting much higher levels of skills.[20] When the time dimension inherent in memory of earlier occupations is added, it is clear that social mobility data are likely to incorporate their own degree of idealization: yet there has been scant recognition of this issue.

If memory is one of the unseen ghosts haunting the social mobility table, history itself is another. Each survey operates from a given moment in time, and life chances differ greatly in the same place in different times: as Tamara Hareven's study of a New England mill town, *Family Time and Industrial Time*, so vividly demonstrates.[21] There is a sense too in which the survey is premissed on an unmentioned history of nation-wide cultural homogenization through the penetration of markets right through the geographical space, internal migrations, mass education, mass consumption, and mass culture.[22] It is even possible to infer from the rigid applications of the same measures between countries with sharply different cultures and economies that the essentials of this historic homogenization are now assumed to be world-wide. But global marketization has certainly not created world-wide social homogeneity: indeed, in terms of living standards alone, it seems on the contrary to work towards exaggerating difference. In the real world, even nearby communities—as we shall see from our Tuscan examples in Chapter 6—can have very different mobility patterns. Helmut Kaeble concluded from his comparative study of social mobility in Europe and America that 'the variety between American cities is so extensive that no consistent American pattern emerges', and the variety in Europe was almost as striking.[23] If father–son occupational relationships can be shown to have similar statistical patterns in France and the former Soviet Union, it does not mean that the same processes underlie the figures. And if the tables for, say, Britain and Japan turn out to be closely similar, we would be a good deal wiser to assume that the tables are missing something vital rather than concluding that the processes of mobility in the two societies are essentially identical.

The technical logic of the survey, in short, randomizes and standardizes at a heavy cost, pressing the mobility researcher to wrest individuals from their family and their local context, to pass over their own descriptions, interpretations, and explanations of their experience and actions, to suppress problems of memory and subjectivity, to minimize the effects of spatial social difference and movement, to focus on occupation as the sum of social status, and to further marginalize those on the margins of the economy. In so doing, it distances itself from issues which are potentially of prime interest for sociological analysis. To point to these built-in limitations does not mean at all that survey research is basically flawed: it is obviously the very best tool to achieve statistical description; but it cannot do everything.

There are indeed imaginable projects which the survey method alone could not possibly study fully. If, for example, we wanted to examine the Jews driven to the holocaust extermination camps in terms of mobility, we could only interview the small minority who survived; and in understanding what they did after the camps, how they migrated and found their feet in new societies, and the kinds of energy which they transmitted to their children, we would need to hear their harrowing experiences, know of their continuing nightmares, sense the ambivalence of their need to transmit and the complex quality of relationships in survivor families. All this would be intrinsic to the mobility processes of the group. It could only be grasped by listening acutely to words.

The repertoire of methods of observations must be enlarged so as to enable sociologists to observe all kinds of relevant processes, and not only those that a survey can record.

## ALTERNATIVE APPROACHES

The alternative approaches presented in this book depend on the use of case studies of families or communities. We have tested them extensively over the years and we believe they possess considerable potentialities for the renewal of research on social mobility processes.

The case study approach can be applied to a wide range of 'objects': we include here one chapter which compares three different local communities, another one studying the mobility of migrants, and a third on dreams of careers which never happened; others would have been possible, focusing, for example, on institutions actively shaping destinies, what Sorokin referred to as 'testing, selecting, and distributing agencies'. Above all, however, we have here case studies of families in a transgenerational perspective. (By 'families' we do not, of course, mean the narrow nuclear family, but cross-generational kin networks of any shape linked by descent or marriage.) This is because we see a family's relationships and inner dynamics as crucial in orienting the lives of its members; it mediates the impact on individuals of social class, schools and education, housing, migration, and labour markets, and therefore also provides an especially effective viewing-point for observing their interaction. Working with family histories, we have indeed often realized how the distance between micro and macro social phenomena is much shorter than was usually thought until the gap began to be narrowed by Giddens's effort to incorporate the self and intimacy as elements in social structures.[24]

While the case study approach enables us readily to encompass underlying processes and the particularity of contexts which the survey discards from its field of observation, such an intensive approach cannot at the same time claim to statistical representativity. The road to generalization will therefore be a different one, although—especially if we bear in mind how few of the earlier classics used statistics—not necessarily less fruitful. Against the well-entrenched dogmas of the scientistic paradigm, let us simply recall that in the natural sciences the principal means for establishing causality is the controlled experiment, rather than the survey based on a representative sample. The experiment is one of the key instruments of psychology too, but it is (fortunately) impracticable for other social scientists. In some ways the comparative case histories used in both economics and sociology have often been seen as substituting for the lack of controlled experiment. Besides, in contrast to most scientific experimentation, the objects of investigation can themselves speak about why they behave as they do. As Weber had well understood, the subjective dimension of the socio-historical world, which underlies not only perceptions and representations but also agency, needs to be seized and utilized. While we cannot expect ordinary men and women to offer us full-blown sociological explanations of their behaviour, they are also certainly not cultural dopes—and indeed the poorer they are the shrewder they need to become to survive at all. We see their interpretations as vital first steps to our own: first- and second-order hermeneutics respectively. They are the best short cut towards grasping the local rules of the games of generalized competition.

The primary goal of the case study approach is not to prove, but to make sense of the phenomena by proposing interpretations.

Case studies undoubtedly allow us to develop rich hypotheses about mobility processes; thus they are in harmony both with the classics of sociology, and with its contemporary 'interpretive turn'.[25]

Interpretations are not mere speculations; they must be grounded in observations. But, as any historian knows well, any interpretation will include wider hypotheses that cannot be directly tested; rather it is by confronting various interpretations about one and the same set of socio-historical phenomena that the best interpretations stand out, and that the others get discarded.

Our approach in constructing case histories is to collect life stories. For us the crucial features of the life-story method are that the interviews are in-depth, no more than semi-structured, allowing informants full room to convey their own experience and views; and that the analysis is based on the interview text. It is important to distinguish this method from that of the life-history or event-history questionnaire which has been used in some recent surveys. While this is certainly an interesting development which opens up new possibilities for mutually complementary work, the two types of interview are not substitutable.

In this volume we use life stories as evidence of facts (situations, contexts, conducts) along with perceptions and evaluations. Since the mid-1970s, the 'life-story approach' has developed fast in many countries, most notably France, England, Germany, and Italy. The bibliographies of review papers now comprise hundreds of references. Within this whole literature one can discover two main orientations. The first approach, particularly strong in Germany, focuses primarily on the subjective meanings that a particular person gives to her/his past and present life; it is almost a form of social psychology. The second, which is the approach used by most of the researchers in this volume, takes interviewees as informants about the various contexts which shaped their life: thus they are used as sources to reveal what happened to the interviewee, how and why it happened, what he/she felt about it, and how he/she reacted to it or 'proacted' to realize his/her projects. This orientation thus aims at gathering both factual and interpretative information, in the same way that ethnographers learn about a micro-culture by asking their informants not only to explain but also to describe it as factually as possible.

This second orientation has proved its validity and its ability to generalize, provided enough testimonies are collected and confronted, provided also that 'negative cases' potentially disproving the researcher's emerging interpretation have been actively searched for. When new testimonies merely confirm such interpretations, through recurrence of descriptions of the same situations, actions, relationships, and processes, it may be taken that the point of saturation has been reached, thus validating the interpretation. It is through such a process that, for instance, the hidden mechanisms and dynamics that make for the survival of the artisanal bakery in France have been discovered: eighty life stories with bakery workers, bakers and bakers' wives were enough to grasp the inner logics of a branch of industry which employs 200,000 persons.[26]

Let us take another example, which concerns entry into the labour markets. The great difficulties that young people, especially those with low credentials, have to find stable jobs in a context of high unemployment and underemployment have generated in France as elsewhere a flow of statistical studies, transversal at first and later on longitudinal, designed so as to map up the occupational careers of individuals. But these studies remain unable to explain what distinguishes those young men and women that prove able to stay employed and those who fail to do so: neither the structural approaches, which focus on the characteristics of labour markets (supply of jobs), nor the strategic ones, which focus on the objective characteristics of young people (credentials, previous job history) succeed in identifying causal processes which could explain the observed patterns. Survey data analysis failed to discover discriminating background variables to explain why some of these young people could find jobs and stay employed—usually through high turnover—most of the time, while others experienced long periods of unemployment.

Aware of this failure, the sociologist Nicole-Drancourt has designed a research project through which, in the French provincial town of Chalon-sur-Saône, the occupational trajectories of 115 young people aged 30, who had all left the school system with low credentials more than ten years earlier, were first recorded with life-history questionnaires, and a subsample of 52 were then reinterviewed at length.[27] The resulting in-depth life stories led to the identification of a specific logic, generated through the interactions of local job opportunities, gender, the differing habitus of young people, and their varying paces of maturation into adulthood.

Four distinct groups stand out. First, a strong minority of the young women are eager to work as soon as they leave school, and neither early pregnancies nor initially poor jobs seem able to deter them from looking for employment. They tend to choose male partners with lower levels of credentials and skills, who will therefore be unable to force them to stay at home after childbirth—practically all these women had become mothers by the age of 20. They move from one job to another, get training on the job, learn the rules of the place, and eventually, thanks to their eagerness to work and flexibility, end up in stable occupations.

Second, the larger group of women mess up their entry to the labour market for a variety of reasons: school failures, early maternities, failed love affairs, and/or identity problems. For a while they become unemployed housewives; but this helps them to gain maturity, and to develop strategies to go back to the labour market. At age 30, they are all employed, but in precarious and less convenient jobs (shifts, night-time, week-ends).

Among young men, the dichotomy is between those who are eager to work no matter what, and those who are looking for the proper job. The former use all their network links to move from one job to another, exploring the planet of work until they find the right place to land. The latter usually have utopian aspirations; when confronted with the realities of poor work they show very little psychic resilience and may prefer to stop working for weeks, months, or even years, indulging in sports, music, or whatever. Paternity does not seem to help them feel more reponsible. Their quest for identity lasts for years and may lead them into marginality and exclusion; more often however, a slow process of maturation and adjustment of aspirations to actual opportunities eventually leads them to reject their previous amateurism and stabilize their life course in their late twenties.

Thus besides gender, which reflects the existing gender division of labour, it is the relation to work and to the self that seems discriminating; and the latter appears connected to the experiences of early socialization.

One of the most striking conclusions of this research is that what statisticians, economists, and sociologists alike would define as objective resources (human capital, opportunities offered by local labour markets) and constraints (financial and moral obligations to make a living) are so much mediated by the *perceptions* young people have of them that they remain ineffective and almost unreal as such. Situations which would appear highly similar to the outsider are perceived very differently by various young people, depending on their relation to work and to themselves.

In terms of quantification, fifty-two young people from a provincial French town do not seem to count for much. But their stories tell much more of the connections between different spheres of their lives than the bare statistics could possibly convey. They generate interpretations which would be worth following in say Bavaria, Sicily, the English Midlands, or Detroit, as well as other regions of France itself, helping to elucidate the effects of different national institutional arrangements and local contexts. The two methods, surveys and case studies, could then move forward in mutual support.

We can indeed be even more precise about the respective virtues of the two kinds of life-history instruments, the life-history questionnaire and the life story, for there have been projects using them both. In a national French study of how people overcome crises such as unemployment, divorce, accidents, or deaths within their families, event-history questionnaires including some open-ended questions were used with the whole sample, and a sub-sample of thirty was reinterviewed with in-depth life-story interviews. Comparing the two forms of evidence, the researchers concluded that the in-depth interviews were both more subjective and more 'objective' (or rather, more factually informative) than the answers to the questionnaires; and indeed, that the subjective–objective dichotomy was itself highly misleading.[28] With the questionnaires it was possible to glimpse informants trying to give fragments of explanation in the small space allowed by the open-ended questions. But when given a full chance to explain particular events in their lives in the in-depth interviews, the same respondents were able to develop much more coherent descriptions of the context of the event, the complexities of their situation arising from constraints and from previous commitments, the influence of their relationships with others, their perception of alternative courses and their hopes at that time, and the reasons why they chose one course rather than another. They thus not only explained the meaning which the event had for them, but provided the missing contextual information for why they reacted to it as they did. Such descriptions cannot pretend to encompass all the relevant causal factors, if only because not all could be visible to the subject: but they are indeed more informative and accurate precisely because they allow much more space for the expression of the interviewee's subjectivity. Statistics can rely on the virtue of the representative sample; but only case studies allow us to reach in-depth, to descriptions of complex situations and conducts, and beyond that to the level of social processes underlying them.

Life stories bring home the complexity of the sequences of cause and effect in human lives. In choosing particular courses of action, structural constraints such as economic needs interact with value orientations, moral obligations, self-determined goals, and the individual's own perception of the situation and choices ahead. The actor's subjectivity, and the subjectivity of others in close relationship, are part of the objective situation, and in a crisis may pull in the opposite direction to more material factors. While some of these factors are relatively stable, others, such as accident or illness, while logically explicable in themselves, impinge on individual lives in an unpredictably random way, above all in terms of precise timing. Chance indeed must be part of even a fully determined world as soon as independent tracks of causation cross each other. A whole life may be reshaped by a minor illness at a crucial turning-point, or by an unexpected encounter leading to a job offer. Thus the more closely one examines the sequence of events in a life, the further one is forced to move away from the linear causalities on which quantitative data analysis is grounded.

We may illustrate the point from the family story which we analyse in Chapter 3. In a small French town at the turn of the century a young man from a peasant background has set up his own bakery, which becomes his life project. He has four sons. The first two learn the trade with him, and it is assumed than when the father eventually retires one will take over the bakery. The two younger sons have been kept longer at school and move on to become bank clerks. But then the First World War strikes. One after the other, all three older sons are drafted to the army. By 1918 two have been killed, and the third has returned home as a broken man. The father then asks the fourth son to abandon his promising and enjoyable job in the bank and to join him in the baker's shop. The son has little choice: he is faced not only with the economic needs of his family, but also with a special moral obligation, because he was spared the horrors of war, to show as much courage as his brothers. Reluctantly he joins his father to become in his turn a baker.

The causes here are multiple, and they show not only how a macro-event such as a world war can realign life courses at a micro-level, but also the centrality of moral commitments in shaping action; and beyond this, how a local system with its own self-regulating logic—here a family business, and under an authoritarian leadership—can sustain its own goals with an obstinacy against the odds, capturing the life energy of the remaining and unwilling son for itself.

This is a single story, but in terms of the nature of causality its implications are general, and replicated in many others in this volume. Years of working with life histories and family case studies have made such complex tangles of causality and self-determination familiar to us, leaving us increasingly dissatisfied with the simpler notions of causality which underlie much empirical sociology. On the one hand, the model of a social world moved by determinate laws, inspired by Newtonian physics, scarcely acknowledges the role of living, self-determined actors; while on the other the more biological Parsonian concept of such actors, whether individuals, families, or institutions, as self-regulating systems, underrates the contradictions and conflict within them and between them. Neither view could incorporate the unpredictability of history, of change over time, and its radical undermining of the social structures themselves. Some of the more recent developments in scientific thinking, such as Prigojine's chaos theory in thermo-dynamics and the open systems approach in biology, for us resonate much more closely with the open-ended world of unstable equilibrium which we discover in our case studies.[29] We sense in these theories—although this is not the place to pursue such a point—a potentially fruitful new language for the discussion of causation in sociology. But we are in no doubt that case studies, while always particular, at the same time expose very clearly the general nature of causality in the intricate interweaving of processes in mobility itself.

## CASE HISTORIES OF FAMILIES

More specifically, however, given the emphasis in so many of the detailed studies in the chapters which follow, more does need to be said here on family and intergenerational transmission. Survey research on social mobility has typically treated families as black boxes, whose inputs are a handful of variables such as father's occupation, and whose output is the occupation of the 'only child' pinpointed by the random sample. Case studies of families allow us to open those black boxes and to see what takes place inside. We can at last look at their strategic efforts, the roles played by women and men, and by different generations, in the transmission of skills and resources, ambitions and dreams, and compare such efforts at transmission in various social milieux. We can explore the relationship between early socialization and adult occupational success or failure.[30] We can track down why there might be sharp differences between the fate of different siblings; or whether it is mothers, fathers, or their interaction, whose influence is strongest in creating the family's microclimate. By relating families to their social and local contexts, which are bound to be highly differentiated by class and other macrostructural variables, we can begin to discern what kinds of games families are forced to play, and what are the unwritten rules of such games.

To make sense of such concrete observations, a rich conceptual toolbox is essential; and conversely, concrete observations seem one of the best ways to enrich it further. We have found the set of concepts developed so far by Bourdieu to deal with the process of 'reproduction' to be quite useful; in particular the distinction he proposes between three main kinds of family assets or 'capital' as he calls them: economic capital, cultural capital, social capital.[31] Concrete case studies allow us to discover still other kinds of 'capital', to understand better how all these resources are actually put to use, and in which conditions family strategies succeed or fail. For such resources are not the kind of things which can be passed on by a single act; transmissions themselves are long processes which include the preparation or 'production' of the potential receiver as well.

Indeed we conceive of families as units of production of their members' energies, or as one of us[32] has termed it in his earlier work, of 'anthroponomic production'. Anthroponomic production, which for instance transforms infants into social adults, is very specific, and as every mother or teacher knows, demands great effort. Producing people implies both nurturing their physical growth and shaping their cultural and psychic energy. Its instruments are not only material resources such as housing and income, but also, for example, language, local environment, and parental time and effort in caring for children, socializing and instructing them, and developing their specific abilities and character. Because the material and cultural resources which parents have at their disposal depend heavily on class and other structural features as well as on particular family traditions, we have always to conceive 'the family' as in a plural form: families.

In the anthroponomic perspective an essential point is that families are differentiated not only by the extent of economic, cultural, relational, and other resources which are available, but also in the degree to which they exploit them. A relatively poor family may concentrate its resources on promoting the educational advancement of a selected child, while on the other hand a more favoured family may throw greater resources into immediate consumption. Each family is to an extent a particular open system, organized around its own values and priorities as well as its different material, cultural, relational, moral, and psychic resources. Hence, as mobility statistics indeed show, given levels of parental 'capital input' do not translate neatly and mechanically into given outcomes. Transmission is a subtle process which operates over a long period. As will be shown in some of the following chapters, parents cannot hand down social status to their children: they can provide them with some resources, which the children may or may not appropriate for themselves and put to effective use.

In understanding this variation a crucial role is played by the emotional and moral bonds which much more powerfully than mere instrumentality hold families together. Such bonds are always an element in family transactions, and often overwhelmingly: for example when resources are pooled to cushion a member who has collapsed or to care for a handicapped child or ageing parent. Such actions are primarily determined not by 'rational choice' or interest in a purely instrumental sense, but by the framework of moral norms, emotional bonds, and the reasons of the heart. This is an essential dimension of intergenerational relationships and transmission which has so far remained absent from the literature, including Bourdieu's extensive writings on the various forms of capital, which retain a model of man as governed by self-interest.

An interesting new perspective on this, resulting in interpretations which tally closely with our own, has very recently been developed by Bloch and Buisson from Mauss's famous anthropological study of the gift and the obligations which follow from it.[33] They suggest that familial solidarity hinges on the intergenerational gift, the feeling of recognition and dignity as a human being that giving activates in the receiver, and the moral debt and urge to return that this feeling activates. All of us are given life by our parents, so that the process starts universally; but only some of us accept it as a gift. It is those who do so, often—but not always—because they have been sufficiently wrapped in love, who later feel the need to give back to their own children, grandchildren, and significant others the unlimited caring which they received in childhood. The nature of the gift, of parental loving and caring and recognition, helps to explain why at the extremes some adults struggle forward as ego-centred semi-isolates, while others immerse themselves in altruistic commitment to the intergenerational family network. We should add, as Thompson has shown in his comparisons between Scottish fishing districts, that different forms of parental caring and recognition can infuse whole cultures and help to shape economics at communal level too.[34]

In our own interpretation of emotional bonds, however, the theoretical perspective which has provided the most fertile ground has been the family systems approach developed in the practice of family therapy, which sees the family as an interlocking structure of intergenerational emotional relationships, each dependent on the other, so that changes in one part imply changes in another. We explain it more fully when discussing intergenerational transmission in Chapter 2. It has been particularly helpful in highlighting for us the importance of not only parental models, but also from grandparents, aunts and uncles; of the influence of rivalries between siblings; and of the extraordinary power of family 'scripts' in influencing destinies down the generations.[35]

## FOLLOWING PATHWAYS

We bring together in this book a set of case studies which not only share common assumptions but also have a linked origin in a series of research projects over a long period, in which all but one of the authors have been in different ways involved.

Not all the authors of the chapters which follow share our own theoretical perspectives. They are, however, united not only in exemplifying a qualitative approach to social mobility, but through an exchange of mutual influences in research over a long period. Daniel Bertaux, Isabelle Bertaux-Wiame, and Paul Thompson were developing the life-story and oral-history methods when they met in the mid-1970s, and subsequently worked together in 1985–8 on the Anglo-French 'Families and Social Mobility' project which is described in Chapter 2. They are together responsible for half of this book. Chapters 3 and 5 also come directly from the 'Families and Social Mobility' project. In addition, Brian Elliott's project on Scottish migrants in Canada was inspired by it. Then in the early 1990s both Thompson and Bertaux responded to the new opportunities for in-depth research in linked work on transgenerational social mobility in Russian families. But while Thompson again used life-story interviews in a project with Ray Pahl,[36] Bertaux went on to develop case histories of whole families as a method for investigating social mobility, and is currently using this in research on 'One century of social mobility in Russia': of which Chapter 8 is an outcome. Rudolf Andorka's parallel chapter on Hungary is based on exactly the same method. Lastly, two other chapters derive from earlier research by Paul Thompson. His comparative study of Scottish fishing communities was the starting-point for Giovanni Contini's investigation of three Tuscan communes; while David Vincent's chapter on shadow occupations is based on a reanalysis of the national sample of oral-history interviews on 'Family Life and Work before 1918' collected by Thompson in the early 1970s.

The final chapter by Mike Savage, a methodological reflection specially commissioned for this volume, is thus the only one not arising from this group of projects. All the other chapters are directly based on research using in-depth interviews. However, it should be noticed that they also vary methodologically. Thus while all the other projects use life-story interviews concluding in the present, Thompson's early interviews for the 'Family Life and Work before 1918' project were conceived as 'oral-history' interviews, so that the narratives (although not the information on occupations) were cut short in 1918: which now seems regrettable. This project also stands out in being based on a substantial national quota sample of 444 interviews.[37] The hundred families interviewed for the 'Families and Social Mobility' project were chosen on a random sample base, thus again combining the strengths of both qualitative and quantitative approaches, but here the unit was the family found through the middle generation informant, with an older and younger generation member of the same family also interviewed wherever possible. Subsequently, but without random sample bases, this multigenerational family approach was used by Elliott in Canada, and by Pahl and Thompson in Russia; and it has also been applied very fruitfully by Chamberlain to study West Indian families on both sides of the Atlantic.[38] With this approach, the units of information are one full interview only for each generation, although this interview will include systematic information on other members of the family. With the case histories of families used by Bertaux in Russia and Andorka in Hungary the unit becomes a family tree, entered here through a member of the younger generation, stretching back to the grandparents and including siblings, aunts, uncles. The aim is to sketch, by interviewing whoever seems most informative, not only each informant's own life story, but the destinies of all their close kin: a task which generally women informants seem to accomplish much better than men. The points of entry—young women or men—have been chosen from available random samples to ensure diversity.[39]

In terms of themes, the chapters can be conceived in pairs. Chapters 2 and 3 are both concerned with intergenerational transmission and with the roles of women in mobility. In Chapter 2, using the whole British 'Families and Social Mobility' sample, Paul Thompson explores the differences between the smoother life careers of men and the broken trajectories of women, especially through the impact of marriage. He shows how, when the full family pattern is examined, intergenerational occupational transmission can be found in four-fifths of the families, and in more than half these transmissions run over three or more generations. Moreover the transmission of women's occupations proves important not only for women but also for men. More broadly, both men and women typically find alternative occupational and personal models in their families, and their choices, as also their decisions to follow or reject parental example, are likely to be based on emotional as well as social factors. In general, however, this British sample suggests that the strength of family ties is more likely to inhibit than to encourage occupational upward mobility. The social risers come typically from small, or even broken families; and often they are migrants.

In Chapter 3 Daniel Bertaux and Isabelle Bertaux-Wiame analyse a single case of intergenerational transmission from the French sample: a family from central France with a male lineage of five generations of entrepreneurial activity, beginning as millers, moving to bakery, then to a seed and fertilizer business, with the informant (a member of the fourth generation) to the sale of cattle fodder, and finally with his son to an estate agency. Close examination of the resources passed on by one generation to the next reveal that besides the family's slowly and painfully accumulated economic resources, the inheritance of a local network of peasant families as clients played a crucial role.

This case also brings home the importance of marriage. A good working partner was essential for the survival of such small businesses. But equally interesting is the effect of the marriage of the informant himself to a socially superior wife, which in this instance leads to the effective social absorption of her husband and his children into her family: the most effective upward step taken by any of these generations.

With the next two chapters we look at some of the different kinds of desire which underlie social mobility. In Chapter 4 David Vincent looks at the 'shadow careers', the hopes of other occupations, expressed by British men and women born at the turn of this century. He emphasizes the modesty and practical realism of most people's unfulfilled dreams. It is striking, however, that this poverty of aspiration was still more marked among women than among men. In examining the constraints which prevented the realization of occupational dreams he finds economic need an important factor especially in larger families. But it appears that parents were generally a confining and conservative influence, and especially for girls. Even when new career opportunities for women were available, parents might refuse to allow their daughters to take them up. For such girls, the past lay like a dead hand on their prospects. The long-lasting presence of such unfulfilled dreams even in later life is indeed striking: as a limb which has been severed still induces suffering, they remain integral to the personality. It is also very likely—although Vincent was unable to check this—that these unfulfilled dreams were projected onto the next generation, determining the professional orientation of at least one of the children.

In Chapter 5, Isabelle Bertaux-Wiame and Paul Thompson explore the symbolic and practical importance of housing in mobility in Britain and France. For many families, their house was the crucial symbol of their social standing, often over generations. Indeed maintaining the family home could become an objective in itself, even to the point of economic disadvantage. For others the house could be a demonstration of upward social mobility, even if they had remained at the same occupational level. Some used house-moving as a deliberate step-ty-step strategy for upward movement, both in terms of investment and social status. This again proved often to be a transgenerational ambition. By contrast, yet other families suffer from a rootless lack of attachment to houses and places, or from the divisions and moves to inferior homes which follow the break-up of marriages. This chapter also touches particularly on the role of housing for the upper classes in both countries: not only the ancestral country house or château, but also the town house, and the role of second homes in sustaining large extended family networks.

Thereafter we look further afield. In Chapters 6 and 7 we see two aspects of the importance of place: in staying put, and in moving. Giovanni Contini examines three Tuscan communes, a tannery town, a knifemaking town, and a mining village. Buoyed by the fashion for leather clothes and the highly flexible nature of its integrated network of small firms, the tannery town still thrives. The artisanal production of knives, by contrast, has been unable to ward off industrial competition, leaving young people with their best option as migration to the city periphery factories nearby. In the third commune, once a strongly integrated mining community, the closure of the mine has left the young of this isolated mountain village workless and hopeless. Thus both in the past and the present, each commune created sharply different structures of opportunities for its inhabitants. In the first, they had the chance of upward mobility locally; in the second, by commuting or short distance migration; but in the third they had no local chances at all. This comparative study of three places within the same Italian region vividly demonstrates the extraordinary heterogeneity of local structures of opportunity, which surely ought to be investigated by sociologists, yet are averaged out and thus invisible through national surveys.

With Brian Elliott's Chapter 7 we follow a group of Scottish migrants from Britain to western Canada. He examines the different kinds of social resources which they brought with them, from advice on immigration and immediate housing on arrival by kin, to job recruitment through less direct connections, and the part played by ethnic Scottishness as a social asset. He again shows strikingly how mobility strategies are often transgenerational. He also emphasizes the importance of distinguishing the role of women from men. Women were more likely than men to bring readily transferable occupational skills, such as in nursing or secretarial work. Equally strikingly, they tended to have more effective social capital, above all because they were likely to have maintained bigger kinship networks.

The next two chapters are on Eastern Europe, and both concern the impact of political revolutions. It is paradoxical that—with the exception of Sorokin—social mobility scholars have paid little attention to the impact of revolutions on social mobility flows. Yet they are fascinating, not only because they are often brief phases of exceptionally rapid mobility, both up and down, but also because they lay bare the former arrangements for intergenerational transmission of desirable status—arrangements destined to remain as veiled as possible from public scrutiny.

In Chapter 9 Rudolf Andorka shows how in Hungary after 1945 most families were more affected through the industrial and educational changes brought by the new regime than by its politics. Upward mobility through the political system was not as common as one might have expected. Certainly some families were very badly hit for political reasons, their members suffering strong demotion, and even death or exile, earlier from the Nazis and then under the Communist regime. But if they survived this traumatic phase, in the long run they were likely to recover their social position.

In Russia, on the other hand, as Daniel Bertaux shows, the former upper and upper middle classes suffered for a much longer period after the February and October 1917 revolutions. The older generation, deprived of their financial resources and usually their homes, were reduced to the level of mere survival, fearing and frequently experiencing imprisonment, deportation, and death. In general it was uncommon for such families to recover their social position before the grandchildren's generation. The women fared somewhat better than the men, as they were considered as less dangerous and neglected. Some married into the new order. And most were able to pass on to their children some of their moral values and high culture, even though the children were at first barred from higher education and forced instead into factory work. Most of the men's lives were more decisively destroyed; but a few of them too did eventually succeed, in part through using opportunities for 'worker' education, but most crucially through joining the Communist Party, in reinserting themselves in the upper ranks of the new social structure. They threw themselves idealistically into its work, and rose through their drive and intelligence to leadership. But in order to do so they had to learn the rules of an entirely different game of social competition: the game of politics.

Lastly, as a complement to this Introduction, in Chapter 10 Mike Savage considers some of the limitations of the survey method in mobility research, and argues for its combination with qualitative approaches. He applies to social mobility an argument for methodological flexibility which has won authoritative backing in other fields of sociological research.[40] It is in this spirit that we offer this book, in the hope that it will inspire other sociologists towards the richly revealing and highly significant findings that a broader-based approach to social mobility will enable.

## NOTES

1. Paul Thompson, 'Life Histories and the Analysis of Social Change', in Daniel Bertaux (ed.), *Biography and Society* (London, 1982), 289–306.
2. Daniel Bertaux, *Destins personnels et structure de classe* (Paris, 1977).
3. Alexis de Tocqueville, *Democracy in America*, trans. George Lawrence, ed. J. P. Mayer (New York, 1969) (first published in French 1835); *The Old Regime and the French Revolution* (New York, 1955) (first published 1856).
4. Vilfredo Pareto, *The Rise and Fall of the Elites: An Application of Theoretical Sociology* (Totona, 1968) (first published in Italian 1901).
5. Pitrim Sorokin, *Social Mobility* (New York, 1927).
6. Emile Durkheim, *The Division of Labor in Society*, trans. G. Simpson (New York, 1933) (first published in French 1893).
7. Talcott Parsons, *The Structure of Social Action* (New York, 1937).
8. Karl Marx, *Capital: A Critical Analysis of Capitalist Production (Das Kapital)*, trans. S. Moore and E. Aveling (London, 1887) (first published in German from 1867); *The Class Struggles in France, 1848–1850*, trans. H. Kuhn (New York, 1924).
9. Karl Marx, *Grundrisse: Foundations of the Critique of Political Economy*, trans. M. Nikolaus (London, 1973) (written 1857–8).

10. Max Weber, *The Protestant Ethic and the Spirit of Capitalism*, trans. Talcott Parsons (London, 1930) (first published in German 1904–5); *Economy and Society, an Outline of Interpretative Sociology* (New York, 1968); Georg Simmel, *Philosophy of Money*, trans. T. Bottomore and D. Frisby (Boston, 1982) (first published in German 1900).
11. Daniel Bertaux, 'Sur l'analyse des tables de mobilité sociale', *Revue française de sociologie*, X–4 (1969), 448–90; 'Nouvelles perspectives sur la mobilité sociale en France', *Quality and Quantity*, V–7 (1971), 87–129; *Destins personnels*; Rudolph Andorka, 'Mobilité sociale, développement économique et transformations socio-professionnelles de la population active en Hongrie. Vue d'ensemble 1930–1970', *Revue française de sociologie*, vol. 13, suppl. (1972), 607–29; John H. Goldthorpe et al., *Social Mobility and Class Structure in Britain* (New York, 1980).
12. John Goldthorpe and Robert Erikson, *The Constant Flux: A Study of Class Mobility in Industrial Society* (Oxford, 1992), xvi–429.
13. Peter Blau and Otis D. Duncan, *The American Occupational Structure* (New York, 1967). Leonard Broom and F. Lancaster Jones, *Opportunity and Attainment in Australia* (Stanford, Calif., 1977). David L. Featherman and Robert M. Hauser, *Opportunity and Change* (New York, 1978).
14. Daniel Bertaux, 'From Methodological Monopoly to Pluralism in the Sociology of Social Mobility', in Shirley Dex (ed.), *Life and Work History Analyses: Qualitative and Quantitative Developments* (The Sociological Review Monograph Series, 37; Routledge, London/New York, 1991), 73–92.
15. Joseph Schumpeter, *Imperialism and Social Classes* (Oxford, 1981).
16. See Chapter 2, note 7, for a description of this research and its sample.
17. Ray Pahl, *Divisions of Labour* (Oxford, 1984); *After Success:* Fin-de-Siècle *Anxiety and Identity* (Cambridge, 1995).
18. A. B. Sørensen, 'Theory and Methodology in Social Stratification', in U. Himmelstrand (ed.), *Sociology: From Crisis to Science?* (London, 1986). Hans-Peter Blossfeld, Alfred Hamerle, and Karl-Ulrich Mayer, *Event-History Analysis: Statistical Theory and Application* (Hillsdale, NJ, 1988). Karl-Ulrich Mayer and Nancy B. Tuma (eds), *Event-History Analysis in Life Course Research* (Madison, 1990).
19. Elliott G. Mishler, *Research Interviewing: Context and Narrative* (Cambridge, Mass., 1986); Paul Thompson, *The Voice of the Past* (Oxford, 1988); Raphael Samuel and Paul Thompson (eds), *The Myths We Live By* (London, 1990).
20. Paul Thompson, 'Playing at Being Skilled Men: Factory Culture and Pride in Work Skills among Coventry Car Workers', *Social History*, 13 (1988), 45–69.

21. Tamara K. Hareven, *Family Time and Industrial Time* (Cambridge, 1982); Helmut Kaeble, *Social Mobility in the Nineteenth and Twentieth Centuries: Europe and America in Comparative Perspective* (Leamington, 1985); 'Eras of Social Mobility', 119–35.
22. Daniel Bertaux, 'Mobilité sociale: l'alternative', *Sociologie et sociétés*, numéro spécial *La construction des données* (Montréal, 1993), XXV, 2, 211–22; 'Families and Social Mobility: The European Experience', *Innovation*, 7 (1) (1994), 89–104.
23. Kaeble, *Social Mobility in the Nineteenth and Twentieth Centuries*, 'Eras of Social Mobiity', 119–35.
24. Anthony Giddens, *Modernity and Self-Identity: Self and Society in the Late Modern Age* (Stanford, Calif., 1991),
25. On the case study approach, see Jacques Hamel (ed.), 'The Case Method in Sociology/La méthode de cas en sociologie', *Current Sociology*, 40 (1992). The 'case study' is, roughly speaking, another name— perhaps a more accurate one—for referring to what has been often called 'qualitative research'. Good textbook introductions to 'qualitative research' are: Anselm Strauss, *Qualitative Analysis for Social Scientists* (Cambridge, 1987); or David Silverman, *Interpreting Qualitative Data: Methods for Analysing Talk, Text and Interaction* (London, 1993). The first focuses on Strauss and Glaser's 'grounded theory' approach, while the latter covers and actually synthetizes the growing body of methodological discussions around 'qualitative methods'. Neither of them however says much about working with either life stories or family histories, which seem particularly well adapted to a case study approach to social mobility processes, as we hope this volume demonstrates. On the use of life stories for sociological research, one may refer to Paul Thompson, *The Voice of the Past* (Oxford, 1978 and 1988); Daniel Bertaux (ed.), *Biography and Society* (London, 1981); Ken Plummer, *Documents of Life: An Introduction to the Problems and Literature of a Humanistic Method* (London, 1983); Norman Denzin, *Interpretive Biography* (London, 1989); Gabriele Rosenthal, 'Reconstruction of Life Stories', *The Narrative Study of Lives*, 1 (1993).

Given that the main mental block inhibiting the development of the case study approach lies in the issue of generalization, the on-going discussions about the micro–macro link are also relevant: see Jeffrey Alexander, Bernhard Giesen, and Neil Smelser (eds.) *The Micro–Macro Link* (Berkeley, Calif., 1987); Randall Collins, 'The Romanticism of Agency/Structure versus the Analysis of Micro/Macro', *Current Sociology*, 40 (1) (1992), 77–98.

See also Anthony Giddens, *New Rules of Sociological Method: A Positive Critique of Interpretative Sociologies* (London, 1976) and *Central Problems in Social Theory* (London, 1979), for a conception of

sociology that, while not focusing on methods as such, implicitly restores the case study approach to full legitimacy.
26. Daniel Bertaux and Isabelle Bertaux-Wiame, 'Artisanal Bakery in France: How it Lives and Why it Survives', in Frank Bechhofer and Brian Elliott (eds), *The Petite Bourgeoisie: Comparative Studies of the Uneasy Stratum* (London, 1981); Daniel Bertaux, 'Life Stories in the Baker's Trade', in Daniel Bertaux (ed.), *Biography and Society* (London, 1981).
27. Chantal Nicole-Drancourt, 'Mesurer l'insertion professionnelle', *Revue Française de Sociologie*, XXXV–1 (1994), 37–68; Chantal Nicole-Drancourt and Laurence Roulleau–Berger, *L'Insertion des jeunes en France* (Paris, 1995).
28. Françoise Battagliola, Isabelle Bertaux-Wiame, Michelle Ferrand, and Françoise Imbert, *Dire sa vie* (Centre de Sociologie Urbaine; Paris, 1991).
29. Ilya Prigojine and Isabelle Stengers, *Order out of Chaos: Man's New Dialogue with Nature* (London, 1984); Edgar Morin, *La Vie de la vie* (Paris, 1980) and *The Nature of Nature* (New York, 1992).
30. Paul Thompson, *Living the Fishing* (London, 1983); 'The Family and Child-Rearing as Forces for Economic Change: Towards Fresh Approaches', *Sociology* 18 (1985), 515–29.
31. Pierre Bourdieu, *Distinction: A Social Critique of the Judgement of Taste* (Cambridge, Mass., 1984); *La Noblesse d'Etat: grandes écoles et esprit de corps* (Paris, 1989).
32. Daniel Bertaux, *Destins personnels*; and 'The Anthroponomic Revolution: First Sketch of a Worldwide Process', *The Annals of the International Institute of Sociology*, IV (1994), 177–92.
33. Françoise Bloch and Monique Buisson, 'La Circulation du don', *Communications*, 59 (1994), 55–72.
34. Thompson, *Living the Fishing*.
35. A. Bentovim, G. Gorell Barnes, and A. Cooklin (eds), *Family Therapy: Complementary Frameworks of Theory and Practice* (London, 1982); Karl Menninger, *Love against Hate* (New York, 1958); G. Spark, 'Grandparents and Intergenerational Family Process', *Family Process*, 13 (1974), 225; 'The Power of Family Myths', John Bying-Hall interviewed by Paul Thompson, in Raphael Samuel and Paul Thompson (eds), *The Myths We Live By* (London, 1990), 216–24; Paul Thompson, 'Family Myth, Models and Denials in the Shaping of Individual Life Paths', in Daniel Bertaux and Paul Thompson (eds), *Between Generations: Family Models, Myths, and Memories* (International Yearbook of Oral History and Life Stories, 2; Oxford, 1993), 13–38.
36. Ray Pahl and Paul Thompson, 'Meanings, Myths and Mystification:

The Social Construction of Life Stories in Russia', in C. M. Hann (ed.), *When History Accelerates: Essays on Rapid Social Change, Complexity, and Creativity* (London, 1994), 145–77.
37. Paul Thompson, *The Edwardians: The Remaking of British Society* (London, 1975 and 1992); *The Voice of the Past.*
38. Mary Chamberlain, 'Family and Identity: Barbadian Migrants to Britain', in Rina Benmayor and Andor Skotnes (eds), *Migration and Identity* (International Yearbook of Oral History and Life Stories, 3; Oxford, 1994), 119–36.
39. Daniel Bertaux, 'Familles et mobilité sociale. La méthode des généalogies sociales comparées', in Nunes de Almeida *et al.* (eds), *Familles et contextes sociaux. Les espaces et les temps de la diversité* (Lisbon, 1992), 297–317; 'Social Genealogies Commented and Compared: An Instrument for Studying Social Mobility Processes in the Longue Durée', special issue, Marco Diani (ed.), 'The Biographical Method', *Current Sociology*, 43 (2) (1995), 70–88.
40. See Julia Brannen, Martyn Hammersley, and Alan Bryman, in Julia Brannen (ed.), *Mixing Methods: Qualitative and Quantitative Research* (Aldershot, 1992).

# 2

# Women, Men, and Transgenerational Family Influences in Social Mobility

PAUL THOMPSON

The currently dominant school of social mobility research has dug itself into a pit so deep and narrow that it has lost sight of what should undoubtedly be some of the principal themes in its field of investigation. Over the last twenty years social mobility researchers have developed increasingly impressive statistical methods, drawing on standardized questionnaires rather than in-depth interviewing, for analysing one single issue, *individual* occupational mobility—and this mobility has been evaluated, essentially because of the difficulties in statistical analysis caused by the broken careers typical of women, primarily through the occupations of men.[1]

The case for researching the social mobility of women alongside that of men is incontestable. Indeed, those such as John Goldthorpe who have argued to the contrary reveal, through espousing such self-deceiving intellectual gymnastics, the straitjacket into which they have forced themselves.[2] Fortunately a number of other recent survey studies have shown the mobility of women can be profitably studied.[3] Certainly the Goldthorpe school has shown that women's voting behaviour is better predicted by their husband's occupation than their own: but that hardly disposes of the issue. It is not at all difficult to pick other aspects of their social behaviour where women's own occupations are a better predictor: of what organizations they join, for example, or, more fundamentally, of the timing and number of children they bear.[4] But in any case, debating along such lines is chewing over a red herring. If we are interested in individual mobility patterns in the general population, there can be no possible justification for excluding the mobility of the female half—or to be precise, majority—of the population from the investigation. It is not possible to predict a woman's own career through her husband's class. Women's own mobility patterns differ in many ways from men's, partly because men and women are clustered in different parts of the occupational structure: and hence they also shape men's chances. Overall, 'people are distributed to places through time according to processes that are powerfully shaped by gender'.[5] Men's and women's mobility patterns interlock in the jigsaw, and to understand the whole, it is imperative to examine both.

This chapter has a double and closely linked purpose. The first is to illustrate through our life-story interviews some of the ways in which our understanding of social mobility processes is advanced by examining the experience of women as well as of men. But precisely because, as we shall see, women's mobility is inextricably bound up with their familial roles, the significance of the part they play remains equally central to a second principal theme. This is the importance of transgenerational family influences to individual mobility.

The nature of transmission between generations within families has been an issue surprisingly neglected by sociologists.[6] Yet for two reasons it raises issues which ought to be of crucial concern. First, it is fundamental to the human condition: it bridges the gap between the need for continuities in culture, the core of human social identity, and the brevity of individual human life. And secondly, because in Western societies it is a widely shared assumption that parental influence can be crucial in shaping their children's adult lives, it is a key theme both in everyday gossip and in national debates on the politics of law and order and social policy.

It was with both the role of women and transmission between generations as key themes that we set about the Anglo-French comparative study using life-story interviews, carried out with Daniel Bertaux and Isabelle Bertaux-Wiame, on which both this chapter and the two which follow are based. Here I shall draw entirely on the British sample of one hundred families.[7]

Before outlining some of the conclusions which we have been drawing from this material, let me first give a sense of its character. Telling one's own life story requires not only recounting directly remembered experience, but also drawing on information and stories transmitted across the generations, both about the years too early in childhood to remember, and also further back in time beyond one's own birth. Life stories thus are in themselves a form of transmission.

The same is true, of course, of the remembering process and conversation between interviewer and interviewee through which a conventional social mobility survey questionnaire is filled in. The problems of retrospective memory apply equally to both, although this is a major issue which mainstream social mobility researchers, in contrast to life-story sociologists and oral historians, have generally chosen to ignore.[8] Mobility surveys, indeed, clearly reflect the subjectivity of memory, which even as regards present occupations can be acute. I discovered, for example, in a research project on car workers, that there are two sets of incompatible contemporary statistics on the percentage of skilled workers in the industry. The census, based on self-reporting by the workers, gives almost double the proportion as the Ministry of Labour statistics, based on the returns of employers, whose interest is to minimize rather than maximize pretensions to skill.[9] Yet nowhere have I found a discussion of these extraordinary discrepancies in data presumed reliable.

The principal difference between life-story and survey interviews is rather that the processes through which the survey data are created are not recorded, and so rarely analysed. When it has been analysed, the survey interview has turned out to be typically much more of an interactive semi-structured genre than mainstream methodological texts would either recognize or condone.[10]

With tape-recorded life stories, by contrast, we are in a position to read and listen to the exact words which were spoken during the interview, and to recognize the complexity of the material which we interpret. A life story can certainly provide valid and rich raw material for both social history and for the interpretation of social mobility. But it is at the same time equally a personal self-analysis, and an example of oral literature. It can be read for its 'objective' factual content, or for its 'subjective' clues to consciousness and to family or collective myth.[11] Indeed, a life story in its own multiplicity sums up the complexity of the transmission of family influences across the generations. With this caution in mind, let us turn to our two principal concerns here.

## MEN AND WOMEN

Life-story interviews can not only indicate, like survey data, ways in which women's and men's occupational mobility patterns differ.

They can also help us to explore how men and women, parents and children, help or hinder each other's mobility, and the sustained strategies, the missed chances, the dreams and disappointments, through which occupational careers are reached. The importance of looking at both genders in relation to each other, and the strikingly different impact of family commitments on men and women, becomes evident as soon as we compare the broad profiles of the occupational careers of our middle generation, born in the 1930s and 1940s.

Almost all middle generation male informants had experienced real although usually modest improvements in their occupational position in terms of income, conditions, and security since they first started work. This clearly reflects a favourable historic moment in terms of the changing economic structure of Britain. This generation entered employment from the 1940s to the 1960s and benefited from the long post-war boom. It is noticeable how working-class young men in the northern industrial regions often gained from post-war policies promoting regional growth, especially in the public sector. Many took advantage of the new job security and opportunities for advancement offered by the nationalized coal, gas, and electricity industries, state education, local council work, and to a lesser extent the National Health Service. Advancement to supervisory or lower managerial posts in the public sector was also open to children from working-class families. Their experience contrasts sharply with that of the younger generation of such families in these regions today, who, because of recent decline both of industry and of the public-service sector, have become especially vulnerable to downward mobility through unemployment.

Men from middle-class families found opportunities in both public- and private-sector middle and upper management. Because of the vulnerability even in the earlier period of small businesses, and the relative lack of opportunities which they offered for promotion, those who joined larger enterprises fared best. There were a few cases of downward mobility (inter- and intra-generational) due to the failure of small family businesses. But most middle-class men also saw a definite if undramatic improvement in their position.

The experience of the middle generation women was notably different. Their occupational careers typically peaked early, by the age of 30, and then plunged downward. It is of course well known that men and women's career opportunities remain differently structured, with women concentrated in lower status and lower paid occupations, both in the manual and non-manual groups. Part of their problem was thus the traditional gender bias of the occupational structure itself. But equally important were the implications for them of marriage.

Many earlier social mobility studies tended, because of their concentration on male occupations, to give misleading impressions of the impact of marriage on women. Certainly if we accept that on marriage women simply assume their husband's class, it has been demonstrated that marrying provides an important opportunity for upward or downward mobility. Women have had a slight tendency to marry men with better education and better jobs than themselves: a tendency which of course partly reflects the lower average occupational levels of women in the whole socio-economic structure. Other social mobility studies have focused on the possibilities of upward or downward mobility at marriage as evaluated by comparing women's father's and husband's occupations.[12]

As soon as the woman's own occupational trajectory is added, however, a much more negative picture emerges. American studies have shown how high-achieving women are not only less likely to marry, but if married more likely to become divorced, and more likely to become victims of violence.[13] The British material also reminds us that a significant number of women had both fathers and husbands in manual occupations, while they were themselves white-collar workers. In their cases marriage was a counterweight against potential upward mobility through their close association with a male of lower status. But the depressing effect of marriage is much more general than this.

Above all, focusing on occupations at the moment of marriage obscures how typically marriage, especially through leading to motherhood, causes a marked downward social mobility in the woman's own career (even when she has a higher occupational status than her husband's), through periods of not working, part-time working, and general lowering of occupational ambitions. The rare survey studies which have pursued this demonstrate the outcome clearly.[14] Among our own informants, the impact of motherhood on long-term career applied whether or not the woman returned to work in the same occupational class, or took up a lower status job. Almost invariably, whether professional, white-collar, or manual workers, women informants had experienced careers broken at the birth of their first child. They had ceased full-time work for periods varying from four to sixteen years after the birth of their last child. In none of our sample families was any doubt expressed that motherhood should take priority over a woman's career. This assumption and practice is the most universal of all the impingements of the family on individual social mobility which we have observed. While men's occupational decisions certainly took some account of family needs with important consequences for their careers, none had comparably drastic effects.

This impression is reinforced if we look at the minority of families—twenty-eight rising and sixteen falling—which did experience intergenerational occupational mobility. Examining them brings out the interlocking of familial and economic structural factors in mobility. Thus upward mobility was concentrated among those in London and the South-East and markedly lower in industrial regions. Conversely, there were twice as many fallers in the industrial regions as in London and the South-East, and half the South-East fallers turned out to be returning migrants pushed out by adverse post-colonial changes in the Empire. But given that the mobile are always a minority, structural factors can only partly explain their particular cases. They were also notably distinct in familial terms. Where the mobility was downward, family difficulties seemed to have been invariably associated, both for men and women. There were recurrent instances of familial ill-health, violence, marital conflict, and divorce. The fallers also had twice as many children as the risers.

Among the risers, however, the familial pattern was only clear among the eighteen men, all of whom appeared securely married (only one in a second marriage) to women either also in middle-class occupations, or in three instances full-time housewives. For them, marriage had reinforced successful careers. The ten women risers had rarely had this kind of backing. Every one of them, in fact, made their crucial upward move in occupational status either before marriage, or in three instances after divorce. All but two had married men whose eventual occupational status was below their own. Three had only a single child, and four had divorced. For two of these women it was indeed only *after* separation, as independent women no longer responsible for children (who were grown-up in one case, lost to the husband in the other) that they were able to become rapidly upwardly mobile.

Four specific cases may illustrate the contrasts. Roderick Parker is an electrician's son who became an architect through evening classes and a pupilship in private practice. He also succeeded in marrying his principal's niece, who was a top private secretary. He describes his marriage as intimate and affectionate, with a joint sharing of responsibilities: 'best thing that ever happened to me'.[15] Moving between only a few firms, he has risen steadily to the point where a partnership was within reach.

Ted Bridges, son of an aircraft technician, seems by nature more of an isolate. He breathes the rootlessness which we have found often associated with sharp mobility in either direction. As a boy he was not close to either parent, failed the eleven plus, did poorly at school, and left at 16. He was a rebellious teenager, ending up in a Detention Centre after being involved with a friend in an insurance fraud. But he had one certainty, that he wanted to be a journalist— 'I used to love writing'—and he had already begun to work his way up from reporting for a local paper to his present top job as a national sports editor. On the way he has married a professional librarian, who also has a working-class background. They have moved frequently for work, and it is important for Ted to feel they could easily move again to 'grab experiences... opportunities'. Hence Ted keeps family and friendship ties to a minimum, and they have only one child. He is the ultimate mobile man, feeding on the 'wide horizon' which means most to him in life. But he has been fortunate, and helped, by being able to carry his supportive wife and child with him.[16]

We may compare these mutually supported ascents to the solitary struggle of Jenny Manning. She could hardly have suffered more from the men in her family. She was abandoned by her father in infancy, after he had been imprisoned for assaulting her mother. She was taken in by her grandmother, but then her grandfather exposed himself to her. And after returning to her mother as an older child, she was sexually assaulted by her stepfather. She had to abandon school in order to act as housekeeper for him and her now alcoholic mother. She escaped from home into the army, and there she fell for early marriage to a dancing soldier; but all too soon he degenerated into a free-drinking, unfaithful builder's labourer. She finally decided to escape him too, but misjudged her moves, and in the ensuing battle lost her three children. Earlier on, Jenny had worked in unskilled jobs, such as a cleaner, waitress, or envelope-stuffing at home. She was over 30 when alone, and drawing on her own experiences of suffering, she began her present career: she is now a professional social worker.[17]

Jenny's experiences, though not unique, represent the harshest end of the spectrum in terms of her relationships with men. At the opposite end of the spectrum, in this respect Sue Keeler is right in thinking, 'I was lucky'. She is indeed the one woman riser who as an adult has been crucially helped in her career by a man in her family. Yet revealingly, this essential figure was not her husband. She is married to an electrician, and both her parents and his were working class. Her own father was positively discouraging:

My father seems to think I've got too many ambitions for myself and me family... I think he saw me as just slotted into a three-bedroomed semi somewhere, and that was it, go to church, your voluntary services work and... a couple of kids—I wasn't supposed to be ambitious for myself. I was supposed to spend my life revolved round my husband and me family.

But Sue was clever, and succeeded in getting to Grammar School, and from there to working in local authority administration. She was 24 when the first of her two sons was born. She assumed that was the end of her career:

I thought I'd packed it in, and that was it. I'd never work again.
And I'd been at home a month, when they came and asked me, would I go back part-time?

That was the first turning-point. 'I kept my hand in.' More surprisingly, with a month here, a month there, part-time work brought unexpected advantages: 'it gave me the opportunity to jump around and get different experience.'

The second turning-point came when her younger son was aged 7. Very unusually, the Keelers had earlier decided to join forces with Sue's widowed father-in-law and buy a larger house jointly together. He was a retired fisherman, originally from an east coast background, and as is not uncommon with such maritime families, very domesticated, a good regular cleaner and cook.[18] Sue was still working part-time. Then the chance of a much better full-time job with the county council came up: 'That's what really encouraged me to go out back to work full time. It was his idea, he encouraged it... He said, "Why don't you take it love? The kids are all right."'

She did take it, and the children flourished with their fisherman-grandfather as a second mother. Sue has now risen close to the top of the council hierarchy. Yet she still speaks of her personal success as if it needs excusing, collectivizing. 'I'd become quite attached to my independence, I didn't want to give it up... Perhaps I was selfish, but I wanted to hang onto something. And everybody backed me. My husband backed me... He always says he fancied a millionairess.' Sue ignores the contribution which she has made herself through her own professional energy and ability; while she expresses gratitude to her husband, simply for passively accepting her achievement.[19]

In short then, men typically rise backed by a helpmeet; but women, by contrast, are either handicapped by marriage, or have to find a way out of it or around it. For most of our informants the gendered expectations of marriage were so ingrained that they were unquestioned. It is as difficult to imagine Ted Bridges, for all the support he has gained through marriage, denying the label of 'self-made man', as it is inconceivable for Sue Keeler to call herself a 'self-made woman'.

These contrasting assumptions underlie the way in which even the most ambitious women would allow their own careers to take second place to family needs. A particularly striking instance of this is provided by Leah Percy, whose own occupational rise is one of the most remarkable stories of our older generation—and whom we shall re-encounter in Chapter 5.

Leah was born in a small Northumberland colliery village during the First World War, into a community dominated by men's work. Her father, husband, and son-in-law were all miners. There was little work for women, and families could only get houses if their men worked for the mine. For the men, the pit offered a universe of powerful social solidarity, but there was much less to reward the women. Most lived out their lives as houswives to their men.

Leah herself had a different inspiration, for she came from a family of strong women. She was especially close to her grandmother, whom she described as 'domineering', but nevertheless as the source of her own ambitiousness. 'She left her mark on me... She made me independent... She would say, "Set your sights high."'[20]

As a child, Leah had dreamt of becoming a dress designer, and was making the family's clothes from the age of 9—'I was very creative'—but her father refused to let her take up an uncle's offer of support. The uncle had said, '"I'll willingly pay for her to go to—": father said "No" ... I felt cheated.' Thus foiled, she went to work in a sweetshop instead, and while working there she met her future husband. Marriage gave her a new dream, which later on, when he fell ill, she proposed to realize: to set up an ice-cream shop together. Once again, Leah was frustrated by her family's men:

> He didn't want to manage a shop. He didn't want to be told. He says, 'I'm not going to give my life to business.' And that was number one regret. I felt bitter. I felt dreadful, really dreadful. I've always wanted a business.[21]

Instead, for twenty years she earned extra money through taking in dressmaking at home.

Yet astonishingly, Leah's ambitions were never extinguished. She was to win out in the end. But she was now a mother too. Very significantly, she first of all threw herself into the encouragement and realization of her own children. Her own parents

> had no ambition for me ... They weren't interested in anything. Somebody's got to be behind the children, or they do nothing. So I wanted my children to do well for themselves ... I determined that my life would be completely different: ... I was gonna be as good a mother as possible.

In particular, she pushed them forward through education. 'From the moment my son was born, I planned education for him, if he had the brains': and indeed he has become a research mathematician. She wanted her daughter 'to do exactly the same, but she was contrary, she was awkward'.[22] She insisted on leaving school early and marrying a miner. The best Leah could manage was to get her to buy her own house.

Only then did Leah feel it was her own turn. She had taken in dressmaking 'right until my son finished university. He left university, Peg married, and I was free.' She had 'done my job, I'd brought them up, I'd seen them to their own places'. So now 'it was up to me to do something for myself. It was either do that or stagnate.'[23]

Leah had never been taught dressmaking. At the age of 48 she went to college. Her husband 'didn't like it one bit ... The times he said, "Pack it in" ... It only made me more determined.' His life was 'simply going to the pub: and I didn't fit in with that ... We were like ships that pass in the night.' Leah not only went on to qualify, but immediately was picked out to become a teacher. She remained there for twenty years. She sums up her experience: 'You've got to make a life for yourself. I had a good life, after they went away... Once I started going to college, I felt a different person... I had another life.'[24]

## TRANSGENERATIONAL INFLUENCES

So far we have traced these examples as accounts of individual mobility. But the fuller evidence of the life-story interview shows us very clearly that the process of upward mobility, the dynamic which generates a riser, cannot be fully understood within the sphere of work alone. In particular, as we have illustrated, personal and family relationships play a crucial role, and they work very differently for women and men. These cases also reveal a second key characteristic: for it is apparent that in three of them there is not only an individual but also a transgenerational mobility project. Now this has indeed emerged as a typical feature of upward mobility, and equally, although unintentionally, of downward mobility. But it is a vital element in the normal processes of mobility whose force traditional research, because of its narrow focus on the transmission of occupations, has severely underestimated.

Our own starting-point has been a broadening of the concepts used in analysing social mobility, which becomes immediately possible once the focus is shifted from individual occupational mobility to families. Occupation ceases to be the sole indicator of social position: family housing, education, culture, and inheritance can also be taken into account. The role of women, instead of being largely ignored, becomes central both as child-rearers and as transmitters of both family influence and their own independent occupational culture (as in the cases of women teachers). Equally important, with the much deeper and subtler material provided by life-story transcripts, motivations, relationships, and emotions also become accessible. We see our task as to identify, through the close analysis of this rich and varied data, the processes of intergenerational transmission.

The family is of course only one among many channels of transmission between generations, ranging from the almost universal role of peer groups to the more particular parts played by educational institutions, apprenticeship, churches, and so on. Our focus here is simply upon the role of the family in transmission: and it certainly remains a broad one. For family is still the principal channel for the transmission of languages, names, land and housing, local social standing, and religion; and beyond that, and for our purposes here crucially, also of social values and aspirations, domestic skills, and those taken-for-granted ways of behaving in parenthood and in marriage which Tocqueville called 'the habits of the heart' and for which Bourdieu chose the old word 'habitus'.[25]

The word 'family' also carries many different meanings. Here we use it in the sense of a network of individuals related by kinship and including two or more generations. It is a network with no clear boundaries, since these shift with each individual viewpoint. 'Family' is a cultural image; but it is constructed by real individuals. Transmission is similarly double-faceted. Most parents select only certain aspects of their family culture which they intend to transmit, and suppress others: even to the point that they may deliberately attempt in some respects to transmit the opposite of what they themselves inherited. Thus the 'family strategies' of which social scientists and historians write are normally not so much collective as overlapping individual strategies drawing on a family culture which is also only partly shared. One of the fundamental dynamics behind transmission is the search for individual self-perpetuation. Physically, a child is of one's own flesh, as the same smile, or eyelashes, or big feet may betray. Parents also hope to hand on some of their social characteristics, or their unrealized ambitions: whether for fame as an artist or for independence as a woman or for comfort in living or for love in marriage. But it is the children who must decide whether to take up what parents offer, and to make it their own, or to turn it down. Transmission is thus both individual and collective; and it takes place through a two-way relationship.

So far, research on intergenerational transmission has tended to be narrowly specialized. It is compartmentalized into studies of language learning in infancy, of cultural adaptation by immigrants, of inheritance laws and customs, of inequalities in wealth, of cycles of social deprivation, of occupational social mobility, and so on. Hence the insights won in each field rarely influence the work in another, and separately they fail to provide an overview of transmission and especially of the family dynamics which are crucial to it.[26]

In studying the process of familial transmission it is remarkably difficult to find helpful theoretical frameworks. The work of Erik Erikson, for example, concentrates too narrowly on the life course phase of reproduction, physical 'generativity', rather than the much more prolonged transmission of culture to the succeeding generation.[27] Bourdieu's concept of 'cultural capital' offers a promising perspective, but he has not pursued it with any closer study of transmission within families. It is also disappointing that so few of those French scholars who have pursued the pioneering work of Maurice Halbwachs on memory as a social phenomenon have focused on the transmission of family memories.[28] Equally, there has been little sequel to the earlier American sociological studies by Ralph Turner, and especially by Bossard and Boll of the different life paths taken by siblings in large families, which examined family interaction in terms of role theory.[29]

We have gained more insights in practice from the 'family systems' approach which has been developed by family therapists, and views each family network as an interlocking and mutually influential system of emotional and social relationships. Although the family systems approach fits well with interactionist perspectives and also with the role theory commonly used in sociological work on marriage, and also with more recent research on the distribution of power in families, it goes beyond it. Such studies do not take the individual family as a system in its own right.[30]

The family systems perspective has been developed for treating those in difficulties: thus the therapist assumes that the member of a family presenting for treatment may be manifesting the symptoms of disturbances elsewhere in the system. The dominating ageing businessman father, for example, suffers acute but inexplicable pains because his son is a grown-up but still obedient boy who will not take on responsibility. A series of deviant patterns has been identified, particularly in relationship to broken families: the child who becomes a parental figure, for example, not only taking adult roles at home but declining to go to school, or the child who fills the empty place as a substitute quasi-spousal confidante in bed or out.

Writers on family therapy have emphasized the need for both differentiation and transmission between the generations. They point to the difficulties which can ensue when children's lives are pinned down by trying to assuage the unsoothed pains of parents' own lives or by following the voices of ancestral 'ghosts'. They have identified how one family member may take on the role of the family conscience, or peacemaker, or historian, and how the family story itself may become a compelling 'script' which successive generations—in extreme cases over a century or more—appear compelled to follow.[31]

In interpreting the intergenerational transmission of occupations, our approach differs in three crucial ways from the assumptions which have been typical of social mobility. We are able to broaden the spectrum. We are able to trace transmissions which transmute or even reverse. And we can begin to unravel the doublesided impact of family culture on mobility.

Most social mobility studies have focused on the intergenerational transmission of occupations solely between fathers and sons, or sometimes also between fathers and sons-in-law. Life-story interviews enable us to trace the transmission of occupations across a whole family tree, including women as well as men, and siblings, uncles and aunts as well as grandparents, parents, and children. The abundance of family occupational transmission becomes immediately obvious: whether or not the first individual we interviewed was mobile, in four-fifths of our families there is some intergenerational transmission, and in more than half the transmissions run over three or four generations. Occupations are transmitted between women, and between women and men, as well as between men. Equally important, in more than a third of the families there are parallel transmissions of different occupations. As a result, the family offers a choice of models. For some, this choice can provide an important catalyst for mobility.

For a middle-class instance of such a choice, we may return to Roderick Parker. His family has four transgenerational occupations. Roderick's paternal grandfather was a builder, one of his uncles was a building worker, he himself is an architect, and his sister's elder daughter has married a builder. His father is still running his own electrical business at the age of 74 and his sister married a man also with his own electrical business. His mother was a nurse, one of his father's sisters married a male nurse, his sister also trained as a nurse, and her younger daughter has married a male nurse. Lastly, his maternal grandfather was a Birmingham Water Board inspector, his sister's husband worked for the Welsh

Water Board after his business collapsed, and their elder daughter is a Water Board secretary.[32]

Equally important, the choice of models offered by the family is not only of occupation but also of many of the other forms of attitude and behaviour which are typically subject to transmission. We have seen the crucial influence of Leah Percy's grandmother in forming her own ambitions. Work models also interact with models of attitude and feeling: so that emotional closeness or, conversely, rejection may underlie why a particular family occupation is taken up or not.

We can see this illustrated in the story of Betty Smith. She is a woman who achieved social mobility after leaving her lorry driver husband. All but one of her six siblings is in manual work and the only exception married a costermonger. Her father was a labourer, normally taciturn, but occasionally violent after drink; her mother an illiterate housewife. Neither her siblings nor her parents encouraged her. Betty from childhood had 'wanted to go into an office; but they wouldn't let me, because the money was more in a factory'. It was only much later, as a separated woman, that she rose to become a supervisor and bookkeeper, and she described this as a 'dream come true by sheer luck'. But it is striking how she picks out as the most influential member of her family her mother's sister, who also achieved fulfilment as an independent woman: 'it was all the scandal at the time, no one got divorced. She just used to enjoy life, really enjoy it ... She was always the gay one, always for a laugh. A right flirt, she was terrific. She was my favourite.'[33]

The transmission of intergenerational influence thus may take several different forms. Straightforward imitation is simple enough to trace statistically, but in other cases it is only through the life-story interview that we may understand the strength of family influence underlying a choice of different occupation. Sometimes this takes the form of a transmutation. Edward Field's father, for example, was an ambulance driver, and in becoming himself a professional physiotherapist with the navy he feels he has fulfilled their hopes for him:

> I've always been in the service of others, I suppose. I think this is what they were interested in. My father was in the St John's Ambulance Brigade and he spent a lot of time looking after other people. Even when my mother died, he became a guide for a blind lady and he was honoured with the Order of the Serving Brother of St John . . .

And I think that is what they expected me to do as well . . . I think they would have been quite proud if they'd been alive to see what I'm doing today. I think so.[34]

In other cases, parents were determined that their children should take a different path, and not follow them into traditional family occupations. Ben Bradgate, a north country miner like his brothers, had had little choice but to follow his father into the mine. His parents had 'come to the conclusion, like, long before I was going to school, there's only one thing for us all, pit'. His father had two relatives among the under-managers of the colliery: 'so what would you do if you're a family with a lot of kids and they want a job? . . . He took us all.' Ben himself only got out to a surface job when he was almost 50. But he was determined that his own sons should not follow his path, and in this he succeeded:

before either of them left school, I said, 'I can't rule you, but my advice to you is to try and keep away from pit work. I can't make you, but I don't advise it'. Cos I'd done my life in it.[35]

Here is a strong instance of intergenerational transmission which would be untraceable in a statistical mobility survey.

It would be a mistake to infer, however, that there is a strong and simple relationship between family influence and upward mobility. Indeed, Ben's older son is not in fact a riser: on the contrary, as an unemployed factory worker he is a faller. Certainly some wish for change is typical of most intergenerational relationships. But in most of our families such aspirations, although usually bringing improvements in the quality of life, were less likely to have a decisive impact on occupational social mobility.

Indeed among these British families it appears that at all social levels family culture, rather than feeding upward mobility, has normally worked more conservatively and protectively. Well-educated parents ensured that their children were educated too; entrepreneurial families attempted—with mixed success—to maintain their small businesses as builders or specialist craft producers or shopkeepers. Working-class children followed their parents into the steelworks or the mill or the car factory. Nearly half of our middle-generation informants, forty-four, were stayers. Let us take two instances.

The Pascoes are a transgenerational small business family. Dawn Pascoe was brought up in a Lancashire pub where her mother was the landlady. Her grandfather had been a Manchester fish market salesman and one of her great-grandfathers another publican. Dawn's mother helped her to start off on her own making handmade bonnets. She gave this up when she married a self-employed tailor—whose mother had run a sweetshop. Dawn's younger son Mont and his wife now run their own butcher's and greengrocery shop together. Mont had learnt the ways of family business through the time he spent with his father as a boy. He loved going to his father's attic workroom, 'a marvellous place . . . It was right high up . . . You could see all over Manchester.' And in the evenings his father would bring 'a lot of work home and sit at home at night and do coats and jackets, he had this boxroom'.

Mont had already begun part-time work as a butcher's assistant before he left school aged 15, and his father then supported him through a five-year apprenticeship. He worked for three different chain stores, rising to the level of butchery manager. By now he had met and married Jan, who had worked as a taxi-driver and barmaid. With another partner they launched out on what has proved a successful independent business. Mont may sometimes have other dreams, but he is clearly swimming happily in his familial element:

I go to work in all my stuff and I come home full of blood and fat and grease in my hair, and I often think it would be nice to go to work in a suit and commute on a train with my paper . . . But I still enjoy what I am doing.[36]

At a working-class level we can again observe essential continuities alongside aspirations for a better life in the family of Pat Sims. She belongs to an industrial Lancashire family for which we have evidence on four generations. In one way, in her choice of husband, she rejected her family model. Her parents had a classically role-divided marriage: her mother responsible for everything at home, while her father, who had separate friends, never helped—'he didn't know what a duster was', never even joined his wife and children on holiday, never told them his wage, preferred to spend his free hours in the pub—'he was a man's man: always in a vault with other men'. Pat chose the very opposite type: 'me friend more than me husband', a shy, gentle, home-centred man, who shares all the family decision-making and helps with the housework and especially with the children.[37]

Interestingly, however, he also shares two important experiences from childhood with Pat. They both suffered serious illness as children, and they were both brought up in multi-generational households. Both experiences help to tie them into a family culture whose very warmth tends to inhibit mobility; indeed can actively discourage it.

The interconnecting influences of the wider Sims family are clearly expressed in repeating patterns of family occupations. It is noteworthy that here none of the connections are in the direct male line, and so they would not have been perceived by a conventional mobility study. Yet on Pat's mother's side, her grandfather and two uncles all worked in chemicals for ICI. The other connections are all made through the women in the family. Her husband was a plumber; so is her daughter's boyfriend. Her husband is now an airport driver; her sister's husband has followed him into the same job. Her son is a process operator for Shell and her niece is marrying his mate. But the most sustained of all these work transmissions is among the women themselves, in service and catering. One of Pat's grandmothers was in service. Her mother worked for seven years in a local restaurant and cake shop. Both Pat and her sister worked later in the same shop. And now Pat's daughter wants to study Home Economics at a polytechnic.

Pat has no brother, so like these family transmissions she herself would be a non-observable case in a males-only mobility survey. Our approach reveals a striking sociological phenomenon; and it also provides the clues for understanding it.

For the Sims family both recurrently helps its members, and holds them back. Thus when in childhood Pat's sister 'had high ideals' they teased her, calling her 'lady Dorothy'. When her husband worked for a time as an independent building craftsman, she herself liked to feel that his financial incompetence in undercharging and failing to chase debts showed his attractive side: 'he's not a businessman . . . You've got to be a bit hard, haven't you?' He gave up. Similarly, they soon abandoned a new house on a housing estate: 'I felt isolated . . . I didn't like being stuck out there.'[38] They remain much more at ease enmeshed in the wider family network.

However sustaining, there is a danger in such a strong family cohesiveness. Because of the geographical shifts in the industrial structure, unwillingness to move may make it more difficult to stay at the same occupational level. The family can then be left high and dry by structural economic change and the ebbing of job opportunities in their area. The danger is further increased when the familial inheritance is in important respects negative.

Thus Terence O'Hara is the grandson of a skilled Irish stonemason and son of a South Wales labourer who himself, after a job as an unskilled bakery worker, has been unemployed for the last thirty years. His wife and daughter who have both worked as cleaners and his son are all also unemployed. In each generation this family has suffered instances of serious illness or death by accident. One daughter who lives with a violent boyfriend also accuses her father of attacking her as a teenager with a carving knife. There are broken marriages in both the older and younger generations. And right through runs a transgenerational thread of excessive drinking: Terence's grandmother, father, himself, and his daughter's boyfriend are all picked out. All these handicaps combine with the pull of—in Terence's words—'a close family' to rule out any thought of mobility. 'We never did let it worry us.' When Terence was a child, there were five family households within a hundred yards. And although the neighbourhood patterns have changed today, they remain as reassuring as ever. As his daughter puts it, 'To be honest, most of my friends don't have fathers. Either their parents are divorced or their fathers are dead.'[39]

The Horsleys are Londoners who have also suffered transgenerationally from poor relationships and ill-health. They have lived and earned as manual workers in the same part of the East End for at least three generations. Both the men and the women are poor communicators. As Sidney puts it, 'we weren't a family for sitting down and talking. I've never been a good talker.' His father combined a similar laconic manner with violence. 'Everybody hated him . . . He was such a strict person like, you weren't allowed to say nothing to him. Otherwise you got a wallop.' Worse still, his father attacked his mother, and sexually interfered with his sisters. Three of Sidney's four sisters and both his brothers-in-law have broken marriages. And as a final handicap, Sidney's father was forced into early retirement by illness, and Sidney himself suffered health problems from childhood.[40]

In other families, similar difficulties are combined with alcoholism. Another typical repeating pattern is when successive generations escape from unhappy childhood homes into early pregnancies and marriage, leading in turn to another unsatisfactory or broken marriage.[41]

Separately such handicaps do not make downward mobility inevitable: falling is normally associated with a conjunction of factors. In any case, while certainly representing strong family transmissions, the patterns transmitted are paradoxically of familial disintegration.

When in fact we look at the families of both fallers and risers we find that typically there are breaches, either within the family itself, most often through divorce, or from the entrenched local network, typically through migration. It appears that a cohesive family culture typically becomes dynamic only in response to sharply changing social and economic contexts.[42]

Geographically mobile fallers, unless they belonged to army families, typically only moved short distances. We found a more consistently positive association with upward social mobility among long-distance migrants (that is, both from outside Britain, or internally from beyond their region of origin). Clearly these informants had been originally pushed to move, either by lack of economic opportunity, from rural agricultural decline or industrial unemployment in Britain or abroad, or from racial persecution, in eastern Europe or East Africa. With some families the disruption of the move was followed by downward mobility, as for the children of a senior India police manager who, on colonial independence, returned home—and also divorced. But we found even more cases in which cutting loose from previous cultural backgrounds was used positively to seize new chances. This was possible through two kinds of dynamic within the families. External immigrants from overseas usually had an entrepreneurial or peasant culture of collective advancement, but with the effort often shifting in the younger generation from family business to professional ambitions. Thus the grandparental generation of the Simbal family were carpenters in India, who at India's independence and partition in 1947 moved to East Africa. With his older brother, Mohammed ran a successful business selling watches, until he came alone to England in the 1970s, where he continued as a watchseller. His two sons, however, have both been able to become graduate specialists in computing.[43]

We found a second type of advancement, by contrast, with the small minority of upwardly mobile families from classic industrial working-class backgrounds. A group of Welsh and English families, mostly originating from mining communities with declining work opportunities, had positively encouraged their children to better themselves through education, and most often specifically to become teachers. Some of these upwardly mobile internal migrants had moved as children with their families, while others had left their communities to pursue their education and careers.

These two means of social mobility are of course well known and have been described in many classic social studies of immigration and education. We were surprised, however, to find them almost exclusively among long-distance migrants. We had anticipated, partly on the basis of earlier research in France and Québec, finding many instances of family projects of upward mobility through education or business. Neither minor entrepreneurial activity nor the conscious use of the education system as a mobility path appear common among second (or more) generation urban British working-class families in our sample. The comparison with France is helpful here. In France a much higher proportion of families are of peasant, small shopkeeper, or artisan origin, and have so carried more entrepreneurial and adaptable attitudes into the cities and industry. It has been noted how the younger generation of the working-class steelworker families of the Meuse, facing redundancy, have switched from a strategy of family support within the community to finding new professions through education, again with strong parental support.[44] It seems likely that the most typical relationships between social mobility (or its absence) and British family culture reflect the earlier establishment of an urban and industrial working class and a relatively slow pace of change up to the late 1970s.

It would thus seem that in the context of a relatively stable society such as 20th-century Britain, the normal effect of family culture and cohesion is essentially conservative and protective rather than dynamic. Furthermore, the larger and more rooted a family, the more this will be. The ties may be loosened in a number of different ways: through migration, through being a small one-child family, or even through family breakdown. We may cite, as the exception which illustrates the rule, the case of a trans-generation Coventry family of car workers with a lone sibling riser, 'the clever bod of the family', who had gone to university and on to a professional career.⁴⁵ He turned out to have been brought up outside the family, after suffering from polio as a boy. In another instance, an illegimate railwayman's son, because he was blind was also sent away, educated in special schools, and ended as a civil servant. One way or another, it appears that the loosening of family ties may often be an essential prelude to upward social mobility, either backed by family support or through lone determination. Equally, the loosening may be a necessary consequence.

Either way, however, mobility is typically also a long-term transgenerational process. We found, as might be predicted, a strong association of falling with divorce, which had in some cases resulted in the downward mobility of a previously upwardly mobile informant. More surprisingly, in view of the extensive literature on problem families, the risers also include several children whose families were broken in childhood. Equally strikingly, whether the mobility is upward or downward the association with divorce recurs with the family of marriage. In the same way, if we look at family size the associations are also transgenerational. Risers tend both to grow up as children in much smaller families than fallers, and to have markedly fewer children themselves.

Another transgenerational effect which can lie behind both rising and falling is the parent who has not accepted the social implications of an occupational position. In a number of families a key role was played by an aspiring mother, who had acquired middle-class values either because her own parents had been middle class and she had married a lower status husband, or because of working in service or as a teacher or a nurse: a broader version of the 'sunken middle class' mothers first noted by Jackson and Marsden.⁴⁶ Less often noticed is the reverse instance of the father who rises occupationally to a managerial level, while his wife and children remain culturally embedded in their original working-class neighbourhood, so that the children become occupationally downwardly mobile. In both, it is important to note, it is the mother's culture which prevails over the occupational inheritance.

Finally, there are indeed families which appear to thrive from positive transgenerational attitudes, such as love and encouragement in childrearing, or commitment to religion, or to work. Often they are existing middle-class families whose children succeed in maintaining their social positions. But one cluster of attitudes, emphasizing the social value of hard work and the importance of education, often linked to a political belief in socialism in at least the older generation, seemed a key factor in a small group of families upwardly mobile from the working class.

The family of Cledwyn Roberts provides a striking instance. And as we unravel the family story, we also see how much more there is to it than the simple upward advance of a son through education.

Cledwyn's paternal grandfather had started life as a labourer on a hill farm, and then migrated to become a South Wales coalminer in the boom years before the First World War. At heart, he never quite settled there. Cledwyn remembers how decades later, he started his own interest 'in the countryside and wild life'. He would

take me for walks on the mountain behind the village. I think being a farming man, basically he missed the farm, and so did a lot of walking on the mountains with his little dog—just trying to get back to the country. Once or twice he did say that he used to find it difficult: what a change it had been from fourteen hours of working in open air to fourteen hours of working in darkness.[47]

Even so, of his grandfather's four sons who survived childhood, three became miners, while his five daughters all went into domestic service and married working men, two of them also miners.

There were, however, two breaches in this pattern. First, Cledwyn's father temporarily left the mines to work in London for a year, as a hotel servant, and there met his mother who was a hotel chambermaid. Although Cledwyn's mother's family was also working class in occupation, it is noticeable that his maternal grandmother had been a schoolteacher before she married. Cledwyn thinks that his mother 'received informal education from my grandmother, who had done a little bit of teaching, and certainly she was able to assist me in doing my homework more ably than my father was'.[48]

It was however Uncle Evan, Cledwyn's father's younger brother, who led the family's rise by winning a scholarship to the local grammar school, and then to university and a teaching job. But he could not have followed this educational path without the help of his family, and indeed 'part of my aunt's contributions from service went to keeping and funding my uncle in his education, in university'.[49] Later on Evan helped others in the family in turn: Cledwyn's father, for instance, in buying his house.

Uncle Evan married a teacher, but had no children of his own.

However their example inspired three of his eight nieces to become teachers, as well as Cledwyn himself. 'There was a very strong drive towards education, in that particular generation in the mining valleys... There was this big push by the parents for education—to improve children's chances.' The attitude was reflected in the comnunity as a whole by the provision of nursery schooling for all children and also by the exceptionally high proportion of grammar school places, which reached a quarter of all children by the 1950s. Cledwyn's own parents certainly 'had hopes for me', and for his sister:

in their generation, becoming a teacher was one of the great aims for the children... You find them all over Britain, brainwashing the English. Become a professional, have a professional qualification. I think this was an ambition they had.[50]

Cledwyn followed his uncle's educational path. But there was one point when, as a teenager, he hesitated. After all, the majority of sons did stay in the community and he wanted to stay with them. This time the crucial influence came from his father:

Education was thought of as how to move out of the valley. When I was about 15, I wanted to leave school. Some of my friends had left school: they were earning money—and I wanted to leave school. And he took me down the mine on a Sunday, and he took me in.
  It was an old mine. So we went down and we had to go three miles to where they actually dug the coal. And the last 300 yards you were crawling, and there was water. And he said, 'Now, this is what you've got to look forward to'. So I stayed in school.[51]

Today Cledwyn lectures at a college in England. He has emphasized to his own children 'the value of education for providing better jobs and also just for the sake of education, to make a better person'. And his daughter, now a university student in turn, can also find encouragement in her grandfather. She describes him as a tiny man, a 'very strong socialist', now retired, who

likes sitting indoors and reading and listening to his music, and pottering about in the greenhouse. He's quite old-fashioned in his ideas. He is really nice. He takes a great interest in our education. He's always asking mum and dad what's going on. When we used to have reports he liked to read them and comment on them. And if they were good he'd give us a present.[52]

Upward mobility through education is a well-known phenomenon: but as this instance indicates, it can depend on much more than formal education itself. Certainly the educational chance itself was crucial. But Cledwyn's own rise was clearly equally influenced by a transgenerational family culture, in which his grandfather, his uncle, and his father each played important parts; and so have his grandmother, his mother, and his aunt. We note too how not only has Cledwyn migrated himself to England, but so, temporarily but crucially, did his father.

Mobility, in short, is generated or impeded by subtle interactions between the chances and dangers created by changing economic and social structures and the particular transgenerational effects of family cultures. We see the further exploration of these intergenerational patterns of both continuity and reversal as a crucial task for sociologists of mobility.

## NOTES

1. e.g. P. M. Blau and O. D. Duncan, *The American Occuptional Structure* (New York, 1967); J. H. Goldthorpe, C. Llewelyn, and C. Payne, *Social Mobility and Class Structure in Modern Britain* (Oxford, 1980); R. Erikson and J. H. Goldthorpe, *The Constant Flux* (Oxford, 1992).
2. For the earlier debate on women and social mobility, see J. H. Goldthorpe, 'Women and Class Analysis in Defence of the Conventional View', *Sociology*, 17 (1983), 465–88, and replies.
3. Shirley Dex, *Women's Occupational Mobility: A Lifetime Perspective* (London, 1987); Pamela Abbott and Roger Sapsford, *Women and Social Class* (London, 1987), 47–87; Gordon Marshall, Howard Newby, David Rose, and Carolyn Vogler, *Social Class in Modern Britain* (London, 1988), 63–87.
4. Diana Gittins, *Fair Sex: Family Size and Social Structure, 1900–39* (London, 1982).
5. Marshall, Newby, Rose, and Vogler, *Social Class in Modern Britain*, 84.
6. Daniel Bertaux and Paul Thompson (eds), *Between Generations: Family Models, Myths, and Memories* (International Yearbook of Oral History and Life Stories, 2; Oxford, 1993) 'Introduction', 1–12.
7. 'Families and Social Mobility', funded on the British side by the Economic and Social Research Council, and on the French side by CNRS.

The Research Officers on the project were Catherine Itzin, Graham Smith, and John Creswell. Interviews were also carried out by Michele Abendstern, Research Officer on our parallel project on 'Life Stories and Ageing', and by Sandra Lotti, Marion Haberhauer, Kay Sanderson, and Bob Little. The Research Officers also carried out some of the preliminary analysis, Catherine Smith focusing on women's occupational mobility in relation to marriage, and Graham Smith on geographical mobility and especially emigration.

The analysis is based on interviews with the core sample of 100 families, in which we carried out 102 middle-generation interviews, 45 with the older generation and 47 with the children's generation. The families include some lone informants, as well as others in which three generations were interviewed. In one family three informants were interviewed in the middle generation. In several of the older generation interviews a spouse of the main informant also participated (but is not included in the figures above). We interviewed fifteen additional families in Scotland (15 middle-generation informants, 6 with the older generation and 8 with the children's generation) who have not been included in our main analysis. We did, however, use the entire set of older generation informants in our book, Paul Thompson, Catherine Itzin, and Michele Abendstern, *I Don't Feel Old: The Experience of Ageing* (Oxford, 1990).

The original research design was to select in both Britain and France subsamples of 100 men and women aged 30 to 55 from large-scale national sample-based surveys, and to carry out life-story interviews with them and in addition with a second informant from an older or younger generation (over sixteen) of the same family. Our intention was in this way to combine the strengths of the in-depth qualitative approach and the random selection of the quantitative survey. The national surveys used were the TRA study in France and in Britain the Stagflation project directed by Howard Newby, David Rose, and Gordon Marshall.

On the British side, this strategy was adhered to, although it had to be modified in the face of a number of difficulties. In particular, we found that an unexpectedly high number of informants—especially in inner city polling districts—had moved and were untraceable. Where contact was made, we found that some people were unwilling to undergo another long interview; while some others claimed never to have been interviewed for the earlier survey—and in a few cases, given the discrepancy between the basic survey data and themselves, this seemed likely.

As the fieldwork proceeded, it became clear that there was also a class bias in refusal rates. We were surprised to find that the lowest refusal rate was among the professional and managerial classes, who proved willing to give substantial time to talk fully about their work and family lives. We therefore introduced a stratified occupational quota to ensure an appropriate class balance.

There were also indications from a number of contacts which were made where informants eventually refused to be interviewed, that refusals could also be due to family secrets (such as illegitimacy). The sample is in any case biassed towards intact families by being based on couples (and so excluding single parents), and the refusals are likely to have increased this. Others were unable to be interviewed because they were too rarely at home (lorry drivers, shift-workers), or overwhelmed by current pressures (such as a Welsh housewife managing a pub and also caring for a sick mother, or a Scottish city family with too many children in too little space). On the other hand, some people did want to be interviewed partly because they had such family problems which they wished to talk about. There are clearly inherent difficulties in achieving a satisfactory sample of any fieldwork which demands long and intimate interviews with informants, as indeed, although perhaps to a lesser extent, with briefer survey interviewing. We are nevertheless in no doubt that the random selection of informants to be approached has added to the validity of their evidence.

The quality of the interviews obtained is high. Rather than the three hours of interview envisaged, older and middle-generation interviews are typically of four or more hours each, resulting in 70 to 150 pages of transcript. Each interview combines an account of family background and occupations with a full life story, covering childhood, working life, marriage, and childrearing. All the interviews are fully transcribed.

Unfortunately, it has not been possible to analyse the interviews comparatively in the systematic manner which we had originally intended. On the French side, a severe lack of funds and other difficulties resulted in only a third of the interviews originally intended being carried out, and they are also clearly unbalanced as a sample. In other respects the collaboration proved very stimulating. We were able to work closely together, both during the preparation of the research design and the drawing up of the interview guide, and during the preliminary analysis of the earlier sets of family interviews. Subsequently we have also carried through a comparative analysis on one theme, the relationship between families, housing, and mobility, which we publish as Chapter 5 of this book. We have also continued to pursue the theme of families and intergenerational mobility in parallel projects in Eastern Europe. This long-sustained close contact has resulted in a continuingly creative exchange of ideas. It highlighted many assumptions of social structural features or influences which we took

for granted in our own countries, and it stimulated the theoretical interpretation of our findings.
8. For a full discussion of remembered evidence, see Paul Thompson, *The Voice of the Past* (Oxford, 1988), chapters on 'Evidence' and 'Memory and the Self'.
9. Over 50% of manual workers compared with 20%: Paul Thompson, 'Playing at Being Skilled Men: Factory Culture and Pride in Work Skills among Coventry Car Workers', *Social History*, 13 (1988), 45–69.
10. Elliott G. Mishler, *Research Interviewing: Context and Narrative* (Cambridge, Mass., 1986).
11. On the mythical element in life stories in general, Raphael Samuel and Paul Thompson (eds), *The Myths We Live By* (London, 1990); and on family myths in relation to this set of interviews, Paul Thompson, 'Family Myth, Models, and Denials in the Shaping of Individual Life Paths', in Bertaux and Thompson (eds), *Between Generations*, 13–38.
12. David Glass, *Social Mobility in Britain* (London, 1954); Abbott and Sapsford, *Women and Social Class*, 56–8; Marshall, Newby, Rose, and Vogler, *Social Class in Modern Britain*, 68–9.
13. K. A. Moore and I. V. Sawhill, 'The Impact of Occupational Conditions on Family Life', in Patricia Voydanoff (ed.), *Work and Family: Changing Roles of Men and Women* (Palo Alto, Calif., 1984); Tichi Sugimoto, 'Status Relationships in Marriage: Risk Factors in Spouse Abuse', *Journal of Marriage and the Family*, 43 (1981), 675–92. British men and women are more likely to stay married to spouses in the same class; those that divorce are also more likely to move up or down through remarriage: Máire Ni Bhrolcháim, 'Changing Partners: A Longitudinal Study of Marriage', *Population Trends*, 53 (1988), 27–34.
14. Dex, *Women's Occupational Mobility*, 40–4; Abbott and Sapsford, *Women and Social Class*, 79.
15. Interview 5103 BM, 91. All names cited from interviews are pseudonyms. All interviews are deposited in the British Library National Sound Archive.
16. Interview 5101 BM, 58, 122, 129.
17. Interview 5004 BF.
18. Paul Thompson, *Living the Fishing* (London, 1983); Trevor Lummis, *Occupation and Society: The East Anglian Fishermen, 1880–1914* (Cambridge, 1985).
19. Interview 5409 BF, 30, 51–2, 60, 62, 65.
20. Interview 5415 AF, 11, 16–17.
21. Ibid. 23–4, 57.
22. Ibid. 52, 202.
23. Ibid. 37, 69.
24. Ibid. 63–4, 68–9, 100.

25. Alexis de Tocqueville, *Democracy in America*, trans. G. Lawrence, ed. J. P. Mayer (New York, 1969), 287; Pierre Bourdieu, *Distinction: A Social Critique of the Judgement of Taste* (Cambridge, Mass., 1984); and *Esquisse d'une theorie de la pratique* (Geneva, 1972).
26. Recent sociological work includes studies of inheritance in Janet Finch and Jennifer Mason, *Negotiating Family Responsibilities* (London, 1993); and Isobel Allen and Elizabeth Perkins (eds), *The Future of Family Care for Older People* (London, 1995). An interesting account of the transmssion of parental ambition is Dona Pilling, *Escape from Disadvantage*, National Children's Bureau mimeo, 1986.
27. Erik Erikson, *Identity and the Life Cycle* (New York, 1959).
28. Bourdieu, *Distinction*; Anne Muxel, 'Family Memory: A Review of French Work', in Bertaux and Thompson (eds), *Between Generations*, 191–7.
29. Ralph H. Turner, *Family Interaction* (New York, 1970); James H. Bossard and Eleanor S. Boll, *The Large Family System* (Philadelphia, 1956).
30. I discuss the relevance of the systems approach, and illustrate it with an Italian case, in *The Voice of the Past* (Oxford, 1988), 152–4. See also below, note 31. I have been particularly influenced by a workshop by Jeremy Holmes on family therapy and the older generation, and by a series of workshops and joint research activities with Gill Gorell Barnes of the Institute of Family Therapy, London, Natasha Burchardt and Gwyn Daniel of the Oxford Family Therapy Institute.
31. G. Spark, 'Grandparents and Intergenerationsal Family Process', *Family Process*, 13 (1974), 225; Karl Menninger, *Love against Hate* (New York, 1958); Carl Whitaker, *Marital and Family Therapy* (Chicago, 1970); I. Boszormenyi-Nagy and G. Spark, *Invisible Loyalties* (New York, 1973); John Byng-Hall, 'Family Legends: Their Significance for the Family Therapist', in A. Bentovim, G. Gorell Barnes, and A. Cooklin (eds), *Family Therapy: Complementary Frameworks of Theory and Practice* (London, 1982), 213–28.
32. Interview 5103 BM.
33. Interview 5005 BF, 30, 58, 60–1.
34. Interview 5406 BM, 25.
35. Interview 5412 BM, 32, 87.
36. Interview 5501 BM, 11, 39.
37. Interview 5502 AF, 18, 35; BF, 70.
38. Interview 5502 BF, 24, 64, 66.
39. Interview 5805 BM, 36, 44; 5805 CF, 48.
40. Interview 5013 BM, 24, 26.
41. A good example from our interviews is Meg Jacks's family: Thompson, Itzin, and Abendstern, *I Don't Feel Old*, 106.

42. Studying in an earlier period, Colin Bell found that while middle-class stayers might be geographically mobile or not, individuals upwardly mobile from working-class backgrounds were all geographically mobile: *Middle Class Families* (London, 1968), 167.
43. Interviews 5206 AM and 5404 BM.
44. Michel Pinçon in Paul Bouffartigue *et al.*, *Comme on fait sa vie: Familles ouvrières, histoires d'aujourd'hui* (mimeo, Paris, 1984), 437–540.
45. Interview 5614 AF, 5–6 (a son of the interviewee).
46. Brian Jackson and Dennis Marsden, *Education and the Working Class* (London, 1962).
47. Interview 5301 BM, 13.
48. Ibid. 16.
49. Ibid. 11.
50. Ibid. 11, 28.
51. Ibid. 42.
52. Ibid. 76; CF, 5.

# 3

# Heritage and its Lineage: A Case History of Transmission and Social Mobility over Five Generations

DANIEL BERTAUX AND
ISABELLE BERTAUX-WIAME*

At face level, this chapter is a case history of a French male lineage from a rural background, which was able over several generations to create a small family business, develop it, and eventually move into the ranks of the educated middle class: a pattern of slow upward mobility rather typical of French society. The chapter describes how this was achieved, focusing on the transmissions and reappropriations of family assets in successive generations. Through this analysis, the unexpected nature of this family's central asset is uncovered.

But this chapter was also first written in its original French version as a contribution to the debate currently referred to as 'structure versus agency'. During the 1980s, intense discussions took place around this topic within French sociology, in which all leading scholars participated: Bourdieu, Crozier, Touraine, Boudon, Morin. Such discussions revolved around the opposition between the structuralist approach, which had been dominant during the two preceding decades, and the (re-)emerging actionalist approach. Since the French readers to whom the chapter was initially addressed were perfectly aware of the foreign parameters of the debate, readers were expected to make the links themselves, which were not recalled in the paper. A reader, however, less aware of this intellectual context, might at first miss the chapter's metatheoretical aspects.

*An earlier version of this paper was published in French in *Life Stories/ Récits de vie*, 5 (1988), 8–25.

The debate which this chapter addresses has been at the heart of sociology since its beginnings. On the one side have been those who hold that social phenomena are determined by underlying laws (Comte), functions and constraints (Durkheim), structures (Levi-Strauss, Bourdieu), systems and sub-systems (Parsons, Luhmann); and on the other, those who believe that, ultimately, they are the results of human action or micro-interactions, from Simmel and Mead to Touraine, Morin, Boudon, the constructivists or the 'rational choice' theorists of today. It has never been solved; very few scholars were able to hold the two opposite points of view simultaneously (Marx and Weber are the two most obvious exceptions). Quite a number of theoretically minded contemporary sociologists are however trying to move beyond the opposition between structure and agency: it is this topic which led Giddens to develop his theory of structuration; which inspired much of Alexander's thinking in the 1980s, and which underlies Bourdieu's best theoretical piece so far, *The Logic of Practice*.[1] All these works stand in the background of the present chapter as silent sentinels.

The case history presented here aims at contributing to the debate, in an original way: by looking at a very small piece of social historical reality, and finding out which of the two grand theoretical approaches, structuralism or actionalism, appears to be most successful in making sense of *what really happened* in this small piece of reality.

Following Bourdieu's example in *The Logic of Practice*, a wholly structuralist interpretation of the observed phenomena is first attempted. It appears to be very successful in this case, as it discloses core underlying patterns of socio-structural relationships in the local society that would have remained undiscovered otherwise. At this point it seems as if the structuralist approach is vindicated by this case study. However, since some phenomena on the margins of the case remain unexplained, a new approach focusing on agency and strategies is then taken; and unfolding through its own logic, it is extended to the analysis of phenomena hitherto conceived as structurally produced, which suddenly appear in a wholly new light...

Thus the chapter has been constructed as an intellectual experiment in confronting the two main streams of sociological thinking on a (deceptively simple) case study.

We include it in this volume for a double reason: not only because its substantive topic is the social shaping of life trajectories, that is, of 'social mobility'; but also because, at the epistemological level, it addresses a central debate which, while being at the very centre of general sociology, has hardly been explicitly dealt with in the literature on social mobility, although the issues it addresses obviously underlie the ways in which social mobility phenomena and processes become conceptualized.

## FAMILIES AND SOCIAL MOBILITY

For those sociologists who first attempted to think concretely about social stratification, the basic unit was not the individual but the family. With the development of representative sampling techniques, however, in which the basic unit is the individual, that sociological approach has vanished. Yet is it not an unnecessary loss to see a conceptual framework rejected and condemned to oblivion simply for technical reasons?

In recent years, we have attempted to reconstruct and develop this 'family-based' perspective for questions relating to stratification and social mobility. In this view, social status, for instance, is construed as a property of family groups rather than of individuals, taken separately: the latter simply have an occupational status, which is not the same thing. The idea of social status as an attribute of the family leads to the notion of family social trajectories as a sequence of social statuses for a 'family' (the fact that a long-range view of the 'family' as a 'unit' reveals its successive subdivisions and recompositions at each generation in no way cancels out the idea of its continuity, but makes it more complex and interesting). We also assume that in a class society—in contrast to a society of castes or corporations—a desirable social status cannot be passed on as such from parents to children: parents can only provide access to or pass on resources or assets (be they economic, cultural, relational, related to socio-spatial location, ethnicity, and so on), on the basis of which a social trajectory remains to be constructed. There is nothing mechanical about reproduction: it is a dynamic process, in which individuals can best be conceived as players involved in the social games of generalized social competition.

On such elementary principles a sociology of stratification and social mobility may be reconstructed in which, at last, women have their place, as do family ties and so many other phenomena (such as how brothers and sisters raised together branch out into different schooling, vocational and—in the last analysis—social trajectories). An appropriate type of observation corresponding to this theoretical perspective is required, then, and it is for this purpose that we have developed case histories of families as a new tool for observing the processes involved in social mobility.[2]

It is a fact that these case histories of families constitute an extremely fertile means of access to the processes by which the social trajectories of individuals and families are shaped. This is particularly true for what we may call the processes internal to families and individuals themselves, as opposed to the external processes (including those connected to local labour markets and structures of opportunities, or collective historical events). In the case of employees, for instance, while the course taken by their career after their first job depends essentially on external processes, that first job, on which their entire subsequent career rests, seems to be determined to a large extent by their family background and personal school achievement. The family of origin, where primary socialization takes place, is indeed characterized by its level of economic, educational, and cultural resources, as well as of access to public facilities and to different segments of the labour market (such levels vary enormously from one family to another, in accordance with class position, at least in France); and also by the highly contrasting cultural micro-climates, even within the same social milieu. Children who grow up within these micro-climates with their tremendous diversity and contrasting resources internalize and eventually embody these differences. The statistical variable 'father's occupation' can only be a very rough indicator of such multidimensional variations.

But case histories of families do much more than unveil what is hidden behind the social origins of an individual: they produce a change in the angle of vision, so that instead of focusing our attention on individuals and their trajectories, we look at the relations between parents and children (or more generally, between ancestors, collaterals, and descendants). We view socialization processes as structured around the transmission of role models, attitudes, values, and taboos, and of linguistic, perceptual, cognitive, educational, communicational, and emotional resources (or handicaps), along with economic and patrimonial resources. What is passed on here is transmitted more or less consciously, more or less voluntarily (in some instances transmission may be completely involuntary, sometimes even amounting to the reverse of consciously pursued objectives); 'reception' and appropriation by the intended recipients, the children and grandchildren, also appears to be quite variable. Be this as it may, what each child retains will condition, to a large extent, his or her personality and school career, as well as integration in the working world (and therefore, the point of departure of the person's vocational trajectory) and beyond that, social integration.

The conceptual framework behind our work on case histories of families is therefore one of the 'shaping of social trajectories', focused on the idea of transmissions. In collecting these histories, we leave our interviewees in full control of their narration whenever possible. The interviewer simply uses the memorized interview guidelines as reminders for introducing themes in the course of the conversation. The reconstitution of the family tree, or genealogy, reaching back at least to the two pairs of grandparents of the person interviewed (ego) and including all descendants of both of these couples as well as their spouses, often affords an opportunity to prolong the interview.

What interests us here is the question of analysis: how can the wealth of sociological facts implicit in any family case history be made explicit?

Clearly, the best method is comparative analysis. Let us take the example of ten families in which the 'grandparents' were peasants at the turn of the century, and compare their destinies: comparison will show the respective weight, for the subsequent differentiation of the vocational trajectories of their members, of external and internal factors, of initial differences in resources, however slight, as well as of local contexts, family micro-climates, and other specific events.

Once a relatively good understanding is achieved of the type of destiny that was probable, possible, or out of reach for people of given social origins at a given time—that is, of the 'champ des possibles', or range of possible destinies, as Sartre puts it—the same may be done for other social milieux. Only then can we go on to the next stage, involving the comparison between ranges of possibilities of different social milieux in a given period.

Before we reach that point, however, it is important to gain an understanding of what each case history of a family has to say, and more specifically, of its sociological significance. The lack of a comparative dimension, showing 'how variables vary', constitutes the main difficulty at this point. The fact that sociology lacks a tradition of case studies is a further handicap. Cursory application of the Aristotelian rule that 'there can be no science without generalization' leads to excessive incitement to ignore specific cases, whereas it is quite obvious that every specific case contains a 'general' dimension. Each history of a family is only partially unique; it has some points in common with many other histories, and much in common with a few other family histories. The 'general' dimension does not reside exclusively in large numbers; it must also be ferreted out in specific cases.

The family history that is analysed below—or rather, the account of that history by one of its members—was collected in a small town in central-southern France, called 'Sauveterre' in the rest of the text. We chose it because we felt it clearly illustrated one facet of the phenomenon of transmissions in general: the transmission of capital in a craft. Four successive generations of its men were craftsmen: one was a rural miller, one a backer, the third a seed merchant, the fourth a small manufacturer of cattle feed. Since we wanted to see how a small 'family' business determines or influences the destinies of the family descendants, the history of this family seemed to demand a thorough analysis.

As we proceeded, we discovered that this case history also afforded food for thought on a much more general question: what governs individual trajectories—the individual's agency or socio-structural relationships? Posed in this simple form, the alternatives may seem caricatured; nevertheless, the question underlies each and every concept used by sociologists of social mobility. The concepts of reproduction, barriers to mobility, and social homogamy (in choosing a spouse), for instance, are clearly conducive to the structuralist–objectivist views, whereas concepts such as achievement, status attainment process, or strategy reinforce the opposite conception. The structuralist approach so popular in French sociology in the 1970s can be exemplified by the old saying, 'It is not the peasant who inherits the land, but the land that inherits the peasant': in focusing on this case history we wanted to find out whether the same may be said of a line of descendants of craftsmen.

## A BUSINESS LINEAGE OF FOUR GENERATIONS

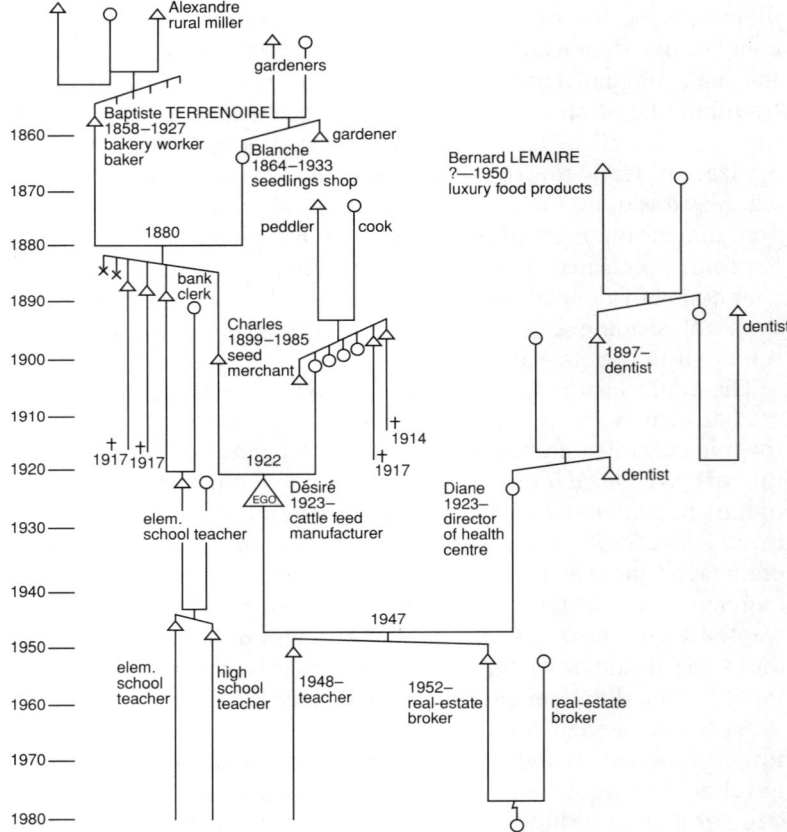

FIG. 3.1. *Social Genealogy of the Terrenoire Lineage*

The graph on p. 68 illustrates what we call a *social* genealogy, that is, a genealogy in which not only persons' names, but also their main occupations appear on the graph and their links become visible. The conventions used by ethnographers to represent kinship relations have been kept, but the graph has been drawn against the background of historical time.

Sauveterre, October 1987. The speaker is Désiré Terrenoire, a 65-year-old retired man:

My father died a little over a year ago. He was born here, in 1899, and died in 1985 at the age of 86. His father, who was my grandfather, was born in the countryside nearby in 1858, to a family of farmers . . . and small-scale millers. At the time, in the village of Beauvallon, the little mills were used not only to grind flour, but were also equipped to make cider and walnut oil, and there was also a small dye-works. That was all done at the mill off a small stream that teemed with fish. It was a real fisher's paradise: full of trout, according to my grandfather.

The grandfather, Baptiste, was the last-born of a family of seven children. At the death of his father, Alexandre,[3] the rural miller, Baptiste was still a youngster. His mother remarried a farmer, also a widower, with six children (six other children were born to this second marriage). Baptiste was brought up by his grandmother, since 'there were problems at home'.

Towards the age of 17 or 18, Baptiste left for Sauveterre as a baker's apprentice. Several years later, in 1880, the young man opened his own bakery, on the outskirts of the town, right on the road leading to his native village.

The house was very tiny, the bakehouse was on the ground floor . . . It's quite complicated, because the house is located at the crossroads. The Rodez road side is higher than the other road, so there are actually two ground floors . . . there are different levels. The bakehouse was on one side and the bakery shop on the other, but above the bakehouse. There were two other rooms.

He was 22 when he set up trade. He married a girl of 16, whose parents were gardeners: 'they sold seedlings for vegetable gardens'.

At the time, my grandfather was a tall, rather handsome man and my grandmother had noticed him. But she had always seen him dressed in his baker's clothes. When they got married he put on a wedding suit and she hardly recognized him. For their honeymoon, they took a carriage and travelled a few kilometres, and on their wedding night he got up at two in the morning to go back and make his bread! My grandmother told me all that.

The family life was entirely organized around the bakery. The young woman ran the store, but Baptiste sold most of the bread on his rounds through the country, with a horse-drawn cart, in the afternoon.

My grandmother was a very lively, dynamic person. She ran the bakery, and a grocery store as well. They also sold farm produce, seed, and fertilizer. My grandmother was a very good, very active businessperson at the time, and she thought nothing of travelling to Bordeaux to buy seed, or to Toulouse to buy noodles, or fertilizer, to handle dealings, and she did that all alone.

My grandfather only worked at his bakery, making bread, and he also had a little garden. He loved that, he loved gardening. He grew huge amounts of strawberries, to the point that he sold large amounts of them. He had organized his garden with reservoirs for watering: he had a well, the land was very fertile.

Baptiste and his wife Blanche had six children, two of whom died in infancy. There remained four sons, born between 1882 and 1899. The elder two left school early and stayed with their father, to make bread. They were drafted immediately when the First World War broke out. Both fought in the trenches for three years, and were killed in the great battles of the year 1917. The third son had also been drafted during the war; he came back alive, but broken by the experience. Charles, the father of our interviewee, was the youngest of the four. He finished elementary school, attended high school for two years, and took a job as a bank clerk in 1915. But when the war was over he had to leave that job, which he had held for nearly two years, and liked, to help his father at the bakehouse. In 1922 he married Camille, a girl who worked as housekeeper in a private home on the same street.

My mother came from a neighbouring region, her family was large and not very well-to-do. She had to 'go into service' very young, at the age of 11. Then, towards the age of 15 or 16, she came to town to work as a maid, for people who lived on the same street as my father. That's how he met my mother.

The two families set up an arrangement. Since the baker and his wife lived over the bakery, the son occupied a house purchased by

## Social Mobility over Five Generations

the father a few years earlier, a bit down the street. Charles's older brother, a bank clerk, who had also married, lived there already. His wife was a postal employee. In 1923, one year after their marriage, a son—Désiré, the narrator of this story—was born to Charles and his wife Camille. To the keen regret of his parents and himself, Désiré was an only son.

Four years later, in 1927, his grandfather Baptiste died. A complete reorganization ensued.

Since the grocery store and the farm produce business had expanded somewhat, my father hired a journeyman baker and a maidservant, who worked in the store and in the house. Both of the employees took their meals with us: that was family life. In fact, I still see the baker's man, who was two years older than my father. He is 90 or 91 now. He made most of the bread. My father helped him at the oven, but he did most of the work, and before him it was my grandfather. My father mostly took care of the business, selling and managing the grocery and the farm produce store, and he went on the rounds with the bread.

The parents, Charles and Camille, moved in over the bakery, while Désiré's grandmother came to live with him: it was she who took care of him.

I was tremendously coddled by my grandmother. I was with my parents until the age of 4, then my grandmother raised me until I was 9 or 10. I was really coddled... too much so. For instance, she had asthma—at the time that was quite exceptional, in fact—and she took the cure at a spa in Luchon, and I went with her. I went there with her for three consecutive years. I was happy, because she didn't just take the cure, we also went touring in the area, just the two of us. I was between the ages of 7 and 10. I went back to the same place 50 years later, I was with my wife, and I saw the lady at the hotel—she was a girl at the time—who remembered my grandmother. People noticed her, because she was so dynamic... She talked a lot, she liked to learn things, she kept informed about politics, she was not marked, politically, but she was interested... That was quite unusual for a woman in our region at the time.

Not only was little Désiré surrounded by affection, he was also 'looked after' by a teacher related to his family. The (secular) elementary school he attended was named after a nephew of his grandmother, a soldier killed during the First World War. The nephew's brother taught there. Désiré, well supervised, has good memories of his school years.

I was 10 when my grandmother died, I was exactly 10. I was enormously affected by her death. She was an energetic woman, as I've said ... She saw her death coming, and she was quite religious, in fact—she wasn't over-devout, she was Catholic but very broad-minded—and she insisted on having her two grandsons present when she received the extreme unction, it was very ... she was a very energetic woman ... That did mark me, after all, that marked me.

When the grandmother died, the estate accumulated by grandfather Baptiste was divided up between Charles and his brother. Charles kept the building with the bakery. His son Désiré moved into a small room there, on the second storey; the building in which he had lived with his grandmother became the property of his uncle on his father's side (Charles's brother), who also had only one son. Charles also kept a third house, purchased by Baptiste on the same street for use as a warehouse. In the following year he purchased the house alongside the bakery, to have more living space, because 'it was really tiny'.

Désiré passed the 'sixth form' entrance exam successfully. He continued his studies up to the baccalauréat with no great difficulty, with the support and encouragement of his family.

My father would have liked me to be a teacher. In fact, I didn't have any definite idea of my own ... so, we were three friends, and after the bac, one of us said: 'why don't we go for the entrance competition ...?' (I was 18.) 'why don't we go for the entrance competition for cadet officers at the Marseilles merchant marine school?'. For inland people, that was pretty surprising.

Still, there were a few precedents, here: I had an older friend who was a sea-going officer, and I knew his parents very well.

The three friends passed the competitive examination, which was relatively difficult (only 60 of the 300 candidates qualified). After two years of studies, Désiré failed the final examination.

We were young, we weren't limited, and we could easily have made another try at the exam; but this was in 1943, and I was 20. There was the Occupation. Now, in '42, I had registered with the Compagnie des Messageries Maritimes, not that I was obliged to do so, and I was supposed to leave for Black Africa, but the boat never succeeded in leaving the dock, I stayed there for a month and a half, waiting. As a result, in '43 I was requisitioned for the Compulsory Labor Service [STO] on the Baltic Sea, as cadet in the German navy. [NB: after the collapse of the French armed forces in June 1940, France was occupied by German troops and remained so until the summer of 1944].

The prospect of being drafted into the German navy was far from attractive to Désiré Terrenoire: like many other young people at the time, he preferred to take to the maquis. At the end of the war, he took advantage of an opportunity to take accelerated courses for army cadets. In 1945, as second lieutenant in the artillery, he enlisted with the Far Eastern expeditionary corps, and awaited his departure for the Pacific. But when the Japanese capitulated, his enlistment lost its raison d'être.

I could have signed up for Indochina, but I didn't want to. I realized that the military career was not for me. They sent me to Rodez, near home, and I spent nearly three months there, waiting for my discharge. I had a few things in mind for my future, I had found out that I was very free-spirited, and that I couldn't pursue a career in the army, or anything like that.

During those months, Désiré Terrenoire filed a request for some 'trade licences' different from those his father had, which would enable him to go into the seed business. When he was finally discharged, he returned to Sauveterre with that new asset in his pocket, and entered his father's business, but with an idea of his own: 'I had set my mind on making cattle feed'.

He also had other reasons for returning to Sauveterre. He had met a girl of his age, Diane Lemaire, who was in high school with him at the time:

I hardly knew her. For her eighteenth birthday, she had a party, and she invited me, just like that, like some ordinary comrade. She had invited my friends, who she knew much better than me, and I was with them at the time, so she said, 'You can come too', just that simple, that's all. We went out together for six years after that birthday party, with ups and downs. I was a cadet in Marseilles and it was very simple, I didn't want to get married: it's incompatible with the Navy. We married in '47. She had gone to medical school, but in '47 she hadn't quite finished her studies. She passed her thesis the following year, in '48. Our first son was born shortly afterwards.

Diane came from a prominent family in Sauveterre. Her father and uncle were dentists there. She herself worked for several years as school doctor in a neighbouring town. But in 1952, when her second son was born, she put a temporary end to her medical work. Two years later she was asked to head a regional medical centre.

She then successfully passed the state degree required for the position. She is still in charge of that centre, which has expanded over those thirty years.

When they were first married, the young couple lived in one of the Terrenoire family houses (the one next door to the bakery). Soon afterward, however, another arrangement was found. When his wife's grandfather sold some business premises, Désiré Terrenoire purchased them, along with the adjoining house, that belonged to an elderly aunt. This enabled him both to move closer to the downtown area and to pursue his idea: to use the business premises to make cattle feed and sell it directly to farmers. He achieved this very gradually, between 1952 and 1958.

There was a man here who had a cattle-feed manufacturing business, a large one for the region. It made practically all of the cattle feed for the region, and my idea was precisely that since it covered everything, there was probably room for someone smaller. At one point I thought about being an officer in the gendarmerie, but . . . I could easily have done it, but actually one or two years later, because it's difficult to mount a business at the beginning. I realized that it was difficult, but in the back of my mind, so to speak, I always thought I would make cattle feed.

Mr Terrenoire was right about farmers' new needs. But he was not the only one: the local co-operative also began to make cattle feed. He then attempted to form an alliance with it, but was unsuccessful.

So I made cattle feed, to the point where my little business was doing well, and I was cramped for space. I had to think about expanding. I applied for land in the industrial tract, so I could put up a larger workshop. But to set up a little factory, even a relatively small one, required a heavy investment; I was already 44 or 45, and I was reluctant.

This was in 1968. Désiré Terrenoire hesitated for several reasons. His business had taken on regional proportions, thanks to fruitful connections with another firm established at the opposite end of the region. After some conflicts with its managers, however, he was anxious to break those ties. At the same time, a change had occurred at the head of the local co-operative, and he knew the new director personally. When the director proposed a merger—that is, that he become an executive in the co-operative and bring his clientele with him—he accepted immediately.

My entire business went into the local co-operative, which was a large one. I was taken on as business manager, and I could then turn my own facilities

## Social Mobility over Five Generations 75

into apartments, for rental. I stayed with them for ten years: and I took early retirement, because of some rather serious medical problems. [Mr Terrenoire had a mild stroke, from which he had not entirely recovered at the time he was interviewed.]

Désiré and Diane Terrenoire had two sons, who grew up in the downtown house. The eldest son entered medical school, and then decided to become a teacher. He is a bachelor, in poor health; for the time being he is not considering either marrying or pursuing his professional training. His father had an interesting remark to make about him: 'He was kind of depressed, so the best thing for him was to become a high school teacher in the Education Nationale (the state-supported school system).' The youngest son studied architecture, taught in a technical school for a while, then returned to Sauveterre to work as a real estate broker. His young wife also works in the agency: they have a daughter about 10 years old. The couple live in the downtown house.

As for Désiré and Diane Terrenoire, they are now living in a villa they built on a hilltop. It is there, in the large, sunlit living-room overlooking all of Sauveterre and the surrounding countryside, that Désiré told the history of his family, waving his arms as he pointed out one place or another, such as the plush home of his parents-in-law, visible in clear weather, or some more distant places like his great-grandfather's village, Beauvallon, the birthplace of the male lineage, vaguely glimpsed beyond the fields and woods.

## STRUCTURES, THE RANGE OF POSSIBLE DESTINIES, AND THEIR DETERMINATION

We are looking at four generations of men of the same lineage. Baptiste had two sons who reached adulthood; his son Charles had a single son, Désiré; and the latter had two sons, Emile and Etienne. This is what makes the case history of this family relatively easy to comprehend.

### THE SEQUENCE OF TRADES

There is no doubt that this is a line of craftsmen and small businessmen, all self-employed and directly involved in the daily workings of their family enterprise.

One might think that the craftsman's trade would be passed on automatically: but this is not the case here. The Terrenoire were neither millers nor bakers for generation after generation (Charles Terrenoire stopped being a baker, in the strict sense, as soon as he could). Each generation seems to have had its own vocational project, its own strategy for accumulation, and to have distinguished itself from the previous one by developing a different activity, by innovating; it galvanized itself around its own specific stakes.

If something was passed on from one generation to the next, it does not seem to have been in the form of transmission of sameness, as is the case when 'the land inherits the peasant', or when the son of a notary public becomes notary public in turn.

Faced with the data he or she has collected, the first job of the sociologist, as we conceive of it, is to look for socio-structural determinations: this is the structuralist moment.

In this case, we first note the technical proximity, or 'kinship' of the trades. Miller, baker, grain and seed seller, and manufacturer of cattle feed all have something in common: they all deal with grain. Exactly a century later, and *mutatis mutandis*, the great-grandson actually does exactly the same work his great-grandfather, the miller, did: he grinds grain. The miller did it for human consumption, the cattle-feed manufacturer makes food for animals.

There is a possibility that the similarity is purely formal: further scrutiny is required to discover whether or not there is continuity in this sequence of subsequent trades.

The main point is that not only are all involved in the processing and/or commerce of grain and its derivatives, but further, although the Terrenoire family, in the person of Baptiste, migrated from a rural setting to an urban one in 1875, its activities continued all along to be oriented towards farmers.

In the rural context from which Baptiste came, dealings were actually done without the mediation of money. One of the best examples is, precisely, the local wheat–flour–bread circuit: each peasant would bring his wheat to the mill and would recover the flour (his own flour) in exchange for a few measures of wheat. He could then either store the flour at home and bake bread on the farm, or take it to the baker in town and recover the equivalent over the course of the year, in the form of bread. Not a cent was paid at any point in this complex circuit; the exchanges were spread over the entire year, and were obviously grounded in the peasant's trust in both miller and baker.

When Baptiste went off to town, he apparently broke with this type of transaction: what are small towns in rural areas, if not market-places? But the reality is quite different. Both the location chosen by Baptiste in building his bakery (on the outskirts of the town, on the road leading to the region from which he originated) and some incidental remarks in his grandson's account seem to indicate that from the outset this 'urban' bakery was purposely oriented towards a rural clientele; that is, towards those peasant families who no doubt already knew Baptiste to be son of Alexandre, the miller.

The rounds through the surrounding countryside, made by Baptiste every afternoon in his horse-drawn cart, become fully meaningful in this light: he was making the rounds of his clientele, of the goodwill indirectly inherited from his father. Now, the reader will remember that his wife sold farm produce, fertilizer, and seeds. Who were her customers? Certainly not the townspeople, but the same farmers to whom her husband sold his bread.

Charles, their son, took over these activities and developed them. His own son remembers that clearly:

In the old days bread was made with leaven (...)
(My father) sold leaven sometimes, to customers who made their own bread. There (were) many country people who made their own bread and bought leaven from the baker. I clearly remember when I was young, seeing my parents sell leaven to farmers for their homemade bread... Later on, (my father) gradually changed to using yeast.

*Do you remember whether your father sold to the farmers or the people from (Sauveterre) on credit?*
Yes, he sold on credit. Often the farmers paid for their bread in kind, either in wheat or in flour; that was called exchange, and it continued until somewhere around 1950–1960... My parents had a little notebook, in which they wrote down deliveries.

As for Désiré, who had first worked with his father, Charles, he set up his own business, manufacturing and selling cattle feed. And who would his first customers be—one must surmise—but those same peasant families, those same farmers whose great-grandparents brought their wheat, loaded on a donkey's back, to the miller of Beauvallon, Désiré's great-grandfather.

There have been many changes over these four generations. The goods sold to farmers are no longer the same, the horse-cart was replaced by a gas-propelled car, then by a gasoline-run truck. But over and beyond those changes, there is continuity to be found in the network of intertwining acquaintanceships between the Terrenoire family following its move to the town, and the peasant families who remained on the land. This web of relations, although invisible, immaterial, elusive, none the less forms the stable core of the variously transformed types of business run by the successive generations of the Terrenoire family.

One realizes, then, that the series of transformations undergone by the Terrenoire family business was not the product of whim. On the contrary, it corresponded quite accurately to the successive phases of development of farming in general (on the regional, national, and even European levels) in the course of a century. To be more explicit: it was only at the beginning of the 20th century that the gradual improvement in their resources enabled peasants to buy bread from a baker instead of having their wives go through the tiresome, fortnightly process of home-baking. After the First World War, the practice of buying selected seed slowly tended to replace use of one's own, thus creating the market for seed. And after the Second World War, the increasing affluence of the entire French population drastically transformed consumption patterns. Meat, especially beef, became affordable to city-dwellers, and peasants followed the market by shifting from mixed farming production geared to home consumption to cattle-raising: hence the growing market for cattle feed. The continuity of the Terrenoire business resides in its function, involving the processing of grain and its resale to farmers in a given area. Milling, bread-making, the selection of seed, the making of cattle feed are four activities of the same kind. Each of them arose at a historically appropriate time, and at each point there was a member of the Terrenoire family ready to be one of the first people present on that new market.

The above analysis yields a measure of the exceptional continuity of the Terrenoire enterprise, from generation to generation. The capital handed down from one generation to the next was not simply confined to physical plant or money, it was also, and above all, a capital of interpersonal relations, of relations between families, woven over the generations, in a world characterized by its stability, and by ongoing relationships through which goods, of various sorts, depending on the period and consequently on the demand of farmers, would circulate. In other words, what is known as goodwill.

But this 'social capital' only retains its value as long as there is a Terrenoire son who takes advantage of it personally. This is its specificity, and it is therefore a highly determining factor which, all else being equal, will tend to 'catch' an heir in each generation. This somewhat self-reproductive structure seems to account accurately for what appears to be a true occupational genealogy, a lineage of trades, with the successive shifts simply reflecting adjustments to the market.

Perhaps the most surprising point is the immaterial nature of this structure, which reinforces its self-reproductivity. Any material capital might be sold, and its monetary value recovered, thus freeing the heir; but a clientele, with goodwill of that sort, cannot be sold, or at least not at its full value.

To fully comprehend the sociological significance of this phenomenon, a break with our spontaneous view of business activity is required. No activity is more anonymous, in our present-day world, than selling: the customers have only brief, limited, impersonal and practically entirely instrumental contacts with the supermarket cashier, the newspaper vendor or the gas station attendant. But in the traditional world to which this family case history belongs, selling—commerce—meant very much the exact opposite. That meaning may be found in some old French expressions which have been handed down to us: He (or she) is 'd'un commerce agréable', or 'le commerce des hommes', in the sense of keeping company with people. In that world, business was only done among people who were old acquaintances and trusted each other, and moreover, who knew that their partner would not disappear unexpectedly. The social dimension was indissolubly contained in every dealing.

Economic transactions and relations were still embedded in social transactions and relations. To push the point, one might advance the hypothesis that the Terrenoire men did not derive their social status from their occupational status but, conversely, that their inherited social status—the position in a locus of mutual sociability and family statuses—enabled them to pursue and develop their professional activity.

What was really passed down within the Terrenoire family? Was it not a position on the local market, rather than physical plant or financial capital; a position inseparable from the Terrenoire line of descent? Seen from this angle, we understand the extraordinary self-reproductivity of that 'structure', and the concept of reproduction becomes fully meaningful. Over and beyond the differences in their successive trades, we discover a hard, permanent core; and these differences, far from resulting from personal 'orientations' of the men involved, suddenly appear as shifts expressing the extent to which these men were held in the grip of the gradually changing economic market. The changes themselves seem to be dictated by the objective evolution of the productive forces and of standards of living: here we have the triumph of materialist determinism and structuralist thinking.

## EXPLORING THE RANGE OF POSSIBLE DESTINIES

This structuralist moment has led us to discover, or at least to hypothesize a stable structure, the network of relationships established over the years between the Terrenoire family and the peasant families in the Sauveterre area. From the sociologist's viewpoint, what is passed on from father to son in this lineage is the centrality of their position within that network. Structuralist thinking ultimately leads to a complete reversal of perspective: the fact that in each generation a male Terrenoire decides to take up the family business and to reorient it according to his ideas is only a consequence of the 'structure'. Actually, it is the family business that captures the son, and thus inherits an heir.

The structuralist model has the merit of consistency. This quality is its strength, and makes for an initial break with appearances. But we cannot stop at that point, for the vision of the world it yields may be distorted by its (momentarily necessary) search for consistency. As soon as we return to the concrete case histories, the real contradictions, forgotten for the needs of the structuralist moment, crop up again sharply.

The fact that Charles worked for two years as a bank clerk before being called back to the bakery by his father seems to indicate some looseness in the structural reproductive mechanism. Somewhat similarly, Désiré left Sauveterre to engage in a career as a naval officer, which adventure lasted from 1940 to 1945 (from age 18 to 23): again, this seems to indicate a lack of predetermination here.

Furthermore, the 'reproduction' of the particular structure identified above seems to have ceased definitively when Désiré closed the Terrenoire business in 1968: one of his sons became a teacher, while the other became a real estate broker, neither of which occupations has anything to do with grain .

Perhaps what is most surprising, here, is what Désiré—an only son—has to say about his father's wishes: 'My father would have liked me to be a teacher.'

This is an astonishing statement indeed, with regard to the structuralist model outlined above, and one that seems to ruin its consistency, since it indicates that the very agent through whom the parallel lines of reproduction ran did not want to foster reproduction.

But that statement is less surprising for anyone who is familiar with the ambivalence of modern-day craftspeople and small-business owners towards their trades, at a time when they are in competition with the major industrial or commercial firms. On the one hand, they complain: 'we are being ground under with taxes and social benefit contributions ... we work hard to fatten the state ... competition with the "big guys" makes it increasingly hard to succeed ... never any vacation ... working twelve hours a day, six days a week, and not even any decent old age pension ...' Which complaints, when expressed in the presence of their children, inevitably end with: 'I do hope you will do some other work.' French shopkeepers and self-employed craftsmen both resent and envy civil servants 'who live off our back' but have stable jobs, holidays, and good pensions; now, teachers are civil servants ...

For, alongside of this complaining, another discourse unfolds, expounded by every individual who exerts some control over his or her working conditions: a discourse that places emphasis on some satisfactions, connected either to the positive side of the day-to-day work or to an overall assessment of the course of a lifetime: 'we worked hard, but we did achieve something.'

And still, this is only one example of the many 'double messages' that parents communicate to their children, and which are obviously not confined to the families of craftspeople and small-business owners. Precisely because of these fundamentally ambivalent relationships, it is essential to go beyond the structuralist phase, which is necessarily deterministic. We have described the ambivalence of self-employed craftsmen's relations to work, and of what children are told about it (and therefore, of children's relations to their own future occupation). However, the field of application of the concept of built-in ambivalence of social relationships is considerably broader (for instance, in the employer/employee productive relationship, the employer is both a supplier of work and an exploiter of the employee).

The ambivalence of social relationships is only one of the reasons why life is not predetermined; another resides in the multiple levels of determination, resulting in the repeated occurrence of situations in which the determinants exert pressure in opposite directions. Paradoxically, this 'contradictory overdetermination' creates space for liberty under constraint, since the actors are forced to choose, so to speak.

And so, for each individual a range of possible destinies opens up at each point in time. The youthful years of Désiré Terrenoire are a perfect illustration of this apparent state of indetermination, with several tracks being followed for a while, then dropped, or even simply considered: 'there are ups and downs in any lifetime: at one point I thought about being an officer in the gendarmerie, but . . . I could easily have done that.'

One of the tasks of the case history approach to social mobility processes should be precisely to attempt to think out the concept of a range of possible destinies. Certain 'possible destinies' are more probable than some others, and much more probable than a number of others, depending on the concrete context, the social setting, age, sex, and so on. But what remains to be uncovered is precisely wherein that difference in probability resides. Be that as it may, an attitude grounded in a too narrowly 'positivist' conception of reality and confined to studying only the actually attained destinies appears, paradoxically, as unrealistic, since the unachieved possibilities are an effective part of reality. If this were not the case, predicting the future would be child's play . . .

## THE CALL OF THE FAMILY BUSINESS

We have not yet exhausted the dialectics of the external and the internal, of objective and subjective determinations, the structural and the innovative. As Désiré Terrenoire told us, when he discovered that the adventurous path he had dreamed of following would lead him straight into a military career, 'I found out that I was very free-spirited'—that is, too free-spirited to accept military discipline. And where did that free spirit lead him? Back to work with his father.

One is tempted to postulate the existence of a force, exerted by all family businesses, calling all descendants back to their destiny. And yet a close look at the indications yielded by this single case history of a family is enough to show how complex the issue really is.

The way the destiny of Charles, father of Désiré Terrenoire, was shaped provides the clearest example of the self-reproductivity of the family business form:

(My father), this is a real story. My father did not intend to become a baker. It was one of his brothers who was supposed to take over. But he had two brothers killed in the war. He himself was a bank clerk. He had started working at 16 or 17, but when the brother who was supposed to take over the bakery died, he took over the heritage ... He absolutely had to help his father.

This is indeed a perfectly clear case. The founder of the bakery had 'chosen' an heir, no doubt his eldest son, to whom he had taught the trade. In doing so, he excluded the other three sons from the family heritage: the second son was also trained as a baker—just in case?—but the two younger sons were encouraged to become bank clerks. (This choice was probably related to the bakery itself in some way: the baker may have resorted to a bank loan to build his oven, and had realized the importance of being on good terms with the local banker.)

When the business catches one of the sons as heir, the choice excludes the others. In other words, as soon as there are several children, the reproduction of the family business generates both inclusions and exclusions, determines the destiny of one child whereas it strengthens the indetermination of the destinies of the others. It is only because there were only one or two sons in the latter generations of the Terrenoire lineage that this phenomenon is not clearly visible here.

The case of Charles illustrates this logic by rebound. Excluded from the heritage by his birth rank, as the youngest of four brothers, and actually glad to escape from the confinement to which people in small-scale bakeries were condemned at the time—they worked seven days a week—Charles was suddenly called back to it at the death of the brother for whom the heritage was 'destined'. Once heavy-handed contingency had shattered his plans, the full force of the call made itself felt. Under the circumstances, there was no avoiding it: that would have meant betraying his father, as well as the memory of his two elder brothers.

Charles worked in the bakery as little as possible. He married at an early age: the young couple might have been expected to form a working couple. Another possibility would have been for his young wife to go to work with her mother-in-law, at the farm-produce business the latter had created. Neither was the case, however, and it was the third, and a priori least probable solution that prevailed: Charles went to work with his mother, whereas the young daughter-in-law formed a team with her father-in-law. The division of labour that was set up then, with its hybrid working couples, was to condition the destiny of Désiré, the yet unborn child.

Désiré, raised by his grandmother—and he probably inherited his liking of travel from her—did indeed find himself faced, at adolescence, with a transformed form of the family business. The pivotal activity on which the enterprise rested was no longer the bakery founded by his grandfather, but the business founded by the grandmother, and run out of the same tiny building: in the space of a single generation, the family business had been through a first metamorphosis. It should be said in passing that these 'generational' metamorphoses are possibly the necessary condition for the heir's subjective—that is, symbolic—investment in the undertaking. The fact of doing something new, of his own, enables him to take possession of it subjectively. Ironically, if the innovation introduced by the heir is to make him successful, it must be perfectly in line with the evolution of the market, and therefore objectively foreseeable, whereas if that heir intends to take possession of the business by investing his personal fantasies in it, he may very well lead it to ruin. Praxis, generally viewed as the opposite of the structured 'pratico-inerte' (the given) is never as effective as when it is embedded in the invisible fabric of an objective structure.

Whereas his father, Charles, had first been excluded from the heritage and then suddenly called back to it, apparently against his will, Désiré, the only son and therefore only heir, although dissuaded by his father to take over the trade, finally went back to it.

His case illustrates another form of expression of what we have named the call of the family business. It was not his birth rank that made Désiré the heir, nor was he called back, like his father; in a sense he discovered the resource represented by the family business, on which he had long turned his back.

That resource was manifold. First, a family business provides employment, and is therefore a source of income. Désiré Terrenoire did have a trade—officer in the artillery—but the drawback of soldiering is the existence of some occupational hazards in wartime: war had just broken out in Indochina, and he may not have been very anxious to go there.

Along with the offer of a more or less permanent job, the family business provides somewhat special working conditions: you work at home, with your own kin. The adjustment period is reduced to a minimum, and communication is theoretically at its best. And on top of this, since Désiré is the only son, there is the prospect of eventually becoming the head of that business.

In Désiré's case, however, this objective job offer carried still another asset with it: the potentially free nature of the work. It is probably not by chance that he used precisely that term to explain why he left the army: 'I was too free-spirited,' he says repeatedly. He, the prodigal son, actually took care not to return empty-handed, but with those trade licences he had obtained, and which would also make him somewhat free of his father.[4] The initiative led to a second metamorphosis of the business, and since it was Désiré's own achievement, it enabled him to identify with the enterprise.

But this case history of a family provides us with a third and more unexpected form of the call of the family business. It involves Désiré's second son, Etienne. Born in 1952, Etienne studied architecture after his 'baccalauréat':

but... how should I say? He saw that the profession was really... there were too many people. He became a real estate broker in Sauveterre. He has an excellent position, across from the town hall, in one of the buildings I own. The house belonged to my father-in-law, who was a dentist, and we bought my brother-in-law's share of it. He (Etienne) is also a condominium manager, his customers trust him. He is very well integrated. He could have taught in a technical school, but he's like his father, very independent. He didn't want to continue teaching. Now he is really very happy.

My daughter-in-law works with him, she specializes in managing rentals. My son mostly takes care of selling. He is an estate manager. He is doing well. And his daughter does well at school.

It should be remembered that the remains of the family business, founded by the grandfather, Baptiste, in 1880, had been 'realized'; that is, sold, or rather, exchanged, by Désiré Terrenoire for a post as business manager in 1968. Hence there was nothing left of it in 1978 at the latest, when Désiré Terrenoire went into premature retirement. Now it was at about that time that one of his sons went into an independent profession, as condominium manager, estate agent, and real estate broker.

There is no direct, objective link, apparently, between the two businesses, except for the fact that the very building in which Etienne worked was loaned to him by his father. In reality, however, when rereading the entire interview one is struck by the frequent mentions of the real estate investments made by the Terrenoire family. Grandfather Baptiste set the example, with his successive purchases, on the same street, of one house, followed by a second and a third one next to the first. His son Charles bought a fourth one, on the same street, and perhaps others that were not mentioned. Désiré Terrenoire bought a large house belonging to his wife's aunt; in 1968, he transformed the cattle-feed manufacturing facilities into residential buildings, for rental; then his wife contributed her share of inherited real estate. Was it by chance, then, that their son set up business precisely in the real estate sector? Or was there some calling effect here as well, not the call of the family business, this time, but the call of the family estate?

It is true that almost all well-to-do business and craft families invest their savings in real estate—this trend is particularly strong in France—without one of their children necessarily becoming a real estate broker. It would be absurd to generalize on the basis of a single case. What is interesting in the connection between the accumulation of a heritage of real estate over three generations, on the one hand, and the profession of the great grandson Etienne on the other, is the discovery of how long a time span is bridged by transmission. For what an ancestor accumulated long ago may determine the vocational trajectory of his great-grandson, through a series of metamorphoses of the heritage.

With this series of examples, we are led to fill in the notion of determination with a meaning specific to the social sciences. For too long a time, determination was synonymous with constraint: such was the case for Auguste Comte and Emile Durkheim, Friedrich Engels and the French structuralists, but also for neo-positivists working with survey data. The epistemological views of the physical sciences were smuggled, so to speak, into a sphere where they did not apply. This led to a conception of the social sphere as composed exclusively of constraints imposed on agents, who are obliged to conform to the norms of their social group, under the threat of sanctions. Now, punishment aside, there is at least one other way of obtaining desirable behaviour: that is the reward principle. Since social life is not reducible to constraints, but also contains resources, the existence of resources to which the agent may gain access by means of some specific behaviour may 'determine' that behaviour just as reliably, if not more so, than the fear of punishment.

This new meaning (reward) of the concept of determination would definitely be meaningless in the physical sciences; but was the old one (constraint) meaningful for the social sciences in any other than a purely metaphorical sense? Is it in the same sense that social beings, on the one hand, and objects in the physical world on the other, act 'in compliance with the laws that determine their movements'? When we claim, then, that an earlier generation may very well 'determine' the shape of the trajectories of future generations through what it passes on to them, we do not use the term determination to designate a constraint only, but also a desirable resource susceptible, precisely because it is desirable, of generating foreseeable conduct.

## MARRIAGES, SOCIALIZATION, AND THE APPROPRIATION OF CHILDREN

We have reasoned so far as if the existence of the Terrenoire line of descent was self-evident, whereas for two reasons it is actually an unusual case. First, it was built around the transmission of a family business; and secondly and above all, from the demographic viewpoint, each generation raised only one or two children to adulthood, and all were boys.

These two peculiarities do indeed make the Terrenoire family something of an ideal type, and that in fact is why we chose it. But even in this case, there is admittedly a considerable gap between actual kinship relations and the construction of a lineage.

Brief mention must be made of the fact that Charles had a brother, who worked as a bank clerk throughout his life, never left Sauveterre, had two sons—cousins of Désiré—both of whom are teachers. They too are full-fledged members of the Terrenoire family. They are defined here as a 'collateral branch' first of all in relation to our narrator—this is the narration effect—but also because it was Charles who was heir to the family business accrued by Baptiste.

It is definitely the business heritage, then, however transformed, that created the Terrenoire line of descent described here. But no lineage can be perpetuated without spouses. At each generation, the heir to the lineal heritage introduces, by marriage, a person from another family. And the children of that couple are then a part of both families, at least formally speaking. This formal symmetry in marriage cannot be transformed into the representation of a lineage unless a principle of pre-eminence governing the relations between the two families is established, a pre-eminence defining the children as 'belonging' only to one of the two.

The Terrenoire family provides a most striking illustration of what is commonly known in France as the pièce rapportée phenomenon (the 'added piece' is the outsider who 'marries into' a family); that is, the situation of the spouse who enters a closely knit family all alone ('rapporté: something added for completion', according to the Robert Dictionary).

This was obviously the case for Camille, the mother of Désiré Terrenoire. He himself has little to say about her. She came from a large, rather poor family:

> The railway line was built somewhere around 1900... My mother's parents travelled [with the construction crew], along the line. My grandfather worked on the track, and my grandmother ran the kitchen [for the workers]. That explains why my mother herself and some of her sisters were born along that line.

Camille went into service as a maid at a very early age, in Sauveterre, far from her parents. Her marriage finalized that geographic move. Moreover, she 'had nothing', as they say, and by marriage she entered a relatively well-to-do family of crafts/business people. There is no doubt that she contributed enormously as a worker in the Terrenoire family business, to the point where her son was raised by her mother-in-law between the ages of 4 and 10; she was absorbed, so to speak, by her in-laws' business...

The situation was different for her mother-in-law, Blanche. Her grandson depicts her as a very energetic, dynamic, innovative woman. Above all, she created her own province within her husband's enterprise, copying and developing the type of business—farm produce—that her own parents ran. And in fact, it is that business, rather than the bakery, that her son eventually took over. Like her husband, Blanche came from a somewhat proprietied family. In short, this couple of grandparents seems to be more balanced.

But what is the situation for Désiré Terrenoire himself? As an only son, he seems to be the continuer—but also the liquidator—of the Terrenoire lineage, built around the constitution and transmission of a productive heritage. He succeeded in mounting his own business:

I already [in 1945] thought about making cattle feed.
*And therefore about creating your own business?*
Absolutely, (but) in the relatively long term, because that required investments that I didn't have. And my wife, who is my age, had gone to secondary school, and because she was really a good student... she was a class ahead of me, she got her baccalauréat at 17, we didn't know each other... That's paradoxical, we actually spent six or seven years at the same school, she was a class above me...

In response to a question about the creation of his business, Désiré launched into a long digression about how he met his wife, their long engagement, their marriage in 1947, and so on. And finally:

And somewhere around 1950 or '52, the factory—my wife's grandfather's little factory—was put on sale and my father-in-law said to me, 'Look, that's what you should buy'... The facilities weren't too large, but my wife's grandfather made luxury food products and dried mushrooms. He was one of the world's largest exporters of dry mushrooms. He was the exclusive supplier of the Tsar of Russia... So I bought the factory, thanks to my father-in-law, I must admit, and to my father.

That indeed was the period when Charles Terrenoire sold the bakery: there is no doubt that the money helped purchase the industrial site. The productive capital of the Terrenoire family underwent a last metamorphosis, at the initiative of Désiré—and, as he himself mentions, with the help of his wife's family.

Désiré purchased the house alongside those buildings at the same time:

(When we were newlyweds) we lived in small quarters on 4, Rodez road [next to the bakery]. We stayed there for five or six years. (Then, since) we had bought that site from my wife's grandfather, I must say there was the workshop, but there was also a very lovely house next door, and it belonged to my wife's aunt. And we were able to buy it: we paid a life annuity. So we lived in that lovely house for—... until '71.

(In 1968), just after my merger with the co-operative, I bought the land we're on (now), with a view to building a house... This house was ready in 1971, and we've lived here ever since.

And my youngest son lives in the house we were in previously.

Both of Désiré's children were therefore raised in a house that came from their mother's side. It is in that same house that the son who appears to be the designated heir now lives. His real estate brokerage is located in a downtown building 'that belongs to me', says Désiré but actually belongs to the two parents, half by inheritance, half by redemption of the heritage.

In addition, it should be said that Diane Terrenoire comes from a prominent Sauveterre family, several members of which had studied in Paris. Is it mere coincidence that Désiré says, and repeats, 'my wife was a class above me'? Might there be some unintended added meaning, since 'class' refers not only to the classroom but to social class as well? All of this points to one question: is there a possibility that this time it is Désiré Terrenoire who is the 'outsider', or 'pièce rapportée', in his own marriage?

Actually, the contemporary part of his account—starting with his marriage—may be reread in that sense. Had we collected an account by his wife or one of his sons, we would no doubt have noticed the same change in perspective as the reader of Lawrence Durrell's *The Alexandria Quartet* finds when he goes from the first volume (written in the first person) to the second, and discovers that what he had taken for the hero of the story was only a secondary character, unwittingly manipulated by forces far beyond his reach and awareness. Without going into the details, we will simply state that many features of the story told by Désiré Terrenoire take on new meaning, and 'fall into place' when seen in this perspective. Following this reinterpretation, his undeniable social ascent also seems to be the result of his marrying well.

The marriage was certainly due to his personal qualities, for the most part: his imposing bearing, particularly when in uniform, the romantic image tied to the choice of a sea-going trade, his social poise, perhaps derived from the summers spent with his grandmother Blanche ... In any case, marriage introduced him not only to a more affluent family, but to one that had long been a part of the local bourgeoisie. That family was to help him to succeed professionally. And as often happens in such cases, he moved near his wife's family; his children became the grandchildren of his wife's family; the lineage which he was the last to uphold yielded to his wife's line of descent, the Lemaire lineage. His children bear his name, of course, but most probably for his family-in-law 'they belong to the Lemaire family'. The younger son, in particular, is perpetuating the Lemaire lineage.

The broader issue raised here through a specific case history and the concept of the outsider (pièce rapportée) involves the rivalry between lineages within a marital union. While marriage is the formal consecration of the union of two families, it is quite common—and inherent in the situation—for those two families to engage in secret rivalry, the real long-term stake being their symbolic appropriation of the grandchildren.

We consider the question here as a sociological rather than a psychological one. The promising young man from a modest background who marries a middle-class girl may well play the dominant role at home, he will still always be an outsider. The chances are that the couple will end up being housed with the help of the wife's family, located 'in exchange' near that side of the family; and that their children will see their maternal grandparents more often, and perhaps in a more formalized ritual. The relative frequency of visits to grandparents and the provenance of living quarters constitute two excellent indicators, at least in France, of the relative strength of the two lineages vying for the symbolic appropriation of the grandchildren.

Only over the long term can the effects of the imperceptible workings of socialization be assessed. The man who dominates his partner in their everyday life is astonished, later in life, at having fathered children who bear no resemblance to him and may even seem to be strangers. What are socialization processes, if not a mysterious alchemy, with constantly interacting psychological and social elements, tending to trade forms with one another. All adults in a concrete family group—thus including all those members of the extended kinship network who interact significantly—are present for the others as both psychological and social individuals, and actually only allow some portion of those complex, ambivalent entities composing both their social identity and their psychological 'identity' to transpire through each of the differentiated roles conferred on them by their status.

These interactions are extraordinarily difficult to grasp in action. And yet, it is to a large extent through their workings over the long term, that destinies are shaped. Like Minerva's owl, case histories of families cannot exhibit the extreme complexity of socialization as it proceeds, but they have the merit of yielding a view of the effective results of that socialization.

## TRANSMISSION AND TRANSMISSIBILITY

Considering the absolutely focal position occupied, within the field of sociology of social mobility, by the relationship between social origin and social position at adulthood, as well as the roughness of the empirical indicators used to 'measure' these two 'variables', it is more essential than ever for us to reflect on the concrete mediations through which personal destiny is affected by origins (the family of birth, socially situated).

The present chapter is an attempt to reflect on this relationship through the concept of transmission. The question turns out to be quite complex, even when confined solely to the transmission of a productive heritage. How complicated would it have been had we concentrated on the transmission of values, attitudes, and prejudices, and if we had had to deal with large numbers of siblings?

The initial hypothesis inferred that social status is a family attribute—therefore the attribute of a small group—and that it cannot be transmitted as such. Only its component parts, be they economic, cultural, interpersonal, geographic, or other, may be passed on. Upon completion of our study, we find that even that element for which transmission would seem to be simplest, easiest, and most direct—capital, in the economic sense of the term—

apparently must undergo a metamorphosis if it is to be reappropriated by the following generation. Because transmission of sameness reifies the heir (treats him as an object), it seems to carry the kiss of death. To become the subject of the heritage, the heir must act on it by leaving his or her mark on it.[5]

If this is the case for productive capital, one of the most objectified forms taken by any component of social status, one would assume that the same must be true for other, less objective components. Parents who are determined to transmit their—possibly frustrated—liking for higher education, business, some art or sport to one or another of their children will most probably meet with a patent lack of enthusiasm in the potential recipients. Whence the first hypothesis: transmission of sameness is the exception rather than the rule.

A much more common occurrence is probably the transmission of equivalents. The baker's son who becomes a seed merchant, the son of the small manufacturer who becomes a real estate broker, the dentist's daughter who becomes a doctor: three examples among thousands of transmissions of equivalents. The writer's son who becomes a reporter, the cutter's son who becomes an engineer, the nurse's daughter who becomes a radiologist, the policeman's son who becomes an internal revenue agent, all are examples where something is retained and, inseparably, a transformation takes place. What is retained may be the occupational status (the physician's son who becomes a lawyer) or the vocational locus (the nurse's daughter who becomes a doctor), and compose the core of the equivalence. The new element, involving both the rejection of the past and innovation, enables the heir to take possession of something that actually was passed on to him. The point is not simply that he must 'make something of what was made of him', as Sartre put it so aptly, but that he make something of what has been passed on to him.

At this stage, we feel it necessary to introduce an essential concept: namely, transmissibility. Its point is to remind us that all of the elements composing the social status of the family of origin are not equally transmissible, and that this is the case irrespective of the receptiveness of the potential heirs.

A few gross examples may be given, for the sake of clarity. Cash is 100 per cent transmissible from parents to children. Real estate is 80 per cent transmissible in France (there is a 20 per cent tax on inherited property). But what is the degree of transmissibility of high academic or intellectual achievement, or of a gift for some art? Of skill in a trade? Of a prominent political position? Of integration in an exclusive social milieu? However great the will—and the ability—of the older generation to achieve this transmission and the ability—and the will—of the descendant to receive it, the transmissibility of these resources or assets is extremely variable. Their transmission may be greatly facilitated or inhibited by various contexts. The transmissibility of an element of status as a resource is directly proportionate to its degree of objectivation, and reversely proportionate to its degree of subjectivation; and this is perhaps one of the reasons that encourage people to try to convert the other elements of status—academic achievement, political position, reputation—into money, an entirely objectivated and therefore transmissible form. In short, the relative degree of transmissibility seems to be an essential feature of those resources that parents attempt to pass on to their children. For this reason, it may be said that one can only pass on what one really possesses, and more accurately: one only really possesses what one can give away.

It is because many elements of status have a low degree of transmissibility that transmissions are so frequently implemented by transforming a resource into a condition for action. For instance, the capital accumulated by Baptiste, followed by Charles, generated some income, which was used to place Désiré in academically conducive conditions in the best secondary school in town.

This 'strategy', which aimed at having him go on to higher education, was relatively unsuccessful as such, for he became neither a teacher nor an officer. But conversely, that strategy put him in the right place to marry well. In both cases, however, for a successful education as well as for successful marriage, he was obliged to go through a period of personal praxis. Seduction, like academic success, could not be achieved without a modicum of effort of his own. His parents and life itself had created a range of possible destinies for him, but it was up to him, through praxis, to transform a potential into actual fact.

These remarks simply point to a direction through which we may surmount the dilemma of structuralism versus voluntarism; for the sociology of social mobility, the latter translates into the opposition between the 'reproductive' view and the 'competitive' view of social mobility. We have attempted to demonstrate that socio-structural components may be found in those decisions and acts apparently most clearly powered by will: and conversely, that praxis may be found in the very heart of what, viewed from afar, seems to be pure reproduction by direct transmission. The idea, quite self-evident in fact, that a life trajectory may be determined—or rather, conditioned—much more easily by the supplying of a resource than by the imposition of a constraint lends an entirely new content to the concept of determination: one that includes both the socio-structural dimension and praxis.

## ON QUALITATIVE ANALYSIS

If we were to advance a conclusion to this chapter—which would be contradictory to its spirit since, conversely, it attempts to open doors—we would not review all of the notions and hypotheses advanced here, but rather, would take a look at the very concept of qualitative analysis. Never before, as strongly as during the present case study, had we felt the need to name the phenomena identified, to operate apparently arbitrary comparisons, to reverse the usual perspectives, simply to see whether the opposite angle was meaningful (and it usually was). And as it comes to the close, this study imparts the impression that theorization plays exactly the same role with respect to 'qualitative' material as statistical methods do for quantitative data.

Indeed, the foremost difference between quantitative material and the material derived from direct observation does not reside in the fact that the former, as opposed to the latter, are intended to be quantified, but rather, that quantitative material claims to be post-theoretical—the verification of hypotheses—whereas 'qualitative' observations are pre-theoretical. In the latter case, analysis and theorization are synonymous, and take place in a dialectical to-and-fro movement between observation and conceptualization. Whereas the quantitative paradigm involves the identification of statistical relations of covariance between factors defined prior to data collection, qualitative analysis aims at discovering what it's all about: at identifying relationships, processes, causal links, contradictions, shifts in meaning, all visible only through the shadows they cast. This is the practice so admirably illustrated by the work of Clifford Geertz.[6]

This conception of sociological practice is certainly nowhere near the scientistic view, which would have sociology become 'a science among others'; that is, a science bent on discovering invariable laws. But perhaps the time has come for us to acknowledge the existence of a third space, outside of those spaces occupied by the natural sciences and by literature and the arts: one that possesses its own regimen of truth. It is precisely because that space contains criteria for comparing the relative value of various interpretations of a same phenomenon that the interpretative imagination may be given free rein.

*Translated by Helen Arnold*

### NOTES

1. Pierre Bourdieu, *The Logic of Practice* (Stanford, Calif., 1990), first published in French as *Le Sens pratique* (Paris, 1980); Anthony Giddens, *Central Problems in Social Theory: Action, Structure and Contradiction in Social Analysis* (London, 1979), and *The Constitution of Society: Outline of the Theory of Structuration* (Cambridge, 1984); J. Alexander, *Action and its Environment* (New York, 1988).
2. Daniel Bertaux and Isabelle Bertaux-Wiame, 'Artisanal Bakery in France: How it Lives and Why it Survives', in Frank Bechhofer and Brian Elliott (eds), *The Petite Bourgeoisie: Comparative Studies of the Uneasy Stratum* (London, 1980); Daniel Bertaux and Isabelle Bertaux-Wiame (in collaboration with Paul Thompson), *Familles et mobilité sociale: Une enquête comparative*, Research Project, CNRS, 1984; Daniel Bertaux, 'L'Indépendance, la délinquance, et les deux salariats', *Annales de Vaucresson*, 26 (1987), 279–95; 'Familles et mobilité sociale: La Méthode des généalogies sociales comparées', in Nunes de Almeida et al. (sous la dir. de), *Familles et contextes sociaux: Les Espaces et les temps de la diversité* (Lisbonne, 1991), 297–317; and 'Social Genealogies, Commented and Compared: An Instrument for Studying Social Mobility Processes in the "longue durée"', *Current Sociology*, special edition, Marco Diani (ed.), 'The Biographical Method', 43 (2) (1995), 70–88.
3. The actual first names have been changed, and we took this opportunity to use names whose alphabetical order designates the order of the generations: the miller was given a name beginning with an A, his sons' names begin with a B, and so on. This system was extended to their wives (Blanche, Camille, Diane).

4. For a sociologist, the trichotomous classification of occupations prevailing in Italy is extremely interesting: there are independent workers, civil servants, and 'dependenti', i.e. dependent wage-earners. This distinction amongst wage-earners, between those who are dependent because they are constantly threatened with the loss of their job, and the civil servants who have the benefit of job security and are therefore somewhat 'independent' within the wage-earning category, seems extremely relevant. There is nothing surprising in the fact that Désiré's father encouraged him to become a teacher; from the craftsman's or businessman's standpoint, a civil-servant job combines the advantages of job security with those of a degree of independence. Risk-free independence, the perfect combination.
5. As Goethe puts it so aptly:

| Was du von deinen Vätern | What from your ancestors |
| Ererbt hast | You have inherited |
| Erwirb es | Earn it thoroughly |
| Um es zu besitzen. | To make it your own. |

6. Clifford Geertz, *Interpretation of Cultures: Selected Essays* (New York, 1977); *Local Knowledge: Further Essays in Interpretive Anthropology* (New York, 1985); Barney G. Glaser, *Theoretical Sensitivity: Advances in the Methodology of Grounded Theory* (Mill Valley, Calif., 1978).

# 4

# Shadow and Reality in Occupational History: Britain in the First Half of the Twentieth Century

DAVID VINCENT

This is a study of social mobility which existed only in the mind. Its central concern is with occupations which were never found, with work histories which never took place. The analysis explores the origin, substance, and function of the imagined alternative careers which men and women carried with them as they conducted their actual careers in the British economy from the years before 1914 until the early decades after the Second World War.

At first sight, such an enterprise appears to be substituting one set of illusions for another. It has long been a criticism of quantitative approaches to social mobility that the sophisticated graphs and tables bear only a distant relation to the working lives they purport to explain. In the marriage registers, which supply the bulk of the data for the study of mobility in past societies, fathers who may be dead are contrasted with sons who may be nowhere near their 'destination', always supposing they have one to reach.[1] The transitions are plotted across vertical occupational or class hierarchies[2] whose construction may owe more to the theoretical assumptions of the observer than the operational strategies of the observed.[3] Analytical tools, such as log linear analysis, may appear to substitute statistical artefacts for the real lives of actors whose behaviour and aspirations are more often imputed than described.[4]

The dangers of abstraction can be justified by the need to count what can be counted, and may be reduced by infusing the mobility models with more empirical evidence of the actual values and practices of individuals and groups in specific social and historical contexts.[5] Nevertheless the perceived limitations of quantitative methods have in recent years led to a search for alternative approaches to intergenerational and intragenerational work histories which depend on descriptions and explanations supplied by the actors involved. These are derived by interview for the era which the tape-recorder can reach, and for earlier periods may be mined from surviving literary genres, particularly autobiography.[6] Such categories of source material offer the possibility of charting more intricate webs of movement across and between generations and of examining in much greater detail the patterns of meaning which were invested in them. However it should not be supposed that the move from numbers to narratives involves a straightforward transition from the artificial to the real.[7] Setting aside the critical issues of the shaping intervention of the publisher or the interviewer, and the conditioning effects of literary form or spoken convention,[8] there remains the question of the practice of the witnesses as historians. Whether they are setting forth an integrated story of a complete life, or supplying more fragmented responses to an interview schedule, they are all engaged in the basic task of retrospective analysis. As such, every account they give is suspended between what was and what might have been.

The possibilities which most attract scholars to these forms of evidence depend on the capacity of the subject to stand back from a bare narrative of events. If the sheer complexity of the forces which shape and constrain a work history are to be charted, then there has to be a weighting of the comparative influence of parents, schooling, gender relations, family economies, occupational structures, and local and national labour markets as they change over time. For the witness, as for any professional sociologist or historian, each statement of cause involves the assumption of an alternative trajectory which failed to happen. If the early death of a mother, for instance, is held by the respondent to have wrecked the daughter's prospective career, then the substance of the frustrated possibility needs to be shown. This task informs and is informed by the central question of what the witness wanted as a 'career',[9] how ambition was shaped and changed over time, and what verdict was drawn from the outcome of a lifetime's economic endeavour. Aspiration patrols the shifting boundary between dream and reality. Neither actuality nor desire can be obliterated entirely—the most grandiose dreamer must sooner or later eat, the most confined labourer will have some sense of a better world—but the relation between them can only be established by the study of the component members of a particular generation in a specific social and economic context.

In this case the evidence is supplied by the first and to date last major national survey by taped interview carried out in Britain. Between 1969 and 1973, Paul Thompson and his collaborators at the University of Essex recorded the recollections of 444 respondents who had grown up before the First World War.[10] The sample was designed to give proportionate representation by gender, region, and occupation, and the questions ranged over a wide range of practices and attitudes of both the individual witnesses and where possible their relatives. Although the exercise bore the title of 'Family Life and Work before 1918', some aspects of the interviews usually continued well into the post-Second World War era, and the respondents were throughout reviewing their past in the light of their outlook at the time the questioning took place. Much of the evidence on social history was subsequently published,[11] but the material on the working lives of the subjects and their kin was not systematically exploited and in the intervening two decades has become a historical record in its own right.[12] For this study, the replies to the occupational questions have been reanalysed, with attention paid both to the sequence of jobs which were held, and the alternative visions of employment which illuminated the witnesses' careers.

The form and function of shadow careers generates three broad questions: the interaction between school, family, and wider economic, social, and political forces in shaping work histories; the relationship between individual time, family time, and the history of the economy in general and of the separate occupations within it; and the perceived balance between structure and agency as the witnesses strive to make sense of what did and did not come to pass. The following discussion begins with an investigation of the substance of the shadow occupations, the frequency and the size of the gap between the actual pathway through the economy and the projected variation. It then looks in more detail at how choice was shaped and restricted during the process of entry into the labour market, and at how in later years the shadows deepened as the cohort of men and women developed a more mature understanding of their occupational fate, and a clearer conception of what might have been possible. Finally it examines the meanings invested in the shadow careers, and the conclusions which were drawn about the failure of the real world to live up to their hopes and plans.

## SHADOW CAREERS AND DREAMS

The group of individuals interviewed for the 'Family Life and Work' project belonged firmly to the 20th century. They were representative members of virtually the first generation in British history characterized by the universal experience of education. Compulsion had not been fully introduced until 1880, and it had taken a couple of decades for the attendance officers to impose their authority. It was not until 1914 that the illiteracy figures in the marriage registers finally fell below 1 per cent.[13] They all went to school, and almost all had some engagement with the labour market in the years that followed. This was true not only of the men who in most cases struggled to earn a living for more than half a century, but of the women who in the course of their lives lived through a slow but sustained growth in the range and availability of paid employment. In the sample, only one in nine of the female respondents failed to make any contribution to their family economies as either a child or an adult. Even the one titled lady interviewed in the survey made a tentative venture into the world of work, spending a few years as a nurse, partly for the sake of the company.[14]

At the very least this meant that almost every one of the respondents was aware of some possibilities of employment beyond their own career or lack of it. Very few replied to the question about alternative occupations with a flat denial of any conceivable alternative. Those that did were for the most part trapped in enclosed rural economies which had once been the common circumstance of the majority of the labouring poor. One such was a Shetlander confined to fishing or crofting.[15] There was, he said, 'nothing to choose out here.'[16] Other men grew up into single-industry economies, especially mining, where there was no point in even contemplating a different path. There was 'no other industry for miles around', explained a miner who had reluctantly followed his father underground, and retired from the same pit forty-nine years after.[17] Such a fate more often befell women in agricultural communities, where the restricted choice of jobs was compounded by limited educational opportunities and greater pressure to stay at home and assist dependent relatives. At best the choice was between casual agricultural work, domestic service, or, as in the case of a girl who worked as a surface tin miner until marriage, labour in the local industry. The wages were poor, but there was nowhere else to go: 'there wasn't nothing, except service.'[18] The less fortunate fetched up working in other people's houses—there were, recalled one servant, simply 'no opportunities in the village',[19] and the less fortunate still never escaped from housework in their own homes. The rare girl who made her way up the educational ladder was still faced with an overwhelming sense of restricted career options. A woman who reached the summit of most girls' ambitions and became a qualified teacher, replied dismissively that it 'was the only thing that anybody with any brain could do really'.[20]

This is not to say that every other respondent surveyed a wealth of choice at every occupational turn. Rather that they were able to step aside from their employment, however brief or unchanging it might have been, and construct some other occupational scenario. Even those with nothing to choose between were aware, at least by the time that they were interviewed, of some sense of loss. The most trapped were separated from the others by the desperate vagueness of their aspiration. A woman who never managed anything more than a little secretarial work for the family firm, longed for anything 'out of the home'.[21] Another who had been kept back to look after her father, taking in some dressmaking when she could, replied that she would have preferred any occupation with a little company: 'I used to envy girls that went out to work.'[22] The simplest possible response was given by a woman whose ambitions had been thwarted by her mother's invalidity: 'I would have like to have been something else.'[23] Such circumstances had kept their victims so far from the labour market that it was scarcely possible to give any shape to ambition. All that was left was a deep sense of waste, as in the case of the farmer's daughter whose mother would not let her explore the world beyond the fields: 'Well I had to stay home, dear, instead of doing what I wanted, using my brains—I had to stay home and milk cows and do all sorts.'[24]

Once out of the domestic arena, it was easier to define aspiration. A checker in a textile factory worked for forty years at the same task wishing that instead he had become a skilled fitter: 'Aye that were my ambition.'[25] What is striking about the dreams revealed by the respondents is their modest practicality. Apart from a flighty teacher who expressed a preference for the position of King's mistress '—I hear they used to have a nice time—',[26] The hopes were grounded in the real world. There were no fantasizing millionaires or film stars, instead a generation of men and women looking for careers which were just over the horizon. Two-thirds of those identifying specific jobs wanted to move across the class divide, while the remainder envisaged some movement within their class. The fitter's mate saw himself a carpenter, the wheelwright a clerk, the clerk an accountant. It was a form of relative occupational deprivation.[27] Advance was conceived in terms of steps rather than leaps. The unattained only had meaning if it could be connected to what had been achieved.

At its most confined, the distance between the actual and the desirable was virtually invisible to the naked eye. Contentment for a life-long pottery worker would have been a move from the small potbanks in which he worked to one of the handful of prestigious firms which dominated the industry.[28] Fellow potters might see this as a serious ambition rendered almost impossible by the clannish recruitment practices of the potteries;[29] outsiders would find it difficult to comprehend the substance of either the dream or the obstacle to its fulfilment. Even where the preference embodied a transformation of status which would have registered on any social mobility table, it generally contained an element of rationality. The two working men, for instance, who aspired to positions in the old professions, had both displayed ambition and ability during their working lives, rising to the limits of their given career ladders. 'What I would have liked to have done', recalled the first of these, 'was to go to school and university and entered the church.'[30] What he had actually done was work his way up the ranks in a textile factory, finishing as a foreman warehouseman. If the final promotion left him some way short of the ministry, it was a real advance: 'I wasn't labouring when I finished. It was a good move.' The second had wanted to be a lawyer, but 'the finance wasn't there';[31] instead he had begun on the railways as a goods porter and climbed rung after rung of the long hierarchy until he reached his summit as an inspector five years before retirement.[32]

The comparative poverty of aspiration was still more marked among the female respondents. In general terms, the careers revealed by the survey were characterized by fracture and meander.

Whereas half the men enjoyed what may be termed 'gold watch' careers, periods of work for the same employer which lasted for at least three and sometimes for as much as five decades, only 7 per cent of women did so, and then usually at the cost of marriage and family.[33] Instead instability was the rule, and it is perhaps not surprising that the unfulfilled preferences were for forms of employment which could maintain some continuity during the almost inevitable disruptions of family life. An occasional domestic servant and waitress wished she had been apprenticed to a trade, 'because you can always go back to those'.[34] By the beginning of this period the centuries-long erosion of skilled female occupations had left only the attenuated and declining trade of dressmaking, which was still the conventional basic aspiration of a mother for her daughter. It was both an extension of domestic labour and a bulwark against the danger of being driven out of the labour market by domestic responsibilities. Thus a women who had never managed anything more than paid child-minding, apart from munition work in the war, always regretted that she had been unable to 'go in for dressmaking or millinery'.[35] However as these apprenticed personal trades were contracting, they were being replaced by two modern certificated occupations, which in a sense were also extensions of domestic skills. There were enough imagined nurses in the sample to staff a small phantom hospital. The frequency of this stated aspiration may have owed as much to the growth of the National Health Service in the decades immediately prior to the interviews as to the number of openings in the Edwardian economy. Nevertheless by the early years of the century it had become a sufficiently real and respectable profession to inform the dreams of cohorts of adolescent girls as they struggled to free themselves from family responsibilities.[36] 'Yes, I'd liked to have gone as a nurse', replied another who had become only a nursemaid, 'but you know in those days the eldest daughter was considered—it was considered right for her to stay at home.'[37] For those with the middle class in their sights, the permanent qualifications of the professional teacher seemed in general more secure than the increasingly available posts in offices.

Amidst these logical and limited goals, however, there were also the professed alternatives which were equally modest but wholly illogical, at least in terms of the models of behaviour which inform conventional social mobility research. One of the women who actually became a teacher wished she had spent her working life on a farm.[38] A man who had reached the respectable white-collar position of ledger clerk, confessed that, 'I think I might have liked to have done manual work.'[39] These interviews strongly suggest that more respect needs to be paid to impenetrable private predilections in the generation of career aspirations.[40] Here we have the potbank fireman who really wanted to be a colour mixer in the same factory, the telegraphist who longed to be a musician, the fitter who dreamed of being a driver, the driver who saw himself as a club doorman in the West End. When a former policeman states that his real desire was to be a fireman, there is no point in trying to explain his preference or generalize from it.[41] The nearest these private dreams come to recognizable patterns of aspiration is in the occasional wistful vision of a more romantic alternative to the grinding virtue of their working lives. There was the woman married at 18 to an invalid husband and thereafter toiling at a variety of manual occupations until she was 70, all along wishing she had had a career on the stage.[42] And there was the accountant beset by nagging doubts that perhaps he had not filled life's cup quite to the brim: 'My parents had always stressed the value of less money for a secure job, and apart from a very short period in my life I have always been fully employed and I've been very grateful for it. And looking back I suppose there are moments when I would have very much liked to have had a more adventurous and more colourful sort of life, but of course, I'm now reaping the fruits of . . . shall we say the years of monotony by the things that a secure job has.'[43]

A third of the respondents in the sample presented some discussion of career alternatives. Only a handful explicitly rejected the question on the grounds of an overwhelming liking for the occupation they had actually followed. Again there was a strong element of purely idiosyncratic preference in their commitment to occupations which most had not actually chosen to follow. It was not just that the passage of time habituated some workers to their destiny where it alienated others, as with a life-long miner who had gone reluctantly underground, but in the end had no desire for anything else, '`cos I'd just gradually got nestled into it.'[44] Rather it was a pleasure amounting at times to a passion for trades which simply suited the aptitude or temperament of those who followed them. These were the round pegs in the round holes. It might be a profession of recognized status and reward, as in the case of the respondent who flatly stated, 'I was born to be an architect and nothing else',[45] but more often these were occupations whose beauty lay solely in the eyes of the beholder. 'I had a very happy time', replied a lorry driver;[46] 'I liked it grand' insisted a saddler who had followed his father and brothers into the trade;[47] there was no point in a different prospect argued an engineer, 'because I like me work'.[48] Where reasons were given they did not necessarily enlarge the argument: according to one of several contented railwaymen, 'I thoroughly enjoyed my life on the railway as a fireman and driver. Thoroughly enjoyed it because you were travelling all the time.'[49]

Railwaymen, if they were successful, travelled in more than one dimension. The one discernible pattern amidst these preferences is occupational advance. Another railwayman recounted a lifetime spent climbing through the grades from train register boy—'I did all these jobs you know, up and up'—and as a consequence could say of an alternative career, 'I never dreamt of it.'[50] This tendency was particularly noticeable among the small group of entrepreneurs in the sample, whose commitment to their businesses had absorbed all their ambitions. One respondent who 'never wanted a different occupation' recounted how he had taken on and enlarged his father's wholesale firm: 'It's progressed very much, very much. But I've always been interested in progress you see. I've always wanted to do more and more. I've always been creative.'[51] It is here that we find the small group of women who were wedded to the work histories they recounted. A barmaid who had risen to become licensee of her own pub until her reluctant retirement at 71, looked back without regret: 'I loved it, I enjoyed every moment of it.'[52] It was not a matter of money so much as the fascination of developing your own enterprise. Thus it was with an energetic Scot who had been the guiding force in the butcher's business she ran with her husband. Amongst her many achievements was making the first black pudding in Dumfries; as to another occupation, 'I never gave it a thought.'[53]

## CHOICE AND CONSTRAINT

The men and women in the 'Family Life and Work' survey had lived through a series of major secular upheavals, including two world wars and the Great Depression, but as they reviewed their work histories, the most dramatic period was usually located in their early teens. It was at this time, around the end of the first decade of the century, that the tensions between the three great forces in their youth—family, school, and the economy—were resolved in ways which had a lasting effect on the paths they followed and the shadow careers which accompanied them.

The expressed wishes of parents were at once the most direct and the most distant influences on the aspirations of their children. In a practical sense their intervention was vital.[54] The methods by which the respondents found their first proper jobs indicate just how limited were the advances made by the bureaucratization of employment. For every post provided by formal devices, three were located by the applicants themselves, their parents, their siblings, their uncles and aunts, and other friends and neighbours.[55] Compared with earlier generations, a greater role was being played by agencies such as the labour exchanges which opened their doors in 1909, or by juvenile bureaux and county education committees,[56] or by influential individuals in the community such as schoolteachers and clergymen, or by commercial devices such as typing agencies, servant registries, and newspaper advertisements, but they were still operating on the margins of the problem. Whereas children might be left to their own devices as they fixed up the myriad of part-time or temporary jobs which usually surrounded the final years of schooling, the pursuit of their first main job would generally be conducted with the controlling assistance of parents, older siblings, or nearby kin.[57]

Few ambitions could be realized without the help of the extended family, but it is evident that those amongst whom the children had grown up did little to enhance their aspirations. The most that happened was that the boys were pushed towards occupations offering the greatest security—a skilled trade or for the better educated perhaps a position in one of the rapidly expanding credentialized occupations such as the railways or the post office. Thus for instance one boy was permitted to find his own initial job selling fruit on a market stall, but when it was time to enter the real world, his desire to become involved in the fledgling film industry was firmly quashed, and he was put in for the civil-service examination to become an assistant postman, and so were his brothers in their turn.[58] As he explained, 'my father was keen on all the family going into something where there's a pension attached to it for after life.'⁵⁹ For most daughters it was assumed that their future husbands would provide for their life after marriage. Some mothers strove to find them a trade, but where resources were limited, the prospects of the sons were always paramount. 'She gave all the boys a chance for a trade', recalled one witness, 'and when I wanted to be a dressmaker she said boys needed it for their future but girls married for their future.'⁶⁰ Instead she was kept at home to help run the family until she was 17, and then allowed a brief job as an office girl in a grocery before returning to housework to await her marriage.

The best that can be said for the parents is that they were being both realistic and responsible. They knew from their own long experience of the labour market what were the feasible limits to ambition; it would be no favour to their children to fill their heads with dreams of the unattainable. What may be said against them, as against any older generation in a time of changing opportunities, is that they were a confining and conservative influence in the career development of their sons and perhaps even more so of their daughters. Men and women who finally left the labour market when Harold Wilson was Prime Minister had their occupational aspirations shaped by parents who had begun work when Gladstone was in office. In structural terms, the restrictions were at their most acute where offspring were compelled to take over a family business which belonged intrinsically to the 19th century rather than the 20th. One son who hankered after clerical work was forced to train as a wheelwright in order to take over his father's declining business. The nearest he got to realizing his alternative ambition was when he became a part-time sub-postmaster in order to eke out his increasingly meagre earnings.⁶¹ Another was trapped in the family wholesale trade which was succumbing to the development of motor transport, and it was not until his father finally retired that he was able to retrain as a doctor, 'what I'd always wanted to.'⁶²

Daughters were less often hampered by the weight of inheritance. Instead they found themselves held back from the opportunities created by the new century. The generation of girls in the sample grew up just in time to exploit the rapid growth in office work,⁶³ a world which their parents neither knew nor understood. Sixty years later a witness recalled how her one chance of a career disappeared when her father refused to let her make use of the shorthand and typing course she had attended.[64] Another was prevented from joining the ranks of the newly organized profession of midwifery because her mother simply did not know how to deal with the application forms and entry requirements.[65] The past lay like a dead hand on the prospects of such girls. With the critical decisions on their future being taken when they were still too young to form or enforce their own judgement, they were critically dependent on advice and encouragement which was rarely forthcoming from their parents. Unlike earlier generations, every daughter had been to school, but the great majority lacked the assistance they required to exploit the limited possibilities their education had given them. All her life one witness felt bitter about the way she was prevented from escaping the traditional fate of mill-town girls: 'I don't remember father ever suggesting that we ought to strike out, we ought to be ambitious. We were never taught to be ambitious and we were never taught to be pushing ... there was no guidance from mother because—perhaps I ought not to blame her because she'd never known anything else. Father was the one who might have taken the initiative but didn't ... There was very little guidance in those days because there was no bridge whatever between leaving school and being dumped into a factory. None whatever. ... I couldn't say there was any real encouragement or guidance to do anything else, only follow the pattern of going into the mill ...'[66]

Within the family, the best source of a challenge to the poverty of expectations was their own age group. The decline in the size of working-class families was only just beginning, and in urban areas, kinship networks were historically at their most dense.[67] There were usually older siblings or cousins already in the labour market whose reported experiences would be eagerly sought. Their pathways provided the most practical prospectus of the breadth of career possibilities, and they were in a position to give a more realistic assessment of the enticing world which lay outside the playground walls. If their new-found wealth encouraged the earliest possible abandonment of lessons, their accounts of physically demanding, dead-end work could have the reverse effect. For a girl growing up in a textile community, the one alternative vision of her future was supplied not by her parents but by her sister who had preceded her into the local industry: 'it was only when I came very near school leaving age that my sister—the elder one Kathy—was so anxious that I should try to get a scholarship in order to do better than she had done by being pushed into the mill'.[68]

The scholarship in question was of recent origin. At the beginning of the century, the state had made a tentative effort to establish a stairway up from the ground floor of the educational system. It was approached through a very narrow doorway. In practice, the Balfour Act of 1902 created more shadow than real careers as for the first time gifted children caught sight of still largely unattainable futures. Of the first cohort of children to benefit from the Act, only one in fourteen elementary schoolboys and one in twenty girls reached a maintained secondary school, and only 1 per cent of boys and as third as many girls made it all the way to university.[69] Most poor but able children received an education merely in what might have been possible. Where these dreams were nurtured by an ambitious teacher, the experience was profoundly unsettling. The promising pupil could vividly remember half a century later the brief moment when an authoritative but almost inevitably hopeless vision was conjured forth. A life-long gardener had not forgotten his schoolmaster's words: 'He said to my mother he said, "your boy writes a lovely civil service hand, he is too good for what they call a knock about job", you know, but that's what happened in those days and that was it. My Mum was glad of the few shillings.'[70]

Schoolteachers were free to generate visions of alternative careers, but powerless to implement them. They might have more ideas than the parents, but the material resources of the family were always the controlling factor. If the children were only dimly aware at the time of what they were missing, they knew well enough why the decisions were taken. 'Somehow I had an idea at the back of my mind I was fit for better things', recalled a textile worker, 'but it wasn't possible, for home circumstances for one reason because being a big family my money was necessary... I should have wanted keeping while I was training. And as I say, the family needed money—so I was anchored.'[71] The varying fortunes of siblings could suggest alternative avenues, but their most important role in occupational planning was their mere presence in the family. Another mill worker's dreams of escaping the local occupational tradition similarly foundered on the rocks of the domestic economy. 'I'd have liked to have gone on [to] further education and become a schoolmaster. Yes I would. But I never got the opportunity, with being such a big family they couldn't afford [it], the schooling was very difficult in those days.'[72]

Not all homes contained large numbers of children, even in the classic pre-20th-century reproductive model. Chance played an important part in determining the size of the completed family, and with it the opportunities for investing in the future of the next generation. It was largely to guarantee that resources would still be available for the increasing cost of preparing their offspring for the labour market that the middle class began to take effective steps to limit their numbers during the closing decades of the 19th century. By the Edwardian period, the more prosperous sections of the working class were coming to accept that the capacity of a family to 'get on' depended on restricting the number of pregnancies.[73] Credentialism went hand in hand with birth control. The poorer children in the sample illustrate the lottery which still prevailed in families which had yet to adjust their reproductive behaviour to the logic of educational reform. There might be a dozen siblings competing for the family income or none at all; at the critical moment of decision over a scholarship, taken when the child was still only 12 or 13, the family might be disrupted by the birth of yet another child, or the illness or even death of a parent. The daughters were most at risk. Their entitlement to a career was at best fragile, and was easily overridden by domestic crisis. One girl had the opportunity to stay on at school and take the civil-service examination: 'at the time I couldn't do it. 'Cos the children were all bad. Well I was awful sorry for that because it would have been a good chance for me.'[74] Instead of becoming a clerk in the post office she spent her working life laying out and washing the dead in the neighbourhood. The common refrain of the would-be nurses in the sample was the need to confine their caring skills to their own family. In one case the mother had become an invalid,[75] in another the daughter had to stay home because she was the eldest,[76] in another it was because she was the last-born: 'I had my own ideas about what I'd like to be but I wasn't allowed—I had to stop at home because I was the youngest of the family.'[77]

There was regret, a sense of loss which lasted a lifetime, but rarely any censure. Retrospection could generate criticism of the parents' restricted vision, but it could never reconstruct their limited resources. All the children knew the material realities of their home, and accepted that their parents could not surmount them at the behest of a well-meaning teacher. Instead the pain of frustrated hope was softened by the sense of satisfaction or even pride in being able to make a vital contribution to the family's survival. A shoemaker wished he had more education, which would have enabled him to escape the family trade, but none the less recalled that when he brought home his first earnings, 'I felt like a hero.'[78] An insurance clerk who had been prevented from staying on at school to take a proffered scholarship because his mother was a widow, still remembered his feeling when he was first able to stand in for his missing father: 'It was quite a change from school and I remember being very proud to pass the half crown to my mother as my first manly earnings. Like I imagined a savage youth would feel when he brought home his first tiger. It made you feel into a man—a status symbol.'[79] The anger and recrimination was the province not of the child but the frustrated teacher, who had a sharper understanding of what the pupil was losing, but a weaker grasp of the reason why. In the case, for instance, of the girl who was forced to become shop assistant instead of staying on to train for the teaching profession, it was her schoolmaster who, 'never forgave her parents for taking her from school' to help in the family business.[80] The pupil caught between the warring adults was just left 'very upset', and with a tendency throughout her life to compare her actual work history with its more secure and better-paid shadow.

Critical career decisions were in most cases taken long before the individual in question was capable of forming a mature view of the occupational journey which lay ahead. The witnesses looked back with rueful affection at their youthful impetuosity. Rather than prolonging their education to prepare themselves for adult life, so many left in order to feel adult before their time. The shift from being a dependent to a contributory member of a family economy represented a major advance in self-perceived age. 'I were a big man when I went half-time',[81] recalled a former textile worker, although he missed school when he left for good. However absurd such feelings might seem when viewed from real manhood, they were a real presence in the transition to the world of work. A sometime plumber and actor could well remember the end of his first week as an apprentice: 'I was quite proud to bring home the pay packet to my mother.'[82] Perspectives changed with the advancing years. A girl wanted to get out of school and 'go a-working' as soon as she could, 'older, you know, I felt older', but later saw the early end to her education as the cause of her restricted occupational horizon. She might have looked for an alternative to mill work, 'if I'd've been better educated, you know. If I'd gone to any classes and so on, but you just did it, you see.'[83]

The passage of time turned children from willing collaborators to regretful critics of the curtailment of their career prospects. The would-be university student and vicar whom we saw 'anchored' by his family to the textile industry, none the less said of his entry into the mill, 'Oh it was grand for a beginning.'[84] Children may instinctively have grasped the realities of the material pressures which determined their departure from school, but they were rarely able to estimate the full range of the alternatives which were being closed down. There was little opportunity for contemplation. 'I had to go in and work, earn some money, that's all people thought about those days', said a former shop assistant, 'Get a job and get on with it.'[85] The decades to come provided the opportunity for more spacious reflection. Only once the road had been taken up was it possible to see clearly those roads which had not been followed. 'I've realized since I got older', admitted a former mill worker, 'that I could have gone a lot further if I'd had further education.'[86]

At the ages of 11 or 12, the sun was directly overhead and the shadows were short. For those who happened to find themselves in careers which continued to suit their needs and inclinations, the passing years caused no regrets. It was always possible to become habituated to unexpected situations, such as the man who had been made a table polisher entirely by accident, and had remained in his job for the following forty years.[87] After a while, he explained there had been no reason to think of alternatives: 'not when once you got used to it and got to know everybody and all that.'[88] There were those, however, for whom time served merely to lengthen the shadows surrounding their working lives. In part their discontents were generated by the disruptions of the crowded history of the first half of the 20th century. A young grocery worker was content with his lot until he went off to fight the Germans, but found himself unable to settle to his dull routine on his return to civvy street. The First World War was particularly unsettling for those women who were suddenly translated from traditional 'female' occupations into munition factories and other work hitherto reserved for their menfolk. For a brief period they performed their patriotic duty in jobs which in general provided more variety and interest, better company, sometimes improved status and almost always better pay. Then the Armistice was signed and they were thrust back into roles which now seemed a little less inevitable than once they had.[89] This cohort were well into middle age by the time Britain went to war again, and most had abandoned their main jobs on marriage, either staying at home to look after their families, or re-entering the labour market on a casual basis. Here the disruption was of a different form as mobilization offered purposeful careers, especially in administration, which unlike the First World War jobs, did not necessarily end with peace.[90] Some discovered latent skills and ambitions and worked on until retirement a decade or so later. For the men who were now too old to fight there was also an opportunity to explore alternatives. An engineer who had been thrown out of work during the Depression was taken on as a government instructor, thus discovering what he had always suspected that he was a born teacher.[91]

The Depression itself did more to terminate old aspirations than to generate new ones. It confirmed one respondent in his regret that he had not received enough education to place him in a more secure sector of the economy,[92] but even in the marginally less disrupted years in which this cohort was growing up, every child knew that a white-collar job or a time-served apprenticeship offered the safer future. It was not so much mass unemployment itself, as the underlying changes in the nature and provision of work which created the real sense of unfulfilled aspiration. At its most general, the feeling was captured by the witness who had spent fifty-two years working his way up the complex hierarchy of the co-op retail system. He had finally reached his goal as a manager, but had increasingly begun to wonder whether this was what he really wanted. 'Had there been modern opportunities', he said of his ambitions, he would have liked a clerical job, 'or the teaching profession or something like that'.[93] The years through which the respondents had lived had altered their sense of the possible. As they concluded their careers, it was difficult to resist the temptation to compare the perceived opportunities facing a young teenager in the Edwardian economy with the prospects awaiting a school-leaver in the 1950s and 1960s. Take for instance the skilled skip maker, who at the time had been very grateful to find a good opening from school: 'you were jolly lucky to get a trade, to be respected as a craftsman.'[94] For the next fifty years he had plied his trade in the same factory, his sense of security and self-respect increasingly challenged by the growing variety of work available to the 'younger generations', who, as he wistfully remarked, seemed to be having 'more excitement' in their working lives.

During the long years between the first encounter with the world of work, which often occurred while the child was still at school, and the final departure from it, which for most of the men and some of the women took place half a century later, the determining factors of family, education, and the labour market were interrogated afresh in the light of changing circumstances. The outcome might be the erosion of established satisfactions or the confirmation of long-held grievances. Where once the teenager had dreamed of a possibility, he or she could now see it as a living reality. One of the fiercest protests against a terminated schooling was entered by a miner's son who was unable to escape his destiny despite the educational reforms a few years earlier. He had passed the examination to the local grammar school, 'but my father said no come to work underground. And three weeks before I was 14 father brought me a shovel size two... Then I was 14 on the Wednesday, my father took me to Ton Hir on the Thursday. I was very annoyed. It very near broke my heart.' For a while he used to return to the classroom when the colliery shut for some reason, but finally had to settle down to what turned out to be forty-eight years in the pit, a fate which became no more acceptable as the years passed. His concluding view was that 'I'd loved it if I'd had the opportunities that young people get today.'[95]

With this miner, as with the sample in general, there is the sense of a generation suspended between its predecessor and its successor. Expectations were shaped and constrained by essentially Victorian parents, and then reopened and reassessed by children of the mid-20th century. A single life embraced a hundred years of hopes and aspirations. As they raised their own families, and in some instances watched their own children raise theirs in turn, old tensions were played out from a different perspective and in a new context. A woman who had traversed a standard sequence of unskilled factory jobs before marriage only began to entertain an alternative scenario for herself when she was forced back to work in a laundry in the 1930s to meet the expenses incurred by her son's scholarship to a grammar school. 'I would have liked another occupation', she concluded, 'but I'd have had to have a different education.'[96] Whilst the Fisher Act of 1918 and the Butler Act of 1944 created new horizons for fresh cohorts of pupils, they merely deepened the shadows of many of their parents. As she saw her daughter enlarge her future, a former mill-worker began to rewrite her own past. Had such an education been available to her generation, 'we'd have got better jobs, we wouldn't have had to go in the mill.'[97] She now knew with absolute certainty that her life-long secret ambition of working in a hospital had been both feasible and unattainable.

The envisioned work histories all began in the classroom. An electrician who had spent forty-two years working his way up to chargehand in a factory was concerned most of all to change what had happened in the critical months before he entered the labour market: 'I think I could have gone farther had I took on a bit more education.'[98] The turning-points which failed to turn were located outside the career itself. A miner who had worked at the coal-face until 1954, when a broken arm forced him to become a pit instructor, rested his case for an alternative trajectory on the short years of his time as a schoolboy: 'I regret—I reckon I should have been a—a little bit better if I hadn't missed my schooling. I mean, I was witty enough and all that ... if I'd had a better chance, I should have been something better—bit better somewhere, shouldn't have been worse anyway.'[99] This conviction that education and its absence held the key to shadow careers arose partly from the fact that this generation had been born late enough to glimpse the reality of a scholarship system, and had lived long enough to see the beginning of its transformation into comprehensive secondary education and post-Robbins universities. Where their parents had little reason to expect anything of value from their only nominally universal and compulsory schooling, and their children could take for granted the existence, if not the award, of scholarships, the witnesses in the sample saw novelty everywhere in the education system, and potential in everything.

They had entered the labour market as credentialized recruitment practices and formal promotion systems were beginning to spread out from the limited innovations of the late 19th century. In practice there were fewer paper-based openings in the Edwardian period than may have appeared in retrospect, but over their working lives there had been a radical expansion in the range of occupations which required certificated qualifications for entry and for subsequent advance. The transformation in prospects was perhaps greatest for women as nursing, teaching, and typing provided more and more alternatives to factories and personal service. One respondent had led an essentially Victorian working life as a factory worker, domestic needleworker, and cook, regretting all the while the absence of the means to join the modern world: 'I certainly would have liked to have had the education to have got an office job.'[100] Another nurtured the ambition of replacing her traditional fate as a domestic servant with the shining new career of qualified social work.[101] Within a given occupation, the issue of promotion threw a retrospective shadow over a limited education. Credentials which had been good enough to secure entry began to seem less adequate as the prospect of upward mobility came into view. A factory machinist who had been eager to leave school and start his apprenticeship later came to regret his impatience which over a working life of fifty-five years had prevented him from reaching a 'higher pinnacle' in his trade.[102] A ship's engineer who had 'never liked school' found in the end that he lacked the education to sit the examination to become a chief engineer.[103]

## RESIGNATION AND REGRET

Substantive knowledge emerges from the shadows. An interrogation of the gaps between actuality and desire exposes the fault lines in the making of careers. A body of information which can only be derived from some kind of narrative discussion of a working life challenges the teleological assumptions inherent in forms of social mobility research based entirely on quantitative analysis. Neither the substance of aspiration nor the means by which it is generated and frustrated can be read from tables of inflow and outflow from one occupational or class position to another. There is no a priori reason why the existence, range, or intensity of ambition should be a constant over time, or across a population differentiated by age, gender, and fortune. Rather it may be argued that the wellsprings of longing are contingent on a particular set of constraints and opportunities, and on the ways in which a given set of individuals handles the outcome of their endeavours in the labour market.

In the case of the 'Family Life and Work' respondents, it has been possible to see how the tensions in the relationship between family, education, and work turned a cohort of men and women into counterfactual historians of their own lives. Unfulfilled ambition was scarcely the invention of the early 20th century, but it can be shown that the particular disjunction between expanding chances and constricting resources created shadow careers on a scale not experienced by earlier generations. Where scholarship, examination, and bureaucratized entry and promotion held out the prospect of children making their own escape from their background, in practice the limited ambitions and still more confined resources of the home denied the possibility to all but a fortunate few. At every turn, the expansion of perceived alternatives far outstripped the capacity to pursue them.

There was little anger in the interviews about the existence of unfulfilled aspiration. This reflected an inherited fatalism, which was only slowly being challenged by the rising expectations of the 20th century. The balance of resignation and regret was best caught by a woman who had 'known nothing all me life but hard work', as a domestic servant before marriage and a daily cleaner thereafter: 'I grieve sometimes and wish I could have had more of life than I have done. But it's no use wishing for it, I've got to make the best of things.'[104] There was no consistency in the substance of the ambition, only a growing assertion of the right to entertain one. At issue was not necessarily wealth or worldly success, but the freedom to define your own occupational goal, whatever it might be. A disappointment suffered in childhood had gained greater resonance by the time the witnesses were interviewed. Thus a woman who had been prevented from becoming a dressmaker, and had been kept out the labour market altogether until wartime, was able to draw a more general lesson from her disappointment: 'so I never really had the chance to do what I wanted to. And I think it's a great mistake. I think every child should be given what they think they're going to be good at or could do—let them do it and if they make a mistake, it doesn't turn out all right, well you've given them their chance.'[105]

Freedom meant responsibility, and it is striking that there was little self-criticism in these accounts. Very few of the witnesses attributed any blame to themselves for their failure to follow their preferred occupational course. Occasionally there was regret that more effort was not given to lessons, or that more attention was not paid to the advice of parents, but in general, structure was thought more important than agency in explaining the existence of shadow careers. For the same reason, parents were rarely censured. Material forces combined with sheer happenstance had determined whether the individual would ever be in a position to give expression to his or her inclinations and talents. This was a generation who believed they should have been able to choose, but not that they had ever done so. If education was seen as the key to opportunity, this was for the future, not the past. They had done their best with what they had been given, sometimes with pleasure, more often with indifference or frustration. Amongst those who had been shown alternatives they could never follow, there was an abiding sense of waste. In the words of a man who had been denied a scholarship by the poverty of his widowed mother, 'I think I would have been the type of mind that could have been much more usefully employed.'[106]

## NOTES

1. A. B. Sorensen, 'Theory and Methodology in Social Stratification', in U. Himmelstrand (ed.), *The Sociology of Structure and Action*, i. *Sociology: From Crisis to Science* (London, 1986), 78.
2. See e.g. G. Payne, *Employment and Opportunity* (London, 1987), 155–88.
3. R. Brown, 'Work Histories, Career Strategies and the Class Structure', in A. Giddens and G. Mackenzie (eds), *Social Class and the Division of Labour* (Cambridge, 1982).
4. For a discussion of the employment of log linear analysis for this purpose, see A. Miles, 'How Open was Nineteenth-Century British Society? Social Mobility and Equality of Opportunity, 1839–1914', in A. Miles and D. Vincent (eds), *Building European Society* (Manchester, 1993), 25–30; M. H. D. van Leeuwen and I. Maas, 'Log-Linear Analysis of Changes in Mobility Patterns', *Historical Methods*, 24 (1991), 66–79.
5. For a pioneering attempt to undertake such an exercise, see J. H.

Goldthorpe, *Social Mobility and Class Structure in Modern Britain* (Oxford, 1987), 217–50.
6. On the extent of working-class autobiography, see John Burnett, David Vincent, and David Mayall, *The Autobiography of the Working Class*, i–iii (Brighton, 1984, 1987, 1989). For an application of such material to the study of social mobility, see Miles, 'How Open was Nineteenth-Century British Society', 30–5.
7. On the escape from 'naive realism' in the treatment of oral life histories, see Raphael Samuel and Paul Thompson (eds), *The Myths We Live By* (London, 1990), 2. For criticism of the notion of biographical reality in written life histories, see A. Fleishman, *Figures of Autobiography* (Berkeley, 1983), 13–14; M. Sprinkler, 'Fictions of the Self: The End of Autobiography', in James Olney (ed.), *Autobiography: Essays Theoretical and Critical* (Princeton, 1980), 322–3; J. Pilling, *Autobiography and Imagination: Studies in Self-Scrutiny* (London, 1981), 116; R. Elbaz, *The Changing Nature of the Self* (London, 1988), 1.
8. For a discussion of these issues, see Paul Thompson, *The Voice of the Past* (Oxford, 1988); David Vincent, *Bread, Knowledge and Freedom* (London, 1979), 3–11; K. Plummer, *Documents of Life* (London, 1983), 99–106.
9. On the development of the ideology and practice of careers in this period, see David Vincent, 'Mobility, Bureaucracy and Careers in Twentieth-Century Britain', in Andrew Miles and David Vincent (eds), *Building European Society* (Manchester, 1993), 217–39. Also M. B. Arthur, D. T. Hall, and B. S. Lawrence (eds), *Handbook of Career Theory* (Cambridge, 1989), 7–25.
10. For brief descriptions of the survey, see Paul Thompson, 'Memory and History', *SSRC Newsletter*, June 1969, 16–18; Paul Thompson, *The Edwardians* (London, 1975), 7–8. I am very grateful to Paul Thompson for generously allowing me access to this material, and to Mary Girling for facilitating visits to the Essex Oral History Archive.
11. Most notably in Thompson, *Edwardians*; J. Gillis, *For Better, For Worse: British Marriages, 1600 to the Present* (New York, 1985); S. Meacham, *A Life Apart* (London, 1977); C. More, *Skill and the English Working Class, 1870–1914* (London, 1980); T. Thompson, *Edwardian Childhoods* (London, 1981).
12. See Vincent, 'Mobility, Bureaucracy and Careers', for a general exploration of the value of this archive for the study of careers.
13. David Vincent, *Literacy and Popular Culture* (Cambridge, 1989), 21–32, 46–9.
14. 'Family Life and Work' Interview (hereafter FLW) 398.
15. Paul Thompson, *Living the Fishing* (London, 1983), 308–30.

16. FLW 174.
17. FLW 458.
18. FLW 439.
19. FLW 38.
20. FLW 21. By 1914 three-quarters of all teachers were women, although more women than men were also unqualified. Asher Tropp, *The School Teachers* (London, 1957), 118. Jane Rendall, *Women in an Industrializing Society* (London, 1990), 75.
21. FLW 267.
22. FLW 320.
23. FLW 119.
24. FLW 456.
25. FLW 237.
26. FLW 250.
27. On the restricted ambitions of those at the lower end of society, see W. G. Runciman, *Relative Deprivation and Social Justice* (Harmondsworth, 1972), 222–45.
28. FLW 254.
29. Richard Whipp, *Patterns of Labour: Work and Social Change in the Pottery Industry* (London, 1990), 74–5.
30. FLW 67.
31. FLW 74.
32. On the creation of new career hierarchies on the railways, see Frank McKenna, *The Railway Workers* (London, 1980), chs. 3, 5, and 6.
33. Vincent, 'Mobility, Bureaucracy and Careers', 224–32.
34. FLW 261.
35. FLW 141.
36. Between 1901 and 1931, the number recording themselves as nurses in the census more than doubled, rising from 65,500 to 138,670. Brian Abel-Smith, *A History of the Nursing Profession* (London, 1960), 117.
37. FLW 200.
38. FLW 436.
39. FLW 161.
40. The essential 'indeterminateness' of the liking of work, the absence of any necessary connection between pleasure in an occupation and longer term issue of achievement or ambition was observed in the pioneering work of E. K. Strong Jr. *Vocational Interests of Men and Women* (Stanford, Calif., 1943), 15.
41. FLW 84.
42. FLW 335.
43. FLW 183.
44. FLW 274.
45. FLW 351.

46. FLW 82.
47. FLW 239.
48. FLW 340.
49. FLW 43.
50. FLW 305. On the development of hierarchical career structures in the leading sectors of British industry, including the railways, see Andrew Miles, Michael Savage, David Vincent, and Hiranthi Jayaweera, *Pathways and Prospects* (forthcoming, Cambridge, 1997).
51. FLW 218.
52. FLW 342.
53. FLW 366.
54. The contemporary view of outside reformers was that the value of parental assistance at this point in a child's life was at best nil. A. Freeman, *Boy Life and Labour* (London, 1914), 124.
55. Vincent 'Mobility, Bureaucracy and Careers', 220–4.
56. The growth of their work is surveyed in, Revd Spencer J. Gibb, *Boy-Work, Exploitation or Training* (London, 1919), 102–37.
57. On the persisting influence of family on locating a career, see F. M. Earle, *Methods of Finding a Job* (London, 1931), 51. Cf. the similar findings in Tamara Hareven, *Family Time and Industrial Time* (Cambridge, 1982), 364–6.
58. On the emerging career structures in the Post Office, see M. Daunton, *Royal Mail* (London, 1985), 36–81.
59. FLW 77.
60. FLW 125.
61. FLW 10.
62. FLW 33.
63. G. Anderson (ed.), *The White Blouse Revolution* (Manchester, 1988), 4–13; T. Davy, ' "A Cissy Job for Men; a Nice Job for Girls": Women Shorthand Typists in London 1900–1939', in Leonore Davidoff and Belinda Westover (eds), *Our Work, Our Lives, Our Words* (London, 1986), 124–44.
64. FLW 326.
65. FLW 414. On the consequences of the 1902 Midwives Act, see Jean Donnison, *Midwives and Medical Men* (London, 1977), 159–75.
66. FLW 72.
67. Wally Seccombe, *Weathering the Storm* (London, 1993), 135–8.
68. FLW 72.
69. J. Floud, 'The Educational Experience of the Adult Population of England and Wales as at July 1949', in David Glass (ed.), *Social Mobility in Britain* (London, 1954), 117–18. The figures are for the cohort born before 1910. See also G. Sutherland, 'Education', in F. M. L. Thompson (ed.), *The Cambridge Social History of Britain 1750–1950* (Cambridge, 1990), iii. 162.

70. FLW 5.
71. FLW 67.
72. FLW 122.
73. Seccombe, *Weathering the Storm*, 176–9.
74. FLW 434.
75. FLW 119.
76. FLW 200.
77. FLW 68.
78. FLW 257.
79. FLW 108.
80. FLW 362.
81. FLW 181. This was virtually the last generation to experience the part-time system, which was abolished in 1918. See Marjory Cruikshank, *Children in Industry* (Manchester, 1981), 85–7, 94–8.
82. FLW 410.
83. FLW 78.
84. FLW 67.
85. FLW 416.
86. FLW 122.
87. For a discussion of the frequency with which school-leavers fell into life-long jobs by sheer chance, see Gibb, *Boy-Work*, 96.
88. FLW 95.
89. Gail Braybon, *Women Workers in the First World War* (London, 1981), 173–210. For the painful aftermath of the war in an élite sector of women's employment, see Meta Zimmeck, '"Get Out and Get Under", the Impact of Demobilisation in the Civil Service 1918–32', in Anderson (ed.), *The White Blouse Revolution*, 89–120.
90. Jane Lewis, *Women in Britain since 1945* (London, 1992), 70.
91. FLW 172.
92. FLW 72.
93. FLW 190.
94. FLW 206.
95. FLW 423.
96. FLW 92.
97. FLW 132.
98. FLW 214.
99. FLW 278.
100. FLW 333.
101. FLW 210.
102. FLW 296.
103. FLW 167.
104. FLW 213.
105. FLW 141.
106. FLW 108.

# 5

# The Familial Meaning of Housing in Social Rootedness and Mobility: Britain and France

ISABELLE BERTAUX-WIAME AND PAUL THOMPSON

Families differ greatly in their relationships to housing. This is because a house is of much greater significance than a mere physical shell providing shelter. A house is also, both externally and internally, a stage on which are played out both the internal roles within the household and the outward presentation of its members to the social community in which it is situated.[1] The special social importance of houses is probably true of almost all settled societies: certainly it is evident outside the West. In Japan, for example, a recent study observes that

> Owning a detached house is different from owning a car. A detached house not only has a higher value as an asset, but also reflects what its occupants think a family is. This may be in part the reason why a house is an object of inextinguishable concern and interest.[2]

In most Western societies the very position and design of a house, both because of its value and all that its style conveys in social terms, contributes strongly to providing the household and its members with a particular position in local society. In both Britain and France, the two countries on which we focus here, a castle, a mansion, or a farm provisionally imply a social position in the geographical locality for *whoever* occupies them. Conversely, for the family itself a house may often be the anchor-point of memories and history, and in extreme cases it may have developed into a family museum so spectacular that it can be opened to the public. On the other hand, more pragmatically a house may also be a shrewd investment and marketable asset which plays a central role in a family's strategy for social advance. Houses, in short, need to be seen as actively reflective elements in social position and movement, very much parallel with the social choices made in marriage, potentially vital at the same time in constructing, confirming, and communicating social position.[3]

We might envisage differences in attitudes to housing as parallel to those in the equally basic culture of cooking.[4] There are again some households for whom common daily meals are central social rituals, and others whose members rarely eat together;[5] families at the one extreme who develop their own distinctive style of home-cooking both for their own pleasure and to entertain guests, and at the other, households whose individual members simply throw their off-the-shelf pre-cooked mass-market foods into the microwave as hunger dictates.

It is clear that such differing attitudes towards housing—and indeed also food—can be crucial features of social mobility. They can at the same time help to constitute and delineate upward or downward mobility. Housing can be a mobility strategy in itself. Strong attachments to particular homes and places can prevent mobility, or shape its goals; while at the opposite extreme, full freedom in physical mobility can often imply a social rootlessness which, in the long run, may prove a handicap to family advance rather than an asset.

These differences in attitudes to housing show up clearly in the extent to which houses are emphasised in autobiographies, whether in written form or recorded through life-story interviews. In the following discussion we draw on both published autobiographies and also on life-story interviews, recorded in most cases from two or more generations of the same families, as part of our research study on 'Families and Social Mobility' in Britain and France.[6]

We can immediately distinguish three basic clusters of possible attitudes towards housing. First, there are families for whom a particular house or a parcel or estate of land or an urban neighbourhood are central to their sense of family identity, an attachment which may go back several generations. Secondly, by contrast other families conceive of their own social progress in terms of housing *change*: at the least, through improving their original house beyond recognition, and equally often, through moving from house to house, each new house or locality representing an upward move. For such families, investments in houses are seen as crucial family strategies. Thirdly, and more neutrally, for yet others—and indeed perhaps even for the majority—housing seems much less salient for either identity or strategy: a necessary and crucial base, certainly, whether long-term or transient, which must be secured as part of the essential material base of family life, but once occupied never a key focus for either attachment or effort.

Clearly the first two groups, in contrast to the third, both put a high estimation on the symbolic social value of their houses: but for the first group, this is in relation to rooted attachment, while for the second, conversely, the house provides a key symbol of mobility.

Classically deep-rooted social attachment to a physical home is found today, both in France and in England, at the top of the social spectrum with the landed aristocracy, and in France also among the peasantry, who unlike in Britain, have remained a social stratum of major significance into the late 20th century. For such families their home is not only a practical context for their contemporary lives, but a symbol of their family past which in itself gives them a special place, at least locally, in the social system. Because of this they cannot ignore the demands which the family house and land make of them, for their social place and esteem depend in part on their success in preserving, improving and transmitting to younger generations a family home whose symbolic value may well be far more significant that its material market worth.

The family home does not, however, need to have stood in the same hands for generations to acquire special symbolic value, even to the point of becoming a kind of family museum. In her recent anthropological studies of the French upper middle classes, Béatrix Le Wita has explored the notion of home as a symbol of the individual self, and the realization of this in terms of carefully chosen furniture and ornaments, pictures, objects bought on family holidays, and displays of family photographs, turns many urban homes into comparable symbols of the essence of a family's life and character.[7]

Indeed, it is quite common for relatively modest homes to take on the character of a personal collection or museum which is at the same time a form of life story in itself.[8] This is of course only possible when the family or individual concerned have secured a space within which such a display is possible. Certainly it would have been difficult for those poor 19th-century families who coped with phases of unemployment during downturns in the economic cycle by doubling up in the same dwelling—'huddling up' as it was known.[9] (The strategy is still practised in both Britain and France by some of the poorest households, as of immigrants and others in acute financial difficulties.) It must also be important in terms of socialization into such attitudes that it was still normal in the early 20th century for children to share rooms and even beds. In Britain, for example, while the average household has occupied five rooms throughout this century, the number of people sharing this space has fallen from nearly four and a half to three, giving much more scope for cultivating this space symbolically. One might therefore presume that to use the home interior as a display space is a relatively modern development. Yet in fact, certainly by the 1900s skilled working-class British families already very widely furnished a front room, known as the 'parlour', for such family purposes—and in some homes this room was regarded as so sacred that it could not be used at all for ordinary weekday living. One such Lancashire parlour is remembered as containing

a piano with a fretwork front and a pleated silk back. On top at one side there is a Sunday School hymn-book with tunes and a small Bible; at the other side there is music—'Asleep in the Deep' for Dad, 'I'll Sing Thee Songs of Araby' for Bill, 'The Lass with the Delicate Air' for Lizzie and 'The Lost Chord' for Sarah Anne. In the middle of the room is a table with a plush cloth on it and the Family Bible in the middle and, as it is a weekday, stocking legs cover the table legs. Opposite the fireplace there is a 'dresser' with lustres at each end, a dressed doll in the middle under a glass case. In between there is a framed photo of Grandma and Grandpa. On the wall above there is a long cased clock . . . In the window a pair of lace curtains, a paper blind, an aspidistra and a fern plant on the window sill.[10]

Every item in this carefully furnished room had an iconographic significance which could be elaborately detailed, combining the family's memories with demonstrations of its transgenerational respectability, from the Sunday School hymn-book used by the children to the mother's treasured aspidistra. It was indeed of just such Lancashire families that Gracie Fields sang with fond irony in her 1938 popular hit, 'The Biggest Aspidistra in the World'.

Equally significant for our concerns, the symbolic value of housing in upward social mobility has been widely recognized. Grandiose home entertainment was one of the many forms of self-indulgent display noted by Thorsten Veblen in his sweepingly transcultural and transhistorical *Theory of the Leisure Class*, although surprisingly, he scarcely mentioned the house itself. But in the last twenty years ethnographers in France and Sweden, most notably Orvar Löfgren, have shown how house interiors change as families accept middle-class values. There have also been some more tentative studies of house furnishing in relation to social mobility by American sociologists.[11]

In Britain it seems likely that the linking of the house itself with social advance has unusually deep historic roots in popular thinking. One of the ways in which employers sought to control their workforce in the early days of the industrial revolution was through the provision of housing, from which oppositional families could be easily evicted. Hence one of the primary aims of the first British working-class political movement, the Chartists, was cottage-building. It is surely no co-incidence that the region with the highest level of working-class home ownership at the beginning of this century was that of the militant South Welsh mining valleys? Indeed it was Merthyr Tydfil, where the ironworkers and miners had confronted the notoriously dominating Guest family as ironmasters, and which had the highest proportion of home ownership of all, already 58 per cent in the 1900s, that sent Britain's first Labour M.P. Keir Hardie to Parliament in 1900.

In the same spirit today we can find Catherine Cookson, currently proclaimed as Britain's best-selling popular novelist, writing of her heroine in *Hannah Massey*, the story of an aspiring northern working-class family, of Hannah's long-nurtured plans to buy a house on Brampton Hill. She

> wanted prestige, and she went for it in the only way open to her, a bigger and better house. Truly she believed that a woman was known by her front door. That her ambition could have been achieved by the educational betterment of her sons she refused to acknowledge ... 'My sons will fit at Brampton Hill, Rosie, as they've fitted in to Grosvenor Road. There's no better dressed nor finer set of men in this town'.[12]

Research has shown how among both middle- and working-class home-owners, house ownership has become a symbol of social independence and security, of relaxation, and of family life, even to the extent of embodying emotional commitment: 'It's the house you build together. A house isn't just bricks and mortar, it's the love that's in it.' And strikingly similar attitudes were also found in a recently built Australian suburb. Here another woman remarked, 'I've poured a lot of love into the house and it has given me a lot back ... This house represents me.'[13]

In contemporary Britain, with just over two-thirds of homes now owner-occupied, inability of a family to purchase a house has all but become an indication of social deprivation. Indeed David Saunders has argued that housing tenure has now become the principal symbol of social class in Britain, and that those who do not own their own houses will soon be reduced to 'a marginalised minority' or 'underclass'. He sees the failure of a family to achieve house ownership as typically one among multiple deprivations, including unemployment, ill-health, lack of cars and telephones, and a fatalistic ideology: hence 'tenure divisions are coming to reinforce and express existing social divisions'.[14] His interpretation is a reflection of the same popular attitudes which have allowed the Conservative Party both to promote itself successfully as the party of home ownership, and to introduce increasingly loaded financial incentives, from the longstanding tax relief on mortgage loans for house purchase to the much more recent enforced price reductions to persuade working-class tenants to buy publicly constructed council housing.

It is important to emphasize that this spread of direct house ownership is a recent phenomenon in Britain. At the beginning of this century nationally a mere 10 per cent of housing was owner-occupied and it was normal for urban families of all classes to rent. This renting was almost entirely from private landlords, and for the working classes it was normally on very short tenure. During the present century there has been a double transformation. Home ownership has grown from the top downwards, while the provision of subsidized public housing has spread from the bottom upwards. The gains for earlier generations from secure tenure in public housing need also to be emphasized. Historically council housing represented an important advance on the situation which still characterized the less prosperous British urban class up until the First World War, for whom constant moves to avoid payment of the rent were a regular economic strategy, and a whole culture had gathered around 'midnight flitting', celebrated in poetry and music-hall song.[15] Even in the later 20th century, for such families to be forced to move from their neighbourhood may be a serious setback, a drastic loss of social resources. Meanwhile through the same decades home ownerships climbed, to 24 per cent in 1939, 59 per cent in 1981, and 67 per cent in 1995.

There have been parallel developments in France which have

similarly reshaped attitudes to housing in successive generations and adjusted both the position and the meaning of different types of house, categories of tenure, and family attitudes to the home. As in Britain there was a significant growth in public-sector housing reflecting the political rise of socialist and communist parties, already making an impact between the wars with the building of the first 'cités ouvrières' with rented housing for working-class families in the Parisian peripheral 'ceinture rouge', but much more after 1945. Political measures to encourage home ownership also go back to the 1920s, and in contrast to Britain, one of the most crucial was introduced by the left-wing Popular Front government in 1935. This provided financial aid and cheap plots of land to help skilled workers to build their own homes in the Paris suburbs. The now common system of co-ownership of urban flats through condominiums developed from the 1920s. Although house ownership grew more slowly in France than Britain, the increase was rapid from the 1960s, and is now 54 per cent of all households.[16]

While the public provision of housing has long been a major interest of sociologists working in the field of social policy, before the 1980s few showed an interest in house ownership. Housing has also been surprisingly little studied by sociologists of social mobility, despite the fact that the need to take account of the crucial relevance of housing in the construction of social class has long been argued by a number of important sociological theorists, such as Manuel Castells and John Rex.[17] The significance of housing as part of the 'cultural capital' transmitted by families has also been pointed out by Bourdieu, although it is not a theme which he has pursued himself.[18] It is thus surprising that it is not a main theme of any of the classic studies of social mobility.[19]

There is, of course, a very extensive literature on housing, but most of this concentrates on the physical and financial aspects of housing provision: on architecture, planning, and building; on physical health, sanitation, and the demography of overcrowding; on state intervention, housing laws and legislation, and forms of ownership; and on housing markets, and the provision of capital, through loans, mortgages, or subsidies.[20] None of this usually directly addresses our own concerns. Even a recent collection of sociological papers entitled *The Meaning and Use of Housing* prove largely irrelevant.[21]

There are, however, some rare exceptions. In Britain, some historians of architecture have broadened their approach into social histories of particular building forms: most notably Mark Girouard in *Life in the English Country House* and Stefan Muthesius in *The English Terraced House*. Jerry White's *Rothschild Buildings* is a notable account of Jewish immigrant families and their homes in one East London tenement block, written by an author who has combined work as a public housing officer with writing social history.[22] Among sociologists, Peter Saunders has had a particularly notable interest in the relationship between forms of housing tenure and social class, focusing on the growth of home ownership and its motivations, which is of special relevance for us. Other younger researchers are now following his example with interviewing on the subjective meaning of 'home', both among owners and council house tenants.[23]

In France, there have been valuable recent studies of the way of life of the aristocracy and bourgeoisie, and the transmission of attitudes, practices, and memories between generations, which include discussions of the role of housing.[24] The post-war development of a school of urban anthropology is also a contrast with Britain. It has included the pioneering work of Chombart de Lauwe on Parisian working-class family life and housing space, and more recently of Martine Segalen on families and their homes in the new peripheral working-class suburbs.[25] Most relevant of all to our concerns here is a group of small-scale researches on French urban housing, in which one of us has participated directly, exploring the interaction between choice of residence and wider family relationships.[26]

In particular ways we have found all these studies suggestive. None, however, provides a cross-class perspective on family attitudes to housing; nor is any concerned with how this relates to mobility.

We discuss here four broad types of family attitudes to housing in terms of attachment or movement and their implications for social mobility. The first is entrenched attachment, and the second its converse, mobile rootlessness. The third is step by step strategic movement, and the last a single move, often made after suffering an unsatisfactory situation for a long period.

In principle, each of these types of attitude can be considered in relation to any type of housing. But in practice some housing types are especially associated with particular family attitudes. Thus the châteaux and country houses of the landed aristocracy, and the family farms of the peasantry, are characteristically symbols of entrenched attachment, while the secondary homes of the urban middle classes in the countryside, even when of great symbolic importance for family identity, do not root the regular lives of family members. Urban neighbourhoods and houses in general have less clear implications for family attitudes: the whole range is possible (see Table 1).

Similarly some attitudes to housing are much more typical of particular social groups, while other attitudes are more diffused. Thus the most deeply-rooted attachment to houses is found in long-established aristocratic families; and it is precisely because of this that families seeking to establish themselves in the upper class or *haute bourgeoisie* provide the most striking instances of the deliberate construction of homes to create symbols of the family's social identity, often incorporating a mythical history of the family's past: yet another form of *The Invention of Tradition* documented for the

TABLE 1. *Housing types and attitudes to housing and mobility*

| | Entrenchment | Step-by-step | Final solution | Rootlessness |
|---|---|---|---|---|
| Country house and park/le château | * | | | |
| Family farm and land; la terre, le lieu | * | | | |
| Second home in country | * | * | | |
| Rural primary house | | | * | * |
| Urban neighbourhood/ le quartier | * | * | * | |
| Urban primary house | * | * | * | * |
| Urban second home | | * | | |

late-19th century by Hobsbawm and Ranger.[27] It is a little further down the social scale, among the middle and lower middle and upper working-class strata, that we most often find housing treated primarily as a form of investment, an economic patrimony, whose transmission to younger generations is expected to be carried out through the sale of the house itself and its conversion into liquid capital.

Among urban working-class families, by contrast, the home and its setting are less likely to be seen in terms of a potential social advance, but more as a defensive bastion, a protective resource not only in the material shelter offered by the house itself but also in the accumulation of friendly social networks which can be used for economic exchange and finding jobs as well as for sociability. The house and its setting is an instrument of social integration, and a fortress against the many possible catastrophes which the family may suffer. Thus for them, as indeed also we shall find for the French urban *bourgeoisie*, social roots in a particular urban neighbourhood are crucial to their social position and way of life.

As a last preliminary we need to emphasize that in using the word 'family' we do not intend to suggest a unity in either strategies or attitudes towards housing among all family members. Certainly attitudes are transmitted and exchanged between generations within families, and relate very specifically to practices of co-residence. But they are certainly not held uniformly among family members. Our interpretations are deduced from individual life stories, which make it clear how different family members may hold views more or less strongly, share or reject attitudes. Some of these differences are themselves clearly socially patterned: for example, characteristically we find differences in attitude between men and women. The attachment of siblings to a house may vary because some have much longer memories of it than others. There are also differences following from inheritance practices.

In this respect the legal traditions in France and Britain differ sharply. In Britain the only restrictions are by custom rather than by law, and the upper classes have built up elaborate means including special legal devices to ensure that their principal family houses and land are handed down through male primogeniture to a single heir. This means that there are inevitably differences in attitude to houses between an eldest son and his younger brothers. In France, by contrast, the law has adopted middle-class custom and attempts to enforce equal division between the heirs, only a quarter being reserved for free disposition. An inherited house or land must thus either be shared between siblings, or sold, or—as is common in farm families—one sibling must buy out the others.

These various dimensions result in a complexity of possibilities which could only be given justice at much greater length than here. Our own purpose is instead to offer a framework within which such questions can be taken forward, and which will, we hope, encourage the further exploration of this neglected but complex dimension of social standing and social mobility, in which material practice and symbolic identity are so subtly intertwined.

In the discussion which follows, we attempt to sketch out this complex relationship between families and their homes, suggesting some of the principal variations in terms of both social group and also type of property, by considering in turn, first various forms of rooted attachment; then, more briefly, some characteristics of the rootless; and finally, contrasting types among those families for whom particular houses are always marketable items in their broader life strategies. We begin then with forms of attachment, considering first of all primary and secondary homes in the country, and then in the town.

## COUNTRY HOUSES AND CHÂTEAUX

We begin therefore with the countryside. There is good sense in this, since our contemporary urban populations not only have their demographic roots in the countryside, but have also often retained rural themes in their attitudes to housing. While in France, however, rural attitudes survive extensively in the towns among families of peasant origin, in Britain, no doubt partly because there has never been a revolutionary challenge to the values of the old landed upper class such as happened in France, there has been a much wider diffusion, in various reduced forms, of aristocratic attitudes to housing.

For English aristocratic families the country house, the family seat, the mansion in its park surrounded by hunting grounds, has been a pre-eminent symbol of status and identity for at least five centuries. The destiny of the house and estate were considered so much more important than the comfort of individual family members that inheritance practices ensured not only that the estate and most of the family's financial capital were passed on intact to the eldest son, but also, through the system of entail, the heir himself had only limited rights to spend or dispose of family property, but was more in the role of a custodian for future generations. Such attitudes are beautifully symbolized in *Orlando: A Biography* (1928), the novel which Virginia Woolf wrote about her friend Vita Sackville-West, in which her family home, Knole in Kent, comes alive as the book's hero/heroine, of ambiguous, shifting sexuality like Vita herself, but also of almost perpetual longevity. In aristocratic autobiographies too, the house can take a quite exceptional place. Lord Willoughby de Broke, for example, gives the opening chapters in his *The Passing Years* (1924) not to his parents and his childhood, as is usual in the autobiographical genre, but to detailed descriptions of his family's four principal houses. Other autobiographies show how, again in a manner very rarely mentioned by writers from other social groups, aristocratic families would use seasonal holidays at the country house as occasions for gathering together younger descendants and passing down their family traditions, memories, and histories.[28]

Maintaining such houses has become an increasing struggle during the 20th century, demanding large expenditures on domestic labour and building repairs. Some of the most spectacular great houses have been converted into tourist enterprises, vying to pull in fee-paying crowds through publicity stunts. The autobiography of the Duke of Bedford, *A Silver-Plated Spoon*, is a showman's story, sold at Woburn Abbey alongside the entrance tickets and the special offer, for a handsome fee, of an evening dinner with the duke himself.[29] His chief rival showman, the Marquess of Bath at Longleat, has lions in his park too. In a quieter style many other lesser country houses have been rescued through a dedication by their owners which has often deflected their lives from other paths and become an overriding commitment.

The symbolic power of the English country house extends, however, well beyond its longstanding owners. Until the First World War, it was expected that any newly wealthy family who hoped for ennoblement should first buy a country house. In recent decades, sometimes families have bought seriously neglected country houses, making restoration their own personal project. In the towns too, the change of fashion by the mid-19th century from classical town-centre terraced housing to romantically picturesque suburbs of detached houses in gardens was, in part, a realization of rural ideals, encapsulated in the phrase, 'the Englishman's home is his castle'. On the other hand, the suburban 'castle' in Britain rarely creates a transgenerational family attachment; middle-class children, when their parents die, more often sell it than move back into it.

Nevertheless, the echoes of aristocratic attitudes to housing can be found at all levels in our own life story interviews. Thus Rudi Fine, son of an immigrant Russian cabinetmaker and born in the slums of east London, successfully worked himself up as a businessman and was able, with his wife, to create a very active social life based on his London home: 'we kept an open house ... People in the movement, people who were interesting—artists, lawyers, solicitors, sculptors ... Tremendous discussions went on all the time ... We were great talkers in those days.' Yet well before he had retired, they moved their main home to the countryside, buying a small manor house and patching together a reduced social life with ex-Londoners:

I wanted to move to the country in nice surroundings. I wanted to feel free and open without any worry ... If I've achieved the one thing I wanted to achieve, then that is a nice home in the country.[30]

For Dick Tiverton it is easier to see why the move into a country home was positive. He was the child of a large Liverpool Scots working-class family who were constantly on the move. He describes his mother as 'one of those gypsies. If she thought there was a better house that suited her, we'd be off. My father just didn't bother. He took it for granted that she'd be on the move again.' But Dick met and married a fellow-socialist from a family of teachers, and through their influence became a teacher himself. With this added income they were able to move from a small bungalow to an ample old stone house in the countryside, which as a widower he has divided with a married daughter who is also a teacher. His son, in turn living in a bungalow, feels frustrated that he has not got the money to buy a similarly ideal home: 'I wanted a big rambling house and a big rambling garden.'[31]

There are resonances of the same ideals even further down the scale from their aristocratic sources. For the Steels—of whom more later—their 'super house' owes its qualities above all to its woodland setting right on the edge of a town. And the restless, but still working-class Caradogs have found an unexpected anchor in an isolated riverside lock house, where the only sound is of the watershoot: 'immediately I thought this is lovely', as Phoebe put it, and her daughter, now back in the town, finds it equally 'a joy to go over there'.[32]

What of republican France, where the hereditary aristocracy were decisively topped from the apex of social and political power two hundred years ago in the Revolution, and many of their heads literally severed in the ensuing years of the Terror? Certainly in France, in contrast to Britain, real or cardboard hereditary peers no longer stud the national and local institutions of economic, social, and political life. The contemporary French ruling class is, without a doubt, 'la grande bourgeoisie française'. But even so, the old aristocracy have left their shadow in attitudes to housing: for in France, the social resonances of 'le château', whether its inhabitants are from genuine noble families or not, remains still potent today.

For a family genuinely descended from the former pre-revolutionary nobility the château may be, in fact, their crucial remaining claim to social distinction. Viewed in purely economic terms, most châteaux are handicaps rather than assets: costly to run and keep in repair, too large, often lacking in basic modern comforts, and too far from economic centres to make it practicable to live there and earn a good living from business. But on the other hand, to lose the château is to lose the symbol of their family history and lineage which is the key to their continuing social esteem in the region. This is why such families typically take great trouble to ensure that the ancestral home passes to an heir among them who will cherish it, and even make great sacrifices to ensure that it remains in the family's hands.

This is indeed a point on which there is a similarity in attitudes on both sides of the Channel: witness the recent disinheritance of the drug-addicted Marquess of Blandford, heir to the Duke of Marlborough and the noble palace of Blenheim in Oxfordshire, built for their ancestors as a parliamentary thank-offering for the defeat of the French and Austrians by John Churchill in 1704. Winston Churchill was born in the same house in 1874. The palace requires a worthy heir; so that the eldest son being deemed unfit, primogeniture has been set aside and a suitable replacement heir identified. Inheritance, in short, is a mutual choice. To maintain the lineage and the patrimony, the family has to select an heir who commits himself to this special destiny: 'je reprends le flambeau'.

In France as in England, securing the family inheritance against contemporary economic pressures undoubtedly demands ingenuity. It is noteworthy how many families are willing to sell part of the landed estate, or some of their inheritance of pictures and furniture, in order to protect the survival of the château itself. But this usually is a way of postponing a decision, rather than seeking a decisive alternative strategy.

One of the simplest but most drastic solutions is to capitalize on the historical value of the family home by converting it into a public monument, and securing the economic benefits of this in terms of grants for restoration of the building, in return for allowing visitors. In Britain the custom of admitting tourists goes back at least two centuries, and houses can also be passed to the quasi-public National Trust, a charitable body which has long been controlled and administered by aristocrats and their sympathizers despite being today a mass membership organization.[33] In France it is a somewhat more drastic move 'inscrire leurs biens a l'inventaire du patrimoine français'. If the house is small enough, so that visiting days can be very restricted and the number of visitors untroublesome, such a strategy can be wholly successful. In such instances, the family can remain in residence, and still play their traditional role in local social life and politics. But more often, especially with larger houses, the resort to public funding has the paradoxical consequence, because of the constant trail of inquisitive trippers, of safeguarding the family inheritance at the expense of driving them out of its practical use if they are to preserve any of their previous privacy.[34]

The more ingenious successful alternative strategies are also typically found in France with smaller châteaux. The now greyhaired Marquis de Marchessaux vividly described the day when he had to find a rapid solution or permanently lose possession of his château. Taking inspiration from the business world in which he had hitherto been immersed, he put his home on the list of public monuments, and without even waiting for the scaffolding to come down when the restoration work was completed, he opened the château to the public and hired a team of students in history, archaeology, and architecture to provide expert guided tours for visitors. He added further authenticity by joining the tours himself and interrupting with comments, thus providing a touch of local colour in his own person. Thanks to his enterprising style of management, the unusual twin blue slate-roofed turrets of the château now shine confident of their glowing future, while in the grounds fervent young horse-lovers can indulge their passions in an entrancingly rustic stud farm.

Other French 'châtelains' have converted their homes into a special type of hotel, in which hand-picked guests are invited to participate in the life of an aristocratic household. Although publicized and written up in travel magazines like other expensive hotels, they retain their special appeal precisely because of the direct involvement of the old family.

Yet another tactic is to turn the estate into a nature reserve, echoing the lions of Woburn and Longleat. But this is again a strategy which can subvert its original aims. At the château of Malsy father and son have been in sustained conflict as to how best to preserve an estate noted for its lakes and woods. Originally they succeeded in securing subsidies for conserving the fishing and the woodland game for hunting. The son then proposed to move on to convert part of the estate into a nature reserve for wild animals, and secured business partners for this enterprise, but the father, despite the immense debts which he owed for re-roofing the château, long resisted. For him, the debts were almost a proof of his devotion to the family, and he saw how the nature reserve could prove a diversion from their original intentions: with good reason. For today the family estate, within easy reach of Paris, is regularly visited by waves of tourists, attracted not only by its free-ranging lions, but also by the craft workshops now established in the service wings of the old house. The family home has become, in fact, a family business, to which its members so far seem equally committed.

However, the current does not always run in this direction. Conversely there are examples of families who, having done well as entrepreneurs, decide to symbolize this by re-investing in their roots. Pierre de Meyrac, a young south-west hobby squireen determined to make his new social mark clear, was seeking to achieve this by regilding the old family arms. This implied not only an extremely expensive reconstruction of the château to make it habitable, but also a re-establishment of his family's traditional position as peasants—or rather, now, as gentlemen farmers—in the village. Hence the first part of the château to be rebuilt, and also used weekly by the public, was its chapel. Meanwhile, for several years the young couple and their three children huddled together in the one furnished and heated room in the château, where cooking, children's homework, running the estate and social entertainment all took place. At night, seated in front of a log fire glowing in the magnificent monumental chimneypiece, it was possible to forget that the rest of the château was still unfurnished, unheated, freezing. And it was already a sufficient base from which to act out their recaptured role as local 'seigneurs'. Paradoxically, even at the expense of physical discomfort they were enabled to become themselves socially the embodiment of the historic home, and effectively claim the social standing which it symbolized.

Unlike the ideal of the country home in Britain, however, the model of the French château has not so diffused down the social scale to inspire at almost every social level a widely held idyll of a rural home. It has, as we shall see, some echoes in the urban homes of the French upper middle class. But in the French towns, in so far as rural notions of attachment maintain their power, roots are more often felt in terms derived from the peasantry, from whom in fact a very high proportion of urban inhabitants are recently descended.[35]

## THE PULL OF PEASANT ROOTS

First, however, we need to consider the peasantry in the original rural territory. The primary social attachment of the peasantry is to the land rather than to the buildings on it. It is with the land, with the soil itself, that the peasant works, grows his crops and his stock; it is the primary resource which is both the source of his economic income and standard of life, and his social position. This is why in both France and Britain farmers relatively close to the big population centres have been so willing to sell not only their barns but also their ancestral farmhouses at high prices to become the homes or second homes of workers in the cities. In the same spirit, in the remoter province of Béarn in south-west France, when they speak of 'la ferme Robert' they mean the land—including the currently rented land—as well as the buildings. Interestingly, in this part of France the farms are always known by the names of their current owners. But while the land is named after the man, the barns are known by the women, and after a woman's marriage her patronymic maiden name survives as the title of the barn of her new family home. Faced by such customs, one begins to wonder which is the inheritance and the inheritor: is it the couple who inherit the farm, or the land and the barns which inherit the man and the woman?

The power of this family attachment to the soil is demonstrated in numerous instances in which farms are taken up by heirs, even against all apparent economic rationality. Such cases bring us into contact with an altogether different social logic. 'Here one is somebody, down there, one is no one', one young Béarn mountain peasant told us. Yves Mauléon had returned to the tiny family farm with as much sacrifice and determination as the squireens whom we have already encountered. As with the young descendants of ancient nobles, his family history of attachment to a place not only gave him a powerful sense of family identity and a bond between its members, but also shackled him with a chain capable of destroying any attempt to break free into an independent professional career. It proved strong enough to bring him back from the opposite side of the world, to take over the farm when his ageing grandparents had become too old to run it, even though he had emigrated with the clear intention of settling and making a new life.

Michel Trace was an eldest son who had been similarly pulled back, against all his own expectations, to the family farm while still a young man. He had dreamt as a boy of becoming an army helicopter pilot, and encouraged by his father who saw that this might bring in a good wage, he had set himself on this path by starting an apprenticeship as a mechanic during his military service. But all this was abruptly interrupted by the sudden death of his father. His mother 'called him back' to the farm, where she could not manage to live on her own with just one younger daughter. For ten years Michel worked as a hired farmhand, and he married a woman who was also employed as a farmworker herself.

But as Michel knew, his wife had like himself no wish to continue with such a way of life. For a while she worked alongside her new husband and mother-in-law on the farm. But as soon as his younger sister had married, Michel sold the farmhouse and most of the land. He took a job in a thermal spa hotel in a nearby town, and his wife, once their two daughters were a little older, found service work in a local hospital.

Judged purely in terms of occupation, these moves look like a negative social and occupational shift into insecure low-paid work. But Michel had a more ambitious strategy. While still being a local, 'from here', he tranformed his previous enforced immobility into an active dynamic based on the local social networks and the land itself which he had inherited. He had kept back a patch of the family land, and he used this to develop a new business with his brother-in-law in rearing ducks. He bought an old house and began to renovate it. In parallel with his growing financial success, this new house became a symbol of a proud local rootedness, along with his active participation in community responsibilities, in the sports club, and as a district councillor. After the interview he completed the construction of a new terrace and swimming pool with the help of his local friends. But he has different ambitions for his daughters, of whom one was to leave for university in the following year. Paradoxically, it was his deliberate use of his local roots and resources which had made possible this upward social leap of his daughter into another social world.

In the past it was traditional among peasant families of southwestern France for more than one generation commonly to live in the family farmhouse, following the model of the 'famille-souche' of Le Play's well-known household descriptions. This model encapsulates especially strongly the notion that the family land and its buildings are more important than the destinies of its individual members. But for the younger generations residential independence has become a crucial point in intergenerational relationships. Hence Béatrice Brabant, a young woman farm worker, would not hear of living under the same roof as the parents of the farmworker whom she married: instead she rented a house in the village, off the family land. More typically, when the farmhouse is big enough, often it is now divided into two entirely separate parts, or alternatively, a second house is constructed on another part of the land. In the Lanion family, the succession between generations in different stages was matched by a series of different housing solutions. It was not the eldest of the nine children, but the second son who took over the farm and farmhouse. At this stage the father continued with some farmwork on an adjoining plot of land, where he built himself a new house. Later the fourth son also decided to go into agriculture, so he took over this new house, and worked the land in common with his older brother. The father, on the other hand, built a third house for himself, this time very close to the village: 'it's more convenient when one is old.'³⁶ The intermeshing of family relationships and work on the family farms which characterized the 'famille souche' thus continues, but is now expressed materially in different housing forms.

One of the consequences of the massive immigration of French peasant families into the towns during the 20th century has been that these attitudes to land can still be quite commonly observed surviving in urban settings. It is in this spirit that many families set about transforming waste spaces in the backlands of towns, between railways or canals, into gardens abundant with vegetables and flowers. Even among Parisians, the practice of cultivating a small piece of land for vegetables, 'un potager', remains widespread. Sometimes a family will spend every Sunday in a rented garden of this kind: 'It's like our country home, one could say!'³⁷ Often a hut is built, and even married children will come to help, taking away fresh vegetables in return. The importance to them is far more than economic, for it symbolizes, in contradiction to their daily incarceration in a high-rise apartment, for the women as well as for the men, their continuing links with the land and their childhood roots.

The same attitudes explain the extraordinary achievements of Italian peasant migrants who came from the south to work in the Fiat car factories in Turin. They occupied—illegally—river beds and refuse heaps all over the city, and transformed them into market gardens, which in turn have allowed them to take control of the city's vegetable markets, and provide them with some significant sources of income with which to face the drastic cutback in employment in the factories from the 1980s. On a more modest scale, but nevertheless historically important, was the 'Dig for Britain' campaign during the Second World War, both because of its symbolism and the food supply which resulted, and the allotment movement in British towns, in this case typically legal and indeed using municipal land bought under special legislation.³⁸

In general, however, influence of this type is scarcely traceable in Britain for a number of reasons. First, the principal migration from the countryside to the town was completed much earlier, by the end of the 19th century, so that first-generation rural migrants are now extremely rare in British towns. Secondly, the very early development of an unrestricted land market and the resulting consolidation of landholdings led to a situation in which most of the rural agricultural population consisted of landless labourers. Even farm families were tenants who were not usually able to pass on their land. The main exception is in the crofting districts of the far north and west of Scotland, where a secure form of communal tenancy has survived, and as a result there are strong traditions not only of outmigration for work on the mainland and abroad but also for return migration. Even in these districts, however, the population numbers are so small, and their ideas of communal tenancy so difficult to transfer, that they had no significant influence in urban contexts in late 20th century mainland Britain.[39]

## SECOND HOMES

The image of the countryside is also typically an important factor in the significance of second homes, but it would be misleading to consider them primarily in these terms. Country houses and rural primary homes were bases for work, be it agricultural enterprise or labour or politics, as well as for domesticity and leisure. For centuries the upper ranks of the aristocracy also maintained scarcely less grand urban palaces close to the royal court and seat of government, such as the aristocratic 'hôtels particuliers' in the Marais and the Faubourg Saint Germain in Paris, or in London, Lancaster House or Spencer House in St James—the latter recently restored by Princess Diana. In a more modest way, many of the provincial well-to-do have long rented flats to provide a foothold from which to conduct business or social activities in London, as indeed do a sprinkling of families from elsewhere in Europe and America. To cite one instance, a Greek family who own a chain of stores have flats—or more precisely, multiples of flats for their extended family—in Athens, in the provincial town of their origin, in the mountains, by the sea, on an island, and also in Paris and in London. In a complex housing system such as this, in which different members of the family rotate seasonally between different bases depending on their business and pleasure plans, it is impossible to make clear distinctions between primary, secondary, or tertiary homes.

In the 20th century, however, a much more distinctive pattern of the second home has arisen in association with the increased emphasis for all social classes on leisure as a form of fulfilment, paralleled by the rise of retirement as its eventual full-time realization. This has generated its own specific housing forms in the second home and the retirement home. In principle, in the case of the second home the family divides its work and leisure projects physically, so that, for example, a family who move their main home frequently for work may retain a long-term second home; or, conversely, they may seek a variety in leisure homes that they cannot have in their work lives. In the case of the retirement home, the division is instead temporal. But in practice, the two may overlap: the second home may be bought with the intention that it become, eventually, the primary retirement home. In this light it is noticeable that both second homes and retirement homes cluster, above all, in the areas most closely associated with leisure and holidays: the mountains, and still more, the sea coast. These are by no means always rural districts, for on the contrary, the biggest concentrations of all are in seaside towns, both in Britain and France, many of which have a majority of inhabitants in retirement.[40] Such houses are the concrete realization of earlier holiday fantasies in a full-time, but too often empty, life of leisure.

The split between first and second homes also opens up choices in identification. The difficulties in finding satisfactory housing which is also convenient for work mean that the primary base for practical day-to-day living, such as a flat chosen almost at random in a not yet known neighbourhood, may not offer a satisfactory basis for attachment. This may then be focused on another house, even if it is rarely used. Cécile Normand, who lives in a block of public housing—or 'HLM'—[41] in Paris, pointed to a framed photograph of a small house in a distant village which, for her, summed up all her personal story:

That house, for me it's everything. I don't go there often at the moment because my aunt's still living there. But it's my childhood—I was born quite close by. And I only have to visit it and I feel that I could easily settle down there. Everyone thinks I'm crazy! But in fact, I'm seriously thinking of doing it.[42]

Thus through this house and the sense of roots which it gives her, Cécile can feel her past, even if it be a largely re-invented past, and she can dream of a future, even hypothetically, which lifts her above her present modest daily existence.

Other families, more commonly in France—or Italy—where the

longer summer holiday break and the warmer and sunnier climate makes a permanent recreational base more attractive than in Britain, buy or rent a regular holiday home as a base for vacation operations. This may also be a flat, either by the sea or in the mountains, and is not necessarily a point of identification. Indeed it may be envisaged as simply a temporary facility while the children are young, the expression of needs at a moment in the family life cycle rather than a lasting second home. Henri Germain, a French technician who has risen with the expansion of his firm to become an engineer speaks of the house in the country which he has had for fifteen years:

> When our first child was born, I thought we needed to find a place for the weekends and shorter school holidays. I bought this piece of land and first I built just two rooms and then bit by bit I added more. I did it all myself. The children used to play, there was nature all around... Sometimes my wife went there on her own and I came down to join them when I could. It was all fine, but when the children were adolescents they started not to want to come there. So we sold it.
> 
> Then when my son married, I bought a flat in the mountains, just three rooms, but we all used to squeeze in there!
> 
> And now that I'm retired, my wife and I go there often with our little grandson. And we're thinking that we'll soon get a little place by the sea, although that's not yet quite decided... [43]

So it all revolves around the children and their tastes. The family reassembles in these specially acquired play-spaces as far as the time constraints of work allow them. The places themselves are valued only in so far as they are useful for recreation and so for bringing the family together. It is the past memories and future plans for family fun and sociability which are central to identity, and the actual homes are merely incidental to this.

It is usually quite different, however, when the second house is itself an old family home. One doctor in the south-west of France, Pierre Salviac, has no need to look for a new holiday place in the country:

> When I want to get away from town, we go to my mother's. She lives in a house which she had from her father who himself had had it from her grandfather.
> 
> She's a real matriarch. She can't imagine our going there without inviting my brothers and sisters, most of whom are married,... so the family reunions, when we all get together, are really impressive. It's very impor-

tant to her to have us all . . . She gets help in for these times and everybody contributes. The children love seeing their cousins there . . . At least they know each other, even though their lives are all different and it's hard to meet except when we're with maman.

Now the children are grown up it's a little different. They come less often. But they'll never miss out on one of the big family reunions which we have at least twice a year.

For this family of doctors, belonging to an old family with a long genealogy is an important element in their social standing. The importance of this is brought home to each new generation by these family reunions around the ancestral hearth ('autour de l'aieule'). 'When she's gone, I want to keep the house as a family house so that everyone can still come there.' But because Pierre realizes that his mother, the central personality of the current reunions, will no longer be there to impose order through her authority, he adds uneasily, 'I hope we won't all fall out over it.'[44] His fears are indeed well-grounded, for the inheritance of second homes does often bring acute problems between siblings. In a sense the maintenance of a family second home after the death of the parents demands a suspension of time and of current individual needs in order to perpetuate a collective sense of attachment and family history. There are many families for whom this does not prove possible.

Second homes can also be used to help bridge the social gaps caused by dramatic intergenerational social mobility, whether up or down. This, for example, is one underlying reason for the intense attachment of one high-flying professional Parisian intellectual to a very modest village house. It symbolizes her continuing social attachment to her much more modest origins, and so stands both for her continuing loyalty to the world of her parents and as a measure of the distance which she has travelled from it.

The situation is more complex when the social movement is downwards. Antoine Villneuve is a young Paris teacher who has done much less well than the rest of his family. His father, a well-to-do industrialist, had hoped that he would be a distinguished researcher; but he has chosen a different path. After a brilliant start at university, he decided to distance himself somewhat from his family, and partly for this reason he travelled abroad. On his return, against his father's advice, he became 'animateur culturel' in a working-class neighbourhood on the periphery of Paris. With his young librarian wife, he first rented a room in central Paris but then moved to a three-room apartment in a high block (HLM) close to his work. As there was no room for promotion in the cultural centre, he decided to take and passed the entrance competition for teaching. Meanwhile the birth of an infant daughter brought him back somewhat closer to his family. Becoming a teacher seemed to be a first step in their eyes towards fulfilling his earlier promise. But when he was given, as part of a new incentive scheme for home ownership, the chance to buy his flat on specially advantageous terms, he hesitated, and began to reflect seriously on where his life was leading him. For his wife, there seemed only advantages in buying the flat. But Antoine, who as a tenant had seen the choice as a merely accidental consequence of what was available within his financial means, buying the flat was another matter. As a potential *owner* of an HLM apartment, he suddenly became acutely aware of its inconvenient, indeed appalling, environment. He wondered whether this was really meant to be his destiny.

Fortunately an unexpected solution came just in time. With the death of an aunt, he inherited sufficient money to buy a much more spacious HLM flat, and to pay for alterations, which provided them with separated spaces for family life and for his professional work; a room for the baby with a bed high up, a study for his wife, and for himself, a balcony with flowers . . .

Most important of all, he used the inheritance to buy a house surrounded by a garden in the village from which his family originated. This gave him a key social role in the whole family. Through it he was enabled, in symbolically recapturing this key family space, to claim back his own position in the family lineage—while still remaining a modest city schoolteacher.

In Britain one could find equivalents to all these various uses of second homes. Indeed, perhaps more strongly earlier in this century, the dream of the little place in the country or by the sea was very widespread, and its most elemental realization by the skilled working- and lower middle-class family can be seen strung along the coastline in countless wooden seaside shacks. But for the climatic and seasonal reasons which we have suggested above, the second home in Britain is in general less extensively developed. At present, in any case, English families are more likely to choose one of the regions which they specially favour on the continent, such as the Dordogne in France, Tuscany in Italy, or Marbella in Spain, rather than to buy a house in Britain.

As a result, the most striking examples of second homes in Britain itself as primary symbols of attachment are to be found among successful upper-class families, who usually acquired them before the 1960s, in a period when buying abroad was still unusual, and the English countryside itself seemed more remote than today. The possession of such houses undoubtedly brings important consequences for transgenerational family relationships. Whereas primary homes are typically owned and used by one family member or couple, second homes are likely to be handed down to the entire sibling group of the younger generation, binding them together—as any transgenerational house ownership must—in owning, maintaining, and negotiating the shared use of their childhood holiday home long after their parents have died. The second home can thus become a major source of conflict and stress between them. Alternatively, as their children in turn share it for holidays, it may foster a sense of common identity between cousins, and of shared experience, which is uncommon.

A particularly remarkable instance is provided by the Garnett family.[45] The story of their second home goes back to the 1890s when the families of Sir Edward Poulton, an eminent Oxford science professor, and Dr William Garnett, a Cambridge scientist who went on to be principal of two new northern universities, began to spend their holidays close to each other on the Isle of Wight. Subsequent generations of the Poultons have mostly worked in medicine, the Garnetts in a mixture of science, administration, and politics.[46] Both families, however, have worked above all through their active minds, many of them also moving around considerably as work required; and at the same time, they have shared a keen pleasure in physical sports, team games, walking, and boating. Their holiday contacts were cemented with the marriage, in 1910, of Poulton's daughter Margaret to Garnett's son James Clerk Maxwell; and in 1927 Margaret used her inheritance from a biscuit-manufacturing grandfather to buy a hillside overlooking the sea and build a new house designed by the fashionable architect Oliver Hill. Horestone Point is still the Garnett holiday home, and has now been used by four generations of descendants and cousins. It has bound them together in shared experience and common tradito church', we always went to church, and John insisted that any visitors came too: 'any question of theologies is not a subject of discussion. I don't care what you believe or what you think, the point is, it's good manners to go to church with your grandmother.' And, at least for special occasions, the custom continues: 'on the second Sunday of the August before last, there were forty-nine of the family in the church together: children, grandchildren, cousins, forty-nine. Outnumbered the congregation.' There is also a regular Easter Monday walk across the island, when family stories are told, on a route which has been followed annually since 1913, and at the end 'the rule is, we go to the top of the cliff, but we go whatever the weather, if its snowing, or raining, or beautiful, we go'. But more typically, these group activities are just fun. In summer there is dinghy sailing, with cross-sea expeditions of over twenty boats. 'For eighty years we've played hockey on that beach every Christmas and every Easter': mixed teams of old and young, amateurs and stars. Around the house and grounds a special form of hide-and-seek called 'Rescue' is played 'every evening . . . shrieking children of all ages'. Elaborate plays are acted, of family stories, and at Christmas a nativity play with scenes punctuating the whole day, a real baby, and the three kings arriving with lanterns in the dark. And in any season events are celebrated by flag-flying from the house—'my dad was mad on flags . . . we dress the ship, and we put up all the signal flags for every child's birthday'.[49]

'That house has given the most amazing happiness'; but it has meat much more than that. Three of John's children found their partner through these holidays, 'in enormously romantic circumstances: you're bathing and swimming and sailing, in August, dancing at night'. The family's 'great celebrations' take place here: coming-of-age parties with dancing to a band, marriages and christenings in Bembridge church. Equally after losses, illness, or divorce, 'whatever disasters strike the family, we find ourselves always going back to the Isle of Wight to lick our wounds'. This is also the place of family memorials. 'The island is home . . . That is where we die. . . . One of the greatest securities of life is to know where you're going to die . . . You know where your body or your ashes are going to come to. There is an extraordinary anchor about it . . . The island is the continuity of the family.'[50]

The maintenance of extended cousinage like this is in any case rare in English middle-class family culture; but it could only have developed in this elaborated form with its 'anchor' as a second home.

## URBAN ATTACHMENTS

Let us turn now to primary houses in the towns. Except in the aristocracy, English town houses are rarely used by successive generations of the same family: instead they are pragmatically abandoned as soon as retaining them no longer seems useful. In the same way the social and physical setting of the house, its neighbourhood, is an important factor in terms of the utility and value of the house, but not for the family's long-term identity. On the contrary, being able to sell the house and to realize its monetary value on the market when parents die is in itself one way in which social status is transmitted socially.

The situation is, however, somewhat different in France. Here again, the intergenerational transmission of social standing is closely connected with housing. Sometimes this is expressed in terms of an identification with a housing type, as is most common in Britain, but can be found also in this French example: 'I've always lived in a house with a garden, I can't really imagine any other way of living with children...'[51] But especially among the well-to-do, this transgenerational identification in France commonly takes the form of attachment to a particular urban 'quartier'.

The attachment of many well-to-do French bourgeois families to a neighbourhood certainly carries echoes of the manner in which aristocratic families seem territorially rooted to their rural estates and châteaux. It is not uncommon for a transgenerational group of middle-class siblings to settle close by their parents, even in the same road or the next, not only in order to remain in regular daily contact with each other, but also because belonging to this quartier is felt a vital part of their common identity. The younger members of the family will deliberately choose to remain close by, even if this requires taking a very modest rented flat: it is the social resonances of the address, rather than the character of the home itself, which matter most.[52]

Quite often, of course, the constraints of the market force those in less well-paid work to seek other solutions, such as taking a house in a nearby more popular neighbourhood and converting the

## The Familial Meaning of Housing 153

attic into a flat, or even renting a high-rise apartment further away. But a continuing nostalgia for the old quartier may prevent the full financial exploitation of these new housing solutions. Thus one woman close to retirement was renting an attractive HLM flat, and had been offered the chance of buying it on specially favourable terms. But she could not stop thinking of the neighbourhood where her family had so long lived, much livelier and socially more interesting. She refused the purchase offer: 'To buy an HLM, here—no! Me, if I was to settle down . . . I'd settle in my old quartier. There I'd certainly buy, yes.'[53]

There are also instances of families which maintain a parental home, which had been for decades the scene of regular family reunions, even after the death of both parents, sometimes at considerable financial sacrifice. Thus one top-ranking professional found himself on the death of his father the common heir with his brothers of a manorial house in a Paris quartier. None of the brothers felt able to dispossess himself of this immense dwelling, in which the family continued to gather. Their spouses, by contrast, while well aware of the symbolic value of the house, all argued for a more financially practicable strategy: but they could not overcome the reluctance of the brothers to sell the old family home.

In more extreme instances the urban home may even recapture a younger member of the family in much the same way as a peasant son may be recalled to work the family farm. Maurice Renault was a high-ranking engineer who had worked for thirty years for a major multinational company. He had been brought up in a relatively modest style by his parents living in a town flat, and after his marriage had similarly rented a series of flats close to his succession of different workplaces. But the death of his maternal grandparents precipitated a dramatic change in his life style. For this grandfather had been a formative influence on him. The grandfather had been a self-trained builder, who had built the house himself, and later had used his life's working experience to advise his young grandson on his early studies. So with the house he had inherited a crucial part of his own early history. He could not think of selling it, because its symbolic importance far outweighed its monetary value. But taking it on meant changing his whole life:

When they died, I inherited the house. I could not just leave it like that, and I couldn't afford to keep it as a second home. I had to make a rapid decision. I cancelled the lease on my flat and decided to move into the house. It was the only solution possible.[54]

Here the dead really have seized the living.

It should be stressed, on the other hand, that even in such well-to-do middle-class families, there is an essential distinction in the nature of the attachment. For the old nobility, the crucial importance of the château was the personal position which it brought within local society, and the public family history which it symbolized. Middle-class family history, by contrast, is essentially of private importance, and the family home wins a social position, not as a personal place in a particular network, but as membership of the social group with which the quartier is associated. While the aristocrat takes for granted membership of a social stratum and claims a specific location from which to exercise its rights and duties, the less secure bourgeois more modestly simply seeks an address which confirms class belonging.

In Britain a strong attachment to urban neighbourhoods is most often found among working-class families. Historically, this is a relatively recent development, for as we have noted, up until the First World War a very high turnover of occupants was typical of working-class urban neighbourhoods, and especially in London and other large cities. Bethnal Green, which already had a relatively high proportion of locally-born inhabitants, was an exceptional and extreme case in London before 1918. From the 1920s onwards, working-class geographical mobility slowed drastically, partly because of economic stagnation, but also as a reflection of the spread of public and philanthropic housing, which was managed with the explicit objective of raising social standards, and inculcating respectability, thrift, and temperance among the working-class families who were tenants.[55]

From the 1960s, however, as a result of the general rise in working-class living standards resulting from full employment and rising real wages through the long post-war boom, the more positive meaning of stability as an alternative to impoverished rootlessness began to give way to a more defensive one as the more ambitious, upwardly-rising working-class families increasingly moved out to buy their own houses. Those who were left behind tended to be the less skilled and poorer working-class families. Among them a significant minority have lived now in the same area

## The Familial Meaning of Housing

for three or more generations, and as a result have developed a cousinage scattered right through clusters of nearby streets. In the late 20th century, with the confident years of the long boom now decisively past and the spectre of poverty and unemployment haunting such working-class families still rooted in districts next to now-closed factories, attachment seems much more a form of primitive economic self-defence: for in the last resort, their kin network is their best bulwark against destitution.

As a child in a rough area of a South Welsh town, Paddy O'Hara lived next door to his mother's sister and three doors away from her brother, with his father's sister round the corner; as they married, his elder brother settled round the corner and his elder sister next door but one. Although the neighbourhood was dirty, work hard to get, and Paddy, his wife, and children have been out of work for many years, mobility, whether geographical or social, did not enter their minds. 'We never let it worry us. We carried on with our lives . . . We didnt wanna leave, we had our friends, our relations was there. There was no need for us to leave.'[56] The Sims, a skilled working-class family, seem to be equally enmeshed in their smaller extended family in their neighbourhood of Greater Manchester. Early on in her marriage Pat Sims and her husband did buy a small new house on an estate close to the edge of the city, a bid to move up: but within a year they had moved back at her behest. 'I felt isolated . . . I made friends, they were all youngish, we lived in little cul-de-sacs, . . . but they were the type who were all the time in and out of everybody's house and always falling out, and I didnt want to get involved. One week they liked you and the next week they hated you—that type. . . . I didn't like being stuck out there'.[57] For Pat the security and practical support of living close to her grandmother, mother, and sister were too much to lose.

Such instances need to be balanced against those of well-rooted families who nevertheless moved from their neighbourhood. Often the break may be made between generations. The Roberts had been Welsh steelmakers for three generations, living in rented houses, and for Dawn's husband this was a principle. 'He would never be in debt, and even buying a house was being in debt, so we never bought a house, we've only ever lived in council houses.' When her son married, however, within a year he had moved away and bought his own bungalow: 'the wife fell in love with it and wanted to live here'.[58]

In other families there is an open difference of attitude to housing between the men and the women. Leah Percy came from a small northern pit village, and her father, husband, and son-in-law have all been coalminers; but hers is a family of strong women too. As a child she was especially close to her 'domineering' grandmother, 'and she made me independent... She left her mark on me... She would say, "Set your sights high"'. Both before and after marriage, Leah lived in rented colliery houses. 'If you didn't work in the mines you didn't get a house. And if you had sons you had to ensure that your sons go up to the mine as the father did.' For the men, the pit was the centre of the community's social universe; but there was much less to reward the women.

From childhood Leah had dreamt of being a dress designer, but with parents who had 'no ambition for me' she had to forget such hopes until well into middle age—when she did in fact succeed in becoming a dressmaking instructor. But in the mean time she put her energies 'behind the children... I wanted my two children to do well for themselves'. he pushed her son through education into a professional research career. Her daughter, however, insisted on marrying a miner like herself. Although she liked him, she was 'disappointed in him being a miner'. But even so, on one point her views prevailed. She persuaded the young couple to move out of the colliery houses and buy an oldish six-room house of their own. 'You must own property', she told them.[59]

## ROOTLESSNESS

From the attached, let us turn now to the opposite end of the spectrum: to the rootlessly mobile. Women may gain or suffer from enmeshment, depending on their ambitions and context. In general, they are much less likely to gain if they belong to families constantly on the move. It does not follow that such families have a less strong social identity just because of their greater geographical mobility. Indeed there are well-known social groups, such as the gypsies in western Europe, or the Bedouin in the Middle East, whose whole culture and identity is centred precisely upon their constant movement. They constitute an important reminder that there is nothing 'natural' about human rootedness: it is a particular social adaptation of particular social groups.

Nevertheless, in the general populations of Britain and France rootlessness is not usually conducive to a strongly integrated family life. This is because typically it is the consequence of men's occupations whose requirements overrule family needs. This need not follow from occupational geographical mobility. The Caradogs, for example, are in more than one sense a highly mobile family. More than half the younger generation have gone to Australia, and they seem recurrently attracted to jobs which keep them on the move, as sailors, lorry drivers, AA patrolmen, postmen, motor racers, or railway engine drivers. Saul himself had over ten kinds of job before becoming a river sluiceman. But house moves, by comparison, have been relatively few.

In some occupations, however, instability has been almost inevitable, leaving families with little choice but to continually uproot themselves if they are to continue living together. Up until the Second World War, this was highly characteristic of those middle-class families who provided the colonial civil servants, soldiers, missionaries, and doctors needed to staff the Empire. Many of these families developed strategies which involved twin bases at home and in the colonies, with the children sent away to boarding-schools, so that in practice they might see very little of each other. It may be as a form of compensation that they often developed very strong attachments to remoter kin, and sometimes succeeded in maintaining a family myth of a closeness which in a day-to-day sense was the reverse of their real experience. A remarkable instance is provided by the Summerhayes family, the seven children of an English clergyman born between 1892 and 1905. Taught as children to visit the parish sick and collect money in their individual missionary boxes, they dreamt of a future in which, still sustained by their parents back in the home country, they would go out to work in the Empire: 'We'll be missionaries. And Mummy and Daddy'll sit at home and thread beads, to send out to Africa.' And the dream was realized: as adults they scattered across the world, as doctors, teachers, diplomats, and evangelists, as far apart as Canada, East and West Africa, and Nepal. Even in retirement when they had all returned to England, they lived somewhat apart. Yet throughout they maintained the image of a family who 'always stuck together. People used to say . . . "Oh, the Summerhayes family, they stick together." And we did.'[60]

Our middle-class families include a number who made occupational career moves with, for example, large organizations such as banks or nationalized industry. But such 'spiralists' proved to be very few: our middle-class informants are typically either settled 'burgesses', or moved once or twice only at the start of a career.[61] The most striking exception is the army, when regular and unavoidable mobility affects all levels. Army families stand out in their difficulties in reconciling work and family life. Living in tied housing inhibits them from gaining a foot in the housing market. All those in our sample had lived so far in seven or more homes. They were unable to choose either where or when they move, and this lack of control over their geographical mobility can bring severe problems ranging from disruption of the children's education to uncertainty and instability in the social and working life of the spouse. May Purcell, an officer's wife, has lived in eleven homes in twenty-five years, including two spells in army barracks, and she feels she lacks any close friends as a result. 'Because we've moved around a lot, you lose addresses and you just don't keep in touch. This is really what happens: in the Forces, you make acquaintances.'[62] This uncertainty is also associated with a strikingly higher tendency to marital stress, tension, or breakdown. The occupational culture of the services does not encourage individualistic initiative, and combined with marital disagreement, was often followed in later life out of the army with problems from displacement and loss of initiative.

A second highly mobile group are of rural origin. Typically as young adults they started as farm labourers or servants, sometimes combining this with small farm contract or craftwork. Although as geographically mobile as army families, it was more through their own choices, and this combined with a jack-of-all-trades background tended to make for an occupational adaptability. Their fortunes were more mixed and a few became upwardly mobile—sometimes when parents or grandparents had been small independent contractors, such as saw millers. More often, however, the consequences of their rootlessness were less favourable.

The Massies were a large family of farmworkers from northeastern Scotland. In this region farm cottages went with the job, and it was common for workers to move on regularly, seeking better terms. Alex's stepfather worked sometimes in a jute mill and for a time was a soldier, but mostly as a farm labourer, and by the

## The Familial Meaning of Housing 159

age of 15 Alex had been to six different schools and lived in more than ten homes:

> Oh dear, canna remember, I was in that many places . . . On the farms, ye just kept moving about. Ye didna need to re-engage. My stepfather probably dinna like the way things were going so he just decided to move, he just moved t'another farm ye know. That was the done thing in those days [the 1940s], everybody kept moving about the countryside. It was a tied house and if ye didna work on the farm ye had t'go anyway. That is what they were all going for, better conditions—aye, travelled roond . . . You were just getting familiar wi' the place when you moved away again.[63]

Alex was made to leave school by his parents: 'I would've liked to have stayed longer . . . You were expected to be a man when you were a 12-year-old . . . They wanted me working right away.' In any case, there was little worry in finding work. 'In that time on the farms, they were always needing somebody . . . There wisna the fear o'being unemployed . . . Ye just worked fae day t'day'.[64]

Alex's working life has echoed that of his stepfather, but in the long run his disrupted early life and education have told against him. Up to his late twenties he worked on farms, apart from three years in the army—which he decided to leave after they refused to fly him home from British Guinea when his stepfather died. 'I said to him, "It's the only father I knew", and he says, "Well, that's the word from the War Office". So that was it. That turned me against the army.' Later he moved into Dundee and worked as a bus driver. Finally be became a plant-hire driver, working away from home for weeks on short-term contracts. Now, like his eldest son, he is unemployed, with 'time on your hands, boredom'. His wife, a fellow soldier's sister, is a part-time cleaner. In the early years of their marriage they too lived in a series of farm houses, but since moving to Dundee they have been in council housing. But Alex has experienced this as a step downwards too. In the countryside socially

> och it wis like night and day. I mean at Christmas and New Year and that you used t'hae yer parties in different people's houses and you were all made welcome and everything. Now [in Dundee] you've got to watch every move, ye've got to watch who comes inta yer house. They come in here wi' nothing and they walk oot here wi yer whisky bottle if ye're no careful.[65]

For large and poor families in the early 20th century, entering service, whether in town or country, offered another answer to housing problems as their children grew. Geoffrey Kedleston's father and grandfather had been gardeners. At the age of 14 he was sent away to become a page boy with a Middlesex family: 'my father, as a young boy, worked for them, and they knew of him.' Geoffrey was miserable to be sent from home—'I cried my eyes out'—but, 'my father said to me, "You'll be far better off with your feet under somebody else's table"'. Later he settled with another family, working for them for over twenty years as a footman and butler, and marrying a nanny whom they also employed. As sometimes happened with long-term servants to wealthy families, Geoffrey was rewarded on leaving with a gratuity. With this gift he was able to buy a village post office, which he and his son turned into a very successful business as well as a family home. Eventually they owned two shops and a school bus. As a servant he had worked long hours, up till ten every night, with only one Sunday afternoon off a month. Geoffrey still keeps some of the habits of his footman's calling, meticulously changing his shirts three times daily. But in his case, loyalty and its paternalistic reward paid off, giving him the chance of success in later life, 'the best thing I ever done really'.[66]

Two other social groups for whom attachment to housing was also not central to identity also need to be added, although in this instance without illustration. First, there are those who choose to live in housing whose attraction is partly precisely in its lack of local rootedness, the feeling of being only temporarily at rest in the interval of a lengthy, mysterious, and hence romantic journey. No doubt many of those who live in houseboats, such as those moored along canals or in backwaters of urban rivers like the Seine, dream at night of future travels as the wind laps the water against their boatsides. And the same may often be true of some of the 'travellers'—rather than true gypsies—who live in mobile homes on the land, even though their fantasy becomes strained when they are permanently grounded in 'caravan parks', and many of their neighbours may be living there simply because such housing is relatively cheap.[67]

The last mobile group, whom again we do not illustrate here, consists of long-distant migrants, who have arrived from origins outside of France or Britain. Some of them are on the move because of economic or social disasters which have struck them, others because they belong to cultures where migration is traditional.[68] In terms of housing they also divide sharply between those who behave like settlers and those who retain the attitudes of transient visitors. One of the most perceptive of all post-war British social studies of housing is on a community of Asian settlers who turned the decaying large Victorian houses of a former middle-class Birmingham suburb into multiple homes, Sparkbrook.[69] Of the transient migrants, the archetypal group, because of their tragic destiny reaching back centuries, are the Jews. They have so often suffered persecution and expulsion that they have developed an international urban culture for which housing is rarely more than a short-term hired space. Jewish families rarely cultivate gardens, and they rent flats rather than buy them, always ready to be on the move again. But like so many other migrants, their very lack of physical rootedness makes them place a special value on their religious and cultural traditions, which as they move, they strive to re-create—often to a completeness well beyond that of their historical origins.[70]

## FAMILY PROJECTS

Between the entrenched families and the rootlessly mobile, both of which types are found more often at either the top or the bottom of the social spectrum, lies the middle ground in which we can identify the attitudes to housing which are characteristic of the great majority of families in both Britain and France. For them, their main home is an economic and emotional investment of prime importance. They look for the best place for it—or, at any rate, the most tolerable choice in a poor market. Almost all today share the ideal of a house with a garden, not only in Britain where this represents a long-established aim, but since the inter-war years also in France.

Only a small minority, of course, are able to realize their dreams. And in the interim they make compromise choices. These are shaped in a number of ways. We can observe in many families how customs of living in a particular type of housing—an old house or a newly built one, owned or rented, a suburban detached house or a city centre flat—are passed down as models to younger generations. Sometimes these models are accepted and followed, but in other cases they are rejected, and taken as precisely what not to do. There are also tensions between the needs of different members of a family, often closely linked to life cycle transitions. A familiar example is the dilemma faced by a young couple who enjoy city centre living when their first child is born. Should they put aside their personal preferences, and move to an environment more suitable for bringing up a child?

There are some who devise imaginative strategies to meet this problem. Thus Roger and Alice Comte, a young couple in their late twenties, had lived in flats in central Paris, but felt that they needed a house with a garden for their two small children. Moving into a Paris suburb would have taken them far away from their work and from the schools and community services which they knew. So they chose a fresh compromise solution. They moved into a small provincial town, where living on the outskirts did not imply the social exile which it does with the great metropolitan cities. For them, concern for an appropriate housing solution had led them to break radically with their whole previous way of life and its familiar physical environment.

As the interviews make clear, for most families the birth of children is seen as a crucial turning-point in housing needs. In France the desire 'to have a house when one has a child' was a recurrent refrain. The consequent mobilization of the couple in a joint housing project was also in itself a strong reinforcement of their long-term mutual commitment. It was as if the engagement in such a project was a reiteration of the couple's public and personal partnership. 'Every couple wants to get their own property', a young Frenchwoman explained: 'when a couple are earning two decent salaries . . . systematically, there's this plan in their minds.' The project may also engage the older generation, especially if they can provide sufficient resources to make it quickly realizable.

For some couples, the housing project may have the additional value of helping to solve familial tensions, for example because of the different social backgrounds of the husband and wife. Thus Albert and Brigitte Causse are a young couple who have lived for a dozen years in an old farmhouse which they have progressively restored themselves. Brigitte is a college English teacher, but Albert is a worker in the largest factory in the region. Brigitte's family were strongly opposed to her marriage, partly because she was so young, 'but, good, they've got to know him and appreciate him'. They started their married life in a three-room flat, where their son was very soon born.

They both recognized that they had little chance of occupational advance if they stayed in the region, but they were not prepared to cut off from their kin and migrate.

Leave? Where to? It's good here and we knew it was possible to get a good house one day. We liked old houses, and our great ambition was to find one that we liked and to restore it. Because we could afford that, and also because we could restore it according to our own ideas. My husband knows how to do any building work and I like mucking in . . . We spent a lot of Sundays working on it! But we're happy with the result.[71]

Their attachment to this house with its stables and surrounding land is not because of its current saleable value, but because of the social message it conveys. They are proud of their way of life, and the house is the emblem of the priority which they have given to making their home rather than advancing their careers.

In other instances, different housing models may be adopted consecutively. Thus Nicholas and Suzanne Léger, a young Parisian couple, are currently living in a suburban high-rise apartment. They had very different childhoods. Nicholas has always lived in flats in urban public housing schemes, and his parents had just bought one. Suzanne by contrast grew up in a house with a garden in a good residential quartier, and her father had been prepared to borrow heavily to ensure that his children could enjoy a similar way of life. The couple had absorbed the lessons of both experiences, and consequently saw their present apartment as simply a stage towards the house which was their real aim. Renting cheaply was enabling them to save for the future house. As Suzanne put it, 'I'd like to get away from here. We'll move closer to my parents . . . Not exactly there, but nearby. It's a beautiful district which I love and one can find interesting houses there.'[72]

As can be seen from these two cases, in finding solutions families also differ in tempo. Some are impatient, while others are prepared to seek their goals patiently through a lifetime. Viewed simply in terms of housing and mobility, this may be expressed in two contrasting patterns. The first is characterized by the one big move, the second by the step-by-step pattern.

## ONE BIG MOVE

The one big move may be early for a family with sufficient resources, but much more often it is long-delayed. Indeed, it may be so long in gestation that it takes as much time as the step-by-step moves put together. For example, Alain Meuse, a French mechanic in his forties, married with two small children, now living in a suburb of a provincial metropolis, looked back on a childhood which he felt had been very difficult precisely for this reason:

We were still living in central Paris, in a very small flat, I slept with my younger sister in the bedroom and my parents in the living room. My father was a building worker, and he had only one idea in his head, to build a house for his family. He couldn't talk about anything else at all.

Eventually he bought a patch of suburban land with his cousins, and started to construct the family home on it.

We had to get up very early in the morning to get to this distant suburb where my father had found a piece of land he could afford to buy in order to build. I remember—we had a 2 cv and he sold it to buy the land. I had to help my father with the plastering, the tiling, the painting... Every Sunday we went there and my father worked, sometimes helped by his cousins. Sometimes he went there on his own on Saturday evenings. We spent every holiday there... My sister was there with my mother and they did the finishing touches and the cleaning. It was hard, I couldn't be with my chums and my father was completely aborbed by the house.

The family moved in as soon as the shell of the house was constructed:

It was far from finished when we started living there. My father continued helping my mother to finish the inside work. Then he had to enclose the garden.

Alain recognizes how important this house construction was for his father's identity. 'It proved he was capable of getting somewhere.' Nevertheless, he certainly does not want to repeat a similar housing saga himself. 'I will not follow my father's example. It was very hard for my mother. Everything went into the house... Building or buying a house is a good thing, but not at the expense of one's way of life.'[73]

Similar examples can be found in Britain. Thus Colin Ward has written with eloquent admiration of the English 'plotlanders' of the inter-war years, some of whom spent decades in constructing homes on the cheap rural plots which they had bought on former farmland an hour or more distant from London. They were typically skilled working or lower middle-class Londoners. At first they constructed one-room wooden shacks, but over the years some of them converted these into masterpieces: one carpenter, for example, was working on the reconstruction of a City of London bank, and he managed to transport sufficient old mahogany from the discarded fittings to construct a home of rare opulence. A more modest dream inspired a poem published in the *Peacehaven Post*:

> My little plot I have not forgot
> It is mine I am sure, but I am so poor
> That I cannot afford to build a door.[74]

Such imagination in transforming shacks into good houses has been a particularly important social dynamic in the shantytowns of Latin America.[75] It would be difficult, for example, for a visitor today to the apparently prosperous and well-built southern suburb of Santo Domingo in Mexico City to realize that it had originated in a mass seizure of open land by five thousand in a single day in 1971, and that the houses had been constructed entirely through the self-improving efforts of originally very impoverished families.[76] The seizure of Santo Domingo was the most spectacular of all recent Latin American land seizures, but the story of the neighbourhood can be echoed from many other great Latin American cities. Another particularly well-known instance of tenancious self-improvement is the story of Brasilia Teimosa, a now attractive neighbourhood which originated in a 'favela' of squatters on land dredged from the harbour of Recife, the metropolis of north-eastern Brazil. Its name itself honours the stubborn courage of these poor inhabitants in creating their own new town at just the time when the state with all its power and resources was building its new capital of Brasilia.[77]

While collective pressure has played a key role in shaping housing provision in Britain and France too, this pressure has taken a political form rather than direct action. This means that rather than actively seizing their chances in a dramatic communal move, poorer French and British families have typically secured their own municipal or state accommodation through demonstrating their passive suffering, often for a period of years. Nevertheless such a move, at least until the drastic curtailment of municipal housing provision in the 1980s, from overcrowded or insanitary private rented housing into a new council house, was the most dramatic single step forward for which they could hope.

Kathleen Peel, for example, whose father was a blind ex-barber from Liverpool, was the eighth out of eleven brothers and sisters, and until she was 12 the family lived crowded into a three-bedroomed terraced house with no indoor toilet. She remembers how when they moved into a council house, 'we thought that was wonderful'. Lorna Selkirk, whose father was a jute spinner, grew up in Dundee with her sister and parents in a tenement flat of just two rooms in all: 'my father an' mother slept in the kitchen and my sister and I slept in the room'. As a young mother, she again lived in a similar two-room flat, on the fourth floor of a tenement: 'we had t'humph that pram up and doon four stairs'. Later they found a larger flat, but again with no lift. When at the age of 35 she and her family were rehoused in a new council flat in a 1960s tower block, 'we thought we were in heaven'; even though socially it proved less congenial. 'It was a lot more intimacy in a tenement than what there is up here ... (But) I was never one for socializing, I prefer to stay in my own house.'[78]

The one big move, in short, could be the outcome of very contrasting situations. It could be almost like a gift, a reward passively received for passive suffering; or it could be the fruit of striking personal determination to achieve change and self-improvement.

## STEP-BY-STEP

Step-by-step movers, however, were less likely to be passive or fatalistic. Some it is true were unsure of their strategies and rather driven by events. But many were the kind of families who on their Sunday walk pass by the agent's windows to register the current prices of land and houses and to reflect on the options for purchase. Their struggle to better themselves through housing was typically part of a highly conscious long-term project. When they tell their life stories, housing is an important theme for them, just as houses or neighbourhoods are for the entrenched, but with a difference: it is not so much the home in itself, but the dynamic of improvement, which counts for them. But however self-determined, most had had to endure a long struggle which included setbacks as well as advances.

Thus some had been initally driven to move by unemployment, such as Robert and Claudine Boulay, a young working-class couple who had bought their home for the first time on moving into the Paris region. But this purchase, like the move itself, was an active response to the problems they faced. 'Back there, we'd rented an HLM flat, like our parents. Nobody in the family had thought of buying anything. Last of all a house. My father-in-law had bought some land on the edge of the town, but that was to grow vegetables.' They had decided to buy after the birth of their third child, when they needed a larger flat, and the management had suggested that they should buy it. They felt proud of this achievement: 'it's better to deny oneself a little. We lead a simple life. I make a lot of things for the house.' But already the Boulays see ownership of the flat as simply a step towards other dreams. 'We'll see', he says, 'it's not certain whether we'll stay here. For now, it's good. And there's work here; but later we can imagine ... returning to our own region to have a house with a garden ... I miss a garden. Well yes, maybe a few years on it won't be impossible ... to find a house'.[79]

Still more difficult was the experience of François Beaulieu, a French professional engineer, who had begun work as a technician in his town of birth. His parents had a house there with enough land to have given each of their children a piece of land on which to build their own house. With his wife, who was also local, he had decided to build, and lived in his own house until their second child was born. It was at this point that the region went into economic crisis, he lost his job, and was forced to move to Paris to find work. Here he rented an HLM flat, but his wife decided against joining him.

This made his relationship with housing more complicated. His two children came to live with him for their schooling, so he needed a better home, and having been promoted to the grade of engineer he had the resources for investing in housing. So he bought a four-room flat, which he remodelled along the lines he thought suitable for a divorced father with two children:

We needed bigger bedrooms, so I took away the wall cupboards, I shifted the bathroom wall, I reduced the size of the entrance, I made an American-style kitchen open to the dining room ... A room for living in, because I could cook the dinner, and look after their homework, and after eating, look at television for a while . . . All in the same room, and then everyone could go to their bedroom.

This flat was his main home. But nevertheless it remained important for him to see it as a functional and temporary solution. He regularly returns to the region of his earlier life and his own house by the sea which has now, by force of circumstances, become his second home. In holiday periods he lives in a part of it—the other part is now let. And he conveys to the children the hope that in time this may again become the heart of the family's life. 'The house is important for them.'[80]

While there are some who eventually feel that they have reached their goal, for many step-by-step movers the dynamic is lifelong. Sally Peel, for example, grew up in a large and poor working-class family in an inner city neighbourhood of Salford, and married a baker's van driver. Later he became ill, and she started working as a bus conductress, resulting in regular visits to Blackpool—'I always loved Blackpool'—and she determined to move there. With the help of her sons, she raised enough cash to buy an unfinished house, decorated it, and sold it—'so method in my madness'—and went on to buy her own first house. And still later on, as a widow in her mid-sixties, she organized a successful new life for herself as a landlady and nurse by converting the upper floor of her home into bedsitters, and taking in elderly lodgers. Over ten years on, her elder son has tried to persuade her to move in with his family, and built a new room specially for her, but she absolutely refuses to relinquish the independence which her own house gives her: 'I'm not giving my little home up for nobody.'[81]

In these families, moreover, just as with the entrenched, the attitude to housing is typically transgenerational. Sometimes it is associated with occupational mobility, but often not. The Jordans, for example, are a three-generation family of Midland semi-skilled car workers, but the grandparents had for some years been boarding-house-keepers before the grandfather entered the car factory. Bob Jordan's mother continued to live with them after she married and took over the house when they died: 'I've never left home you see.' Bob himself set up as a home-owner immediately on marrying. 'We bought a house from the word go. That is why because our parents have always owned the home, their own house'. He contrasts that with his father-in-law who has 'done nothing with his life', remaining in council housing: 'he's never worked to achieve anything. They've just spent their money on drink, gambling.' To keep up their payments on the house, when their second child was born and his wife stopped working for a while, Bob took on a second job. He improved the house by building an extended kitchen and a new bathroom suite. After eleven years, they moved on to buy another house. 'It was a step up. It's better, it's closer to the country, it's a better area ... Investment-wise as well, I mean you can't lose.' Yet strikingly, Bob's drive for housing improvement is not paralleled by any work ambitions:

I don't want any promotion. It's not worth it, the pressure that are put on foremen and that sort of people, I don't want. I couldn't handle that sort of pressure now. They worry about the job ... I'm settled now. I'm a car worker. I'm your normal run of the mill working-class bloke that chucks wax at a car all day and is thoroughly bored with it.[82]

Two southern families, the Hands and the Steels, had much more conscious social aspirations, each transgenerational. They also illustrate the centrifugal lure of the suburbs, which for middle-class families goes back to the mid-19th century, but by the early 20th century had become a much more widely held goal.

The Hands were a highly skilled London family: the older generation compositors 'in the print', Jack and his sons patternmakers and engineers. One of four, as a child Jack was brought up in a one-bedroom inner city tenement flat in a block of Victorian Peabody Buildings, the children sharing the bedroom, his parents sleeping on a folding bed in the living room. But they imbibed high ideals. 'My dad was a real white socialist', a local party organizer and speaker, who 'made sure you get an apprenticeship ... then make sure you went to evening school, carry on your education ... As far as socialism's concerned, you've got to educate people to it.'[83]

The family's first step forward, when Jack was 18, their move to a three-bedroom council house, was a fitting fulfilment of local socialist campaigning for municipal house-building; and 'it was a palace to what we were used to'. Jack met his wife an insurance clerk, whom he married five years later in 1938, through the socialist League of Youth, and with her began to construct a more private utopia. They rented a two-bedroom flat on the southern outskirts of London, Jack cycling the twenty-five-mile return journey to work daily: 'we didn't want to live in London.' Eventually they were able to buy the flat, and eleven years later to move out still further into Surrey and buy a three-bedroomed house with a garden. Jack made 'lovely' furniture for it—'he does all the carving on it'.[84]

They brought up their two sons to believe in 'effort', working and saving, and 'to make up their own minds about things'. Both skilled men, each has moved on, the elder to New Zealand, the younger to Kent. This younger son Gerald is now a heating firm's branch manager. Occupationally, he feels his social position has become ambiguous—'I'm still a worker, in a way, but I'm not what they would term working class'—but he sees a clear middle-class identity as a house-owner. Since marriage he has lived in a new two-bedroom terrace house with a garden in a leafy estate 30 miles out from central London.

> I know I owe the money to the Building Society, but it is my own. I've done a lot to it. We've had all the windows done. I've done all the central heating myself. I've heated it all and done all that, cos thats the job. Decorating we've done. We fitted all the kitchen out. We've changed all the bathroom units round to what we want.

And what does he see as his most important future life goal? 'Try and improve it. Improve the house.'[85]

Dave Steel provides a still more striking instance of this symbolic focus on the house rather than occupation. He is the son of a railway electrician who has become a senior managerial mechanical engineer. His mother is a nurse, but his wife Leslie works part-time in a canteen. Occupationally, the family's mobility is therefore confused and his wife especially does not see them as upwardly mobile in class terms. Dave describes himself as 'very, very vaguely—well working class. Yeh, I have to work for a living.' But she is quite clear:

> We're working class: we class ourselves as working class... I wouldn't want to be 'frightfully, frightfully' and all this sort of thing. I want to stay the way I am. I want to be me.[86]

The mobility which is clear to them, and which they jointly celebrate, is in housing. When they met, Dave was a teenage apprentice on a motorbike, and both lived in working-class homes, hers more crowded than his. Yet significantly, Leslie's own parents had already made several moves themselves to win a decent house. When he was born they were sharing with his grandparents. Then they moved into a temporary wooden hut with a corrugated iron roof, heated by a cast-iron stove, which had been converted from a prisoner-of-war camp. This was followed by an unattractive, noisy council flat; and then finally a good semi-detached council house with its own garden. As a child Dave saw class very much in terms of housing: you could distinguish the respectable working-class home

> with the front garden being tended and the roses are there and the lawns cut. And sometimes you'd see them walking around in a suit ... And they'd paint the window frames. And the kids would be a bit quieter.

The upper classes could be picked out in the same way, 'driving around in posh cars and living in great big houses'.[87]

When he married, Dave moved briefly into a rented flat, but soon after was able to get a council house. He and his wife found this 'quite modern but not all that brilliant'; it suffered from damp. Eventually they were able to move into a better, larger council house, which they bought. After an interval they sold it to buy their present home. It was in less good condition, but superbly situated on the edge of a private estate, with 'a super garden with a beautiful oak tree down the bottom', a bridle-path beyond leading into woods, and away from neighbours 'so we could be completely independent'. The house had been 'seriously neglected' but Dave threw himself into its improvement. 'The first two or three years, I spent about £5,000 on it and nearly broke my back on putting it right. But now we've got a super house ...'.[88]

Each of these five family stories of step-by-step mobility was told in terms of success, and the teller and chief actor in most was a man. But this kind of mobility has its dangers too: indeed, carried to extremes, it can injure families, and especially women, as seriously as either rootless mobility or entrenchment. Our final family story is an instance of precisely this.

Oliver Ridings was a Lancashire millworker's son who worked his way up to comfort and prosperity through dealing. He began with fruit and fish and ended with shares, retiring early to a bungalow he built for himself in the Pennine hills. 'I wanted to go out and have a gamble ... buying something and selling it, you see. That was the most important to me.' At other times he dealt in turkeys, in horses—and in houses. His father taught him how to judge a house: 'if the roof's a good one, you'll take no harm'. He looks back contently on 'a grand life. I've had one of the best lives that's ever been.'[89]

Oliver saw in his daughter Barbara 'a bit of a dare-devil', a likeness, 'a chip off the old block'. She returned the compliment by marrying an entrepreneurially-minded mechanic, who for a time ran his own garage, but was much more concerned with building. From a rented flat, they moved into a house of their own; but then, for four years, back into a caravan, while he reconstructed an old isolation hospital, complete with tower, into a house. The strain on Barbara of looking after the children unaided in the caravan, with most of their possessions in storage, proved fatal to their marriage.

> We grew very much apart. The marriage basically was a business, really, going from one achievement to the next achievement. Had we been still together, I don't know where we would have been now, we would have had our own helicopter pad and goodness knows what—it was just ridiculous, striving from one step to the next step and so on.
>
> We both went our separate ways. I'd got to the point where I just couldn't take any more.[90]

They managed just two years in the grand rebuilt house before Barbara finally quitted: moving back into the caravan.

## FAMILY FISSION

With separation or divorce any family housing strategy is likely to shatter. Our concern here has been with couples and their families. But the relationship between families and houses at divorce clearly throws up very similar issues, and indeed deserves further study in its own right. It is obvious that houses are often fought over bitterly in legal proceedings at divorce not only because they constitute the principal material asset of many families, but also because for the now contending partners and their children they are the central symbol of a lost family unity.[91]

The eventual outcome can take many forms depending upon the family's social position, demographic shape, and stage in the life cycle. The balance of power between husband and wife will inevitably be crucial. But the grandparents may again become critically involved, especially if they had earlier helped the couple to set up home: although at divorce, a French study suggests, it is the wife's family who are more likely to mobilize resources in renewed support.[92] The alignment of the older generation may also be crucial in determining the disposition of a family second home: one partner may discover with surprise that a house redolent with conjugal memories always 'belonged' to the other family.

The first house is of course of more central importance. Indeed in East European countries like Poland and Russia it has been observed how in a situation of acute housing shortage a couple is practically forced to stay together until one partner can find alternative housing. Less drastically, a French or British couple who have both put their hearts and energies into obtaining and furnishing a much-valued home may delay separating for many years precisely because of this. Conversely, when the housing project was essentially of one partner or the other, this will make a decision to leave much easier.[93]

For the children of separating parents, whether or not their feelings are taken into account, moving house may exacerbate their sense of pain, loss, and bewilderment. For most children, a house provides a sense of continuity in their lives, at its simplest, physically: a known, familiar environment. For many it is much more than a physical shelter, and also a symbol of a former 'safe, secure little world'. In Britain, as we have found in another research study,[94] although a small minority of children do stay in their original homes right through childhood, for most a parental separation implies two or three subsequent moves. Nearly a third of those whose caretaking parent goes on to remarry will move between four and ten times.

Sometimes these moves became symbolic of resentment of incoming stepmothers, who were blamed for insisting on a move to a fresh house: 'she wanted everything'; 'we wanted to stay in the other house, but she wanted to move, so we did.' The worst moves, however, were those following the breaking up of a family when loss of a parent was made worse by a sharp drop in living standards. Middle-class children might carry with them idyllic memories of a golden past with a 'beautiful' house as their lost home: a seaside house with a huge garden, a playroom with a big doll's house and a wooden rocking horse, where a 'back door opens onto the pebbles'.

For others, the changes might bring real poverty, living in a series of rented rooms: 'we moved in with lots of different families'; 'even, sometimes, one large room divided with a curtain'—'living in rented accommodation, it was always a bit iffy, because if they didn't like kids . . .' Even when a lasting new base was established, there was quite often simply not enough space for the growing children. Siblings had to share beds as well as rooms—'she'd put her legs over me, and grind her teeth'. If they were of mixed sexes this became impossible as they became older. One girl grew up in a one-bedroom flat with her brother, her mother, and from middle childhood, her stepfather. For a while, her brother slept in the bathroom, but as teenagers both he and she were forced to sleep out on weeknights with friends—and she 'used to resent it, being pushed out'.

Conversely, one of the most obvious gains of entering a stepfamily, especially for middle-class children, could be a substantial increase in living space. 'So, all of a sudden we had our own room', remembered one girl, in 'the biggest house in the street', complete with a built-in theatre organ, Daimler car, and thrice-weekly 'treasure' of a cleaner; while another lovingly described the new pleasures of a 'big house, a lot of land, a dog, a cat, a nice area to live in'.

It seems appropriate to end with a dream house. Perhaps it is because our early homes are so fundamental to our evolving consciousness that for most adults houses are the stuff of dreams as well as material shelters. We construct them as cocoons for our emotional security, for togetherness with others, for our sense of self. We use them to project fantasies of living other lives, of belonging to other social milieux. And sometimes these fantasies become real social projects.

Yet this double character of housing has been too rarely studied by social scientists, and scarcely at all from the point of view of social mobility. How the relationship works out differs, as we have seen, between particular families, between social classes, between Britain and France. Thus in France, the peasant tradition of attachment to land rather than to houses has survived into the urban present; the laws of inheritance prevent the devices which enabled the perpetuation of the aristocratic English family country estate; the upper middle classes root themselves much more firmly in particular urban neighbourhoods; and the move towards mass home ownership came later than in Britain. Class and occupational

## The Familial Meaning of Housing

differences are equally crucial. Both rootedness and rootlessness can have drastically different consequences in leading to upward or downward mobility. Again, the 'one big move' to a better house may come about as the passive acceptance of a gift, or by contrast as the fruit of personal determination to achieve change and self-improvement. And while in Britain the country house almost invariably passes down the male line, by contrast the middle-class second home in the countryside can be a collective inheritance and endeavour which bonds a whole cousinage.

While such a mobilization of an extended family is rare, we think it particularly important to emphasize the extent to which housing is a form of maintenance or advancement of social position which very often involves intergenerational models and direct help, and typically represents the joint engagement of a couple rather than a lone individual.[95] It rarely provides an individual path to upward mobility: indeed, on the contrary, it is likely to falter with family fission.

Our purpose here has been, through re-examining the rich material we have in the interviews from our own life story projects and setting it within a comparative Anglo-French framework, to demonstrate how illuminating it can be, both of family dynamics and of the wider social class structure in terms of mobility and continuities, to explore this mutually interactive relationship, both material and symbolic, between houses and families.

### NOTES

1. Erving Goffman, *The Presentation of Self in Everyday Life* (New York, 1959).
2. Kunihiro Narumi, 'Inheritability and Attachment', in Ernesto Arias (ed.), *The Meaning and Use of Housing* (Aldershot, 1993), 341–79.
3. Peter L. Berger and Thomas Luckmann, *The Social Construction of Reality* (New York, 1966).
4. Claude Lévi-Strauss, *Le cru et le cuit* (Paris, 1964).
5. On the French *bourgeois* family, Béatrix Le Wita, 'Des pratiques quotidiennes ritualisées', in *Ni vue ni connue: Approche ethnographique de la culture bourgeoise* (Paris, 1988), 83–92; for the whole range in early 20th-cent. England, Paul Thompson, *The Edwardians: The Remaking of British Society*, 2nd edn. (London, 1992), 11–16.

6. See above, Chapter 2, note 7. For both the British and French interviews, all informants have been given pseudonyms in order to protect confidentiality.
7. Le Wita, *Ni vue ni connue*, 24–5, 38–44, 134–51; Martine Segalen and Béatrix Le Wita (eds), *Chez-soi: Objets et décors, des créations familiales?* (Paris, 1993). The latter collection is mostly French but includes articles by Judith Attfield on the cocktail cabinet in England, and by Orvar Löfgren on Sweden.
8. Ken Plummer, *Documents of Life: An Introduction to the Problems and Literature of a Humanistic Method* (London, 1983).
9. Raphael Samuel, 'House and Home in Late Victorian London', unpublished paper, 1974.
10. Pat Barr (ed.), *I Remember* (London, 1970), 19.
11. Thorsten Veblen, *The Theory of the Leisure Class* (New York, 1899). Löfgren's work in English includes: 'The Swedish Family: a Study of Privatisation and Social Change', in Paul Thompson (ed.), *Our Common History* (London, 1982), 232–48; 'The Sweetness of Home: Class, Culture and Family Life in Sweden', *Ethnologia Europea*, 14 (1984), 44–64; and Jonas Frykman and Orvar Löfgren, *Culture Builders: A Historical Anthropology of Middle Class Life* (Rutgers, NJ, 1987). Also Y. Bernard and M. Jambu, 'Espace habité et modèles culturels', *Ethnologie française*, 8 (1978), 7–20; E. O. Laumann and J. S. House, 'Living Room Styles and Social Attributes: The Patterning of Material Artifacts in a Modern Urban Community', in E. O. Laumann, P. M. Siegel, and R. W. Hodge (eds), *The Logic of Social Hierarchies* (Chicago, 1970); J. S. and N. J. Duncan, 'Housing as Presentation of Self and the Structure of Social Networks', in G. T. Moore and R. G. Golledge (eds), *Environmental Knowing* (Stroudsburg, 1976).
12. Catherine Cookson, *Hannah Massey* (London, 1964; 1990 edn.), 47.
13. David Saunders, 'The Meaning of "Home" in Contemporary English Culture', *Housing Studies*, 4 (1989), 177–92 (the speaker is skilled working class); Lyn Richards, *Nobody's Home: Dreams and Realities in a New Suburb* (Melbourne, 1990).
14. Peter Saunders, *A Nation of Home Owners* (London, 1990), 321–36.
15. Samuel, 'House and Home'. According to Patrick Joyce, even in relatively prosperous and stable provincial Blackburn, in 1868–71, 20% of families moved house each year. In metropolitan London in the 1900s, it was common for a third of the population to move annually in working-class districts. Even in council housing a quarter of the tenants moved annually; but the rate had fallen dramatically to around 5% by 1920 (Paul Thompson, *Socialists, Liberals and Labour: The Struggle for London 1885–1914* (London, 1967), 13, 288). Yet by the mid-century a street of still-mobile families could become regarded,

partly because of this, as notorious: see Jerry White's portrait of *The Worst Street in London: Campbell Bunk, Islington, between the Wars* (London, 1986).
16. Christian Topalov, *Le Logement en France: Histoire d'une marchandise impossible* (Paris, 1987); Jean-Paul Flamand, *Loger le peuple: Essai sur une histoire du logement social* (Paris, 1989).
17. John Rex and Robert Moore, *Race, Community and Conflict: A Study of Sparkbrook* (London, 1969); Manuel Castells, *The Urban Question* (London, 1977), and *The City and the Grassroots* (London, 1983); Nicos Poulantzas, *Les Classes dans le capitalisme d'aujourd'hui* (Paris, 1974); Yves Grafmeyer, *Sociologie urbaine* (Paris, 1994).
18. Pierre Bourdieu, *Distinction: A Social Critique of the Judgement of Taste* (Cambridge, Mass., 1984), and *Esquisse d'une theorie de la pratique* (Geneva, 1972).
19. For example, Pitrim Sorokin, *Social and Cultural Mobility* (Glencoe, Ill., 1959); Seymour M. Lipset and Reinhard Bendix, *Social Mobility in Industrial Society* (Berkeley, 1963); Peter M. Blau and Otis D. Duncan, *The American Occupational Structure* (New York, 1967); David V. Glass, *Social Mobility in Britain* (London, 1954); John Goldthorpe, C. Llewellyn, and C. Payne, *Social Mobility and Class Structure in Modern Britain* (Oxford, 1987); Robert Erikson and John Goldthorpe, *The Constant Flux* (Oxford, 1992).
20. Notable examples by historians are John Burnett, *A Social History of Housing, 1815–1978* (London, 1986); M. J. Daunton, *House and Home in the Victorian City: Working-Class Housing 1850–1914* (London, 1983); Mark Swenarton, *Homes Fit for Heroes: The Politics and Architecture of Early State Housing in Britain* (London, 1981); and David Englander, *Landlord and Tenant in Urban Britain 1838–1918* (Oxford, 1983). A somewhat wider perspective is to be found in Miles Glendinning and Stefan Muthesius, *Tower Block: Modern Public Housing in England, Northern Ireland, Scotland and Wales* (New Haven, 1990).
21. Arias, *Meaning and Use of Housing*. The most relevant paper is by Narumi on the inheritance of houses in Japan. Some other papers discuss the social significance of interior decoration. The volume is not improved by a pervasive tendency to infuse discussions with jargonistic or statistical aridities, so that it lacks both fresh theoretical insight and empirical detail.

    An earlier collection, James S. Duncan (ed.), *Housing and Identity: Cross-Cultural Perspectives* (London, 1981), includes nothing on familial attitudes to housing.
22. Mark Girouard, *Life in the English Country House: A Social and Architectural History* (London, 1978); Stefan Muthesius, *The English*

*Terraced House* (New Haven, 1982); cf. Helen Long, *The Edwardian House: The Middle-Class Home in Britain, 1880–1914* (Manchester, 1993); Jerry White, *Rothschild Buildings: Life in an East End Tenement Block, 1887–1920* (London, 1980). Despite its title, M. J. Daunton's *A Property-Owning Democracy?* (London, 1987) is still concerned, like his earlier research, with the history of public housing.

23. David Saunders, 'Beyond Housing Classes: The Sociological Significance of Private Property Rights in Means of Consumption', *International Journal of Urban and Regional Research*, 8 (1984), 202–27; 'The Meaning of "Home" in Contemporary English Culture'; *A Nation of Home Owners* (London, 1990); Craig Gurney, '"Oh, We Wouldn't Live in a Council House": Contested Meanings of Home and Housing Tenure', paper to British Sociological Association Annual Conference, *Contested Cities: Social Process and Spatial Forms*, Leicester, Apr. 1995.
24. Le Wita, *Ni vue ni connue*; Segalen and Le Wita, *Chez-soi*; Eric Mension-Rigau, *L'Enfance au château: L'Éducation familiale des élites françaises au vingtième siècle* (Marseille, 1990); Yves Grafmeyer, *Quand Tout-Lyon se compte: Lignées, alliances, territoires* (Lyon, 1992).
25. Paul-Henry Chombart de Lauwe, *La Vie quotidienne des familles ouvrières* (Paris, 1956), and *Famille et habitation* (Paris, 1959–60); Martine Segalen with Françoise Bekus, *Nanterriens, les familles dans la ville* (Paris, 1990).
26. Isabelle Bertaux and Anne Gotman, 'Le Changement du statut résidentiel comme expérience familiale', in Catherine Bonvalet and Anne Gotman (eds), *Le logement: Une affaire de famille* (Paris, 1993); Isabelle Bertaux-Wiame, 'Espaces résidenties et identité familiale', in *Les Espaces de la famille*, AISLF, University of Liège, 5–6 May 1994, 21–42; Isabelle Bertaux, 'Familial et résidentiel un couple indissociable', *Sociologie et sociétés*, 4 (1995); Françoise Bloch, Monique Buisson, and Jean-Claude Mermet, 'S'éloigner ou se rapprocher: Le Lieu de résidence, un enjeu dans les relations intergénerationnelles', *Familles et contextes sociaux*, proceedings of Lisbon conference, 10–12 Apr. 1991, 271–8.
27. Eric Hobsbawm and Terence Ranger (eds), *The Invention of Tradition* (Cambridge, 1983); cf. David Lowenthal, *The Past is a Forgotten Country* (Cambridge, 1985).
28. Paul Thompson, Catherine Itzin, and Michele Abendstern, *I Don't Feel Old: The Experience of Later Life* (Oxford, 1990).
29. John R. Russell, Duke of Bedford, *A Silver Plated Spoon* (London, 1959).
30. Interview 5003AM, 35, 58.

## The Familial Meaning of Housing

31. Interviews 5401 AM, 12, BM, 43.
32. Interviews 5207 BM, 24; 5208 BF, 97, CF, 51.
33. With over two million members, and holding extensive landed estates especially along the coastlines and in the most beautiful hill country, the National Trust is now the largest voluntary society in Britain, with more supporters than even the Church of England, the largest religious denomination.
34. Michel Pinçon and Monique Pinçon-Charlot, *Dans les beaux quartiers* (Paris, 1989).
35. In 1955 there were 6,000,000 agricultural workers in France, of whom 90% were family members; in 1980 2,800,000, and the wagepaid workers had declined faster than the family members—Alice Barthez, *Famille, travail et agriculture* (Paris, 1982), 11.
36. Interview 92, ML, 22.
37. Interview TRA. Lasalle, 29–32.
38. David Crouch and Colin Ward, *The Allotment: Its Landscape and Culture* (London, 1988).
39. Paul Thompson with Trevor Lummis and Tony Wailey, *Living the Fishing* (London, 1983); Graham Smith, ' "Fur coat, nae knickers": Working Class Attiudes to Social Mobility and the Family in Scotland', unpublished conference paper, Atelier Constitution des Trajectoires Sociales, Paris, May 1986.
40. Valerie Karn, *Retiring to the Seaside* (London, 1977); Françoise Cribier, *Une génération de Parisiens arrivent à la retraite* (Paris, 1968), and 'La Retraite au bord de la mer et les relations avec enfants', *Gérontologie et société*, 21 (1971), 44–69.
41. 'HLM' is a generic term for a unit or bloc of public housing, 'un logement collectif': the initials mean 'habitations à loyers modérés'—low rental housing.
42. Interview 92, CN, 23.
43. Interview RP, HG, 16–17.
44. Interview TRA, PS, 12–14.
45. Not part of the national random sample. This section is based on an interview with John Garnett, who also showed me a video of a family play, and drew a special family tree with over a hundred names, indicating which had used the house and which had not.
46. William Garnett's son, James Clerk Maxwell Garnett, was principal of Manchester College of Technology, and then secretary to the League of Nations Union: his grandchildren include Peggy, who married the Labour politician Douglas Jay, and was a politician in her own right; and his great-grandchildren Virginia Bottomley, recently Minister for Health in the Conservative Government.
47. Interview, 12, 15, 17, 19, 27.

48. Interview, 3, 10, 12–13, 15, 23.
49. Interview, 7, 10, 15–16, 23.
50. Interview, 5–6, 30–2.
51. Interview RP, Brice, 12.
52. Yves Grafmeyer, *Habiter Lyon: Milieux et quartiers du centre-ville* (Paris, 1991); Jean-Claude Chamboredon and Madeleine Lemaire, 'Proximité spatiale et distance sociale: Les Grands Ensembles et leur peuplement', *Revue Française de Sociologie*, 11 (1970), 3–33.
53. Interview RP, Avray, 3.
54. Interview TRA, MR, 19.
55. Cf. Reinhard Sieder, 'Housing Policy, Social Welfare, and Family Life in "Red Vienna"', *Oral History*, 13 (2) (1985), 35–48.
56. Interview 5805 BM, 36, 44.
57. Interview 5502 BF, 66.
58. Interview 5807 AF, 54, BM, 55.
59. Interview 5415 AF, 4, 11, 16–17, 59, 66; BF, 202.
60. Gloria Wood and Paul Thompson, *The Nineties: Personal Recollections of the 20th Century* (London, 1993), 169, 172. These interviews with the family were carried out for the BBC Television series on men and women aged over 90 years.
61. Colin Bell, *Middle Class Families* (London, 1968).
62. Interview 5203 BF, 73.
63. Interview 6403 BM, 15–16.
64. Ibid. 26, 29, 42, 55–6.
65. Ibid. 74–6, 107.
66. Interview 5204 AM, 4–5.
67. Jean-François Stassen, 'Le Caravaning résidentiel: Du dépaysement à l'appropriation de l'espace', in 'Les Espaces de la famille', AISLF, University of Liége, Belgium, 5–6 May 1994, 195–216.
68. A notable study of transgenerational family migration cultures is Mary Chamberlain, 'Family and identity: Barbadian Migrants to Britain', in Rina Benmayor and Andor Skotnes (eds), *Migration and Identity* (International Yearbook of Oral History and Life Stories, 3; Oxford, 1994), 119–37.
69. Rex and Moore, *Race, Community and Conflict*.
70. Lena Inowlocki, 'Grandmothers, Mothers, and Daughters: Intergenerational Transmission in Displaced Families in Three Jewish Communities', in Daniel Bertaux and Paul Thompson (eds), *Between Generations: Family Models, Myths and Memories* (International Yearbook of Oral History and Life Stories, 2; Oxford, 1993), 139–54.
71. Interview TRA, BC, 28.
72. Interview RP, SL, 28.
73. Interview RP, AM, 24.

74. Dennis Hardy and Colin Ward, *Arcadia for All: The Legacy of a Makeshift Landscape* (London, 1984), 2.
75. William P. Mangin and John Turner, 'Benavides and the Barriada Movement', in Paul Oliver (ed.), *Shelter and Society* (London, 1969), 127–36; N. J. Habraken, *Supports: An Alternative to Mass Housing* (London, 1972).
76. Patricia Safa, *Por qué enviamos nuestros hijos a la escuela? Socialización infantil e identidad popular* (Mexico DF, 1992).
77. Hugo Slim and Paul Thompson, *Listening for a Change* (London, 1993), 'Community History and Mobilisation: Recife, Brazil', 104–15.
78. Interview 5408 BF; 6402 BF, 52–4.
79. Interview RP, RB, 32–5.
80. Interview RP, FB, 7.
81. Interview 5408 AF, 18–19, 36.
82. Interview 5605 AF, 35; BM, 64, 79–80, 82.
83. Interview 5202 AM, 20, 24, 27.
84. Interview 5202 AF, 3, 35; BM, 48.
85. Interview 5202 BM, 23, 60–1, 114, 121.
86. Interview 5207 BM, 123, 125.
87. Ibid. 49, 52.
88. Ibid. 22–4.
89. Interview 5413 AM, 7, 19, 23.
90. Ibid. 34, 45.
91. We have ourselves carried out a separate research project on the consequences of divorce in Britain, including for housing, in a life-story study of fifty men and women, all born in March 1958 and followed by the National Child Development Study longitudinal survey study: see Gill Gorell Barnes, Natasha Burchardt, Gwyn Daniel, and Paul Thompson, *Growing Up in Stepfamilies*, forthcoming 1997. On the consequences of divorce in France for housing, Patrick Festy, 'Statut d'occupation du dernier domicile conjugal et mobilité résidentielle à partir de la séparation', in *Transformations de la famille et habitat*, INED, cahier 120 (Paris, 1988); and 'Mobilité résidentielle des femmes séparées: Une étape dans le cycle de vie familiale', *Stratégies résidentielles*, INED, cahier 2 (Paris, 1990); Claude Martin and Didier Le Gall, 'Familles à beau-parent: Choix du logement et "guerre des meubles"', *Groupe familial*, 143 (Apr.–June 1994), 88–96.
92. Nadine Lefaucheur, *Les Familles monoparentales: Une catégorie spécifique?* (Paris, 1987).
93. Jean-Claude Kaufmann, *La Vie ordinaire: Voyage au coeur du quotidien* (Paris, 1989).
94. See above, note 90. To maintain anonymity the interview numbers of the quotations used here are not identified.

95. British research has found that between a quarter and a third of current home owners started buying their houses as newly married couples with the help of a gift or loan from their families, and a similar proportion is in turn helping their children (Saunders, *Nation of Home Owners*, 161–3).

# 6

# The Local World View: Social Change and Memory in Three Tuscan Communes

## GIOVANNI CONTINI

To the visitor Tuscan—or indeed Italian—villages may be assumed to be similar; and certainly the social mobility researcher analysing a national survey is unlikely to be interested by differences between them. But in fact, as I have discovered, villages and small towns within the same region can have radically different stories of economic and social development and also, as a result, different life chances and patterns of mobility.[1]

In this chapter I compare three Tuscan communes whose recent histories I have researched. The first is Santa Croce sull'Arno, a tannery town by the Arno river and close to Pisa, on a plain where trade developed early. The second is Scarperia, built by the medieval Florentine Republic on the road to Bologna across the mountains to the north, a village of knifemakers possibly from the early 14th century and certainly from the 18th. The third is Abbadia San Salvatore, also a mountain village, but lying south of Siena, on Monte Amiata and from the end of the 19th century until very recently a mining village.

I intend to focus in particular on the relationship between the history of the change in each commune and what can be called 'local world view': that is to say the common beliefs shared by the inhabitants which are both a reflection of the past history of the commune and one of its causes. I also compare local reconstructions of the experience of the past with the viewpoint of a professional historian from outside, in order not only to underline the teleologism and moralism of the insiders' view, but also the limitations of the professional perpective when it treats the local world view as simply 'a fake' or popular 'error' to be unmasked by the enlightened intellectual.

I have been using a variety of sources for my research on the three communes. Demographic data—held in both local and national archives—and business archives have been particularly valuable in building up a convincing reconstruction of past events and social and economic development; while oral sources—interviews orally and visually recorded—have been used both for information of 'how things happened' and also of how people think that they happened. I have also used these interviews in two books which have been published on the stories of Santa Croce and of Scarperia,[2] while a book on Abbadia's local memory is to come out soon. The local administrations of the three communes have been promoting local history research during the last decade. As a result books and articles have been written on Scarperia in the Middle Ages,[3] on Abbadia's mining history,[4] and on the story of the Santa Croce industrial district since the beginning of the 19th century.[5] All these sources have contributed to my research.

I chose these three communes because they represent three different possible developments of the old Tuscan rural village, whose inhabitants in the past were mostly poor day labourers living in permanent fear of unemployment, half industrial workers and half peasants. Today, Santa Croce has become a successful industrial district, while Scarperia, once a flourshing small town devoted to an ancient handicraft, has failed to develop a modern industry. Of the three only the last, Abbadia San Salvatore, experienced large-scale industry in the form of its mercury mine, and it is now facing serious problems following the closing of the mine.

All three communes were symbiotically linked to the surrounding peasant society of the region. They sold some of their products to the peasants—Scarperia's knives, for instance—and their wives went to work in the countryside during the critical moments of the yearly agrarian cycle, when the peasants needed a larger workforce. More generally, many artisans, small industrialists and industrial workers in the three communes came from peasant backgrounds, some because they had moved from the countryside to the commune in order to change their work, others because the arrival of industry in their commune undermined its earlier peasant economy and society.

## SANTA CROCE SULL'ARNO: STORY

The first commune, Santa Croce sull'Arno, is today very rich. Its main trade is the tannery industry. Several hundreds of small firms have arisen during the last forty years, creating an 'industrial district' (in Marshall's term): these small entrepreneurs are able to cooperate in many different and flexible ways to meet the extremely erratic demands of the leather market.

Santa Croce's wealth is, however, very recent. From the origins of the tanning trade in the early 19th century until the end of the Second World War, in fact, the work and housing conditions of its inhabitants were very poor indeed. The tanners had to work in the cold water for hours on end, even during the winter. There was permanent work only for the top craftsmen, so that the great majority of the less skilled had to migrate during the months of unemployment. Some others found work with the local sharecropper peasants at the harvest, the vintaging, and the olive-picking. Many houses consisted of one single room, in which the whole family used to eat and sleep; one window looked out at the front, the other into a narrow alley, blind on both sides, where—as in Boccaccio's tale—faeces were thrown, to be collected from time to time by the peasants, who used them as a fertilizer. After work the men stayed very little at home, preferring to spend their spare time with their comrades talking about anarchy or socialism, singing opera arias, drinking wine—and often getting drunk. Especially after evenings dedicated to wine, wives were frequently ill-treated.

Things started to change after the Second World War. The leather market was very favourable, while in many countries—in Germany, for instance—laws controlling pollution were becoming very strict. As a result the tannery industry tended to move towards those countries less interested in the protection of the environment, such as Italy.

In Santa Croce sull'Arno there were many people ready to seize this favourable opportunity. There were those who had made money on the black market during and immediately after the war, and wanted to invest their earnings; and there were peasants leaving the sharecropping system, who needed to find a new activity for their family enterprise, and had their savings and their key-money to invest. In addition, the tendency to form many small enterprises was favoured by the large firms. In fact, already during the 1930s, the big industrialists had successfully experimented with the subcontracting system, lending money to workers so that they could set up independent tannery shops; as a result the large firms were not forced to employ new workers when business was good, or to sack them when the economic cycle turned bad.

In 1953 an important confrontation took place between the unions and the large firms. The unions, deeply influenced by the Communist Party, wanted to bargain not only over wages and work conditions, but even over the general social conditions including housing problems: the industrialists were asked to build houses for their workers. Although many of the industrialists belonged—and still belong—to left-wing parties, they answered with a lock-out. Although eventually an agreement was achieved, it was never implemented, because in fact the unions were defeated, and never recovered. Nevertheless within a few months workers' wages were higher than those established through the national agreement between the unions and the employers. Many of the workers who were sacked for having led these struggles were given loans, and they too became small entrepreneurs.

This proliferation of small firms, although starting as a ring of subcontracting shops around the large firms, developed into a more 'democratic' system during the 1950s and 1960s, because each small firm developed its own specialization in the leather's cycle, and thus managed to become more independent of the larger firms, which lost some of their previous importance. Subsequently, by the mid-1970s, they managed to win back some of the lost ground by building up a complex system of industrial groups; so that of course in each group the larger firm succeeded in getting more power.

Another interesting feature of the making of Santa Croce sull'Arno's industrial district was the method of its financing. Up until the Second World War no bank had established a branch in Santa Croce sull'Arno. The largest firm played the role of representative for a Florentine bank. Even when the banks arrived, those inhabitants of the commune who decided to start their own business preferred to get loans from friends, relatives, or acquaintances—with bills of exchange—rather than ask for a credit from the banks.

## SCARPERIA

Scarperia is a commune founded by the Florentine Republic at the beginning of the 14th century. The small walled town lies at the foot of the Appenine mountains, and for several centuries, perhaps back to its foundation, its main trade was cutlery.

In the late 19th century, however, after the unification of Italy the number of artisans working in this craft grew dramatically. Boys from many of the peasant families and also from those of other professions were choosing to become cutlers. The trade was family-centred: and while in 1841 there were only 35 families of cutlers, by 1881 their number had grown to 92, and in 1901 to 155. This proved the peak, for the subsequent decline of the trade is apparent from the figures: down to 100 families in 1936, 69 in 1951, and a mere 20 in 1961.

The basis of the success of Scarperia's cutlery trade from the 1840s to the 1900s was also the cause of its subsequent crisis: for the boom was based on an extreme skill and speed in making knives with an archaic technology. Through the last century with this skill and speed Scarperia's cutlers competed successfully in the knife market of southern Italy. They started to copy the traditional jack-knives models of the region: from Naples, Calabria, Sicily, Abruzzi, and so on. But the drawback was that success won in this way did not give Scarperia itself a recognized trade mark: southern models were copied and pushed out the regional originals on the market, but this happened secretly. The excellent chance for building up Scarperia's own reputation and trade mark was lost.

The boom, which had been a response to the opportunity created by national unification and by the abolition of internal import duties, was halted fifty years later by a change in the law. Again, an external factor beyond the control of the small cutlers of Scarperia intervened, this time to close the golden age of their trade. At the beginning of this century a maximum length for jack-knife blades was established by law. As a consequence, the knives became either much shorter or without points, making it more difficult to sell them. The trade entered a period of crisis.

One way of meeting this challenge could have been to speed up the process of technological innovation, in order to reduce production costs. But the cutlers were too conservative, proud of their skills in an extremely archaic technology—the forge for the blades was completely manual, for instance—and too strongly attached to the old system. So they did not wish to risk their money in order to improve their work process. In any case they did not have enough money, and they were not used to saving and investing it. Instead they preferred to spend their money as soon as they managed to get it, organizing feasts and playing cards with their friends. Quite often the family was excluded from these feasts, although wives and children might be starving while the man was eating beefsteaks with his workmates.

Because of the crisis some of the inhabitants of Scarperia tried to set up a co-operative society. This was intended to buy iron for the knife-blades and horn for the handles; also, and most importantly, the society itself was intended to sell the knives. The members were still working in the old way, in small workshops, often in their own homes, sometimes in the kitchen itself. Hence the only advantage of the co-operative was in eliminating the merchants who sold raw materials and bought the knives. These were often the same people and were reputed to have been particularly extortionate.

Had the co-operative been a society for production, it could have introduced technical innovations through the collective purchase of machinery. Equipment such as pressing forges for the blades was very expensive, but only needed by each cutler for a few hours a week. But instead the co-operative's main purpose was the purchase of raw materials and sale of the finished products. As a consequence, the cutlers' own entrepreneurship was discouraged: they were kept away from getting to understand the market's rules and problems. Worse still, both the managers of the association and the cutlers themselves soon made a fool of the co-operative. The managers secretly let the artisans know the names of the customers, and the cutlers asked for this information, precisely in order to supplant selling by the co-operative itself. Not surprisingly, the society soon went bankrupt. And the same thing recurred every time somebody tried to found another co-operative in Scarperia: seven times in sixty years.

Meanwhile the craft continued to decline. Some young cutlers left their family firm after having fought, and lost, a long battle with their fathers to introduce new machinery in the workshop. And at the same time the buoyant local labour market played an important role in the final destruction of the ancient craft. The manufacturing plants in Florence very much appreciated the skills of the young cutlers. And they were happy enough to move closer to the city.

## ABBADIA SAN SALVATORE

In sharp contrast to the stories of the first two communes is that of Abbadia, a remote mountain mining village in the province of

Siena, on the slopes of Tuscany's southernmost mountain, Monte Amiata. Until the end of the 19th century, Abbadia's inhabitants were poor peasants or shepherds. The difference between the rich and the poor lay mainly in the quantity of food. Rich peasant families had plenty of bread, cheese, and wine, while the men of poor families were forced to migrate seasonally to other parts of Tuscany in order to sustain their wives and children.

This archaic social structure was shattered when, just at the turn of the century, mercury was discovered immediately under the village, and a mine was opened. The former peasants, both rich and poor, became miners. Very soon the mine, which belonged to a German company, controlled almost the entire life of the village. Because the original standard of living in Abbadia had been so low, the local Fascist *podestà* (governor), Baiocchi, succeeded in persuading the mine owners to reduce the wages of the workers, which had started at the level of the German miners; and not surprisingly, partly through his economic power outside the mine, Baiocchi was able to divert a large part of the money saved from workers' wages towards himself. He had gradually bought from the inhabitants of Abbadia their small woods, until he became the only owner of the forest. He was then able to sell wooden pit-props to the mine at a monopolistic price: indeed, according to local memory, through trickery he regularly succeeded in selling the same pit-props twice . . .

The village was very isolated. It was distant from the main highway, and far from any large towns. The miners' work was hard and dangerous and their education primitive. The bar was the only place the men could go to for their free time, and in the bar wine-drinking was the main form of fun. Often miners got so drunk that they completely lost their sense of direction, and children were sent to the bar to 'rescue' their drunken father. Drunken miners would bet that they could beat their wives harder than everybody else: and because their homes were close together in the narrow medieval streets, it was possible to verify who the winner was from the painful yells of their wives.

The class composition of the village was extremely simple: workers, foremen, and managers, and just a very few artisans. Hence from the late 1930s it proved a fertile ground for the propaganda of the clandestine Communist Party: Abbadia society matched very well with Jack London's representations.[6] After the war, the now formally established Italian Communist Party (PCI) became the most powerful party in Abbadia. Its membership grew dramatically, and many former Fascists now became communists, so that by the end of the 1940s the majority of villagers were PCI members. When, in July 1948, a young Fascist attempted to assassinate Togliatti, the PCI's leader, in Abbadia the event was taken as the beginning of the Revolution. The village was occupied by armed partisans, and the Christian Democrats and the Fascists were beaten and forced to lock themselves into their houses. When the Carabinieri (the rural police) tried to occupy the village, they were shot at. Two of them were severely wounded, and died. During the days that followed the village was instead occupied by the army. Many of those who had taken guns were imprisoned. There was eventually a trial, which concluded with very severe sentences.

Despite this traumatic event, the PCI's power in the village remained intact, until the recent crisis of the mercury mine. The mine suffered several difficult periods when demand in the mercury market was weak and during these some miners were laid off. But in the mid-1970s the collapse of the market was so severe that it provoked a final crisis which brought the closing up of the mine. Abbadia's industrial history was at an end.

## LOCAL WORLD VIEWS: SANTA CROCE AND SCARPERIA

This is my outline story of the development of each of the three communes. But how do their inhabitants remember and interpret them? Let us begin with Santa Croce and Scarperia.

In Santa Croce, the successful tannery town, people insist on the moral virtues of their fellow-citizens. The big industrialists, friends, and relatives lent money to workers who wanted to work on their own account; and the workers always returned the money lent, whether they were successful or not. The tannery artisans never kept their craft secret, but instead always circulated information about new work processes and market opportunities. Even the poorest tanner used to address the richest as 'tu', using the second-person singular, rather than as 'lei', the third-person singular, which in Italy expresses deference.

In Scarperia, by contrast, the interviewees explain the failure of the local craft in terms of a lack of morality: the artisans never trusted each other, each of them always tried to cheat the other, and those who set up the co-operative were no better. The commune deserved the final collapse of its local craft.

In neither of these two cases does the local and collective elaboration of past experience encompass the role played by external constraints and opportunities in explaining the respective success and failure of the two industrial districts. In Santa Croce the positive changes in the leather market after the Second World War are not mentioned in the stories. In Scarperia the difficulties caused by the legislative changes on the size of jack-knives are also omitted. Thus the present, through a very teleological interpretation of the facts, is seen as the logical consequence of its moral causes: of the reliable or unreliable behaviour of the artisans of the two small towns. Furthermore this moralistic view not only ignores the crucial role played by external factors beyond local control, but also greatly oversimplies local moral behaviour in the past.

Thus in Santa Croce, in practice people lent and returned money back not only because they were 'good', 'generous', or 'honest', but also because they were acting in this way for their own interests. The large industrialists wanted to create a belt of small artisans in order to give them work when the economic cycle was rising, without being forced to take on extra manpower and then in turn to sack workers when the crisis came. They showed little concern at the bankruptcies of the artisans, which were frequent in the 1930s. Friends and relatives who lent money hoped that they would share in the work if the venture was successful. Those who did not succeed returned their loans because otherwise they could not hope for a second loan in the future. Their world was small. Everybody knew everybody: for the dishonest there were no second chances.

In Scarperia, on the other hand, despite what is recounted today, people were not really mistrustful 'by nature'. On the contrary, they were prepared to co-operate, as is shown by the very fact that they tried seven times to build up a co-operative society. The repeated failure of those societies depended partly on external constraints which were difficult to counter locally, and partly on the inappropriate shape of the co-operatives, which discouraged the entrepreneurial spirit of the artisans and pushed the more enterprising to cheat the society.

Thus focused on the present, these local world views transform the past into a coherent continuum, a teleological process which ends, and could only end, precisely in the present. The rise and fall of local industries, which have shaped the destinies of the men and women of each commune, are accounted for, not in terms of external economic or political factors, but of local individual and collective moral worth. Yet this strong reduction of the complexity of past experience is understandable; the local world view, like the anecdotes people tell about the past, has above all a didactic function. It represents the rationalization of what has been done, successfully or not, by fellow-citizens in the past. Its concern is not to reconstruct the whole experience, including the stressful presence of the external constraints—which are stressful precisely because they are beyond the influence of those living in a small, peripheral world. Whoever transmits such a collectively elaborated world view intends to transmit a practical message in order to avoid the repetition of past mistakes and to encourage moves that time has proved to be beneficial.

As sociologists have shown, the belief of neo-classical economists in the 'rational choices' of the social actors is far too optimistic; in practice individuals have at their disposal only a limited range of information, and the rationality of their choices is undermined by this limitation. This is particularly true of the individuals, like the older artisans of Santa Croce and Scarperia, who had very little education, and as a result were nearly illiterate. In such a situation the information embedded in the local world view, orally elaborated and transmitted through face-to-face relationships, played a vital role for them in enabling them to make their own life choices.

The local world view thus reinforced the tendency of the artisans to trust each other in Santa Croce, while in Scarperia it operated just in the opposite way. In the first commune, when people had to trust each other, the commonplace that 'a santacrocese can trust a santacrocese' played an important role, providing a link between the interests of one man and another which could be advantageous for both of them. In Scarperia, by contrast, the common view certainly played a role in preventing the cutlers from trusting each other, even when it was in their mutual interest to co-operate.

In both villages, then, the local world view distils the moral of the story. And at the same time the circulation of this view has a practical influence on the shaping of local development: the history becomes a self-fulfilling prophecy. Like a fly-wheel, the local world view absorbs the evil or the good of the past, projecting them back in the day's events.

These local reconstructions of the past not only played important roles in making things go as they did; they can also have an impact on the professional historian's account too. Usually the social historian who 'reconstructs' a completely extinct past from traditional records finds several causes for change. These are supposed to be assembled according to a hierarchy of significance. Often however the historian has insufficient information to make such distinctions, and will thus present a picture of the past which, however elegant, makes no decisive attributions of responsibility.

The reconstruction of the past by the villagers, as we have seen, is often monocausal and teleological. It is uninfluenced by any academic hesitations: a rough and ready picture of the past intended to be immediately used in the present. This is why local witnesses attribute the greatest importance to the moral qualities of their fellow-citizens and leave out important elements like market constraints, national policies towards the trade, and so on. But we need to appreciate that it is precisely this one-sidedness of popular memory which allows it to play a crucial role in the many small choices which make up the story of the villages. Thus a view which may seem wrong to the professional researcher became true in a sense, and at any rate is now part of the story and thus must be taken seriously within it. The local world view is also important for the external researcher in another sense. It shows how narrow the village world was, and how important, until very recently, was local talk and even gossip for getting the information needed to make personal choices.

## LOCAL IDENTITY AND COMMUNIST IDEOLOGY: ABBADIA SAN SALVATORE

In Abbadia San Salvatore both the mine and the local identity of the villagers were derived from outside. Its story shows, by contrast to those of Santa Croce and Scarperia, how important were their narrow, small, local worlds in which, at the very least, it was possible to make independent economic decisions and to elaborate an autonomous world view. In Abbadia everyday experience was quite different, and this difference affected both the common way of interpreting the story of the village and also, more broadly, the sense of local identity.

Once the mine was established in Abbadia, the traditional local agriculture and stock-raising ceased to provide the main occupations, although it remained a 'spare time' hobby. Former shepherds and peasants, now turned miners, still grew some grapes for their own wine and kept a garden for their vegetables. They were now better protected than before, and they earned more money than any others living on the Amiata mountain. But they had lost their independence. They could no longer decide for themselves when to work, what to do, what to buy and sell. All such decisions were now taken by the staff of the mine; the workers had only to obey the orders, and to show their skills within the strict framework of the mine heirarchy.

When workers in Scarperia or in Santa Croce talk about knife-making or the tannery industry, they say 'we'. In Abbadia, when they talk about the mine they say 'they'. 'We' is used to express the collective association of the workers in the political parties—especially the Communist Party—when they set themselves against the mine, and against capitalist society more generally. In Santa Croce and in Scarperia political experience was important, but local identity was never moulded entirely by a political party's ideology or by the experience of its membership. In both communes, particularly in Santa Croce, social mobility was quite easy, so that party members could leave their original social status, moving up—or down—the local social structure. In both the local world view was rather embedded in the local craft culture.

In Abbadia the Communist Party played a much more important role. There was little chance of individual social mobility here. The class composition of the village was as stable as it was simple: the workers on the one hand and the members of the management of the mine on the other. Furthermore the system of working discouraged the formation of a collective identity through work itself. The miners never experienced a workers' community inside the mine; they worked in isolated pairs, the 'couple' of the miner and his assistant, always together, but cut off from the rest of the workforce.

The loss of their autonomous culture by Abbadia's inhabitants is also indicated by the fact that even their traditional folklore was eradicated from the village. An educated Communist leader who moved to Abbadia during the war and remained active during the 1940s and 1950s remembers that they needed to 'reinvent' the local folklore in order to develop their propaganda, because the old traditions were dead. Only the specific dialect of the village, distinctly different from that of its neighbours, still maintained—and still maintains—some traces of the old story, and of the strong hostility between Abbadia and the next village. The two dialects, indeed, have developed specific features just in order to differentiate one from the other.

It was the political parties which instead became the new core for local identity. Their ideologies provided the world view of their members. The largest party in Abbadia was the Communist Party, and its scope seemed to coincide with that of human society itself. Indeed even its rivals seemed to be born of it. Thus one man who left the PCI after the 'revolution'—the shooting of the two Carabinieri in 1948—told us that the pressures and insults from his former comrades were so intolerable that he was driven to set up a local section of the Christian Democratic trade union: 'If you compel me, I can really do my worst...' Several of those whom we interviewed told us how at some point they were expelled from the PCI: and in each case this is recalled as an incurable wound, a traumatic shift in their life. Such 'rejected' former militants could not find anybody to talk with, nor, given the isolation of Abbadia, could they enjoy any social life elsewere. If they did not join a political strike, they had to come out of the mine completely isolated from their fellow-workers: the human stream of once fellow-miners avoiding the blackleg, condemned to symbolic obstracism.

For many decades, the political ideology of the PCI and the social structure of the village matched each other harmoniously. The Communist worker found in his everyday work a confirmation of his political world view; while the political line of the PCI seemed particularly convincing in explaining how the mine, the village, and Italian society as a whole was working. And for the young men in Abbadia the choice was extremely simple: they all wanted to become miners.

Things started to become confused in the 1970s, when the mine entered its terminal crisis. The opening of new galleries ceased; workers were sacked. By 1980 it was clear that the mine was closing and would not be reopened in the future. At the same time, the PCI itself had also entered a period of crisis, first with the failure of its attempted alliance with the Christian Democratic Party, and then with the collapse of the Communist world in the East.

Local identity, once built on a combination between political affiliation and membership and the simple class composition of the village, disintegrated fast. Even the memory of the past started to vanish very quickly, and the younger generations have little consciousness either of Communist politics[7] or of the mine and of the mining. Now that the road to the mine was blocked, they started to migrate to the larger towns. Those who remained experienced a hard situation: unemployment and the growing marginalization of the village, increasingly perceived as completely isolated from the world, a dead pool. When we interview Abbadia's young inhabitants we often get the feeling that they see themselves as citizens of the global village unluckily projected by a ruthless fate into the middle of nowhere.

The invention of tradition seems a very common phenomenon in Tuscany, and in Italy in general. Even when a village formerly did not differ from its neighbours, as was common enough with villages in peasant areas without any industrial or artisanal tradition, often an element from the past is now picked out as the hub around which a new collective identity is built. Such invented traditions are often by many standards illegitimate, and even ludicrous, but it is impressive to sociologists and anthropologists how much time and money villagers will spend in organizing the 'wild boar festival' or the 'hot sausage festival'. Nearly every Tuscan village has established a 'traditional' festival of this kind during the last two decades. Yet in Abbadia, even this phenomenon is missing.

The future of the village looks as uncertain as its past, and it is becoming more and more bleakly helpless. The local and regional governments tried to introduce small industries to Abbadia, but the outcome was a failure. The whole market had to be invented from scratch, and those who were prepared to try lacked any experience of entrepreneurial culture. Now the rate of alcohol and drug addiction is higher in Abbadia than in any other nearby village.

These three communes are all relatively small centres in a region which as a whole has developed over the last fifty years from a largely rural towards an industrial economy. But despite their common region and also their common past links with Tuscan peasant culture, the paths of each commune, and the mobility chances which they offered, have differed sharply. The contrasts between them indicate how crucial particular localities can be in the shaping of life chances and experience.

## NOTES

1. For a similar exploration of the socio-economic contrasts between different fishing communities, see Paul Thompson, *Living the Fishing* (London, 1983).
2. On Scarperia, see Luciano Ardiccioni and Giovanni Contini, *Vivere di coltelli* (Florence, 1989). On Santa Croce, see Giovanni Contini (ed.), *Santa Croce sull'Arno: biografie di imprenditori* (Florence, 1987). The second book is out of print, and a revised edition will be published soon. More recently a survey of local firms from the 1920s to the 1970s has been made, in order to discover the percentage of firms which were born or died over half a century, their size, etc.
3. See Giuseppina Carla Romby and Giovanna Casali, *Gli statuti dei coltellinai* (Florence, 1990), an edition of the statutes of the knifemakers' guild from 1538 to 1665. For a more concentrated focus on medieval knifemakers, see Giancarlo Baronti (ed.), *I libri di bottega di Giordano di Guido Giordani, maestro coltellinaio a Scarperia (1546–1562)* (Florence, 1991).
4. Luciano Segreto, *Monte Amiata. Il mercurio italiano. Strategie internazionali e vincoli extraeconomici* (Milan, 1991).
5. Franco Foggi (ed.), *Nel segno di Saturno. Origini e sviluppo dell'attività conciaria a Santa Croce sull'Arno*, i–iii (Florence, 1985–7).
6. Jack London's *The Iron Heel* (New York, 1907) was published under the Fascist regime, despite the censor, and this book was used by the clandestine Italian Communist Party as part of its propaganda. Thousands of workers read it. In Abbadia it was a best seller, together with Maxim Gorky's novel *The Mother*, trans. M. Wettlin (Moscow, 1950).
7. As more generally in Italy as a whole, the young had already stopped joining the PCI by the late 1970s.

# 7

# Migration, Mobility, and Social Process: Scottish Migrants in Canada

BRIAN ELLIOTT

Let's begin with a question. What happens when immigrants from an ethnic group commonly regarded as part of the dominant 'Anglo' élite in Canada confront downward social mobility or find the pathways to greater achievement blocked? The question arises out of an on-going study of social mobility among Scots who migrated to Canada in the period 1945–1975. Most came, of course, expecting that in the New World they would be able to 'succeed', but some of them found that there were serious obstacles to the realization of their ambitions. A number, discovering that their qualifications were unacceptable or that both qualifications and experience were heavily 'discounted' by prospective employers, had to accept jobs (at least initially) that were inferior in class or status terms to those they had left behind. Others found that some combination of education, gender, ethnicity, and age meant that their opportunities for career advancement were blocked or that achievement objectives—other than occupational ones—were unattainable.

In these circumstances, what did people do? Some simply left—heading back to Scotland, or setting off for the United States or Australia or some other country in the hope that their luck would be better there. Most, though, stayed and used social and collective resources to overcome or compensate for the difficulties they experienced. The frequency with which migrants and their offspring referred to the threat or the reality of downward mobility or blocked mobility led to the writing of this paper. Risk and reflexivity, two of the features often cited as hall-marks of the 'late modern' era (Beck, Giddens, and Lash 1994) have long been integral to the experience of long-distance migrants and the subjects of the present study were acutely aware that in choosing to leave their homeland they had risked whatever status and security they had, that they had been forced to confront a new social system in which class and culture were no longer connected in the predictable ways they had known and where identities (including their own) were multiple and mutable. They recognized all this and reflected and acted upon it.

Focusing some attention on the cases of downward or blocked mobility turned out to be particularly instructive—as S. M. Miller (1960), many years before, had suggested it would be. But where Miller's interest was in the aggregate rates of downward mobility as the means of assessing the relative openness of stratification systems, ours is in the use of qualitative, biographical data about actual or threatened downward movement as a way of understanding *processes* of social mobility. The data provided by the Scottish migrants to Canada provide confirmation and very clear illustration of the profoundly social nature of social mobility involving, as it does, collective as well as individual effort, and collective as well as individual resources. Collective struggles to advance status have frequently been commented on, but maintaining social standing or coping with social dislocation is, arguably, no less demanding of group effort. Most commonly it is the family—at least the immediate set of parents and children, and very often a wider set of kinsfolk—that is mobilized. In addition, ethnic networks may be activated or cohorts of migrants who have arrived at much the same time may be drawn upon. Collective resources—material, social, cultural, and symbolic come into play. Our primary purpose in this paper is to use case studies to examine the social nature of mobility processes and to emphasize the particular importance of cultural and symbolic 'capital' for migrants negotiating the complex dimensions of stratification in a new land. But to begin, some discussion of the origins, purposes, and character of the broader study should be given.

## THE 'FAMILIES AND SOCIAL ACHIEVEMENT' PROJECT

The study reported here has its origins in a long-standing dissatisfaction with most of the investigations of social mobility that line the shelves. Often, they seem curiously limited, unable to convey the real complexity of mobility processes or the subjective responses to them. Ever since Sorokin's original work (1927), social mobility has generally been conceptualized in a narrow way, in a way which places the overwhelming weight on vertical movements between occupational positions. It is true that Sorokin did discuss horizontal mobility and the importance of cultural mobility, but these matters, along with the interconnections of geographical and social mobility received relatively little subsequent attention. Miller (1956), reviewing mobility research between the 1920s and the 1950s pointed more specifically to what he saw as missing dimensions, to the failure of mobility scholars to address economic and political power and social position within the community. The 1960s certainly saw some major developments in mobility studies, among them Blau and Duncans's massive, path-breaking research on *The American Occupational Structure* (1967), but at the beginning of the next decade we find Anselm Strauss (1971) complaining that the growing methodological sophistication was not leading to any broadening of the way we thought about mobility. In his view, studies in this field remained limited, ethnocentric, excessively quantitative, and boring.

As the investigations have proliferated and the level of statistical analysis has become more refined, so we have tended to reduce the phenomenon to a range of variables that can be employed in either the occupational mobility/inheritance studies or the status attainment researches. Typically, the data are generated through questionnaires or interview schedules that seek and record information about individuals and the analysis—even in the best studies like those of Goldthorpe and his collaborators (Goldthorpe, Llewelyn, and Payne 1980; Erikson and Goldthorpe 1992) generally deals only with individuals, rather than with families or other social groups. In the major Canadian study of social mobility we find, in the concluding chapter, the statement that—'Together these findings underline the importance of the family in the attainment process. We need, however, to know more about the way in which the family exerts its influence' (Boyd *et al.* 1985). And that brings us to the work of Daniel Bertaux and Isabelle Bertaux-Wiame who go beyond the negative criticism to offer specific suggestions about alternative methods that might be used and alternative ways of conceptualizing the process of mobility (Bertaux and Bertaux-Wiame 1986; Bertaux 1991). For them, the use of biographical methods opens up exciting prospects for describing and analysing mobility processes and exploring the possibility of social mobility as essentially a 'family affair'.

The study reported here should be seen as having close links with the joint project that the Bertaux and Thompson have conducted in France and Britain (Families and Social Mobility: A Comparative Study), and with Daniel Bertaux's other work on social mobility. All spring from similar misgivings about the preponderant styles of mobility studies and all use similar 'biographical' methods of data collection—life stories, family stories, family histories, or 'social genealogies'. In fact, the present work can be related precisely to observations that Thompson and his colleagues made about one aspect of social mobility in Britain. Their interviews revealed that for some groups, 'getting on' frequently meant 'getting out'— emigrating. Comparing their English and Scottish samples, they discovered that in Scotland, there were proportionately far more families that had experience of emigration: 'From our Scottish sample... over a third of the middle generation informants recalled family members in their own and in the older generation emigrating in the post-1945 period' (Smith 1990).

And the country to which they most often came was Canada. The process, of course, has been going on for a long time and by 1991, when the Canadian census-takers asked about ethnic identification, they recorded 3,355,000 people in Canada claiming Scottish ethnic origins. Only 4,646,000 people in Canada claimed specifically English origins, a somewhat surprising figure when we consider the fact that in the United Kingdom the English outnumber the Scots by a ratio of 10:1. In part this reflects, no doubt, the disproportionate numbers of Scots who left the UK for Canada, but there are reasons to think that it is also testimony to the durability, portability, and romantic appeal of the rich symbolic culture through which Scottish identities are created and sustained.

The present study then, seeks to examine mobility processes among some of the post-war Scottish migrants. It is organized around four key questions. First, how can we broaden our conception of social mobility beyond the conventional focus on occupation and education? What else do migrants count as significant 'social achievement'? Secondly, is social mobility or social achievement really more of a social, collective accomplishment—more of a family matter, than most of our studies allow? Thirdly, if mobility or achievement is to a large degree a family affair, what exactly is transmitted within families that most influences mobility processes? Fourthly, what distinctive part do women play in mobility processes?

It involves lengthy family-history interviews with at least two members of different generations in each of fifty families who came to this country between 1945 and 1975 and who have children living here. Precise linkage with the British study through the tracing of family members who migrated to Canada has not been possible, since they are too widely scattered. Instead, two 'convenience' samples have been drawn, one in the greater Vancouver region, the other in Kamloops, a city of 75,000 people in the interior of British Columbia, Canada's most westerly province. Some of the migrants who came to Canada in the post-war years came not to the metropolitan areas, but to small, resource-dependent communities. Indeed, for generations of migrants probably the commonest experience of Canada—at least initially—has been in communities strongly linked to one or two resource industries (Lucas 1971). The Kamloops sample will provide some understanding of that, for though it has grown to be a regional centre which today provides a wide array of governmental, commercial, professional, and educational services, its economy is still heavily dependent on the forest industry (particularly on the operation of a pulp mill), and to a lesser degree on ranching and mining. What is discussed here, is based upon interviews with Scots-Canadian families in these two locales, supplemented by information from the leaders of some of the ethnic associations, some historical research (especially on the role of the Scots in Kamloops) and a lengthy autobiography that one of the respondents had completed. While our sample cannot be treated as representative, the processes that are made visible in the case studies deserve description and analysis.

## MOBILITY AND LONG-DISTANCE MIGRATION

The focus is on the Scots, a people for whom migration and social mobility have long been linked. There are accounts of Scots abroad—travelling as merchants or as labourers, settling and setting up businesses and homes in diverse northern European countries since at least the 13th century (Brander 1982). Through the

16th to the 18th centuries they also appear as soldiers of fortune, itinerant clerics and scholars on the continent, and, from the 1620s, as would-be settlers in North America. The arrival of Highlanders in Cape Breton and what would become Prince Edward Island, the migration of many Lowlanders to Upper Canada and the disproportionate number of Scots in the Hudson Bay and North West Companies are too well-known to need comment. As traders, factors, and explorers, as farmers, teachers, and politicians they left their names on the landscape. In the period of most extensive European migration—1830–1914—only the Irish exported proportionately more of their sons and daughters (Anderson and Morse 1990). We can say, with certainty, that from the mid-19th century, awareness of migration—of its hardships and sadness as well as the excitement and opportunities it might bring—was deeply embedded in Scottish life and culture.

Many of the early migrations of Scots to Canada have been extensively researched and reported (Reid 1976; Mackay 1980; Andrews 1989; Morton 1985; Bumsted 1982a/b, Cage 1985), but the flow of Scots in the years after 1945—chiefly in the 1950s and 1960s—has received little attention. Yet these are decades of considerable out-migration from Scotland. In the 1951–61 period, Scotland, with a population of just over five million, saw some 282,000 of its people move elsewhere, either to other parts of Britain or abroad. More than half—142,000 left to go overseas. In the next decade, even larger numbers quit Scotland, 169,000 migrating to other parts of the United Kingdom and 157,000 going overseas (Scottish Abstract of Statistics 1980: 6). These were the boom years in most Western economies, but to many Scots the prospects of work and advancement in Canada and other rapidly growing 'settler' societies surpassed the opportunities at home. Thus, we find that in the year 1957 alone, some 24,000 Scots came to Canada—either directly from Scotland, or via the USA. The data from the Canadian Department of Citizenship and Immigration record the fluctuating but often large numbers of British migrants through the 1950s and 1960s, and since they disaggregate Britain into its constituent parts, it is easy to see that the Scots were always greatly over-represented.

Studying mobility processes among a migrant group has some advantages, for in almost all cases, the move to the new country is occasioned by some strong desire to find better or different opportunities, and commonly there is a good deal of reflection on what has been lost and gained. Most of the respondents were sharply conscious of what they had 'achieved' and what they had 'lost' since coming to Canada, and frequently they construed the former as a collective, family accomplishment. They also made it clear that social mobility requires effort. Reproducing even the standard of living or the social status level held before the move may demand real struggle and the mobilization of resources in a network of family, friends, and acquaintances. For the first-generation migrants the points of comparison are always there; comparison with the way things were in the old country, with the ways they might have been had they stayed. With very little prompting they placed their lives alongside those of their brothers or sisters or other relatives who still lived in Scotland and drew conclusions. This consciousness of social mobility, captured in the biographical accounts enables us to explore experiential and cognitive dimensions that are richly represented in drama and literature, but glossed over in most sociological analyses.

## MOBILITY AND MOTIVES

In almost every interview the first, spontaneous reference to downward or blocked mobility came when a respondent gave reasons for the decision to emigrate. Though the motives for migration were usually complex, the experience or the fear of downward mobility or blocked mobility was mentioned by the great majority of people interviewed. One respondent, David Thompson, who in the 1960s was working in a fire department in a major Scottish city put it this way:

I would have moved up the ranks fairly high, but I would never have got into the upper echelon. But in this country you can go as high as you want... There's that 'old school tie' thing in Britain that stops a regular-type person from moving up into certain brackets.

Later in the interview he returned to this matter again, making it plain that, in his judgement, those who selected people for top positions in the fire service in Scotland looked for social skills, particularly a cultivated ease in exercising authority, that was associated with an upper middle-class background and a particular kind of education or perhaps, a prior career as a military officer. In Canada, he hoped his occupational goals would not be blocked simply because he lacked such a background. Interestingly, this same informant also discussed another motive for leaving the old country: housing. He could see little prospect of being able to afford to own anything other than the small apartment in which he and his wife and their first child lived, and the demand for public housing in Scotland was such that he and his little family would have no hope of being allocated a 'council house'. Housing, he thought, would be much easier to obtain in countries like Australia or Canada, and he was quite happy to go to either. It was his wife who chose Canada, at the point where they had completed immigration formalities for both countries. Over and over again, the quest for decent housing was identified by the Scottish migrants as an important element in their decision to leave. The difficulties in obtaining housing in the old country constituted a much-resented thwarting of their aspirations and the acquisition of good housing in the new country counted as a major achievement. The Thompsons evidently made their decision to migrate jointly, Mrs Thompson's voice in this being decisive in terms of where they chose to go. Here too we find recurrent elements: the familial, rather than just individual pattern of decision-making and the importance of women in the process.

Jack Kay, an engineer-turned-college instructor, also spoke about the prospect of 'not making it'—but in a very different way. He described the fear of not being able to live up to familial and personal ambitions:

My father was one of six brothers. All of these six were successful—some very successful, some marginally so. Part of the reason I made the move (although I might not have been able to verbalize it at the time) was that when I saw all this success related to hard work, I did not want to be in a position to be measured against that.

Mr Kay came from a relatively prosperous bourgeois family, had received a good education at one of the best schools in the city, but what he called the 'internal structure' (we might see it as 'culture') of his family presented him with daunting prospects. How to live up to the family tradition of 'success'? How to cope with all those parental and wider familial expectations? Going abroad would put him at some distance from the interactional pressures.

Jack Kay also gave a second reason for coming to Canada. He was toying with the idea of emigrating in 1957, at the point when many people, in the aftermath of Anglo-French military invasion of the Suez area, were leaving the district of Glasgow in which he lived. A number of them were going abroad, exasperated at the persistence of the Conservative Government's imperialist policies and fearful of another war. So there was also a political motive that informed his decision to leave. The exodus of others legitimated his action. Political motives, linked more or less directly to some mixture of personal ambitions and values, were mentioned by several respondents. A number of those who came to Canada in the mid-1960s did so because they were so distraught at the outcome of the 1964 General Election in the United Kingdom. Harold Wilson and the Labour Party holding the reins of power after many years of Conservative Government, was a prospect that horrified them. They foresaw the implementation of policies which they heartily disliked, policies which, in their judgement would hurt business, favour the trades unions, further encourage dependency on the state and probably inhibit their own chances of 'getting on'. In Canada, they felt, there was more likelihood of an individual 'making it' by his or her own efforts. Mrs Bruce, describing the factors that brought her and her husband to Canada in 1966 explained:

I believe that Harold Wilson was in at the time . . . and it was not our type of government at all. We just felt that people did not have the incentive to try and better themselves . . . We don't really espouse socialism, and in Scotland it's quite a socialist paradise. And, of course everybody, well not everybody, but quite a lot of people, feel that the government should look after them from the cradle to the grave, and we don't feel like that at all. So with that government being in, we felt incentives were not there for young couples who were trying to get on.

Prior to their migration few respondents had actually experienced downward mobility in terms of their own careers. Most were, in fact, relatively successful at their jobs in Britain (at least if we accept their own accounts). A good many clearly benefited from the reorganization and expansion of educational opportunities that occurred in Britain in the 1950s and 1960s, and had moved into occupations that generally were accorded more status than those of their fathers and mothers. But their expectations in terms of careers, income, patterns of consumption, and life-style had been raised, and then inadequately realized or threatened in some way.

The real experiences of social demotion were most commonly reported in terms of declining fortunes in their families of origin, or of marriages to partners whose status and class positions were plainly inferior. Fathers became alcoholics and 'drank away the family fortune'; businesses failed and respondents recalled periods of severe poverty; marriages dissolved and mothers and children were left with few resources. Respondents described the effects of a parent 'marrying down', and the pervasive anxiety this generated about the cultural and educational resources for the children and the social status they would likely have. In these families the concern with social mobility was acute, and long-distance migration had often been considered and even sought over long periods. Others came to Canada in the hope that the move would somehow repair their failing marriages and prevent the stigma and loss of status that divorce would bring. Prior to the reform of the Divorce Acts in England and Wales and in Scotland in the late 1960s (and even long after it in many Catholic families and communities) divorce brought with it a social demotion. Migration, they thought, would free them from family pressures, force them, as a couple on to their own resources. Maybe this would lead to some reconstruction of the relationship, but if not, at least they would be spared the immediate effects of the opprobrium that divorce would call out 'back home'.

Downward mobility then, as a threat or a reality in the lives of our respondents, was a powerful element in many of their decisions to emigrate. For some, the promises of the New World were fulfilled, for others there were set-backs and disappointments. In trying to analyse the accounts of their social as well as geographical relocation, and to understand the relationships between expectations, structural limitations and actual experiences we shall draw upon some of Bourdieu's work (1960, 1973, 1984, 1990*a*, 1990*b*) to discuss the various kinds of resources that are vital in mobility processes.

## MIGRANTS, MOBILITY, AND MATERIAL CAPITAL

Migrants to Canada have not, generally, come from the ranks of the very poor. Not even the Highlanders who fled at the time of the 'clearances', nor the Irish who came in the immediate aftermath of the famine could be counted among the destitute, for nearly all required some money for their passages and most brought with them at least a few tools and maybe some seed and a farm animal or two (Bumsted 1982*a*; Elliott 1988). Those who contemplated emigration had resources, however slim, that were just enough to allow them to rise above the insistence of necessity and contemplate an alternative life. They could envisage the possibilty of choices, of projects of their own devising, and the prospect of a rationally structured, predictable future.

And so it was after the Second World War. Among those interviewed for this project there are professionals, salesmen, teachers and nurses, clerical workers, and a variety of skilled manual workers. A few of them—especially those who were only in their early twenties when they arrived—came with very few material assets. A former Aberdeenshire farm worker recruited under a special scheme, established before the Second World War, but still operating in the early 1950s, had his passage subsidized by the Canadian Pacific Railway and arrived in Kamloops to work in the railyards there with only twenty dollars in his pocket; while clerical and health-care workers and tradesmen came to Canada with their small savings of, at most, a few hundred dollars. Some of the older migrants, and especially the professionals, brought with them the proceeds from selling a house or an apartment, but all had had mortgages and none was in a position to transfer substantial sums of money. No one in this sample came as an entrepreneur. All were using occupational experience and educational credentials as their primary resources to make their way in the New World.

This is not, of course to say that material capital was unimportant, but simply that for this group of migrants it was not the personal fortunes that they brought with them, not their money, stocks and shares, businesses, or real estate that shaped their social trajectories in Canada. Their social and cultural capital were much more important in that regard. But material capital of another kind was significant. The Scots emigrating in the 1950s, 1960s, and 1970s were coming to a country in which many of their compatriots had already established themselves and built (locally and nationally), a powerful economic presence. As industrialists, mercantile capitalists, bankers, and owners of a great deal of land, the Scots had created a kind of *collective* capital on which the newcomers could draw in direct and indirect ways.

The strongest evidence of this comes from the information gathered about the role of Scots in Kamloops. The origins of the Scots influence in the town go back to the exploration of the region by Alexander Mackenzie and Simon Fraser and the subsequent establishment of a North-West Fur Company trading post in 1812. When the Hudson's Bay Company absorbed their North-West rivals, they appointed a series of Chief Traders who were Scots and they plainly favoured the recruitment of fellow-Scots for many of their profit-making schemes. As Granovetter and Tilly note: 'Recruitment networks, supply networks, and the junctions between them are all historical products; when and where they first form considerably affects the subsequent experience of people with them' (1992: 193).

The Scots seem to have established a very effective network in Kamloops and when the settlement was incorporated as a city in 1893, members of the Scottish cultural association (the St. Andrews and Caledonian Society) took control in a very public way. The first mayor and all five of the aldermen were members of the Society. Another of the thirty-nine members of the Society was referred to as the 'King of Kamloops' because he owned the lumber mill, the water system, the electricity company, and a large swathe of the best residential land. He was to become an alderman within a few years, adding this to the many other civic leadership roles he occupied. The Society members laid out the Caledonian Field which became the centre of sporting and social life in the city. For the first two years after its creation, Society members held the Presidency of the Board of Trade and were Magistrates and members of the Hospital Board and other bodies (Weir 1977). There is no doubt that the power of the Scots sprang from the material capital that was accumulating at the nodes of their social networks and being concentrated there through business partnerships, memberships of business associations, and processes of intermarriage. At the turn of the century, in this interior town, Scots-Canadians could access economic capital held by members of their ethnic group. They could (and did) buy land from each other, they provided loans and invested in each others' businesses.

Few Scots migrating to Canada in the years after the Second World War found groups of fellow-countrymen or women or their descendents enjoying such obvious local economic power. By this time the ethnic mix in Canada was very broad and generations of earlier Scots settlers were widely dispersed, intermarried with many other groups and thoroughly assimilated. They were no longer distinguishably 'ethnic'. And the post-war newcomers too would soon be absorbed into the general fabric of Canadian society in the same manner. But the threads of Scots economic influence stretched through the structures of the nation and many local communities in ways that undoubtedly benefited the immigrants. In the 1950s and 1960s the Canadian and British Columbian economies were booming and for the immigrant finding a job was relatively easy. At the time of the interviews, the majority of our respondents did not work for fellow-Scots or even Canadians of Scots heritage, but the accumulated material capital of the earlier arrivals plainly was a resource upon which some of them had drawn when they first landed. In the 1990s there are no 'ethnic enclaves' in Vancouver or Kamloops in which Scots are employed, but in the 1960s, according to some informants, there were Scottish businesses—Canadian branches of Scottish insurance or engineering companies, industrial plants, companies associated with the shipyards and a wide variety of smaller artisan enterprises that were known to favour the recruitment of others from Scotland.

The pattern of co-ethnic employment was more marked in some of the industrial cities in eastern Canada where there were larger, more established and more concentrated Scots communities. Almost half of the respondents in this study arrived in Vancouver after some period living and working in such centres and could describe how bonds of shared ethnicity were invoked in order to obtain jobs, contracts etc. But by the late 1970s, in most of the British Columbian communities, the local networks of Scottish migrants had atrophied as the streams of new recruits dwindled and the opportunities to draw on a pool of collective economic resources greatly diminished.

However, in the course of the interviews the significance of *family* wealth gained in Canada and held within the immediate family networks of recent immigrants became plain. Some 'pioneering' siblings came to Canada, saved their money, bought houses, sponsored brothers and sisters and parents and sometimes provided substantial material support over many years. Sometimes the 'successful' immigrant used his or her resources to 'rescue' family members from downward mobility in both Britain and

Canada by bringing them to Canada or facilitating their movement within the country. Those with resources provided their kin with housing and income, helped them through episodes of illness and job loss, supported divorced siblings (and parents) and provided mothers and fathers who had come to join them with a standard of comfort they did not enjoy 'back home'. Most of these efforts were undoubtedly focused on the relatives here in Canada. The 'falling from grace' of one member threatens the collective identity of the group and undermines the reputation of 'success' that has so often been cultivated with the greatest care by those who went away to find new opportunities.

## SOCIAL CAPITAL

Material capital matters, but other kinds of capital are, perhaps more interesting sociologically. Social capital is a term employed both by Bourdieu (1990a) and Coleman (1990). Both see social capital as resources that are embedded in sets of social relations. 'Unlike other forms of capital, social capital inheres in the structure of relations between persons and among persons. It is lodged neither in individuals nor in physical implements of production' (Coleman 1990: 301). Social capital then is an attribute of whole networks of people. As Anheier and his colleagues suggest (Anheier, Gerhards, and Romo 1995), it refers to the total resources—actual and potential—that can be mobilized through membership of particular networks of actors and organizations. It exists independently of the individuals, but those who have legitimate access to the social network may draw upon that capital and 'cash' it in a whole variety of ways. Different types of capital are more or less 'fungible', that is, convertible into other forms.

Economic capital is the most liquid, most readily convertible form for transformation into social and cultural capital. By comparison, the convertibility of social capital into economic capital is costlier and more contingent; social capital is less liquid, 'stickier', and subject to attrition. (Anheier, Gerhards, and Romo 1995: 862)

In Britain, and, indeed, throughout the English-speaking world, there is one especially well-known form of social capital. In Britain and abroad, the graduates of Oxford and Cambridge universities have available to them a widespread network of social relations, and the mutual acceptance and trust that flow from the presumption of a generic culture. 'Oxbridge' graduates, collectively, can mobilize an enormous array of the most diverse resources.

There are weaker, specifically Scottish equivalents of this, based partly on the ancient Scottish universities, and on the 'F.P.' (former pupil) associations of the élite schools—Fettes, Watsons, Heriots, for example—that are found in many places to which the Scots migrated. Such capital, of course, is accessible only to a small minority. However, in Canada, as elsewhere, other forms of social capital are available to a much broader population through the many Scottish voluntary associations that have local chapters scattered the length and breadth of the country—the Sons of Scotland, the St. Andrews and Caledonian Societies, the Highland and Scottish Dance Societies, the Pipers Societies and a whole host of associations for migrants from particular counties or regions of Scotland. The social capital on which the migrants draw is thus, not all of a piece: it is segmented and stratified, with varying potential for 'conversion' into other forms. It is an extensive and pre-existing resource, differentially available to new migrants via networks, some of which are exclusive and élitist, while others are much more open.

Newly arrived immigrants may try to access this kind of social capital, but many of them have little prior knowledge of it; some will have had their efforts to join the networks rebuffed and yet others, because of their location, will have very little opportunity to draw upon this stock of resources. In consequence, almost all newcomers try to create their own, and this they typically do through urgent relational activity. Migrants, having left the old country, are generally anxious to create new ties of friendship and support. They are very conscious of the small stock of assistance and goodwill on which they can call, and apprehensive about their vulnerability in times of trouble. They have so few who are obliged to them; so few social debts that can be called in. Therefore, they often set about the building of new networks in very deliberate ways—joining associations, signing up for evening classes, inviting workmates and neighbours to share activities with them. This intense and nervous activity reveals the truth of Bourdieu's observation that a social network is the product of an endless effort at institution ... the product of investment strategies, individual and collective, aimed at establishing or reproducing social relationships that are directly usable in the short or long term, i.e., at transforming contingent relationships such as those of neighbourhood, the workplace or even kinship into relationships that are at once necessary and elective, implying durable obligations subjectively felt (feelings of gratitude, respect, friendship, etc.) or institutionally guaranteed rights. (1990a: 249–50)

For some migrants, building the supportive networks begins before they leave Scotland. They write to relatives—sometimes relatives with whom they have had no previous contact—in order to find out whether or not they should come to Canada. They seek advice on how to make a successful application for immigration; they enquire about sponsorship maybe; most commonly they write hoping for the promise of somewhere to stay when they arrive.

The invoking of kinship ties and the rapid assimilation into kin-based networks once they are here seems most common among the working-class Scots. The classic pattern of chain migration and the reliance on the 'auspices' of kinship seems, as Tilly and Brown (1967) argued, most common among working-class groups. Middle-class migrants—the senior-level professionals in particular—have less need of kinship as a source of social capital. They have the material capital to obtain housing and almost invariably they have come with highly paid jobs already assured. They are following what Richard Brown (1982) described as the 'occupational strategy' of social mobility, confident that they are part of an occupational community that has no sharp national boundaries. In their new positions they set about establishing supportive networks largely among their fellow-professionals. It is not only men who do this. In some of the largely female professions women have highly 'portable' skills that enable them to migrate with considerable ease. When, as nurses, physiotherapists, and other professionals they do so, they too rely heavily upon their colleagues as companions and friends. These seem to be the principal sources of social capital if there are few or no kin available.

If migrants arrive without jobs they may be able to use their kin as sources of contacts or even as employers, but more often than not they find work through weaker ties—as Granovetter (1973, 1982) suggested. In the 1950s and 1960s, when Scots were still migrating to Canada in substantial numbers, they often used the ethnic associations as a means of finding out about local job markets and making contacts with fellow-Scots. The Sons of Scotland served as something of a clearing-house for such enquiries: 'One member ran a rubber plant. He employed lots of Scots. A number were prominent business people so they could help newcomers from the old country. One guy was a civil servant. He found lots of people jobs,' said one respondent. An association like the Sons of Scotland could be the means of creating among members of an immigrant group precisely that quality of trust to which both Coleman and Bourdieu refer. A prominent organizer for the 'Sons' told the following story by way of explaining his forty years as a member:

He had joined in order to play soccer. The 'Sons' had a Sunday league for which he was determined to play, even though this went against the strict sabbatarian rules of the fundamentalist Christian sect in which he had been raised. His brother invited him to join. In those days the 'Sons' had various teams; they had a ski-hut, they offered lots of social possibilities.

While playing soccer one day he was injured. His nose was broken and he lost a lot of blood. In the hospital he remembers coming out of the anaesthetic to find the entire team at his bedside. In those days if you needed blood it was expected that you would arrange for a family member or someone else to donate some of their blood as a kind of recompense, as a way of replenishing the stock. Knowing this, the other ten players had come along and each had donated a pint for their team-mate.

He was very moved by this and had felt a deep loyalty to the association ever since. (Field notes. Interview A02).

Mostly though, it is not through the associations but through the family and neighbourhood that norms of altruism, trust, and reciprocity are established. These are the currency of this kind of capital, and within families women have crucial roles in its constitution and circulation. They do this, in part, through the networks of kin and neighbours and friends that they maintain and cultivate and to which they introduce their children. Within these networks, there is usually a relatively high degree of social closure, a condition which Coleman observes, fosters the effectiveness of norms. In these social circles young people observe adults acting in the interests of the group as a whole, acting relatively selflessly. They learn what they can expect by way of help and support. They learn on whom they may depend and for what. They discover resources that are often vital in the struggle to maintain status and may well be instrumental in gaining assistance for projects of upward mobility. There is reason to believe that women very often have more social capital than men. Their social networks may well have wider spans of status and class, in part because, as Portocarero (1987) shows, through occupation and marriage they are more likely than men to have moved from their initial social positions. A similar finding appears in some recent Canadian research on social mobility (Creese, Guppy, and Meissner 1991). This greater social diversity provides ranges of contact, relations of obligation and trust that may well prove useful in the realization of aspirations—maybe their own, but more likely their children's.

Immigrants then are engaged in the building of social relations as essentially a defensive strategy. The social capital created and nurtured in this way may, indeed, have value for projects of upward mobility, but it is created in the first instance as a protective device in a society of strangers. In the early years of settlement, when many migrants find themselves having to take jobs or live in neighbourhoods of lesser status than they had known back in Scotland, these new relations have enormous importance. Years later, after the migrants have changed jobs, neighbourhoods, and even cities, these ties forged in adversity form the basis of enduring friendships and continuing association. This relational capital served as the foundation for the growth of a local, bounded social capital that had great practical significance.

But there is another kind of social capital that plainly needs to be considered. There is a social capital that resides in simple ethnic identity. Being Scots enables newcomers to access a large pool of fellow-Scottish immigrants and, beyond that, all Canadians who more or less overtly present themselves as '*Scots*-Canadians'. The existence of this social capital and the manner of its use and reproduction are observable, in part, in the interactions of erstwhile strangers. The speed with which individuals are located in terms of the areas from which they have come, the places and firms for which they have worked, the schools they attended, the football teams they support, and so on, can be breathtaking. In some instances we can observe, within minutes, men and women who are totally unacquainted, treating each other as intimates—offering food, drinks, gifts, services, help, and advice—and cementing, through little acts of reciprocity, a relationship which may well surmount barriers of class and status that would have been exclusionary in Scotland.

Because Scots in Canada are numerous, long-settled, and well-placed, the immigrant, in almost any area of the country can use his or her Scottishness to draw upon an extraordinarily rich source of support and affirmation. The frequently remarked 'clannishness' of Scots abroad signals a common-sense appreciation of this fact.

## CULTURAL CAPITAL

Pierre Bourdieu, whose name is most closely associated with the term, sees cultural capital existing in various forms: in its 'embodied' state in the dispositions of individuals; in its 'objectified' state in items like books and pictures and instruments and in its 'institutionalized' state in educational credentials (Bourdieu 1990*b*). For Bourdieu, cultural capital plays a crucial role in the reproduction strategies of privileged groups because other, more obvious ways of passing on benefits from one generation to another are often disapproved and controlled to some degree. The transmission of cultural capital which can take place under a meritocratic façade in the schools and colleges is the best (because hidden) method, for the maintenance of privilege. There is much that is appealing and, indeed, useful in Bourdieu's key insight, but there is a fundamental inadequacy in the *unitary* character of the system of distinction, he describes. Interviews with immigrants made it abundantly clear that they are involved in social worlds where a plurality of cultural capitals exists. Among the Scots themselves there is more than one system in play, for while, in Scotland they necessarily participated in a cultural world in which standards were set largely according to the predilections of the English upper class, there are elements of Scottish culture which have remained distinct from the dominant, allegedly, hegemonic English forms, and which are incommensurate with them. As a result there has long been an ambiguity, a lack of fit between the indicators of class and culture which Scots in Britain have successfully exploited. They simply could not be 'placed' by language, accent, or education on the English social map, and thus were free to transgress class and status boundaries to a considerable extent. As Michele Lamont (1992) observes, assessing Bourdieu in the light of her study of the cultural traits of the French and American upper middle class, it is no longer possible to work, as Bourdieu does, with a conception of a society which is relatively closed and involves a stable set of actors. That is not true for most modern societies. It is certainly not an appropriate image of Canadian society, which proclaims itself bilingual and multicultural, and in which the legitimacy and value of cultures other than those of the Anglophones and Francophones is officially endorsed. We are obviously dealing here with a plurality of coexisting cultural systems, and in this circumstance a key issue for newcomers is the convertibility of the cultural capital(s) they bring with them.

To fully understand the ways in which specifically cultural capital is implicated in the social trajectories of our Scottish families we need to explore first how their decisions to migrate were shaped, at least in part, by cultural considerations, and then we can examine their uses of cultural capital in their adopted country. One of the first things we can see in the family histories is the way in which downward or blocked mobility leads, very often, to the mobilization of the family and the development of concerted collective action. In his British study, Thompson observed that few families had definite mobility projects for their members and that generally family cultures (especially in the working class) seemed to operate in conservative, defensive ways (Thompson 1990, 1993). There are exceptions to this, he claimed: 'a cohesive family culture typically becomes dynamic only in response to sharply changing social and economic contexts' (1990: 8).

Downward mobility is clearly such a change in social and economic circumstances, but blocked mobility can also lead to changing and increasingly tense relationships at work, or, indeed, at home when the social and economic and cultural ambitions of spouses are disparate. Many elements involved in downward or blocked mobility can lead to concerted action and even to migration—a new start, in a new country, free from the pressures of kin and acquaintances implicated in the existing unhappy circumstances. Once embarked on the making of a new life in another society the family may continue to act in a planful, calculating, rational way in order to establish itself and adjust to a whole set of unfamiliar circumstances.

In the interviews with Scots migrants we have several examples of downward mobility and blocked mobility as reasons for emigration. Among the first, we find Mrs Lindsay, who 'married beneath her' and who spent many years trying to escape from a loveless marriage and the constant reminders of the social demotion she had suffered. Although material circumstances—the lack of money in a household where the husband's modest wages were all too often consumed by drink or gambling, and the cramped and ugly council apartment in which she was forced to live—plainly mattered, it seems that it was a series of cultural and moral considerations that did most to fuel her burning desire to escape to North America. Her overwhelming concern (vividly expressed in her daughter's as well as her own account of the family story) was with cultural and moral deprivation suffered by her children, raised as they were on the public housing estate, constrained to attend the local schools and to socialize with children whose standards of behaviour and cultural ambitions were so far removed from those she had known in her own education and upbringing. She desperately wanted to send her daughters to the kind of school to which she had gone, to give them access to cultural opportunities that she had had and to protect them from the very different cultural ambience of the area in which they lived. The best she could actually do was insist on some linguistic 'refinement' in the home. As often in Britain, language became a crucial indicator of a claimed status.

Getting to North America became her supreme objective—in fact something of an obsession. At one point she took her children to her sister's house and, leaving them and her husband, she went to New York to work as a nanny in the hope that she could obtain a work permit, and thus be able to have her children migrate with her to a place of 'opportunity'. Her efforts were not successful, but her daughters, raised with this constant motherly project of relocation, soon found jobs in Canada: first, the eldest daughter, then a second one, and by the time they were both comfortably established Mrs Lindsay had divorced, remarried and the daughters sponsored mother and step-father. At last, she had made it. For her this was the great achievement. This was social mobility; not a better job, not riches, but the satisfaction of her personal escape and most of all the joy of seeing her entire family (the third daughter and the son soon joined her) living in a country where they would have choices, where they could easily gain more education, where they could take charge and shape their own life-styles unfettered by the class constraints of a tough Glasgow neighbourhood. What we see here is migration motivated more by cultural deprivation than by material want, and aspirations that have less to do with class position than with life-style and status group membership.

In a second case, Mrs Mackay described how her mother had gone to work as a domestic servant in the home of a wealthy business family in Edinburgh and—to the consternation of his parents—soon married the son and heir. Plainly a case of upward movement in the status order for mother. However, over the next fifteen years and the birth of nine children, the fortunes of the family declined catastrophically as father drank, and neglected and finally lost the business. To survive, mother turned the home into a guest house, but even with this the family sank deeper into poverty. Sometimes there was not enough to eat and not enough to heat the house.

Out of these circumstances came the most deliberate contrivance of a family mobility project so far encountered in these interviews. In their researches, Daniel Bertaux and Isabelle Bertaux-Wiame (1986) explored the possibility that it was not so much individuals who 'got ahead', as whole groups of siblings. In Daniel Bertaux's project with students at Laval, though, he discovered a good many cases in which families acted collectively, not to promote all their number, but to advance the careers of selected siblings—the last child in a farming family, for instance, being the only one sent off to the city and to college. The Mackay case shows a similar focusing of effort. Mrs Mackay recalled how her mother tried to shape the educational fate of her offspring, how she 'sort of picked her children' for different abilities and aptitudes. In particular the sixth child was selected as the one who would become a doctor: 'before he was born (this is one of her great stories) the doctor said, "Now what's this one going to be, Mrs Craig?" "He's going to be a doctor. This one's for medicine". And, by golly, he did.'

In a family with so little money the realization of this ambition meant sacrifices on the part of other siblings: 'In order to take the place of his income coming into the family for that number of years, another of my sisters... had to stop short of her ambition and work, because the woman makes it happen and she had to go out and make a living.' Here the labour and wages of an older daughter were deliberately used in order to build up cultural capital in a younger son. It was a family investment in a form of cultural capital that, at least in the 1960s, was about the most convertible that could be found. At that point, doctors had great opportunities to sell their skills on a world market. Not surprisingly, there was some bitterness in the family about this. But the son who became a doctor emigrated to Canada and together with two other siblings who also came here, he sponsored his mother, father, the respondent and another brother and sister. Thus, though he was not the first to come to the new country, this family member in whom so much was invested became the principal means for arresting and reversing the downward slide in the family fortunes. In this case, straitened circumstances led to a concentration of resources on an individual, and whether or not it was conceived in this way, it played an important part in the geographical and social mobility of most of the children and the support of the parents. Focusing resources and emigrating arrested the social decline of the family and restored its fortunes to some degree.

In these instances, and others where blocked mobility provided the impetus, families acted strategically and developed plans—including plans to emigrate. The fire officer who anticipated that his chances of career mobility would be blocked because he lacked the cultural capital of the British upper classes decided that experience and credentials would be capital enough in a settler society like Canada, that the embodied 'dispositions' acquired in an élite milieu would not be required or recognized there. He and his family laid plans to find a more open society in which to pursue their ambitions. But as he and others would discover, converting cultural capital on the other side of the Atlantic would not be without its difficulties.

## CONVERTING CULTURAL CAPITAL

In many of the immigrant families we find ourselves looking closely at both cultural and social capital, at the ways in which they are implicated in the experience of downward or blocked mobility and at some of the ways in which they are employed to provide alternate routes to 'success', or sanctuary from symbolic violence. The Scots migrants bring with them varying amounts and kinds of cultural capital and it soon becomes clear that while some kinds transfer very readily and may even command a 'premium', others are 'discounted' and devalued. This applies to cultural capital in all three of the forms identified by Bourdieu, but it is easiest to begin with it in its 'institutionalized' state. The diplomas and certificates, the trade qualifications and the degrees from Scotland—these and other forms of certified competence—are not always acceptable in Canada. It often comes as something of a shock when the immigrants realize this, for raised in a culture that retains the imprint of its imperial past, they have naturally absorbed the idea that British qualifications are superior and bound to be welcomed in a society that reflects the political, economic, and cultural dominance of those with British backgrounds. But the acceptabililty of Scottish credentials varies widely, as does the willingness of employers to give credit for work experience in Britain. The example of a Scots born, English-educated school teacher provides some illustration.

A teacher of English and drama, migrating to rural Alberta in the mid-1960s, Robert Johnston found himself accepting a post that was in most respects considerably less good than the one he had left. In his appointment there was no recognition given to his rather special educational qualifications, his time spent at the Sorbonne, his unusual achievements as a teacher in England. In Alberta, he was working in a school with no tradition of drama and no facilities for it. But he soon overcame these obstacles, and before long the school had won provincial competitions for theatrical productions. He was invited to apply for a more senior post in much larger, better-endowed school in a major urban centre. However, in the course of the interview for the job it became clear that the school board would not recognize some of his credentials, would not count some of the seniority he thought he had earned and even assessed his salary entitlements in ungenerous ways. Furious at this failure to acknowledge the kind of cultural capital he would bring to the position he refused the post and quickly resigned his current job. He would leave school-teaching, bitter at what seemed to him to be petty, small-minded, parochial denials of cultural competence—his knowledge of, access to, and ability to transmit elements of the legitimated, 'authorized' high culture.

How did he subsequently make a living? He traded on his dramatic, literary, and singing skills, becoming a writer, performer, and interpreter—an authoritative voice—for Scottish culture. He was a founder of a national foundation for the promotion of Scottish culture in Canada, he made films and records and put on stage and TV presentations. Latterly, he has become an author of popular historical fiction. Thus he created an alternative career for himself. Faced with a loss of a job, income, and status, Robert Johnston successfully made the ethnic culture a resource, becoming someone who actually 'objectified' that culture by giving it concrete and durable expression. To do this in a commercially viable way he needed an audience that consisted of more than the home-sick new arrivals. Given the low levels of immigration from Scotland since the 1970s, he would have had a thin time had he depended on them. Instead his appeal is much wider and it is explicable in terms of the privileged place of Scottish music, dance, games, and literature in the cultural fabric of North America, and Canada particularly. Finding that his cultural capital—his English degree and French certificate—was not fully convertible, Mr Johnston used his ethnic culture, much of which is accorded only a subaltern status in Britain, to make a living.

Robert Johnston's life story reveals that there is more than one kind of cultural capital within the social field of arts and literature, and that in an ethnically diverse society it is possible to use ethnically specific cultural capital, first to mitigate the effects of downward mobility and later to gain recognition as a member of an artistic élite. In their German study, Anheier and his collaborators examined different forms of cultural capital and showed how these 'correspond to a social structure with multiple elites and semi-peripheries' (Anheier, Gerhards, and Romo 1995: 892). Robert Johnston did not become a member of Canada's most prestigious circle of writers and artists whose work is celebrated in Toronto and Ottawa and used to define that which is quintessentially Canadian (more precisely, Anglo-Canadian). Instead, he earned a place in a sub-élite of creators and performers whose work is more 'commercial' and draws on the heritage of a numerous and historically well-placed ethnic group.

Our schoolteacher became a 'professional' Scot, and while no other respondent actually derived a living from Scots culture, others were deeply involved in aspects of it, and profited from it in various ways. A teacher of Scottish country dancing, a world expert and adjudicator whose skills were widely sought, described how, in little more than a twelve-month period she had been in St Andrews in Scotland (where she taught every year), in Japan, Germany,

Hong Kong, and Singapore and several parts of the United States. All to judge and teach dancing. This aspect of Scots culture had provided her with an international reputation, and a world-wide network of friends. In her case, as in Robert Johnston's, cultural capital was readily convertible into social capital and to some extent into economic capital too.

Another case uncovers an unanticipated 'cost' of a certain aspect of Scottish culture and illustrates the fact that Canadian society is sufficiently 'Anglo' for certain regional accents to be read (as they would be in England) as indicators and even determinants of class position. In her fifties, Mrs Angus came to an industrial city in Ontario to join her children. In Scotland she had had a variety of clerical jobs, mostly involving bookkeeping and accounting. Her identity was that of a reasonably well-educated, skilled clerical worker. Her habitat was the office, close to the bosses. In Canada she was offered only manual work, forms of domestic work. She ultimately took a job in a catering enterprise but even here she was sequestered in a 'back-stage' position—not so much out of sight, as out of earshot. The problem? Her strong Scots accent which, in the opinion of prospective employers rendered her unfit for any but proletarian roles, and only those where she did not have to deal directly with a public that supposedly would find her incomprehensible. This was a severe blow to her self-image and a clear illustration of how some cultural attributes are mapped onto a grid of class positions. By no means are all Scottish accents treated in the same way. The fact that a pronounced Glasgow accent can be read as an indicator of low status owes something, no doubt to some negative stereotypes of Glaswegians and anti-immigration campaigns in the 1950s to keep out these 'scum of the earth'. In this period there was, it should be noted, a great deal of very unflattering journalistic representation of Glasgow in the British media, which created moral panics about the levels of gang violence and deprivation in that city. It would seem that some of that was reproduced in Canada. Part of the 'embodied' culture that Mrs Angus carried served to structure her occupational opportunities, to demote her in terms of class and status. Her experience illustrates a process that John Hall (1992) in his interesting critique of Bourdieu's notion of cultural capital refers to as 'cultural structuralism'—the way in which structures of power are infused with and partly shaped by cultural elements.

For Mrs Angus, whose Scottish identity was the source of denigration and reduced opportunities, the Scottish cultural organizations became a refuge. In the industrial centre in which she was then living, the St. Andrews and Caledonian Society was not the vehicle for a local upper middle-class élite (as it is in some metropolitan centres), but a social organization in which many manual workers participated, and in this milieu her accent was not the source of any difficulty, nor was it associated with a subordinate class position. She and her husband became deeply embroiled in the work of the local Society, which in the 1970s was still a large and thriving one. Here she could find affirmation of her worth, restoration of reputation and dignity. For some who face downward or blocked mobility there is the option, provided the community is large enough and the culture sufficiently rich and diverse, of a deliberate immersion in the ethnic world. Here there are other opportunities, alternative sources of status, prospects for alternative careers and achievements that are not registered in the conventional studies of social mobility.

## SYMBOLIC CAPITAL

By contrast, Mrs Angus's husband, also in his fifties when he arrived in Canada in the early 1970s, found that his Scottishness could be a valuable asset. Initially, he too was offered only very menial jobs (he had been a bus driver in Scotland—not an elevated position, but a 'respectable' job and one with a certain amount of autonomy), but soon his Scottish son-in-law recommended that he go to see an acquaintance of his, a prison officer who might be able to find him a better position. The contact at the correctional institution was also Scottish and he arranged for Mr Angus to be interviewed by a senior officer. 'Are you vouching for this man?', the interviewer asked the sponsor. 'No need to sir, he's a Scot', was the reply. Mr Angus got the job and stayed in it until he retired. In this case it was cultural capital in the form of embodied 'disposition' that was so favourably received. Many respondents talked about this kind of capital, about the 'universal' acceptability of Scottishness interpreted as a set of cultural traits that included 'honesty', 'forthrightness', 'having no side', 'generosity', 'warm-heartedness', and 'a reputation for hospitality'. Many believed that these characteristics were expected and that they opened doors. One respondent described how he got his first position on the strength of his willingness to be blunt and somewhat challenging in his dealings with a senior public servant who was interviewing him. Here, learned dispositions prove to be valuable, portable assets. The threat of downward mobility may be avoided by exploiting the cultural preferences of the dominant ethnic group and claiming, simply on the basis of a national identity, that the respected attributes have been inscribed on the self.

This symbolic capital, this bundle of assumptions about national or ethnic characteristics is really the most inescapably social aspect of all those we have considered. In a multi-ethnic society the fortunes of individuals and families may owe a good deal to the societal preconceptions about particular groups. Whether an individual benefits or not from such stereotypes depends largely on the history of this group in the particular society.

The life stories of the Scottish migrants make it clear that we are not really dealing with a single, unified entity when we talk of the culture of the dominant 'Anglo' group in Canada, for each of the nations absorbed into the 'United' Kingdom would claim some cultural distinctiveness. However, it is interesting to note that whereas in Britain Scottish culture is indisputably subordinate to that of the more numerous and politically dominant English, in Canada, symbols of Scottishness are seemingly very closely associated with power, wealth, order, and authority. One has only to rehearse the names of Canadian Prime Ministers and premiers, examine the control of the great trading companies or notice the almost invariable use of pipe bands in public ceremonies to appreciate this. The 'privileging' of this variant of the dominant culture has significance when we are considering downward social mobility.

## CONCLUSION

The fact that some Scots migrants, faced with the prospect of downward or blocked mobility could exploit Scottish culture to create alternative careers (and not just inside the ethnic community); the fact that others could use culture in the form of dispositions and everyday practices as the means of restoring their occupational fortunes; the fact that Scottish culture is objectified in so many forms—dress, music, musical instruments, military paraphernalia and regiments, games, dancing, literature, and song—all this, raises curiosity about the nature of this culture that has been distributed so widely around the globe.

Scottishness, like other ethnic identities, rests heavily on what Hobsbawm and Ranger (1983) called 'invented tradition'. We know that the claimed antiquity of clan-specific tartan designs is a nonsense, a fiction for the tourists, along with much of the other paraphernalia of genealogy tracing, family crests, seals, and rings. We know how much is owed to the romantic movement of the early 19th century in the generation of images of Scotland and myths about its people. But this continuous process of 'invention' has created an enormous stock of symbolic culture that is readily transportable.

Bourdieu (1960), writing about Kabyle society, a colonized people in Algeria, had an important insight which seems relevant in seeking to understand the Scots and Scottish migrants. For subordinated peoples there is an urgent need for recognition, for symbolic capital through which can be made assertions of worth against insistent denial and the pervasive representation of inferiority. For centuries the Scots have faced such representations of inferiority; they simply were not English. Yet, they were not conquered. They were a nation without a state, but they retained some of the distinctive institutions of statehood. In these circumstances and in every period, the English have sought to maintain and extend their domination culturally; the goal has been total cultural supremacy—hegemony. Scottish culture, in its full range from the glories of its 18th-century Enlightenment to its most tawdry and commercialized aspects represents resistance to that. It is this heritage that Scots brought with them to Canada, and on which both recent migrants, and those who identify as Scots-Canadians, draw.

Recognizing the extensiveness and importance of this cultural stock and recognizing too the significance of the associations and networks through which it (and other resources) are nurtured and shared, brings us back to the argument that we need to conduct some of our mobility research in other than the conventional ways for, typically, they miss so much about the collective, profoundly social shaping of aspirations and ambitions and the collective and socially formed strategies for achievement.

## ACKNOWLEDGEMENTS

The research on which this chapter is based was made possible by a grant from the Multi-Culturalism Directorate, Office of the Secretary of State. An earlier version of this paper was given to the Social Inequality Section of the Canadian Sociology and Anthropology Association Annual Conference in Ottawa in June 1993. I am grateful to Daniel Bertaux for helpful criticism of that draft.

## REFERENCES

Anderson, M., and Morse, D. J. (1990), 'The People', in H. W. Fraser and R. J. Morris (eds), *People and Society in Scotland*, ii. *1830–1914* (Edinburgh: John Donald in association with The Economic and Social History Society of Scotland).

Andrews, A. (1989), *The Scottish Canadians* (Toronto: Van Nostrand).

Anheier, H., Gerhards, J., and Romo, F. (1995), 'Forms of Capital and Social Structure in Cultural Fields: Examining Bourdieu's Social Topography', *American Journal of Sociology*, 100 (4), 859–903.

Beck, U., Giddens, A., and Lash, S. (1994), *Reflexive Modernization: Politics, Tradition and Aesthetics in the Modern Social Order* (Cambridge: Polity).

Bertaux, D. (1991), 'From Methodological Monopoly to Pluralism in the Sociology of Social Mobility', in S. Dex (ed.), *Life and Work History Analysis: Qualitative and Quantitative Developments* (The Sociological Review Monograph Series, 37; London: Routledge).

——and Bertaux-Wiame, I. (1986), 'Families and Social Mobility', paper delivered to the XII World Congress of Sociology, New Delhi.

Blau, P., and Duncan, O. D. (1967), *The American Occupational Structure* (New York: Wiley).

Bourdieu, P. (1960), *Algeria 1960* (Cambridge: Cambridge University Press).

——(1973), 'Cultural Reproduction and Social Reproduction', in R. Brown (ed.), *Knowledge, Education and Cultural Change* (London: Tavistock).

——(1984), *Distinction: A Social Critique of the Judgement of Taste* (London: Routledge).

——(1990a), *Reproduction in Education, Society and Culture* (London: Sage).

——(1990b), *In Other Words* (Cambridge: Polity).

Boyd, M., Goyder, J., Jones, F., McRoberts, H., and Porter, J. (1985), *Ascription and Achievement: Studies in Mobility and Status Attainment in Canada* (Ottawa: Carleton University Press).

Brander, M. (1982), *The Emigrant Scots* (London: Constable).

Brown, R. (1982), 'Work Histories, Career Strategies and the Class Structure', in A. Giddens and G. MacKenzie (eds), *Social Class and the Division of Labour* (Cambridge: Cambridge University Press).

Bumsted, J. (1982a), *The Scots in Canada* (Ottawa: Canadian Historical Association).

—— (1982b), *The People's Clearance* (Edinburgh: Edinburgh University Press).

Cage, R. (1985), *The Scots Abroad* (London: Croom Helm).

Coleman, J. S. (1990), *Foundations of Social Theory* (Cambridge, Mass.: The Belknap Press).

Creese, Gillian, Guppy, Neil, and Meissner, Martin (1991), *Ups and Downs on the Ladder of Success: Social Mobility in Canada* (Statistics Canada, Ottawa).

Elliott, Bruce (1988), *Irish Migrants in the Canadas: A New Approach* (Kingston and Montreal: McGill-Queen's University Press).

Erikson, R., and Goldthorpe, J. H. (1992), *The Constant Flux: A Study of Class Mobility in Industrial Societies* (Oxford: Oxford University Press).

Goldthorpe, J. H., Llewelyn, C., and Payne, C. (1980), *Social Mobility and Class Structure in Modern Britain* (Oxford: Oxford University Press).

Granovetter, M. (1973), 'The Strength of Weak Ties', *American Journal of Sociology*, 78 (6), 1360–81.

—— (1982), 'The Strength of Weak Ties: A Network Theory Revisited', in P. Marsden and N. Lin (eds), *Social Networks and Social Structure* (Beverly Hills, Calif.: Sage).

—— and Tilly, Charles (1992), 'Inequality and Labour Processes', in N. Smelser (ed.), *Handbook of Sociology* (Newbury Park, Calif.), 175–221.

Hall, J. (1992), 'The Capital(s) of Cultures: A Non-Holistic Approach to Status Situations, Class, Gender and Ethnicity', in M. Lamont and M. Fournier (eds), *Cultivating Differences: Symbolic Boundaries and the Making of Inequality* (Chicago: Chicago University Press).

Hobsbawm, E., and Ranger, T. (1983) (eds), *The Invention of Tradition* (Cambridge: Cambridge University Press).

Lamont, M. (1992), *Money, Morals and Manners: The Culture of the French and American Upper Middle Class* (Chicago: University of Chicago Press).

Little, J. I. (1991), *Crofters and Habitants: Settler Society, Economy and Culture in a Quebec Township, 1848–1881* (Kingston and Montreal: McGill-Queen's University Press).

Lucas R. (1971), *Minetown, Milltown, Railtown: Life in Canadian Communities of Single Industry* (Toronto: University of Toronto Press).

Mackay, D. (1980), *Scotland Farewell* (Toronto: McGraw-Hill Ryerson).
Miller, S. M. (1956), 'The Concept and Measurement of Mobility', *Transactions of the Third World Congress of Sociology*, 3, 144–54 (London: International Sociological Association).
—— (1960), 'Comparative Social Mobility', *Current Sociology*, 9, 1–89.
Morton, J. (1985), *The Dusty Road from Perth* (Vancouver: Douglas and McIntyre).
Portocarero, L. (1987), *Social Mobility in Industrial Societies: Women in France and Sweden* (Stockholm: Swedish Institute for Social Research).
Reid, W. S. (1976), *The Scottish Tradition in Canada* (Toronto: McClelland and Stewart).
*Scottish Abstract of Statistics* (1980), (Edinburgh: The Scottish Office).
Smith, G. (1990), Personal correspondence concerning the ESRC-funded Families and Social Mobility Project (Scotland).
Sorokin, P. (1915, 1959), *Social and Cultural Mobility* (Glencoe, Ill.: Free Press).
—— (1927), *Social Mobility* (New York).
Strauss, A. (1971), *The Contexts of Social Mobility* (San Francisco: University of California Press).
Thompson, P. (1990), 'Family as a Factor in Social Mobility', paper delivered to the XIII World Congress of Sociology, Madrid.
—— (1993), 'Family Myth, Models and Denials in the Shaping of Individual Life Paths', in D. Bertaux and P. Thompson (eds), *Between Generations: Family Models, Myths and Memories* (International Yearbook of Oral History and Life Stories, 2; Oxford: Oxford University Press).
Tilly, C., and Brown C. H. (1967), 'On Uprooting, Kinship and the Auspices of Migration', *International Journal of Comparative Sociology*, 7 (Sept.), 139–64.
Weir, J. S. (1977), *The Caledonians: A History of the Scots in Kamloops* (Kamloops: Peerless Printers).

# 8

# Transmission in Extreme Situations: Russian Families Expropriated by the October Revolution

DANIEL BERTAUX*

In retrospect, the major social revolutions are seen in their historical truth: not so much as the achievement of the ideals of liberty and equity for which they were waged, and for which so many men and women gave their lives, but as the replacement of one hierarchical order by another. The old power structure crumbles, and with it vanish institutions, social relations, mores, the old social games, in short everything the members of the former ruling class and their allied classes called 'society' and whose foundations they thought to be eternal. A society dies, and the upper-class families, at least those that do not emigrate or are not liquidated by political repression, find themselves excluded a priori from the new society in the making. How do they survive, how do they gradually gain a foothold in the new social relationships, how do they help their children find a place in the new hostile social world? What strategies do they choose, what resources can they count on, how do they use them?

The old strategies for transmitting social status have lost all meaning; and it suddenly becomes obvious how much of their success depended not only on mobilizing family resources (economic means, cultural resources, political and social connections) but on the favourable environment provided by the earlier society: it was *that* social order which, in the end, was for them the crucial collective resource; and *that* is what vanished; all that remain are strictly family resources which suddenly appear laughable.

*An earlier version of this chapter was published in French in 'Générations et filiation', *Communications*, 59 (1994), 73–99.

# Families Expropriated by the Revolution 231

From the standpoint of the sociological analysis of how family social status is transmitted from one generation to the next, then, social revolutions constitute so many laboratory cases, and it may be regretted that the sociology of social mobility has taken so little interest in them: not only because social revolutions, those 'catastrophes' (in the sense defined by the mathematician, René Thom) that snap the thread of history, engender much greater and qualitatively different upward and downward flows of social mobility than those found during smooth economic development; but also because, in those societies with a stable social order that are usually studied by sociologists, contextual continuity is assumed and ultimately goes unnoticed, whereas it is actually the condition that makes most of the attempts at transmission possible.

Let us focus on the two revolutions that occurred in 1917 in Russia. They produced huge upheavals in the social structure, which were aggravated after 1929 with the forced collectivization of land and the Terror of the 1930s. As a result, between 1917 and the Second World War the country experienced considerable downward and upward social mobility. In the framework of this paper, I focus on the fate of families who, before the February and October Revolutions of 1917, belonged to the ruling or simply privileged classes under the Czarist regime. As Pitirim Sorokin, the respected but forgotten founder of the sociology of social mobility, himself born in Russia but driven out by the Bolsheviks at the end of 1922, wrote in 1925:

> The [Russian] revolution reminds one of a great earthquake which throws topsy-turvy all layers in the area of a geological cataclysm. Never in normal periods has Russian society known such a great vertical mobility ... In one or two years ... almost all people in the richest strata were ruined; almost the whole political aristocracy was deposed and degraded; the greater part of the masters, entrepreneurs, and the highest professional ranks were put down.
> Within four years, from 1914 to 1918, almost all the well-to-do and rich classes were made poor ... the entire classes of landlords and well-to-do farmers, entrepreneurs, merchants, bankers, business men, well-to-do or high-salaried state and private officials, employees, intelligentsia and professionals, not to mention the nobility and gentry ... were cut off and turned into poor people. On the other hand, a great many Communists, new business men, profiteers, swindlers and underhanded dealers, who before the war and the revolution had not been anything, now became *nouveaux riches*.[1]

At the time of the Russian Revolution, Sorokin was a junior sociology professor at the University of Saint Petersburg.

> With the assistance of my pupils I carried out in 1921–22 an investigation of the social circulation in Petrograd, during the years of the revolution. Eleven hundred and thirteen persons were subjected to investigation... Every one had at least once changed his original occupation in the period from 1917 to 1921... The average number of changes of profession... amounted to five... The majority became impoverished; a comparatively small section became rich. Their 'social position' also changed sharply.
>
> Two examples will prove the rapidity and sharpness of those changes. A former Senator and Deputy-Minister, during three and a half years of the revolution, has passed consecutively through the following stages: a starving gardener, a prisoner in a concentration camp, a dealer in powder against cockroaches, a clerk in a cooperative shop, a typist in the Academy of Sciences, a teacher in the Agronomic School, a member of the Board of an Agricultural Association, a photographer. A former village lad, eighteen years old, had been consecutively in those years: a Red Army soldier, a factory worker, a party propagandist, arrested and condemned to death by the Whites, a member of a factory committee, an administrator of finances in a provincial town, a Red Army officer, a student, a member of the Provincial Committee of the Russian Communist Party, chairman of the Provincial Extraordinary Commission, a member of the All-Russian Central Executive Committee and a prosecuting counsel.[2]

The data for the study conducted by Sorokin and his students has been lost, but the survey is probably the only empirical study of the awesome vertical fluctuations in social mobility brought about by the war and the two revolutions of 1917. The February Revolution overthrew the Czar and

> all former rulers, down to the policemen, as well as the dominant class, i.e., the gentry, were removed from their position in the legal pyramid... Their places were taken partly by representatives of the middle class of industry and trade, partly by the representatives of workers and peasants, and partly by the persecuted nationalities of Russia... At the end of October there came a new explosion which finally buried the gentry and brought to the surface a new layer consisting of workers, soldiers, lumpen-proletarians and village paupers on the one hand, of international adventurers of all countries... which filled all the commanding posts... Communists, together with the paupers and the dregs of society who supported them, became a new 'gentry'...

## Families Expropriated by the Revolution 233

Many representatives of manual labor—workers and peasants—took to brain work as commissaries, propagandists, factory managers, etc.; on the contrary many intellectuals, like teachers, professors, students, writers, employers and factory managers were compelled to earn their living by manual work and became factory workers, guards, agricultural laborers, woodcutters, dockers, station porters, etc. Both of the former and the latter, according to Zinoviev [at the Eleventh conference of the Russian Communist Party], 'changed their profession nearly every month'.[3]

For Sorokin, writing these lines in Prague in the winter of 1922–3, such upheaval could only be temporary: one day the cycle would have to reverse directions and those professionals (engineers, doctors, economists, administrators, teachers, entrepreneurs, and merchants) once again take up the work which, because of their training, they alone could perform effectively. He thought he already detected the beginnings of the reversal in 1921. And yet, retrospectively, we know that other cycles of exclusion were to follow, with the end of the New Economic Policy, the expropriation of the well-off peasants (*kulaks*) beginning in 1929, the repression of bourgeois specialists and even old Bolsheviks in the 1930s. Even the *children* of the former ruling or simply cultivated classes were affected and would be refused access to the university on the grounds of their class origins.

The importance of investigating these phenomena *in detail* and submitting them to social analysis is obvious. Of all the questions that spring to mind when these are mentioned, questions concerning not only the social consequences of the Russian Revolution but any victorious revolution, here are a few that we still cannot answer. Among the families of the dispossessed classes, which ones chose to emigrate and were able to do so, and which ones were unable or unwilling to leave? What resources were lacking for those who stayed? What kept some from trying to emigrate? Of those who stayed, what distinguishes those who fell victim to political repression, famine, poverty and those who survived? Besides expropriation and direct repression, what other forms of coercion were used—administrative violence, political stigmatization, social exclusion—to bar government employees from their jobs and 'put down' members of the former élites? What strategies of protection, disguise, retraining, reinsertion were they able to contrive for themselves or their children in order to avoid social degradation? Were they able to pass on to their children resources (culture, moral values, relations) that could be used to win a decent or even desirable place in the new society with its new hierarchies? Were these transmissions tolerated or, on the contrary, fought by the new regime, necessarily aware of the danger from former élites attempting to reconstruct part of their power? Confronted by professional competition from old-regime trained specialists, how did the new political élites react, aware as they probably were of the inadequacy of their own technical skills and level of culture?

If war is simply (international) politics carried on in another form, it could also be said, paraphrasing Clausewitz, that civil war is class struggle carried on by other means; and, likewise, just as wars are often continued by the occupation of the losers' territory by the winners, the civil wars that accompany revolutions are continued by many forms of repression of the defeated by the victors, who, once in power, rely on State violence. The only difference is that these post-revolutionary class struggles do not set one nation against another, but oppose social groups within the same people, leaving the members of the losing side at least the theoretical possibility of changing sides. It is these free-for-alls that follow victorious revolutions that will be examined here, from the standpoint of 'social mobility'.

Our data are drawn from an initial corpus of some fifty Russian family histories going back before the Revolution and continuing down to the present day.[4] From this corpus we selected the families whose ascendants included members of the old-regime ruling classes (nine cases). Rather than trying to generalize from such a narrow base, we have chosen to examine these life stories for traces of some of the social processes that had a profound effect on the fate of these families, as well as accounts of the families' struggles to help their children find a new place in post-revolutionary society. In effect, each family's or person's global experience contains a multitude of individual experiences, among which the sociologist's eye can pick out the effects of collective socio-historical processes. There are many of these and they vary with the context and the period; they have a number of facets; and each individual experience throws light on only one small aspect. It is a labour of patience to compare, establish relations, cross-check data and hypotheses in order to reconstruct the social logics of historically situated contexts; a labour akin to the work of the archaeologist, painstakingly piecing together, out of the scattered shards, an ancient vase or mosaic.

In this exploratory paper I will simply suggest a few hypotheses concerning certain aspects of transmission in extreme situations, based on a presentation of a few authentic experiences. I have chosen to present two cases in some detail and to give the basic outlines of three others.[5]

## VERA'S STORY

Our corpus contains examples of privileged families who were unable to avoid social degradation. We have scant access to the most tragic stories, those of men and women who died without children and therefore without witnesses (nevertheless these stories can be told by surviving nieces or nephews). But there are still stories that are sufficiently dramatic to show that reconversion was not always possible.

Let us take the story of the Nilaiev spouses and their children. At the beginning of the century, Mr Nilaiev was a brilliant engineer trained in the new electrical technologies; he was one of the directors of a large industrial firm in Moscow. His wife came from a noble family, and had studied at the famous Smolny Institute for young women of noble extraction. Her husband had no noble blood; but he did cover his wife with jewelry, which he bought on his way home from work. They had four children: Alexandra, born in 1899; and three sons, Illia (1900), Nikolay (1901), and Vassily (1904). They lived in a large villa north of Moscow and had also bought, in Lesnoy Gorodok, a village some forty kilometres out of Moscow on a local railway line, a wooded plot where they built a small one-room dacha at which to spend their Sundays.

When the revolution broke out, Alexandra had just started medical school; the three boys were still in high school. The father's factory was in a state of turmoil: the workers occupied the plant day and night, the owner had fled abroad, the managers were left to their own devices. Every night Mr Nilaiev would return home deeply demoralized, repeating over and over: 'What's going on? What's going on?' In the space of a few weeks he lost his mind and had to be placed in an asylum, where he soon died. Meanwhile the family home was occupied by worker's families, who took over one room after another.

Vera retreated to the dacha with her three sons. The eldest, Illia, who worshipped his father and imitated him, was distraught. And yet he was now the head of the family! Under pressure from his mother, who upon her husband's death was confronted with the loss of the only income for the family, Illia, a bookish and docile boy, always dapper and extremely well spoken, took a job as a factory labourer. His formal speech and delicate manners immediately made him the butt of the other workers' jokes. The tension was too much for him and he soon began drinking when he got home: after a few months he could take no more and he disappeared.

Vera saw where she had gone wrong and steered her two younger sons into crafts: they became lathe operators (Russia has a tradition of household objects made from wood). They were to exercise this trade all their lives.

On one side of the dacha in Lesnoy Gorodok, where they now lived, Vera and her two sons made a garden; they raised chickens and rabbits. Vera was clever with her hands: she knew how to knit, sew, embroider, and dressed the whole family and even sold (for a small sum) to her neighbours items of clothing she made from start to finish.

But then Nikolay became engaged to a girl who had been placed at the age of 14 as a servant with a family in Lesnoy Gorodok. She was a country girl and practically illiterate; but she had caught Nikolay's eye, as he often passed her in the village. Vera was set against this *mésalliance*, but the marriage took place nevertheless. With no help from Vera, with his own hands, Nikolay built a rudimentary *isba* (log cabin) for his wife and himself on a bit of land that his mother had finally agreed to let them use. Two children were born in 1923 and 1924.

Now winters were very cold in the isba, and both children fell ill. Hundreds of prayers would be said for their recovery, before the family icons (some very old and valuable). All for naught: both children died, one after the other. In a fit of rage at divine injustice, Nikolay burned all the icons, which was a considerable trauma for his devout mother. Many years later she would remember that dramatic moment as the point when the thread of her former life was truly severed; furthermore she saw it as her son's conversion to atheism, for which the Bolsheviks were actively campaigning at the time. Nikolay's loss of faith seemed to her the ultimate failure in all her struggles to maintain family continuity.

One day a letter arrived from Moldavia, from her eldest son,

Illia. He described his poverty-stricken life there as a stableman in a *kolkhoz* (collective farm). He had married the daughter of a farm worker; the couple lived in a shed next to the stables. They had two children, but the youngest daughter had died from lack of care, and Illia was worn out. The family got together and decided to bring him back to Lesnoy Gorodok. It was a spent man, alcoholic, unrecognizable, who arrived some time later with his wife and small daughter. He would never recover his equilibrium and even stole from his mother to buy drink.

The years went by, and Nikolay's wife bore three more children, among them Ludmilla (born in 1925), who many years later would be telling this story, interviewed by Marina Malysheva (her grandmother, Vera, lived with her until she died in 1972). Vera's youngest son, Vassily, whom his mother no doubt wanted to keep with her as long as possible, also finally married in 1939 to a girl from the village; they would have a daughter in 1940 and a son in 1941.

When the war broke out, in June 1941, the three sons were mobilized. Restrictions were tightened, the family, now reduced to Vera, her daughters-in-law and their children, had almost nothing to eat. That was when Vera decided to sell her last pieces of jewelry for bread and gruel.

All that now remained of the family fortune were the books, some valuable editions. But the German troops were close, and rumour had it that they were executing all Communists, who could be identified by the fact that they owned books. Any books, as the Germans could not read Russian. As a precaution, the whole library went the way of the stove.

In the end, the German army was stopped four stations down the line from the house. But Vassily, the youngest of Vera's three sons and the one closest to her, had been killed at the front. Nikolay came back alive, but in a weakened state, and died of pneumonia in 1950.

His daughter, Ludmilla, would have liked to go on with her studies. But she was 15 when the war came. She was recruited to work in one of the big Moscow factories; conditions were harsh, and she slept on the shop floor for weeks on end because of the curfew. She finally escaped from the factory in the 1940s by marrying a worker, who found her a job as a helper in the *crèche* at his own factory. She moved into a two-room apartment in Moscow and sent for her grandmother, Vera. Ludmilla's brother and sister, her cousins (the children of Alexandra, Vassily, and Illia) and their spouses all met similar fates: the men became factory workers, with frequent alcohol problems which broke up their marriages and made life difficult for the mother left to raise the children on her own (this was the case for Ludmilla, among others); the women worked in factories, in hotels, as cooks and as childminders. Their own children, born in the 1940s and 1950s, remained in the same social class. Ludmilla herself, now 67, today lives in a small two-room apartment with her daughter and her granddaughter; it is cold and damp in the winter, they have to leave a window open because the gas water-heater leaks.

Nothing remains, then, of the original family's great material resources, which before the revolution placed them in the top centile of Russia's most privileged families. Clearly the husband's depression was a factor that weighed heavily in the family's subsequent fate: with him disappeared not only their source of income, but also the possibility of activating useful relations. (Had he survived the 1917 Revolution, however, he would probably have become a victim of the repression that in the 1930s hit 'specialists' trained under the old regime.) This family was lucky enough to have somewhere to fall back on when the apartments and homes of the aristocracy were requisitioned and occupied by workers and their families; the family microculture was thus preserved. And yet Vera's considerable efforts to transmit to her children, grandchildren and great grandchildren at least some bits of the culture she bore were for the most part in vain. She was unable to prevent her three sons from marrying practically illiterate country girls—who nevertheless turned out to be good solid mothers; Illia was broken by life and lost all sense of morality; Nikolay lost his faith; Vassily did not live to see his children grown up. None of the children in the following generation went on with their education. Such an example allows us to measure the importance of the overall *social context*, without the support of which all attempts at transmission may prove vain.[6]

## LYDIA'S STORY

The second story is that of Lydia Ziemlianine, born in 1914; she was interviewed in Moscow, in 1992, by Victoria Semenova. At that

## Families Expropriated by the Revolution

time she was 78 and lived in a modest apartment; nothing told of her noble origins or her brilliant career as a Soviet geologist. She shares the three-room apartment with her daughter, Irina (born in 1940, a biologist), her son-in-law and their son, Alexander (born in 1969), whom Lydia, like so many Soviet grandmothers, often looked after when he was small.

Lydia recounted her family story:

My paternal grandfather, Fedor L., was very rich. He lived in the provinces, he owned a very fine house with a big terrace and an *escalier d'honneur*. He was a collector of indirect taxes. His first wife had attended the Smolny Institute. She was very beautiful, I saw a photo of her. They had a baby, Konstantin (my father), but she died of galloping consumption shortly after his birth.

My grandfather remarried, he had three other children; but his second wife hated Konstantin. The others had private tutors, but not him, they left him to grow up on his own. This caused him a lot of suffering. He left home (and school) as soon as he could. He took to the road, worked at various trades; finally he joined the Czar's army as a junior officer. He met my mother, Antonina, they got married and she got pregnant with me. That was in 1913. In August 1914 the Prussian war started; he was wounded, a punctured lung; he was sent to recuperate in central Asia because of the warm climate. Mother joined him and that is where I was born.

My mother Antonina came from a well-to-do family; her father started out as the steward of a large estate in Belorussia; then he bought the property. That is where my mother was born, in northern Berezina. At the beginning of the war, her father lived in Moscow, on the income from his estate in Belorussia. He had a big apartment in the heart of the old city. My mother could not stay in central Asia to raise me; she came back to Moscow. We lived at her father's with her younger sister, who was not married.

But the revolution came. I was 4. I remember one winter, it was so cold [1918 or 1919]. All five of us lived in one room. There was nothing to eat in all Moscow; a terrible famine. Below the window of our apartment there was a shed roof; grandfather would throw out seeds to attract the pigeons, and sometimes he would manage to net one.

A cousin came to see us. He was working in the Ukraine on the railroad. Mother, who saw we were a burden on the family, decided to leave with him for a warmer climate, better for me. He found her a job as a secretary on the construction site; obviously she knew how to read and keep books, she had a good education. We lived in one of the big wooden shacks on the site. In the same shed lived the construction supervisor, Savva. He had nine children to support and he was alone. His wife had just died of tuberculosis, she had caught it while nursing her son, who had come back from the front with the disease. Both died the same day. Savva was at his wit's end. My mother helped him look after his children; she was a good seamstress and she made their clothes. Savva and she began living together. Mother had removed my father's pictures from the family album because in all of them he was dressed in the uniform of an officer of the Czar. She destroyed my birth certificate and re-registered me as though I were Savva's daughter.

I was very fond of Savva, both of him and his children. They were all musical! None of them went on with their studies but we have always kept in touch.

We moved with the railroad construction; we went to the village schools. My mother wanted me to continue my studies. When I was 15—that was the end of compulsory schooling—she sent me to my aunt's in Moscow. But my aunt did not want to help me find my way. And I was a hindrance to her. I tried to get into the Pedagogical Institute (teacher training school), but I was too young, for one thing, and especially, there were my class origins! . . . Officially Savva was my father, an engineer trained under the old regime, a bourgeois specialist; they only accepted the children of workers. This was in 1930.

In the courtyard lived a girl who worked in a spinning mill. She got me a job there. I didn't have a choice, I had to earn my way, my aunt made me pay rent and, besides, everyone worked there. I spent five years there, but after two years I managed to enroll in night classes at the rabfak.

The rabfaks, or *rabochii fakultet*, were secondary schools set up by the new regime to bring workers up to a level from which they could continue on to higher education. Of course they were reserved for workers. Having easily passed the successive examinations during the two years of rabfak (as her friends had failed, she repeated the last year with them for the pleasure; the teachers, all trained 'in the old way', were top notch), Lydia won, as a worker, the right to enroll at the university. She chose geology, a speciality not frequently selected by girls ('there were ten boys for every girl').

Lydia herself confesses that she was very interested in boys; she quickly fell in love with one of the students, Evgeni, who was fascinated with geology. He had spent five years working in a coal mine; he too had gone through a rabfak. They became engaged and then married secretly, each continuing to live in their respective student dormitory: both were active members of the Komsomols

(Communist youth organizations) and aspired to join the Party; but early marriage was frowned on.

Evgeni was brilliant and cultivated, and that is what had drawn Lydia to him. He was well versed in the great Russian and Western writers. When he saw he could trust Lydia, who had confessed to him that both of her real parents were of noble extraction, he confided that he, too, was from a noble family and even once a rich one; his time in the coal mine had served to launder his origins.

As soon as they graduated from the Institute, Lydia and her husband would participate in expeditions to the outer frontiers of the Soviet Union (Altai, Siberia) in extraordinarily rustic conditions. Luck smiled on them, as they rapidly discovered deposits of gold and other rare minerals and were entrusted with organizing new expeditions. Evgeni, who had volunteered when war was declared in 1941, would soon be sent back to the expeditions, considered to be strategic for national defence. When Lydia gave birth to a little girl, the child was given into the care of her grandmother, Antonina, who had been living with the couple since the death of her husband, Savva; she raised the child herself. Some years later, Lydia and Evgeni separated, each having developed a relationship with another partner; but they remained on very good terms for the rest of their life, something that surprised my Russian colleague, V. Semenova, who attributed this apparently uncommon civil attitude to the persistence of aristocratic values.[7]

## First Comments

Although this second family history has been highly summarized, it sheds some light on a few important social processes. First of all it provides us with information on the fate of the adult members of these classes that were brought down by the revolution. Excluded from Soviet society, deprived of all income and social aid, Antonina's parents actually starved to death in Moscow. They lacked a son, or a son-in-law, who could have found them a place in the new society, even if it were in a manual occupation, and could have helped them get through the dramatic time that followed the revolution. Theirs was no doubt also the fate of many others of their social class and generation.

According to Sorokin, who quotes Soviet figures, the population of Petrograd fell from 2,420,000 before the revolution to 1,469,000 in 1918, and 740,000 in 1920. Moscow dropped from 2 million to 1 million inhabitants between February 1917 and 1920.[8] Emigration, famines, high mortality, flight to safer places: the Russian cities had become high-risk zones for the former upper classes.

Antonina herself managed to find an entry into the new Soviet society, due no doubt to her courage and her ability to adapt, but at the cost of repudiating her husband and concealing her own identity. And yet she manifestly succeeded in transmitting to her daughter her own cultural and moral resources, which were all she had left of her past.

'The real object of transmission is to pass on', writes the psychoanalyst, Pierre Legendre:[9] 'to pass on *something*, whatever it may be, so as to be able to recognize oneself in one's children.' How can this be done in such trying conditions? Antonina's daughter, Lydia, was only able to attend village schools, changing schools as the railroad advanced. But she had the best of tutors in her mother, and she was a fast learner.

When Lydia was of an age to go on to higher schooling, she came up against a formidable barrier: university was reserved for working-class children. In this case the substitute father was inoperative. Disqualified, Lydia went to work in the factory, as did the vast majority of young people of her age.

Nevertheless and without forming a conscious strategy, she remained on the lookout for opportunities to learn. It must be added here that Lydia enthusiastically espoused the progressive ideals of the new regime and thoroughly internalized them. She was active in the factory Communist youth group. She dreamed of one day joining the Party. What was there to regret in the status of the former nobility, idle and parasitic as it was?

But it is fascinating to see how, at the very time the Soviet regime was the most totalitarian, when the struggles against the 'class enemies' and their children was raging, not only Lydia but many other children of the former élites discovered in the very rabfaks that were created to train their replacements, paths which led to highly qualified positions carrying responsibilities. These falsely 'working-class' children were also more fit for higher education; they were at the top of the class because of the cultural resources they inherited and which set them apart from the others. They were also, by an additional paradox, whole-hearted communist activists.

We have found the same phenomenon in other family histories as well. Such was the case, for instance, of the two sons of a well-known Moscow jurist at the beginning of the century. As I have discussed this example elsewhere,[10] I will only touch on it here. The jurist, a cultivated *grand bourgeois* who received the cream of Moscow society in his drawing-room under the last Czar, was not only dispossessed of his apartment by the revolution (he lived confined to one room with his wife and his books), but deprived of all income: the regime had no place for a specialist in bourgeois law. But his own interest in the history of Russia and France—his library contained a wealth of historical works—would save his two sons. The elder managed to finish his studies in Chinese and became an expert on the Far East. The younger was not as fortunate: he graduated from high school with excellent marks but was rejected by the history department of the university because of his class origins. Like all of his schoolmates from the same milieu, he took a job as a construction worker for the Moscow subway, where the conditions were very harsh. Like Lydia in the preceding story, he too was an enthusiastic supporter of Party ideals, and his natural authority rapidly made him a worker's leader (the bulk of the men digging the tunnels were peasants fresh from the countryside). After many vicissitudes, including deportation to the Altai for 'anti-Soviet propaganda' at the end of the 1930s (a time when a political joke told in public could result in denunciation and deportation), he would end up as a senior Party official at the time of Destalinization.

Lydia's story, that of the successful reinsertion of a young woman of noble extraction into Soviet society, is therefore not unique; which authorizes a few hypotheses of a general order.

## ANALYSIS

The overall situation that forms the backdrop for these accounts of social degradation is that of a society turned upside down by a victorious social revolution. To be sure, Western societies also provide cases of strong downward mobility; for instance, families ruined by bankruptcy, the rapid dilapidation of a fortune by a carefree heir, the premature death of a family head or the gradual loss of drive by generations raised in the lap of plenty, as described by Thomas Mann in *Buddenbrooks*. But each of these cases illustrates the fall of a single family; its social class as a whole continues to prosper. With respect to what happened in Russia after 1917, even the dramatic consequences of something like the 1929 Wall Street Crash pale in comparison. What characterizes the post-revolutionary situation is the *societal*, nation-wide nature of the expropriation and stigmatization. In the Russian case, there would come a remission, provided by the NEP, but it would be of short duration.

In the face of this historical 'catastrophe', three main types of response could be envisaged: emigration, organized resistance, or adaptation to the new situation. Here once again we find Albert Hirschman's *exit, voice, loyalty* typology.[11] In the present article we are interested only in behaviours of the third type. But the two others need to be mentioned, not because they were adopted by tens of thousands of families, but because those families who remained in Russia without trying to resist would be suspected either of having taken part in acts of resistance (civil war) or of having maintained contacts with the members of their own family in exile.

We will therefore focus on those who were caught up in the net of the new regime, and more precisely those who survived the most 'catastrophic' time. *How* did they survive? What resources could they still command in order to attempt to insert themselves into the new social relationships and reconstruct some kind of social status? What channels of insertion were objectively open to them? What could they transmit to their children to help them become fully integrated in the new Soviet society? But first of all, what did this sudden loss of their formal social status mean to them?

This question, foremost in the series, can be answered in different ways, depending on whether these were families of leisure, numerous in Russia due to the nature of the old regime, or families from the economically active classes, among which must be distinguished entrepreneurs and merchants, on the one hand, and professionals and intellectuals on the other.

The loss was the more severe for the leisure classes, who lived on land rents and privileges; it was no doubt they who emigrated or put up armed resistance in the greatest proportions. For them, the new society manifestly had no place, held out no future. Everything that had made up their world, the old regime 'society', had collapsed; many others had known the fate of Antonina's parents, who died from hunger and cold in their Moscow apartment to indifference or general hostility. The harsh new times were exacerbated by the loss of all that founded their former life ('What's going on?', the heartfelt cry of the company manager who identified completely with the old regime, must have been all the more heartfelt for the many landowners who, as in Tchekhov's plays, had not seen the new times coming). Loss of all familiar landmarks: not only sources of income but friends and relations, social milieu; life habits, former beliefs, the comprehension of a social world acquired by experience, all of this was rendered null and void overnight. The new society, brutish and incomprehensible for them, invaded their very private space: working-class families obtained from the municipality the right to live in your apartment, to occupy nearly all of the rooms, to pile up, a family per room, to use the kitchen and bathroom, leaving you to get along as though on suspended sentence, in one room, at the mercy of a denunciation for a critical remark overheard.

The invasion of one's privacy by families of a different social class flaunting their political victory seems to have been a particularly traumatic experience. There was almost no way to avoid it, since the housing market had been abolished: no amount of money could (at least in principle) keep the invaders at bay, nor secure another apartment. For that, you would have had to go through those very officials who had caused your misfortune in the first place and who would, in all likelihood, have eyed your request with the utmost suspicion. Even possessing money was suspect, a sign of belonging to the former upper classes.

We have the case of a family living in a villa surrounded by a splendid orchard in the middle of a town in southern Russia, who managed to keep the entire family home for themselves throughout the 1920s, thanks to the political support of a relative who had joined the revolution in its early days. The slow dilapidation of the orchard, home to a large number of working-class families living in makeshift shelters, was a source of suffering; notwithstanding, the story of this family shows how great a resource continuing control over their *private space* was for them. The mother was able to go on raising her four daughters, to keep them safe under her wing until they could make their own way in the world; their fiancés called on them in a controlled space and even lived there as students—which made it possible to hold off the city officials, always on the lookout for vacant rooms; and this ten-year reprieve was used for their necessarily slow adaptation to the new society.

For most, by contrast, the loss of control over private space, even more than the loss of their source of income, was the greatest trauma; for, among other reasons, without some privacy, it is practically impossible to pass on to one's children—by education but also by everyday interaction and maintaining a style of life that is first and foremost an objective means of their cultural production—the values, orientations, and codes of behaviour desired by the parents, who have nothing else left to transmit. Not only for those families of independent means, but also for the many in which the adult generation was now comprised exclusively by women, loss of family privacy would virtually eliminate all hopes of transmission.

Where there was a trade to hand on, the situation was slightly better. To be sure, many qualifications, such as jurist or theologian, had suddenly lost all value; these would have to be forgotten and replaced with new skills (one of the girls' fiancés mentioned above, a theology student, managed to cram enough applied economy to be recruited by his high-school classmates, now engineers, for the committees planning the housing developments that were mushrooming around the new mines: like Magnitogorsk, or Azovstal). But it was a safe bet that whatever direction the new regime took, it would always need doctors, engineers, architects, agronomists, and teachers. One of our informants, 90 years old at the time of his interview, was the son of a rich fisheries owner in Astrakhan, on the shores of the Caspian Sea. He was steered towards medical school. When his father, who had managed to keep his company afloat during the New Economic Policy (NEP) in the early 1920s at the cost of large bribes, was arrested and tried for corruption, his son was sent to a camp. But as a doctor, he enjoyed a regime of semi-liberty; he was even allowed to sleep outside the camp when his wife visited him.

Another case is that of a sawmill owner in northern Russia whose mill was seized by the state. Nevertheless, under the NEP, he was restored, if not as owner, at least as director of his mill, long enough to complete his daughters' education and to marry them off to his own engineers, while two of his three sons went off to join the Whites in Siberia, then after the resounding defeat of the White army, stayed on and made a new life for themselves under a new identity (one of them would be denounced in the 1930s and executed); here transmission was indirect, it concerned the daughters and was effected not through an occupation but through marriage.

Yet even the common-sense expectations ('there will always be a need for engineers'), like those of Sorokin in 1922, eventually turned out to be overoptimistic. In the 1930s the grave economic crisis that followed the collectivization of land, and which affected not only agriculture but industry as well, set off a search for scapegoats. We know today that it was due to the inability of central planning to handle, in real time, the same amount of information as a market economy.[12] But this was not the perception at the time: the Plan, being more rational than the market *should* have made the economy run without a hitch; and if it could not, it was surely due to sabotage at every level.[13] Suspicion obviously fell first on the specialists from the Czarist period. Thousands were arrested and deported or executed, among whom the above-mentioned engineers who had codirected the construction of Magnitogorsk or Azovstal, or the saw mill owner's sons-in-law. Being in possession of a useful trade was not enough to save them, it only postponed the fatal moment: their class origins caught up with them in the end.

The only one of the sawyer's sons to survive was the youngest and most intellectually inclined, Kostia. He had gone to the trouble of reading not only the new regime newspapers but the Marxist classics. He had become convinced, the only one in his whole family, that the new ideology was consistent and that the new regime was there to stay. Consequently he did not join the Whites, but, on the contrary, when the NEP ended, decided to move to a remote village in the northern forests where, concealing his family origins, he offered his services as a schoolteacher. One of the village houses was turned into a school, and he was given a room. A short time later, he married an almost illiterate peasant girl, daughter of one of the poorest families in the village, and they had several children. He lived in constant fear of one day being discovered, something he was spared: he died at the front in 1941, but he had had time to see his children grow up and to hand on to them his taste for study. Thanks to their good marks at school (and to their mother's secret collaboration with the KGB, which she provided with information on individual villagers' attitudes towards the government), they would later be the first authorized to leave the village—something that was theoretically forbidden by the administration. Considering the times, which were very dangerous for those who, like Kostia, had been put down, this strategy can be regarded as a success.

It is reminiscent of the strategy of Antonina, the young noblewoman who had concealed her first marriage with an officer of the Czar: these are extreme strategies in that they affect personal identity, but they were necessary because this aristocratic identity was a mortal danger. The hardening of the struggle against 'class enemies' did not leave much choice. But the need to conceal one's past, hence an essential component of one's personal identity, means that, beyond the external private space, it is one's intimate privacy that is impaired; and when one is forced to lie to one's children, whose innocence obviously makes them incapable of keeping a secret, the damage is exacerbated.

Upper-class families then had not only to face the loss of their sources of income and their heritage, the devaluing of their cultural resources, the lost effectiveness of their now inoperative social relations, the inversion of the value of their 'social qualification' (their class *habitus*: see the case of the unfortunate Illia); but also the loss of such basic resources as control of family privacy, or the symbolic resource of belonging to a family line with respected social status; and even more generally of being forced to suppress the family memory, which is so crucial to one's identity.[14]

And yet some young people from noble or bourgeois families, like Lydia, Evgeni, or the jurist's two sons, after having spent the required time in manual occupations, manifestly managed to efface their class origins, to find a place in the new society and to make a career for themselves. All four went through Communist youth groups and finally joined the Party, after having been required to provide a detailed biography which included their ascendants. One might think they were motivated by political opportunism; but our findings show that, on the contrary, their allegiance to the new ideals was sincere.

Let us take for example the way Lydia managed to enroll in her local rabfak:

At the factory I met other girls who would have liked to go on with their studies. At the end of the first year, I called together my girlfriends and said to them: 'Girls, we've got to try to get into the rabfak!' They all agreed.

The group of us went to see the director of the factory. He refused. The

## Families Expropriated by the Revolution

classes were at night, but as we worked in three shifts, he would have had to reorganize all of them, and he wouldn't hear of it!

That was the period when every senior Party official was affiliated with a large factory that he was supposed to visit periodically. We had Boudienny. One day we heard he was in the plant, with the director! We got together—there were ten of us: 'Let's go see him! Maybe he'll help us!' The director's secretary wouldn't let us in; we showered her with insults and rushed the door. I still regret that, but it was the only way.

Boudienny was taken aback: 'What's wrong, young ladies?' We explained to him that the director didn't want us to go to night school. The director confirmed this. 'Ten at once, it's not possible; it would disrupt my night shifts'. 'That's your problem, Comrade', Boudienny told him. 'Our problem is that we have no working-class intelligentsia. You must send these girls to school!' Turning to us, he said: 'Have you made out your applications?' He read them and signed them in front of us, and made the director sign, too.

Is it credible that Lydia could mobilize a whole shift, and convince a senior Party official—at the height of the Terror—if this had been only a calculation? What drove her and gave her the necessary daring was the conviction that the ideals of the Party were just, and her trust in its leaders.

Does this mean that the price of her reinsertion was the betrayal of her parents' values, the rejection of everything that her mother had tried to hand on? Things are not that simple.

In the first place, Lydia and those who followed parallel paths were younger than Vera's children, for instance: they had barely known the former society and no doubt saw only its bad sides. But the essential is not there: it lies to my mind in the unconscious transmission of a way of relating to the political sphere.

In Western societies, the political dimension is built into the social structure. It is part of the scenery, and one can live and die without being aware of it; it is the business of specialists, and those who go into political activity proper at one time or another in their life are fairly few in number.

The experience of a social revolution, on the other hand, teaches that politics can kill (that is the lesson of Nazism, too, in its way[15]). This experience is deeply engraved in the awareness of those who live through it. They draw the lesson that people should keep their distance from political activity and they try to dissuade their children from getting involved. But this very fear, or the silence that expresses it, rouses their children's political sensibilities. We noticed this during an international research project on the family origins of 1960s student activists in the United States, France, and other countries:[16] many were born into families of political refugees or Jews who had been driven out of their country by Nazism or Fascism. While some had received an anti-Fascist political legacy from their parents, others were totally unaware of the reasons that had made their parents emigrate; the latter, whose only ambition was to find a place in the target society, had hidden their former political activism or even their Jewishness from their children. Nevertheless, their own children, sensing some mysterious secret, became interested early on in politics and ended up in leftist groups. I believe it is a process of the same kind—the unravelling of some relationship with the political sphere, subconsciously passed on from parents to children—that led Lydia and so many others to engage in political activities, which could only—given the context and the idealism of youth—bring them to espouse the progressive ideals of the new regime. It may be the case that a governing-class habitus, internalized in childhood as a disposition to organize and direct others, has contributed to the process. If this is the case, the strange phenomenon of children of former governing classes integrating themselves into post-revolutionary society through political activism appears less paradoxical.

It was precisely this type of reinsertion through political activism that, in the new society, opened the way to other professional, cultural, or social insertions; the parents were unable to comprehend this, but the children had grasped it instinctively.

In market economies like our own, social integration comes primarily through economic integration. Cultural integration, too, is important, but it is not sufficient in itself, as shown by the case of jobless youth in our societies.[17] As for political integration, it is altogether secondary.

Soviet society, like any post-revolutionary society, centred its new structure around the political sphere; and the concentration of power at the head of the Party-State only exacerbated and prolonged the phenomenon.[18] From the end of the NEP, economic and cultural integration were definitely subordinated to political integration. This would be cruelly felt by the engineers and other specialists trained under the old regime and who thought they had found their place in the new society because of their technical skills:

the lack of political integration eventually made them lose everything else.

## CONCLUSION

The study of 'transmission in extreme situations', as we have defined it here, namely the efforts made at transmission in a societal context thrown into turmoil by a social revolution, is only at its beginning. But it is already possible to see beyond its field proper to the contributions it can make to the study of 'transmission in normal situations': indeed it highlights the considerable importance of the overall *societal context* in transmission.

When this context exhibits a high degree of historical continuity, as in the case of Western societies, there is a tendency to see it as an unchanging backdrop and to no longer perceive its effects. This is particularly evident in the abundant Anglo-Saxon literature on 'social mobility', which focuses on individual competition for the most desirable professional positions.[19] The fact that empirical studies of social mobility have been conducted exclusively in stabilized societies, made 'homogeneous' by a century or two of nation-state building;[20] the stress, for ideological reasons,[21] on *mobility* to the detriment of the reproduction of family resources in the wake of the transmissions; and especially the observation technique systematically used, namely questionnaires administered to a representative sample (a technique which has its own built-in blind spots[22]), all these imperceptibly lead research to focus on the *individual* factors (social origin, education) that might explain the difference in paths taken. Applying to this field concepts borrowed from micro-economic theory, such as 'cultural capital' or 'relational capital',[23] tends in the same direction: in the end, the societal context is reduced to a set of markets, always present from the outset, in which families and individuals compete with other families and individuals endowed with different capitals, which they attempt to accumulate, enhance, and transmit by more or less successful strategies.

To be sure, this approach has led to some conclusive results, especially when structural effects were also taken into consideration.[24] Nevertheless, what it omits is just as important as what it brings to light; namely the specific effects of the historical continuity of societal contexts. Paradoxically it is these effects, invisible because they are always there, that the study of transmission in extreme situations brings out: when a social revolution has destroyed a societal context, even those capitals that families have managed to preserve (culture, relations) become difficult to utilize or transmit. When this happens, it becomes easier to understand just how much, in societies enjoying historical continuity, successful family transmission depends on the features of a favourable societal context: a school system which only seems neutral, but whose content actually favours types of knowledge acquired in families who live out/off the dominant culture;[25] a banking system that favours access to credit by members of already well-to-do families; a fabric of relations which spontaneously restricts the circulation of strategic information to the same social milieu and reserves the best opportunities for the members of this milieu or their offspring: in short the spontaneous self-organization of a ruling class and its middle-class allies in an active, integrated milieu, orienting the collective institutions to their own advantage, accumulating exchange relationships through the daily exercise of responsibilities and sociability, excluding along the way without malice or aforethought—though sometimes with—anyone not belonging, by birth or marriage, to this milieu.

Societal context is not an inert backdrop; it facilitates transmission for families of the dominant classes. It even invites these transmissions, raises them to the status of norm. But it works so naturally that one forgets that it is an active, enabling presence; only when it disappears, something almost unthinkable, does one measure its full importance.

An 'individualistic' approach does not reveal this type of phenomenon, particularly if it consists of merely taking down the facts from a sampling of individual trajectories, however representative the sample may be. If the societal context is to be made visible, if its existence is even to be conceived of, the place to start is not with individuals but with institutions; with instances of social integration, of the constitution of social milieux; in short, from an approach which, from the outset, focuses on collective and societal phenomena, a Durkheimian approach.

Such a method also leads to a better understanding of exclusions, as Robert Castel's recent work has shown.[26] Trading the concept of exclusion for that of 'disaffiliation', Castel shows the importance of relations of affiliation, those ties which form the integrating web of a stabilized society. These are the pathways leading to a place in society; and when they are severed, in particular those provided by professional or family ties, exclusion follows.[27]

In market economies, male social integration is accomplished traditionally through professional integration, while women's takes place through marriage; reciprocal phenomena do operate, even though, until recently, they have been constantly underestimated. Exclusion is simply the converse of integration, it obeys the same logics of affiliation: the economic dimension is the crucial dimension; the family dimension is also very present.

In early 20th-century Russian society, a market economy was just beginning to emerge. Serfdom had been abolished only in 1861; the land belonged to the gentry or was jointly owned by peasant communities; to be sure commerce was booming, and industry was developing fast, but the upcoming bourgeoisie was excluded from the political system. This was a society based on orders, an autocratic system that revolved around the political sphere and not economics.

It was this society that collapsed during the 'bourgeois' revolution of February 1917; but the rise to power of the entrepreneurial class was to be short-lived. The 1917 October Revolution brought in a new social order even more power-centred than the Czarist regime. The end of the market economy was not long in coming; the Party-State became the sole entrepreneur, the only owner, investor, manager, and beneficiary of the entire wealth of the country. The political sphere subsumed the economic (and the professional), the cultural, and all the other spheres of society, including the justice system.

This means that the Western approach to transmission cannot be applied directly to a post-revolutionary society like the Soviet one. In the new order, integration and exclusion, social ascension or degradation are not decided in the economic sphere: these decisions come first and foremost out of the political sphere. This is the key without which it is impossible to arrive at a sociological interpretation of family destinies, of massive exclusion or of individual reinsertions into the new society: they must constantly be thought with reference to political power. Any Western-style analysis of the efforts to transmit family capitals is doomed to fail if it does not take into account this societal phenomenon: the *inversion* of the values of all (upper-class) families' resources. Not only the former possession of wealth: former possession of a large political capital (at the time of the Czar) also became a considerable handicap; renewing contacts with former relational networks became a perilous exercise, as it might be interpreted as an 'attempt to rebuild a dissolved class'. Even professional skills came under suspicion and took on a negative valence: political loyalty had taken precedence over professional skills.

Women from the former dominant classes, in so far as they were systematically excluded from the political intrigues of the old regime, seem to have come off more easily (Alexandra, Vera's oldest daughter, was unable to complete medical school, but she became a nurse and found a job, in the early 1920s, at the Kremlin hospital). No doubt regarded as politically inoffensive and easier to retrain, they could reaffiliate themselves by marrying into the new society (Alexandra married a Communist official). But those whose husband fell victim to political exclusion went through very hard times, commensurate with their loyalty to their spouse. Whatever skills they may have possessed, the majority were forced to earn a living in a manual occupation, deprived of qualifications, autonomy, or responsibility.

As for the offspring of these families, we have seen the difficulties they faced in finding a place in the new society. The resources, notably culture and relations, their parents had passed on to them could not be converted directly into access to qualified professions, for the societal context and its new rules had undergone a radical change. It is no doubt revealing that those in our corpus who had nevertheless managed to overcome the obstacles had spontaneously chosen the Party route. For them, twenty years after the political exclusion of their parents that had preceded all other exclusions, political reinsertion paved the way for the other forms of reinsertion.

*Translated by Nora Scott*

NOTES

1. Pitrim Sorokin, *Social and Cultural Mobility* (New York, 1964) (first edn. *Social Mobility*, New York 1927), 143, 466.

## Families Expropriated by the Revolution 255

2. Pitrim Sorokin, *The Sociology of Revolution* (New York, 1967) (first edn. 1925), 238–9.
3. Ibid.
4. This study was funded from 1991 to 1993 by the Social Sciences department of the French Ministry of Research and Technology, with occasional aid from DGRCST, the Maison des Sciences de l'Homme and the Centre National de la Recherche Scientifique (Programme Europe).
5. These two fragments of family histories, as well as the other even shorter examples, are taken from a corpus of 50 case histories of families conducted since 1991 in Moscow. The methodology, called the method of 'commented and compared social genealogies', consists of constructing case histories of kinship networks; the older members of the network, via their family memories, provide access to the history of their own parents, born at the turn of the century; the inclusion of collaterals makes it possible to observe the histories of parallel and intertwined lines (Daniel Bertaux, 'From Methodological Monopoly to Pluralism in the Sociology of Social Mobility', in Shirley Dex (ed.), *Life and Work History Analyses: Qualitative and Quantitative Developments* (The Sociological Review Monograph Series, 37; London/New York, 1991), 73–92; Daniel Bertaux, 'Social Genealogies Commented and Compared', *Current Sociology/La Sociologie contemporaine*, 43 (2) (1995), special issue, 'The Biographical Method', 70–88. For a large part, the kinship networks explored have been chosen at random, their entry point being a young man or woman chosen from a representative sample of Moscovites born in 1967. It was via one of the grandchildren selected by chance that, for instance, Ludmilla or Lydia, the narrators of the following accounts, were met.

The study takes in all urban social milieux. It includes of course all of the living generations, even the youngest, which is presently going through a societal crisis comparable in scope to that following 1917. For the purposes of the present paper, we not merely chose only lines which came from the dominant classes of the old regime, but also narrowed their histories to the post-1917 years.

The information on the Nilaiev family ('Vera's story') was collected by Marina Malysheva; that on the Zemlianin family ('Lydia's story') by Victoria Semenova. I am indebted to them for a number of relevant comments; but I assume full responsibility for the interpretations and hypotheses put forward here.

6. If I have kept the comments following this first story to a minimum, it is not only for lack of space; it is also because the most important has already been said through the way in which the story is told. As one can well imagine, between the information collected in the course of

the interviews and the constructed version that is set out here, there has been a necessary labour of analysis and composition. The analytical work consisted in patiently piecing together, from the fragments of information provided in the course of the interviews, the stories of Vera and her children. To give just one example, the children's birth dates, which situate each child biographically in the historical temporality of Russia, allow one to calculate their respective ages at *each* subsequent historical moment, which adds precious information to that explicitly provided by the person being interviewed: it is important, for instance, to realize that at the time of his father's death Illia was not 12 or 20, but 17. Likewise, the scant information provided by interviewees on housing made it possible to reconstruct the phases of cohabitation or de-cohabitation, which are crucial; once the data has been laid out on the table, it is possible to get a fairly accurate idea of the *family group history*, which was not apparent in our first readings of the interviews.

Thus step by step we can begin to uncover the relationships which plausibly linked the various events or situations recalled. The story line is fleshed out, becomes more complex; events, situations, reactions, and conflicts fall into place. The inevitable blanks are gradually filled in by increasingly plausible inferences (in the present case, one last interview was held to verify a few 'hunches', which turned out to be accurate).

That leaves the story; one becomes aware that it can be told in different ways, all equally true, and equally incomplete. The thrust of the present paper has led me to focus on transmission, which means that I put this account into 'story form' (*'en intrigue'*, to use Paul Ricoeur's expression) in order to bring out the various moments of transmission—here especially the failures. The reader's sociological imagination will have done the rest, spontaneously linking up those parts merely waiting to be connected.

At this point the commentary becomes almost superfluous, since it comes down to repeating explicitly what the reader has already perceived. But it is relevant to point out that this account, which can be read as a simple story that could have been told as it is, actually contains conclusions from an effort of analysis: in a sense it represents a synthesis of this effort (Daniel Bertaux, 'Écrire la sociologie', *Informations sur les sciences sociales*, 19 (1) (Jan. 1979, 7–25).

7. The second story is told here partly in direct speech. This form should be read as a way of making the story more lively but not as a *verbatim* transcription of an interview.

Certainly Lydia is a better storyteller than Ludmilla; and she is talking about things she herself has experienced, while Ludmilla is reporting what she has heard from her grandmother a thousand times. And yet her interview too is made up of bits and pieces that have had to be pieced together. Although I have stayed as close as I could to Lydia's speech, and especially to its content—which I only grasped after reading the transcript many times—I could not avoid putting it into written form. Oscar Lewis set the example, and felt somewhat guilty about it—see his introduction to *The Children of Sanchez* (New York, 1961)—almost apologizing for having overstepped the rules of scientific procedure (objectivity first) and added the artist's touch to the finished product. But one knows now that the researcher cannot help interfering with the text, if only because of the distance between the oral and the written accounts; between the inevitable form of *oral* discourse, even for a highly literate speaker (unfinished sentences, skipping ahead, going back, parentheses, background constructions, associations of ideas, explanations, assessments), and *written* discourse, which follows much stricter conventions, among which the cardinal rules of linearity and clarity.

Lydia did not say everything I have made her say, then; and yet I have obviously not made anything up, and did not make her say anything she did not say one way or another. Oscar Lewis made his tape-recordings available to his colleagues as proof of his good faith. We too have placed our transcriptions at the disposal of anyone who wishes to consult them; when possible, we also submit the text to the interviewees themselves, as a means of controlling the accuracy of our own interpretations.

8. Sorokin, *Sociology of Revolution*, 244.
9. Pierre Legendre, *L'Inestimable objet de la transmission: Étude sur le principe généalogique en Occident* (Paris, 1985).
10. Daniel Bertaux, 'Révolution et mobilité sociale en Russie soviétique', *Cahiers internationaux de sociologie*, special issue, 'Les Sociétés post-totalitaires', 46 (1994).
11. Albert Hirschman, *Exit, Voice, and Loyalty* (Cambridge, Mass., 1970).
12. Friedrich August von Hayek, *La Présomption fatale: Les Erreurs du socialisme* (Paris, 1993).
13. Gabor T. Rittersporn, *Stalinist Simplifications and Soviet Complications: Social Tensions and Political Conflicts in the USSR, 1933–1953* (Chur [Switzerland], 1991).
14. Daniel Bertaux and Paul Thompson, 'Introduction', in Bertaux and Thompson (eds), *Between Generations: Family Models, Myths, and Memories* (International Yearbook of Oral History and Life Stories, 2; Oxford, 1993).
15. Cf. Nicole Lapierre, *Le Silence de la mémoire: A la recherche des Juifs de Plock* (Paris, 1989).

16. Ronald Fraser et al., *1968: A Student Generation in Revolt* (New York, 1988).
17. François Dubet, *La Galère: jeunes en survie* (Paris, 1987).
18. Moshe Lewin, *La Formation du système soviétique* (Paris, 1985).
19. See e.g. Peter Blau and Otis D. Duncan, *The American Occupational Structure* (New York, 1967); Robert Erikson and John Goldthorpe, *The Constant Flux: A Study of Class Mobility in Industrial Societies* (Oxford, 1992).
20. Daniel Bertaux, 'Mobilité sociale: l'alternative', *Sociologie et societés*, 25 (2) (Fall 1993), 211–22.
21. Charles-Henri Cuin, *Les Sociologues et la mobilité sociale* (Paris, 1993).
22. Cf. Bertaux, 'From Methodological Monopoly to Pluralism'.
23. Pierre Bourdieu, *La Distinction: Critique sociale du jugement* (Paris, 1980).
24. Raymond Boudon, *Education, Opportunity, and Social Inequality* (New York, 1973); Claude Thélot, *Tel père, tel fils?* (Paris, 1983); cf. Cuin, *Les Sociologues*, for an assessment of French and American work.
25. Pierre Bourdieu and Jean-Claude Passeron, *Les Héritiers: Les Étudiants et la culture* (Paris, 1964); and *Reproduction* (Beverly Hills, Calif., 1977) (French first edn. 1970); Bourdieu, *La Distinction*.
26. Robert Castel, 'De l'indigence à l'exclusion, la désaffiliation: Précarité du travail et vulnérabilité relationnelle', in Jacques Donzelot (ed.), *Face à l'exclusion: Le Modèle français* (Paris, 1991), 137–68.
27. In the course of a study on the increasing fragility of the father–child relationship in France, we encountered men 'in free fall': who have lost their job, their family ties, and their home. We also encountered men in precarious situations. This has led us to suggest the concept of *double étayage*, or twin supports—job and family—to characterize the equilibrium, however precarious, which enables an individual, especially male, to 'function well' (Daniel Bertaux and Catherine Delcroix, 'La Fragilisation du rapport père–enfant', report for the Caisse Nationale des Allocations Familiales, 1990; a summary of the results can be read in 'Des pères face au divorce: la fragilisation du lien paternel', *Espaces et familles*, 17, July 1991). Castel's concept of disaffiliation (rather than exclusion) refers to precisely this type of phenomenon; it has the advantage of designating the social content with greater exactitude.

# 9

# Social Mobility in Hungary since the Second World War: Interpretations through Surveys and through Family Histories

RUDOLF ANDORKA

Hungary is one of those European societies for which the statistical flows of father-to-son social mobility are best established. As the patterns of these flows appear to be rather similar to those of west European societies with market economies, it has led some scholars to the thesis that the forces unleashed by economic development *per se* are much more influential on mobility patterns than the actual form of economic relations—whether planned or market-based. But the collection of family histories, which give access to the concrete processes through which lives have been actually shaped, yields a picture with more nuances, as we will demonstrate in this paper.

## HUNGARIAN SURVEYS OF SOCIAL MOBILITY

Hungary has exceptionally rich data sources on social mobility. To begin with, questions on the occupation of the father were included in the questionnaires for the censuses of 1930, 1941, and 1949. Later on, social mobility surveys based on large national samples including women as well as men were carried out: in 1962–4, 1973, and 1983 (Andorka 1972, 1976, and 1983).[1] The data from the 1973 survey were used widely in international comparisons of social mobility (Andorka and Zagórski 1980; Alestalo, Andorka and Harcsa 1987; Erikson and Goldthorpe 1987a, 1987b, and 1992).

The Hungarian surveys followed the approach known as the ISA paradigm: relatively large samples were interviewed on their full occupational and educational histories and the occupation and education of their fathers. These variables were presented in cross-tabulations showing the distribution of social origins of members of the present socio-occupational groups. The socio-occupational categories used to regroup occupations were essentially the same as the ones used in contemporary west European and American mobility surveys, that is to say managers and professionals; lower level clerical workers; self-employed artisans and merchants; skilled manual workers; semi-skilled workers; unskilled workers; and peasants and agricultural workers. The cross-tabulations of social origin, first and present occupation, education, and so on were analysed by the usual outflow and inflow mobility rates and by log linear analysis. The main conclusions from these analyses might be summarized in the following way.

First, the growth of total intergenerational mobility, and the relatively high level of total mobility in the post-war decades, have been primarily due to the rapid structural changes in Hungarian society which followed industrialization. The egalitarian ideology of socialism has had much less influence on social mobility. Thus the thesis earlier formulated by Ossowski (1957) seems to be completely confirmed.

Second, almost half of the total mobility consists of the outflow of peasants' sons and daughters into other strata, most of all into the manual strata. Third, although the inflow from the manual strata into the non-manual strata has been important, the opposite flow, that is the loss of status of the sons and daughters of non-manual fathers, especially of managerial and professional fathers, has been no higher than in the Western capitalist societies.

Fourth, the degree of openness of Hungarian society in the post-war decades, measured in terms of relative mobility chances, has been similar to the openness of west European societies, in other words, that 'socialism has made no important difference'.

Thus the overall patterns of social mobility in the socialist Hungarian society have not been very different from those found in Western capitalist societies. Actually, the socialist transformation in Hungary may have resulted in making social mobility in Hungary more similar to that of advanced capitalist societies than it was in the inter-war period, when many features of the feudal society were still present and the market economy had not fully developed.

However, these conclusions drawn from survey data were so much at odds with the common beliefs held in Hungary that there had been large-scale downward mobility—usually referred to as the process of becoming 'déclassé'—that during the first analysis of the survey data of 1962–4 I already tried to examine the occupational life histories as recorded in the individual questionnaires more closely (Andorka 1968). I found that people of non-manual origin had very often experienced 'counter-mobility' (Girod 1971): that is, after an initial loss of status relative to their fathers, or a phase of downward mobility in mid-career, they more often than not had returned to their stratum of origin. When comparing directly the social position of the interviewed person at the time of the survey and the social position of his or her father, these phases of temporary loss of status were obviously obscured. Thus I concluded that the investigation of complete life histories would be necessary in order to understand the full process of social mobility. However, in spite of several attempts (Andorka 1980, 1982, 1983), I never really succeeded.[2]

More recently, some younger sociologists have criticized the interpretation I gave of the social mobility survey data (Örkény 1990; Harcsa 1990). They have emphasized that during the period of the 'socialist transition'—the Stalinist years from 1945 to 1956—not only the Hungarian bourgeoisie, but also the Hungarian professional class was essentially destroyed by political means and a completely new social élite was created, whose core feature was political reliability (Kovács and Örkény 1986).

Others questioned the idea that the outflow from the peasantry into the working class, which was central to the overall trend of economic and social mobility, could be interpreted as a type of upward social mobility. It was suggested that, on the contrary, those peasants who became workers experienced this mobility as a loss of status (Simó 1984).

More generally it has been suggested that social mobility processes in socialist societies were essentially different from mobility processes in capitalist societies. In socialist societies mobility was 'forced' by political factors, while in capitalist societies it was the outcome of spontaneous processes, and regulated by the impersonal mechanisms of the market (Harcsa 1990).

In this chapter, family histories will be used to clarify these issues, which could not be answered through analyses of survey data. What happened to the descendants of the families which had a privileged position in pre-war Hungary? How did the descendants of the rich peasants branded as 'kulaks' fare after the collectivization of agriculture? Was all social mobility really 'forced' by political factors and actions, or—alternatively—did the typical processes of social mobility in other industrializing societies also operate in Hungary?

## FAMILY HISTORIES AS SOURCES FOR MOBILITY

As mentioned above, the three social mobility surveys contained the complete occupational, educational, and residential life histories of the interviewees. These were collected through standardized questionnaires. But despite my efforts even this detailed data proved unfit for clarifying the issues at stake.

Hence I have tried another approach, which had been successfully tried out by Daniel Bertaux with his students (Bertaux 1981). Basically this method consists in collecting a sufficient number of family histories, with a 'depth' of three generations and a 'width' given by the extension of the case study to collaterals (Bertaux 1995). Each case study brings with it a wealth of information about mobility processes at the micro-level; the number and variety of case studies makes for the possibility of developing hypotheses about social processes.

While teaching sociology at the University of Economic Sciences in Budapest since 1983, I took to asking the students of the course on 'Social structure and mobility', which serves as an introduction to specialization in sociology, to write the social mobility history of one family: they usually chose their own. The protocol was that they should start from a given person (usually themselves), move back to his or her four grandparents, and describe the life histories of all the descendants of these two pairs of grandparents (Bertaux 1995). It was suggested that on the one hand they should try to relate the individual life histories to the immense economic, political, and social changes and historical events of Hungary; while on the other hand they should try to explain the subjective and active side of observed trajectories, the situational and motivational contexts of changes of status, and how mobility was experienced by individuals and their families. The students showed great enthusiasm in working on these case studies.

Close to two hundred family histories were eventually collected in this way. As a sample it cannot be said to be representative of the whole population, since in almost all cases at least one of the grandchildren is a professional—a student of our university. They might be said to represent the social mobility experience of the families of origin of present young professionals; but the social milieux they cover are larger than this specific group.

From the whole set collected, I have selected three case histories for the purpose of this paper. They represent three types.

First, the *Tiller family* belonged to the traditional pre-war Hungarian professional stratum, and have suffered serious set-backs and tragedies since the late 1930s.

Secondly, the *Smith family* originates from the prosperous peasantry, were branded as 'kulaks' in the Stalinist period, and suffered repression; but the lineage achieved an important 'counter-mobility' in the second generation and upward mobility of some of the third generation.

Thirdly, the *Chester family* represents the type of 'ordinary' mobility, which was undisturbed by historical adversities or political change.

In order to include an example of a family belonging to the bottom of the present social hierarchy, I supplemented these three case histories by a fourth which has been collected by a researcher. In this fourth family the grandfather was an agricultural worker who had only a very small farm before 1945, and most of his descendants are workers or at best skilled workers. This is the *Hawk Family*, representing the mobility, or rather the destiny, of the most unprivileged section of Hungarian society.

I have changed both family and personal names. All the four case histories are presented in the form of 'social genealogies' (Bertaux 1995), as graphs showing the kinship relations and, for each person, his or her name, year of birth (and possibly death), years of education, and socio-occupational position of the person at the time of the case study (between 1986 and 1990).[3] Birth and death dates, and also years of education, are lacking for some spouses originating from other families.

The number of years of education relate to the following types of schooling. Six years indicates complete primary schooling before 1948 and eight years after 1948. Eleven years represents eight years in primary school and three years in a skilled workers' school; twelve years, primary school plus four years of secondary school. Sixteen years signifies a higher educational diploma.

In the following description of the life histories of the members of the four families, I will usually deal first with the paternal family, beginning with the grandparents, followed by the members of the parental generation, and ending with the person who wrote the essay, and his or her siblings and cousins. Next I shall treat the three generations of the maternal family in the same way.

## 'DÉCLASSÉS' PROFESSIONALS AND COUNTER-MOBILITY: THE TILLER FAMILY

The direct comparison of the social origins, educational levels, and main occupations of the members of the three generations of the Tiller family yields an image of stable status maintenance in the professional stratum in the mother's lineage, and of one-step upward mobility from the clerical to the professional stratum on the father's side. However, the case histories show that *all* the members of the first and second generations in both lineages suffered serious status losses in mid-career as a result of political events.

Both of Ferenc Tiller's grandparents on his father's side, *András* and *Csilla*, were born in the 1890s into the Jewish petty bourgeoisie. András finished the gymnasium with excellent marks and began to work around 1912 as an employee in the Credit Bank. He enlisted in 1914 and fought the whole First World War, ending it with the rank of reserve captain. After the war he continued his career in the Credit Bank, rising by the late 1930s to the position of head of the savings deposit division. His political attitudes were characterized by cautious conformity to the very conservative ruling ideology of inter-war Hungary.

After the occupation of Hungary by the German Nazi armed forces in 1944, he was suddenly dismissed from the bank as a Jew and had to work as a manual labourer. Within a few months he was actually arrested and deported to a German concentration camp near Hamburg, where he died from wounds caused by torture by the SS prison guards. He was 50 years old.

*Csilla* also worked in the Credit Bank (where she met András) and later in another bank. After the birth of their son Bela in 1926,

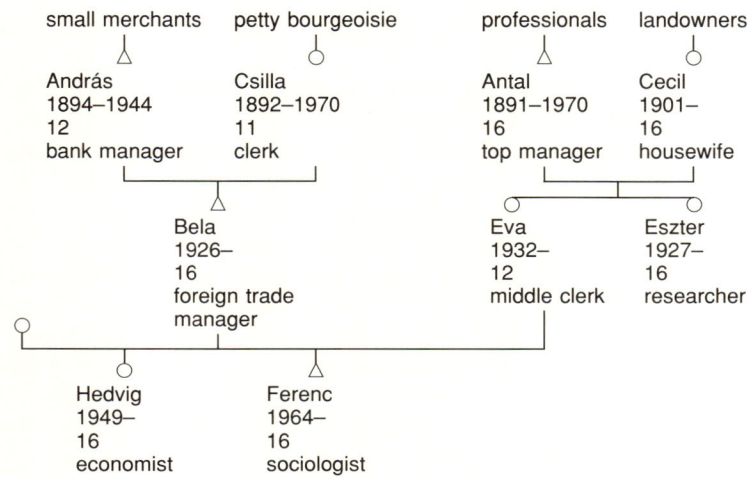

FIG. 9.1. *Social Genealogy of the Tiller Family*

their only child, she became a full-time housewife. Her family belonged to the left wing of the Social Democratic Party: one of her brothers worked in the underground with Janos Kadar, the future secretary of the Socialist Workers' Party, the Hungarian Communist Party.

In 1944 she was forced as a Jew to move to the ghetto of Budapest, but was not deported. Even now it is not completely clear why the ghetto of Budapest was spared complete annihilation. Csilla survived there. She joined the Communist Party in 1946. After the war for some time she made her living by baking and selling cakes, a housewife's skill, raising her son alone.

This only son of András and Csilla, *Bela*, was awarded his gymnasium diploma in 1944. He was already fluent in English and German, which indicates that he had received an excellent education. He was immediately drafted, and for some months served in an army unit doing forced labour: Jews and political suspects were put into these units, where they did not carry arms and were sometimes sent to the front itself where they were exposed to severe risk of death. From October 1944, during the worst months of Fascist terror, he went into hiding, changing places frequently and carrying false identity papers. In this way he escaped death in the holocaust.

He was the only one of the eleven male members of his extended family to survive.

After 1945 he worked for some months as a manual worker, and then took on lower-level clerical work at the Credit Bank. Soon however, thanks to his knowledge of languages, he was able to rise rapidly in the bank. His career was not seriously hindered by the fact that after having entered the Communist Party in 1947, he was expelled from it in 1948 for his 'bourgeois origins'. In 1957 he changed to a job in the state-owned foreign trade company, which he was able to keep despite a 'political inspection' of his past. In the 1970s he was the founder and first director in London of a Hungarian-English joint foreign-trade company. In parallel he got a university degree from the Marxist-Leninist Evening University. At the end of his career he was teaching at several higher education foreign trade schools.

Bela married three times. *Hedvig*, his daughter from his first marriage in 1949, has had a smoother life course. She got a higher education diploma in the foreign trade school, and speaks three languages. She joined the Communist Party and became a professional (cadre) in a foreign trade state company. She married, had a child, and soon divorced.

From his second marriage, to Eva, a middle-level clerk, Bela had a son, *Ferenc*, born in 1964. He went to school in London for some years while his father was employed there, and so speaks English perfectly. He graduated in sociology at the University of Economic Sciences in Budapest. He wrote his dissertation on the deportations of 'bourgeois' families from Budapest to villages in 1951–3, and then co-authored a book on the history of deportations during the Stalinist period, based on recollections of formerly deported persons. In 1989 he went on to post-graduate research in New York.

We now turn to the family of Eva, the second wife of Bela.

Eva's parents originated from even higher status Jewish families than Bela's. Eva's father *Antal* was born in 1891 into a high status and wealthy professional family of Jewish background. His parents sent him to a Lutheran primary school, and then to a Lutheran gymnasium, both of which were élite educational institutions. He graduated in both law and humanities at the University of Budapest, and went on to study at the Handelshochschule in Leipzig, and then at Oxford. He was fluent in English, French, German, Italian, Latin, and ancient Greek.

He participated in the First World War, eventually reaching the rank of hussar captain. (The prestige of hussar officers was higher than that of any other officers for the Hungarian gentry and middle classes). In 1918 he converted to Christianity, which was a sign of his wish to become fully assimilated to Hungarian society.

From 1920 to 1944 he achieved a remarkable career, rising to the position of top manager of a large agro-business company. His lifestyle followed the ideal model of a 'world citizen': a rich social life, travels in foreign countries, and hunting—a typical hobby of the Hungarian ruling class. He was a member of the Social Democratic Party. In 1925 he married Cecil, daughter of a landowner's family. They had two daughters: Eszter, born in 1927; and Eva, born in 1932, the future wife of Bela.

Antal's wife *Cecil*, born in 1901, came from an even higher status family than her husband. Her father was one of the most prestigious and wealthiest inhabitants of Zenta, a town which at present belongs to the Serbian Voïvodina. He owned a very large estate and was director of Zenta's bank. The family had a Jewish cultural background. Cecil was given the best education available; she learned German, French, and English, and graduated from the Musical Academy of Budapest as a pianist (she never performed as a professional pianist, but used to play the piano at home).

At the age of 18 she became the fiancée of a descendant of the Serbian royal family, but her father was opposed to the marriage. She later married Antal, who was ten years older. Her family gave the couple a substantial dowry, which was invested in building an apartment house—to be rented—and a villa in Budapest for their private use.

During the German occupation in 1944–5, Cecil went into hiding with false identity papers with her younger daughter Eva in Budapest itself. In 1945 the Gestapo arrested her husband Antal, not for being a Jew but because of his political activities. He was deported to Mauthausen concentration camp, where most of the Hungarian political prisoners were sent. He survived.

After the war he worked again for some years in agro-business. But after the collectivization of the trading company, he got into conflict with the new director nominated by the government (the former occupation of this 'worker' director was a shoemaker). Antal left the company and made a living as a translator.

In 1951, at the age of 60, he and his family were deported to the village of Mezobereny in eastern Hungary. This meant that he was not permitted to leave the town without permission from the police. They lived in the house of a German 'kulak' peasant, whose 'punishment' was being forced to accept deported families into his house. A former state secretary, a former captain of the gendarmerie, and the owner of the most elegant brothel of Budapest, the famous Madame Frida, all lived with them in the same house. Antal was able to get translation jobs from his friends under a false name, typing on his hidden typewriter (deported persons were not permitted to have one).

In 1954 deported families were authorized to look for accommodation elsewhere. As their own former house had been given by the municipality of Budapest to other families, Antal's family were unable to return to Budapest until 1956. They came first as lodgers, later on as co-tenants.

In Budapest Antal continued to work as a freelance translator, obtaining very important commissions and employing two typists. But only after his death in 1970 was his wife able to rent an independent dwelling. In spite of all the troubles she had experienced in her life, Cecil, who was still alive at the time of the case study in 1990, 'took everything in a quiet and peaceful spirit'.

Antal and Cecil had had two daughters. The elder of them, *Eszter*, was deported in 1944 to Ravensbrück concentration camp. She was only 16. She survived, and after the war studied at the University of Agronomy in Budapest. She then got a job as a researcher in an academic institute.

This status prevented her from being deported to Mezobereny in 1951 with her parents and sister. However, for several months she was sent as an agricultural worker to work in the fields of the research institute. But she soon married a colleague at the institute, and thus regained her former job there. She remained in it up to retirement. She is without a child.

Her younger sister *Eva* survived the period of German occupation by hiding with her mother in Budapest. After having finished secondary school she was unable to obtain a place as a student at the University of Budapest in the Faculty of Humanities, because her 'bourgeois' origin was considered to be hostile to the socialist regime. After working for one year as a clerical employee, she was deported in 1951–4 with her father and mother to Mezobereny, where she worked as an agricultural day-labourer. When they were allowed back to Budapest she returned to clerical work, and stayed in it all her active life, attaining relatively high-level positions due above all to her knowledge of German, French, and English. Her only child was Ferenc.

These life histories from Ferenc's family do help us to understand the apparent contradiction between the empirical results of my social mobility surveys, and current opinion concerning the fate of the Hungarian bourgeoisie and professional class during and after the war. These social strata indeed suffered very hard and sometimes tragic experiences under two successive totalitarian regimes. This vindicates the widespread feeling of loss of status and becoming 'déclassés'. Nevertheless, in this case history all surviving members of this family, after a drastic loss of status, were able—mostly thanks to their knowledge of foreign languages and other cultural resources—to come back to their class of origin at the top of Hungarian society. Hedvig and Ferenc, the only two members of the third generation, are firmly established high professionals; they belong to the intellectual élite of Hungary. If such a pattern of counter-mobility (Girod 1971; Bertaux 1977) corresponds to a social logic, as seems plausible, it could explain why, in the cross-sectional data of the social mobility surveys of the 1960s, 1970s, and 1980s, relatively few downwardly mobile sons and daughters of the class of managers and professionals were found.

Notice, however, that the four grandparents in this case history have had only two grandchildren. This is not a unique case; and it points to the demographic decline of these strata. Their children had themselves few children, probably because of their parents' dramatic life experiences. It may be added that the members of such high strata were probably over-represented among those who were killed during and after the Second World War, and also among those who emigrated from Hungary to the West in the same period.[4]

It can be inferred from statistical data as well as from case histories that the demographic reproduction of the bourgeoisie and of the professional class has been far below the level of simple replacement. This partly explains why, in 1973, only 21 per cent of the male managers and professionals and 24 per cent of the female managers and professionals were of managerial, professional, and other high-status origin. Indeed the majority of persons belonging to this rapidly growing stratum were of lower origin. So while it is justifiable to speak of a 'new' managerial and professional class, it has not developed as a consequence of the loss of status of the 'old' bourgeoisie and professional class, as is usually assumed. It is rather as a consequence of structural factors of mobility: the low fertility of the old ruling classes, whose descendants may have achieved high status without filling in all the available positions; the high rate of emigration of these descendants; and of course the growth of the managerial and professional stratum itself.

## KULAKS: THE SMITH FAMILY

The paternal grandparents of the Smith family, Albert and Csilla both born in 1892, had been peasants with a relatively large farm who were declared 'kulaks' by the local authorities in the Stalinist period. Nevertheless their descendants followed the usual stepwise mobility path of industrializing societies: from peasants to unskilled, semi-skilled, and later skilled workers, some women becoming clerical workers and in the third generation professionals. Their pattern of mobility does not differ essentially from that of the descendants of the maternal grandparents, Antal and Cecil, who had a medium-sized holding and were classified as 'middle peasants'. The analysis of life histories demonstrates that the offspring of the kulak family achieved a social status similar to that of the offspring of the middle peasants, but with greater efforts.

*Albert* and *Csilla* were born in Besenyotelek, a medium-sized village in the Great Plain area (Puszta) in eastern Hungary. The eastern regions and the Great Plain were and still are less developed areas than western Hungary and Transdanubia. Both of their parents had farms of about 80–120 hectares, and therefore were considered locally as rich peasants. Their way of life and their aspirations were, however, typical of peasant culture and aspirations: the supreme norm was hard work on the farm, and the main goal was to enlarge the landed property, which inevitably tended to diminish in size from generation to generation as a result of the partition of land among the relatively large number of children. Albert's and also Csilla's siblings all remained peasants, with the exception of one of Csilla's brothers who went through to higher

Social Mobility in Hungary

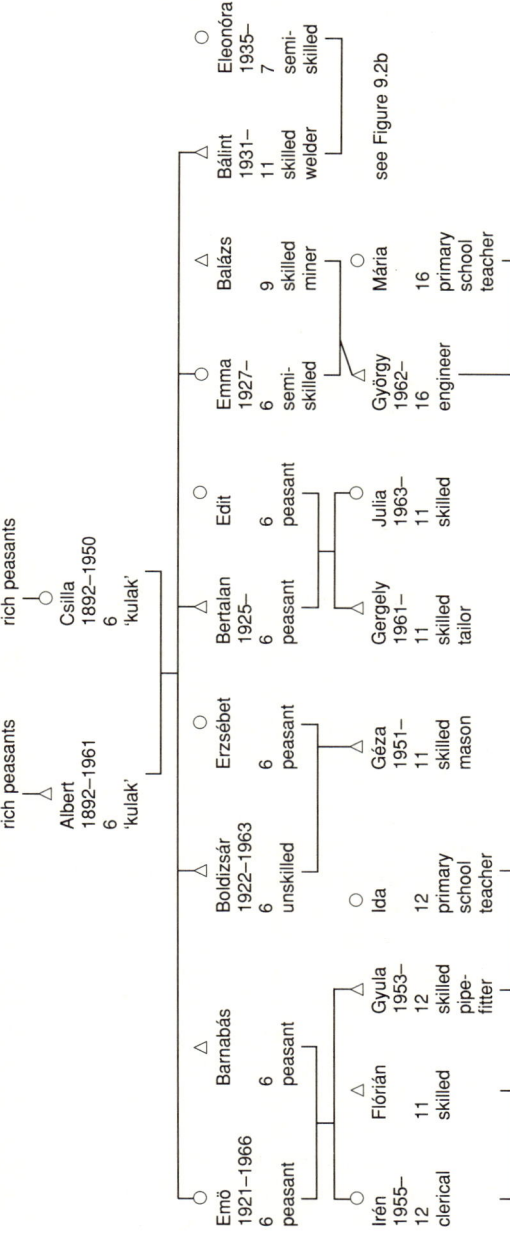

FIG. 9.2a. *Social Genealogy of the Smith Family. Because of the large number of descendants the genealogy of Smith family is illustrated in two separate parts. Bálint and Eleonóra are included in both parts*

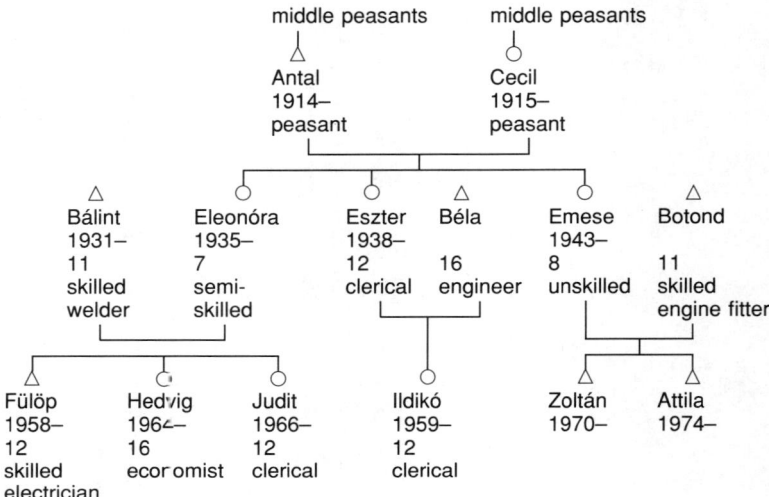

FIG. 9.2b. *Social Genealogy of the Smith Family*

education, obtained a university diploma in law, and became a judge.

Albert and Csilla married after the First World War. They had five children, born between 1921 and 1931. This high fertility is in itself an indicator of their traditional mentality, for peasants living in more advanced areas of Hungary usually had no more than two or three children in the 1920s. The four older children reached the same level of education as their parents, that is six years of primary schooling; the daughters stayed at school for two more 'supplementary' years, but this did not result in a higher level of education.

After the Communist takeover in 1947, when they were both in their mid-fifties, they were immediately declared as kulaks by the local state and party authorities. Kulak families were heavily taxed and harrassed by various other methods, in order either to force them to give up farming, or at least to give over to the state authorities their 'surplus' production—which sometimes included the food needed for the bare survival of the family. The aim of this policy, besides extracting as much agricultural produce as possible for the cities, was to convince poorer peasants that it was preferable to enter the agricultural co-operatives (kolkhozes). During these years the farm of Albert was reduced to seventeen hectares; that was still enough to be classified as a kulak. Albert and Csilla's children persuaded them to apply for entry to the co-operative. Their application was however rejected on the pretext that kulaks should not corrupt the socialist co-operatives. Csilla died in 1950, so that Albert now had to farm his land alone. All his children fled from agriculture; they would return only in the peak summer periods of agricultural work to help their ageing father. In 1959, in the second Kadarist wave of collectivization, his application to join the collective farm was finally accepted; he became a co-operative peasant, but died within two years.

One of their five children, the eldest, *Emö*, remained essentially a housewife all her life, tilling the small household plot and garden around the house, while her husband *Barnabás* worked as a peasant for the agricultural co-operative. They had two children.

*Boldizsár* participated in the Second World War and ended as prisoner-of-war; he was not liberated until 1947. After having returned home he went to work as an unskilled worker in a metallurgical plant in a distant town. His wife *Erzsébet* was a housewife all her life, helping in the small household plot around the house. They had one child.

*Bertalan* began as a self-employed farmer. He was 25 in 1950, during the first wave of collectivization. He left agriculture rather than join the collective farm, and moved as a day-labourer into the same distant metallurgical plant where his brother Boldizsár worked. In 1959, however, he came back to his native village and joined the agricultural co-operative. He married *Edit*, a co-operative peasant.

*Emma* married in 1959 a skilled coal miner, *Balazs*. She remained a housewife for fourteen years after her marriage, and then took up semi-skilled work. Both are at present invalid pensioners: early sick retirement is very frequent among miners. Nevertheless Emma's family achieved more upward mobility than those of her three older brothers and sisters. Their two children have become professionals, while the children of Emma's elder siblings, five in all, became either skilled workers or took up lower level clerical jobs.

The youngest sibling, *Bálint*, born in 1931, after six years at primary school was sent by his parents to a secondary school (gymnasium) in a distant town, where he lived in a students' hostel. However, during the campaigns against kulaks in 1949, he was excluded from the gymnasium as the son of kulaks, just as he was about to complete his diploma. The red 'K' for 'kulak' which was stamped on his cadre sheet was to prove a serious handicap for him in subsequent years. He needed to earn as much money as he could because his parents were facing very great financial difficulties during the worst years of the persecution of the kulaks between 1949 and 1953. So Bálint tried many different jobs: he worked as farm worker, as an unskilled worker in a metallurgical plant, as a truck guard, and so on. In each job he tried to learn new techniques, and this was how, without ever attending courses in worker's schools, he taught himself three manual skills; those of fireman, engine fitter, and welder. After having finished his military service he worked with all these three skills, but also sometimes as a semi-skilled and unskilled worker when these latter jobs offered better wages.

In 1956, in the weeks following the Budapest uprising, as the western frontier was practically open, Bálint pondered the possibility of emigrating in order to escape the handicap of his kulak origin; but he finally decided to stay and to marry Eleonóra, a girl from his native village. After marriage, his first aim in life remained to earn as much money as possible, in order to achieve his dream: to have a separate house for his family. He actually built the family house himself, with the help of family members, as is usual in Hungarian villages. He finished his career as a welder in a metallurgical plant in a nearby village.

The frustration of having been excluded from the gymnasium because of his kulak origin shadowed Bálint all his life. His main ambition was to make it possible for his children to study, and possibly to live during schooling in a town, in a students' hostel.

His wife *Eleonóra* had experienced similar frustrations during her own schooling: in consequence of an illness she had to repeat the seventh year of primary school, and her parents did not have the financial resources to send her to finish the eighth year. This prevented her later on from being promoted to the post of foreman. Therefore she spent all her active life in unskilled and semi-skilled jobs. She was determined to help her own children to complete their secondary schooling.

Let us summarize the histories of Albert and Csilla's children. Their older children did not achieve the slightest upward mobility; on the contrary, they themselves and their spouses remained collective peasants or unskilled workers all their life, thus in definitely *lower* statuses than their parents. As for their last two children, who were younger at the time of the persecution of the kulaks and collectivization of the land, they were able to do slightly better: Emma became a semi-skilled worker and married a skilled worker, a miner; Bálint learned several manual skills and married a semi-skilled wife.

These five children of Albert and Csilla had ten children born between 1953 and 1966. All of them achieved significant upward mobility when compared with their parents. Two girls and one boy became professionals, two girls became clerical employees, and four boys and one girl became skilled workers. Thus none of the ten grandchildren has remained a peasant, semi- or unskilled worker. The spouses of these grandchildren belong to the same social stratum as their partners: the wife of György (an engineer) is a schoolteacher, the wife of Gyula (a skilled worker) is a clerk, and the husband of Irén (a clerk) is a skilled worker.

If we examine the different fates of these ten grandchildren in more detail, we can observe how closely they reflect and indeed develop small distinctions between the statuses of their parents.

*Barnabás* and *Emö*, who were themselves peasants, had two children. Their daughter Irén completed the gymnasium and is a clerk. Before marriage her husband Flórián worked at sea on a Hungarian ship; later he got a job as skilled worker in a nearby town, to which the couple presently intend to move. Irén's brother Gyula is a skilled pipefitter, his wife Ida is a primary school teacher with higher education.

*Boldizsár*, an unskilled worker and his wife *Erzsébet*, a peasant, have had only one son, Géza, who became a skilled mason.

*Bertalan* and *Edit*, who were both peasants, have had two children. Gergely is a tailor and Julia also a skilled worker.

*Emma*, a semi-skilled worker and her husband *Balázs*, a skilled worker, have had only one son, György. He studied in a specialized agricultural secondary school, then in an agricultural higher educational institution, and became an agricultural engineer. His wife Maria is a primary school teacher.

*Bálint* and *Eleonora*, who were so frustrated for not being able to study more, succeeded in realizing their ambitions for the education of their children. All their children have studied in Budapest and lived during their secondary school education in student hostels, thus far removed from the backward village where the family home was located. Fülöp studied in a special secondary school for the power industry. After completing this he took three courses giving him specializations in the same field. He works in Budapest as an élite skilled worker. Hedvig studied in a specialized secondary school for economics and went on to study at the University of Economic Sciences in Budapest. During her university years she lived in a college of the university, which was famous for providing, in addition to lodging, special courses. The students of this college formed the university's avant-garde in contemporary economics and social science. She learned sociology as a second specialization and is at present employed in the Institute of Management Research of the university. It is she who was the author of this case study. As for Judit, she studied in a specialized secondary school for the postal service and has began to work at the central post office in Budapest.

Let us now examine, much more briefly, the case history of Eleonóra's own family of origin. They were also peasants, but less prosperous than Albert and Csilla. Hence their fate, as well as those of their children, provides an interesting point of comparison with the previous kulak family.

The parents of Eleonóra, *Antal* and *Cecil*, were born in 1914–15 in Zagyvaszanto, a village near to Besenyotelek; they were however more than twenty years younger than Albert and Csilla. They farmed their land of seven hectares, a medium-sized peasant farm, undisturbed until 1961, when in the second wave of collectivization they had to join the local agricultural co-operative. Since they were quite poor, Antal sometimes took up some supplementary earning activities, such as transporting goods with his horse-drawn cart, or inn-keeping.

They had three daughters, born from 1935 to 1943. We have already met the eldest child, *Eleonóra*, who could not finish primary school because of illness and her parents' poverty. The second daughter, *Eszter*, after having finished primary school, first attempted to complete a course of typewriting and shorthandwriting, but left it after half a year in order to earn money. She worked as an unskilled worker in a nearby cement plant until she married. Through this marriage she indeed achieved an important social step upward, for her husband, *Béla* came from a professional family, and was himself an engineering surveyor. After the birth of their daughter, Eszter completed secondary studies, and then a typewriting and shorthandwriting school; and she became a clerk.

The third daughter, *Emese* worked seasonally as an unskilled worker in a nearby canning factory till her marriage. She married *Botond*, who was a skilled welder and engine fitter. After the birth of her two children in 1970 and 1974, Emese took up a job as cleaner in the local industrial co-operative.

Antal and Cecil have had six grandchildren. Four of them were already at work in 1989, when the case history was written. The three children of Eleonóra and Bálint have already been discussed above with the family of Bálint: one is a skilled worker, one clerical, and the third, Hedvig, author of this case history, is an economist. Two granddaughters are clerks, and a grandson is a skilled worker. Ildikó, the only daughter of Eszter and Béla, first studied in a school of commerce; she then took up work as a saleswoman. Later she studied at an evening gymnasium. Having obtained the gymnasium diploma she has become a cashier. Thus by comparison with both their parents and their grandparents, the third generation is moving upward.

Thus the mobility history of the two branches of the family, the kulaks and the middle peasants, end up with similar outcomes. This leads us to wonder whether the socialist system, the anti-kulak policy and the collectivization of agriculture made any difference in the long run for the destinies of these two families.

The fate of Antal and Cecil and of their descendants seems in fact very representative of hundreds of thousands of other peasant families from similar backgrounds. The older generation remained peasants all their lives. The second generation, which grew up in the 1940s, could not study further because of their parents' shortage of funds; they remained in the village but moved into industrial jobs or menial white-collar jobs. The third generation had the chance of access to a wider range of jobs, depending on their educational achievements. Living in a village was obviously a handicap, as opportunities for higher education were not at hand. This may explain why Ildikó, the daughter of the engineer, did not get higher education: one may suppose that being the only child, her parents were reluctant to send her away to the town; while by contrast Hedvig, as one of three children, was able to achieve entry to university education by going to a boarding-school in Budapest.

Thus structural factors had a dominant influence on the destinies of the descendants of these two peasant families. The industrialization of Hungary, the decline of the agricultural population, the growth of both the working class and also of non-manual strata had a much more important influence than political events and state policies. It ought to be remarked that the younger the given person was, the better mobility career he or she achieved, as those who were born later entered adult life in a period when the country was economically more developed.

While the economic situation of each generation is certainly better than that of the previous one, it is much less clear that this improvement can be characterized as upward *social* mobility. There is occupational change, from agriculture to industry and on to services; but this change is part of the general trends of change in the social and economic structure. Such occupational change is thus better understood as 'mobilité dans le sens principal', as I put in an earlier paper (Andorka 1972): as 'situs' mobility engendered by economic change, which is a well-known characteristic of developing economies. It would better be referred to as structurally induced situs or economic mobility, rather than as social mobility.

If the collectivization of land had not taken place, the chances are that the destinies of the children and grandchildren of Antal and Cecil, the middle peasants, would have been quite similar. One son might have remained a peasant but, as the comparison with Western countries clearly shows, the others would have entered industrial or clerical white-collar jobs anyway.

On the other hand, the destinies of the children and grandchildren of Albert and Csilla, the kulaks, would probably have been quite different without the collectivization of the land and the establishment of an overall socialist system in Hungary. Again by comparison with, for example, France, where the class of rich peasants went its historical way undisturbed, one could have expected that one or two children of this family would have remained farmers—one through inheritance of the farm, another through marriage with a farmer having roughly the same level of property—and would have passed on their farm to one of their own children. Another child could have become a shopkeeper or a worker and the youngest one would have completed general secondary education and moved into the urban middle class, thus combining both occupational and genuine social mobility.

By contrast, Albert, Csilla, and their own children experienced initial expulsion from the family farm as a very painful experience. Not only did the loss of family property represent a considerable lowering of their objective life chances, which were connected not with cultural resource but with the shares they had in this economic capital; but the youngest son, who had clearly a project of mobility through studying and the capacity to fulfil it, saw his project crushed by the red 'K' stamped on his file.

All the five children had to struggle hard for several decades just to make a living; and if, at the end of their lives, they were better off than their own parents, this was due to the overall process of development which would have taken place anyway, whether through capitalism or through state socialism. So it may be said that for the members of this family of rich but hard-working farmers, collectivization did make a real difference in pushing their life chances downward, making them equivalent to those of ordinary peasants.

Recently Ivan Szelényi (1988) has contended on the basis of the analysis of the data of the 1983 household income and social mobility survey that the descendants of rich peasants were more successful in adapting to the market conditions created by the market-oriented reforms in the 1970s and 1980s.

Two other cultural factors ought to be mentioned. The remarkable willingness of Hungarian self-employed peasants—both rich peasants and smallholders—to work all the hours of daylight and to exploit themselves for the sake of their own and their childrens' betterment certainly played an important role in their ability to survive the hardships of the first twenty years of the socialist system, and in the successful reconstruction of the life chances of the members of the third generation.

At the same time a very strong ambition to assure upward mobility of the offspring was present in the culture of these peasant families. As Hedvig, the author of the family stated, the adults belonging to the second generation all used to suggest to their children that they should study in order to avoid becoming a peasant who has to work 'from daybreak to nightfall'. They also wanted to spare their children very heavy manual work. For them, 'learned persons' had a much higher prestige than the 'unlearned'.

## UPWARD THROUGH EDUCATION: THE CHESTER FAMILY

The two previous family histories appear to have been both strongly influenced by the political history of Hungary. Was it the same for all Hungarian families? It is obviously not possible to answer this question on the basis of only a few histories. But the history of the Chester family is an example of one whose mobility over three generations seems essentially to have been left untouched by political events.

Three of the four grandparents were born in the Tolna country in Southern Transdanubia, which—together with the neighbouring country of Baranya—used to be called the 'Schwäbische Türkei', referring to the large number of Germans who had immigrated there after the liberation of the region from Ottoman rule at the end of the 17th century. Although it is a relatively backward region, the German element of its culture gives a special west European flavour to the mentality of its population which consists, in addition to the autochthonous ethnically Hungarians, and the ethnically German group of Hungarians, of Hungarians who immigrated from Slovakia and Bukovina after the Second World War, when these regions were separated from Hungary, and of Southern Slavs. The mentality in this region might be characterized by the high value given to education and frugality on the one hand, and by the ability to adapt to existing conditions in order to avoid acute conflicts with the political regimes on the other hand.

*András*, the paternal grandfather of Géza (who recorded this case history) was born in 1910 as the fifth and last child of a poor family of agricultural 'cseléd'. These were farm workers who had neither land nor house; they would engage in year-long wage-work contracts on the large estates which provided them with temporary housing (usually outside the village). The cseléd families were at the bottom of the social hierarchy, because they were completely dependent on the landowners. Even the seasonal farm workers who had a house in a village were much more independent than the cseléd, although they were as poor.

After primary school, András was placed as an apprentice with a carpenter of a nearby village. In 1929, at the age of 19 he became a self-employed carpenter; and he remained in this occupation till 1948, when in consequence of the restrictions placed on all self-employed occupations he gave up his workshop. As a consequence of his acute shortsightedness he had not been called up for the army during the Second World War. From 1946 to 1948 he had been a member of the Social Democratic Party, but did not join the Communist Party which resulted from the unification of the communist and social democratic parties. From 1948 on, he was employed by the municipality as a foreman in the local distillery, but in 1960 he returned to the occupation of carpenter on the local state farm, a job which he kept until retirement.

His wife *Csilla* was born as one of the six children of a self-employed cartwright. One of her brothers was an army officer in the pre-war regime; he remained in the army also under the post-war regime. However, he died early, so that his privileged position had no influence on the careers of his nephews. Csilla remained a housewife throughout her life.

Of the two sons of András and Csilla, *Balázs*, who was born in 1931, completed a gymnasium schooling and began work as a semi-skilled carpenter. He then for some time was a clerical employee of the village municipality; and afterwards came back to work as carpenter on the same state farm as his father. Between 1964 and 1969, he attended courses at an institute for the building industry, which gave diplomas for lower level building engineers. He then became a building-site architect, thus winning the status of a professional.

His wife *Eszter* was born into a working-class family. Before her marriage she worked for some years as a semi-skilled worker. Later on, after a long period of caring for her two children, she became a clerical employee in the local state farm where her husband had worked earlier.

The second son of András, *Bálint*, who was born in 1933, completed school at the gymnasium and then began working as a shop assistant with a local shopkeeper. But then the shopkeeper was declared a kulak and lost his shop. Bálint went to Budapest to find a new place in commerce. But after working there for a short period, he was dismissed following a governmental decree demanding reductions in the number of workers in commerce. It was in 1951 and Bálint was 19. He was ordered to learn the skill of grinder, but for health reasons he could not stand it. He therefore returned to his native region and worked at a commercial job in a nearby town, and later in a village. His career seemed at a dead end. In 1952 his strong desire to learn brought him to start a special course which could give access to the medical universities; but he had to stop learning for lack of financial resources. In 1954 he was called

# Rudolf Andorka

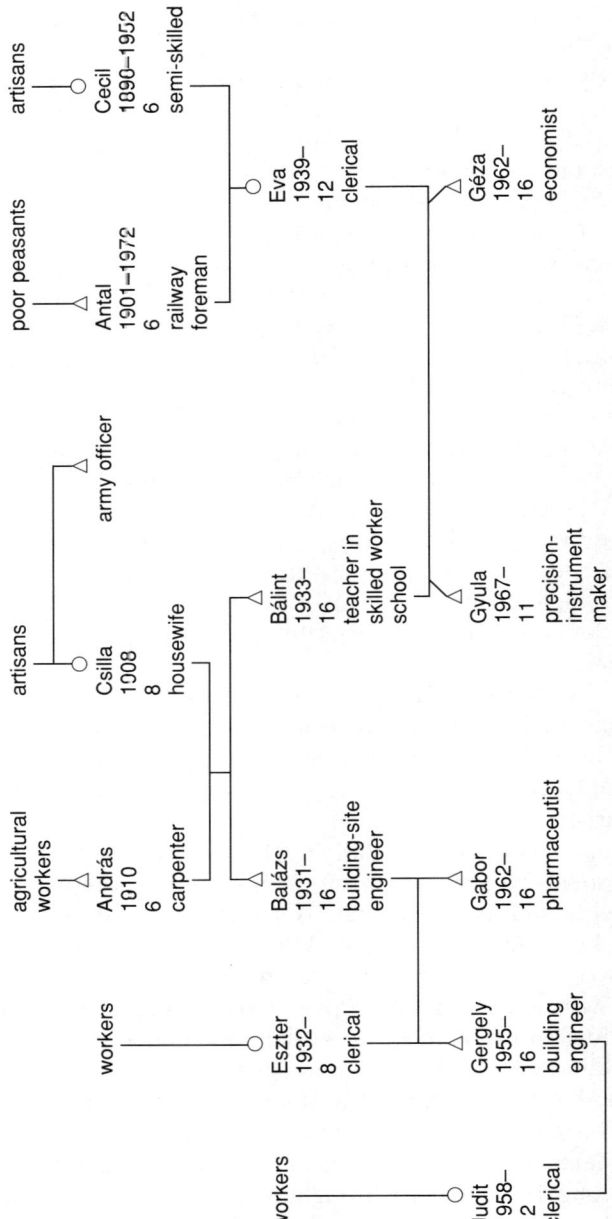

Fig. 9.3. *Social Genealogy of the Chester Family*

up to the army, but a year later he was discharged from the army when, in a period of international détente, the size of the army was somewhat reduced. This spared him being in the army during the revolution of 1956.

For some time he continued to work in state shops; but then in 1960 he became a clerical employee of a village council. And after his marriage with Eva, they migrated to a larger town. Here Bálint took up and completed a training course for teachers. He became a teacher in a school for skilled workers. In 1969–71 he returned once again to education, this time at a tertiary school, and got a diploma in chemistry. So at the age of 38 he became a high school teacher: at last a full professional.

Let us now focus on the parents of his wife Eva. She was the only child of Antal and Cecil.

*Antal*, like András, was born in the Tolna county, but into a German smallholder peasant family, as the third and youngest child. At an early age he decided not to remain a peasant. It was anyway the custom in German peasant families for the youngest sons to learn a craft. Antal worked from age 13 to 23 as a day-labourer. In 1924 he got a job with the Hungarian railway. It was a state-owned company which demanded a high level of skill and discipline from its workers, but provided them with secure employment and many other privileges. Antal began as a track worker, maintaining the stone bed of the railway lines; then moved to the positions of railway line inspector, railway point switch-worker, ticket office clerk in a small rural station, and lastly foreman. Each step forward necessitated the completion of the appropriate course in the company school.

In 1935, under pressure from the assimilation policy of the state-owned railway company, Antal changed his German family name to a Hungarian name. He married Cecil in 1938: he was 37, she was 42. In 1940 he got a job in a village near Budapest; because he was a railway worker, he was not called up for the army. After the war, a large part of the ethnically German population of Hungary was expelled from the country; but Antal, bearing now a Hungarian family name and living outside his native region—where everybody knew him as 'German'—was not expelled. Almost all his relatives living in the county of Tolna had to move to West Germany in 1946, but Antal continued to work undisturbed as a railway clerk in the same village near Budapest.

In 1947 Antal joined the Social Democratic Party, and after the fusion of the left parties he remained a member of the Communist Party, but did not attempt any party career.

His wife *Cecil* was born into a German shoemaker's family of nine children in a village near Budapest. Her first husband had died of tuberculosis; her first child had also died in infancy. Because she remarried to Antal in her forties, they had only one child, Eva, who was born in 1939.

*Eva* never learned German, the mother tongue of both her parents. After finishing primary school she first worked as a seamstress in a factory in the outskirts of Budapest. Later on, after having completed different courses, she became a wage accountant, a materials accountant, and eventually a cost calculator. Between 1975 and 1979 she went back to education at a specialized secondary school for economics and, having completed this, found a job as price computing expert. She married Bálint, the teacher whom we have already encountered.

Of the four in the family's younger generation, three have completed university courses and have become professionals.

*Gergely* studied at the Higher Learning School for Architecture in Pecs. (Higher Learning Schools are educational institutions which provide courses normally of four years, leading to a diploma which has an only slightly lower value than a university diploma.) He works as a building engineer. His wife Agnes, of working-class origin, works as a laboratory assistant in a hospital.

*Gabor* has completed a degree in pharmaceutics at the Medical University of Szeged. *Gyula* studied after primary school in a skilled workers' school and became a precision-instrument maker, which is an élite skill in Hungary. More recently he has been taking an evening course at a special secondary school for engineering, so he too might later study at a university.

*Géza* got a secondary school diploma in a specialized chemical industry school, continued to study for two years at the Technical University of Budapest and changed over to the University of Economic Sciences, where he studied sociology. He collected the data for this case history. After having completed his studies he got a job as teacher at the university.

It seems that the mobility history of the Chester family would have been essentially the same if there had been no revolution after

1945, and therefore no political interference in the processes of social mobility in Hungary.

Every one of the three generations has achieved some upward mobility when compared to the previous one. The two grandfathers, András and Antal, came from poor peasant or farm worker (csebéd) families and learned manual skills. The three members of the next generation all entered non-manual occupations. And three of the four grandchildren have become professionals, and there is a good chance that the fourth one will also make it.

The life histories of the Chester family indicate how important intragenerational and career mobility has been in the past decades in Hungary, and the great role played by education—especially in evening courses during the occupational career—in these mobility processes.

As Géza, the writer of the case history, put it, 'the great historical storms raged high above the family story, but fortunately they left it unaffected'. Both grandfathers avoided—partly by luck—being drafted into the army in the Second World War, where many members of their generation either perished or spent years as prisoners-of-war. Antal was especially fortunate in avoiding being expelled to Germany. The fathers, the two sons and the daughter, being either workers or lower clerical employees, were not exposed to political discrimination in the Stalinist years; the sons and daughter, being of 'working-class origin', avoided any disadvantageous treatment in the educational system.

One reason why the Chester family achieved a somewhat more successful mobility career than the Smith family, might be that the Chester family came from a region of Hungary which was already much more modernized in the inter-war period than the region where the Smith grandparents lived. This difference is suggested by the simple fact that both grandparental couples of the Chester family had only one or two children, in contrast to the three or five of the grandparental families of the Smith family.

More generally, in accounting for the gradual but uninterrupted upward mobility of the successive generations of the Chester family, the key factors are clearly structural changes. Industrialization and urbanization were crucial; and so was education. And within education, the role of retraining courses, perhaps enhanced through the presence of the socialist regime, deserves special notice.

## AT THE BOTTOM: THE HAWK FAMILY

In 1930, 21 per cent of the active earners in Hungary were landless farm workers; and another 15 per cent had a farm smaller than 2.85 hectares, which means that they had to hire themselves out as farm labourers to supplement the tiny income from their farm. These 36 per cent of the population were clearly its poorest part, located at the bottom of the social hierarchy. Through the case history of the Hawk family I would like to illustrate what happened to the families from this lowest class from the inter-war period onwards.[5]

The Hawk family lived in Besenyszög, a village not far from Besenyötelek, where the Smith family lived, in a very backward part of eastern Hungary. Besenyszög was an exceptionally poor village; the majority of the population worked as farm workers on the large estates around the village and as pick-and-shovel men at the drainage and embankment works in the Great Plain area.

*András*, the grandfather of the family, born in 1899, owned a tiny piece of land of less than two hectares, and worked as a pick-and-shovel man in the construction of anti-inundation embankments and of canals for the draining of marshy areas. He was a man of remarkable character and intelligence; and he was eventually promoted to become the local supervisor of canals by the state-owned water management company. This was a manual job, but it required important intellectual capacities, as the supervisor was responsible for the maintenance of the local embankments and canals.

András, who was a devout Catholic, married at 21 to a peasant girl. They had nine children. After 1945 he obtained seven more hectares of land; later on, in 1959, one of his children used this farm to join the local agricultural co-operative.

András was widowed at the age of 47; his youngest daughter was only four. As a widower he brought up his children on his own, and was even able to give all of them a cow as a wedding present. He had become an elder of the local Roman Catholic church. It is also characteristic of him that neither he nor any of his children or grandchildren ever joined the Communist Party, which in principle was supposed to attract poor farm workers.

The life histories of his nine children and of their spouses can be summarized shortly as follows.

*Barnabás* was a lifelong pick-and-shovel man; after the retire-

Social Mobility in Hungary 287

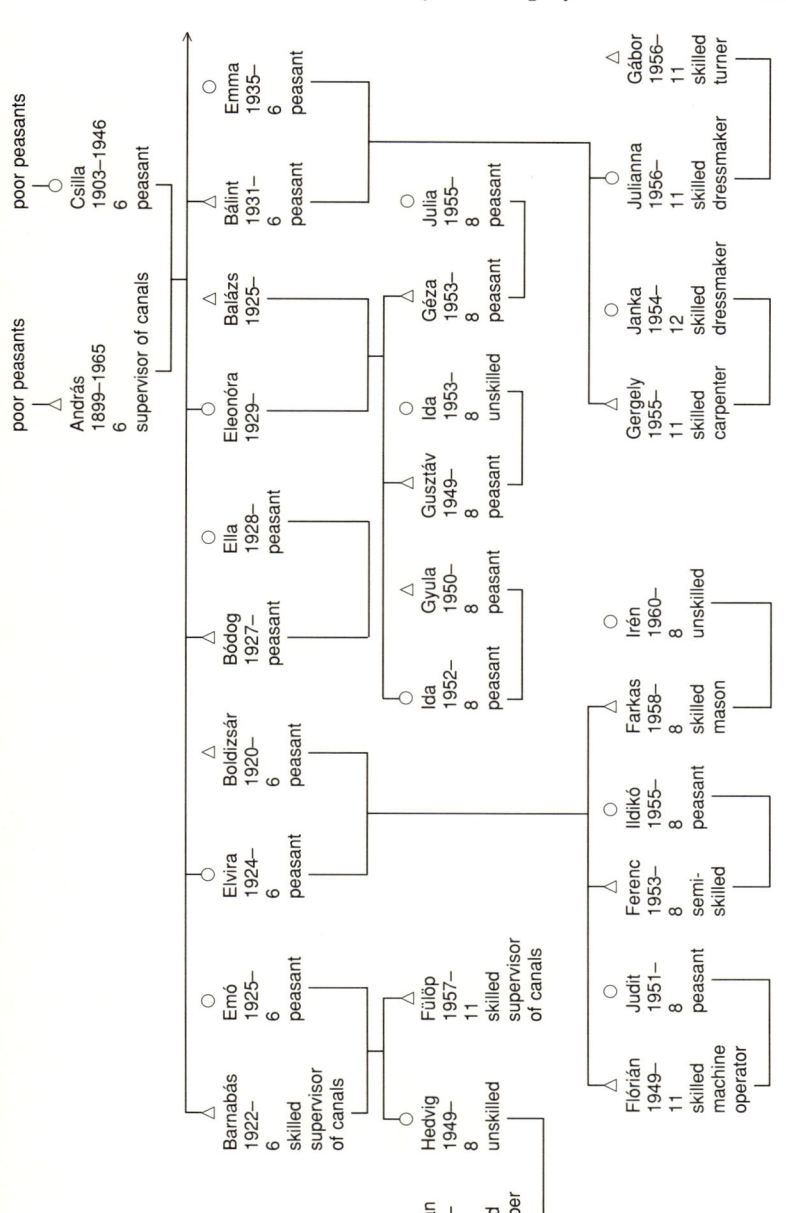

FIG. 9.4a. *Social Genealogy of the Hawk Family*

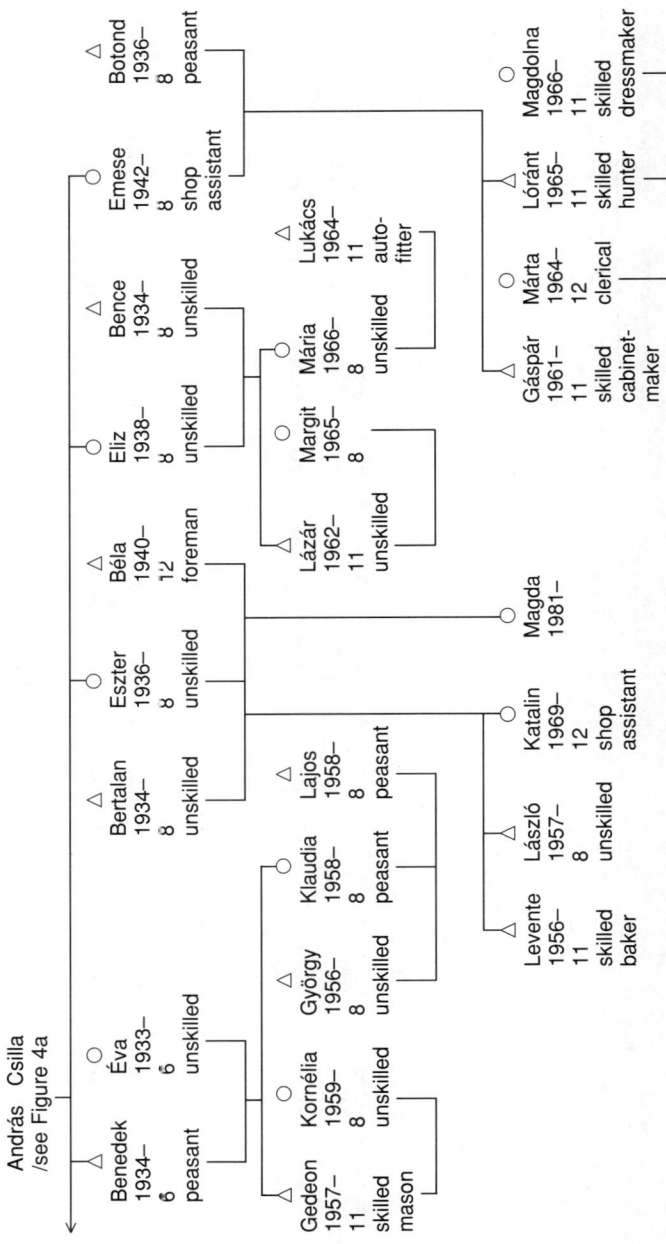

FIG. 9.4b. *Social Genealogy of the Hawk Family*

ment of his father he followed him into the job of local supervisor of canals. His wife *Emő* was born into a farm worker's family; she worked partly as a farm worker, partly in the household plot given by the water management company to the supervisors. *Elvira* married *Boldizsár*, who was the village drummer, publicly announcing the decisions of the municipality in the streets, and also carman for the local administration; later on he bought his own cart and two horses, thus becoming self-employed.

The third child, *Bódog*, was the 'black sheep' of the family, because of his heavy drinking. He had many different jobs: as carman, pick-and-shovel man, shepherd. His wife *Ella* was a seasonal farm worker.

*Eleonóra* worked as farm worker in the local state farm and agricultural co-operative created in 1945. She married *Balázs* who was a carman in the state farm and later in the co-operative; at the end of his career he became a shepherd. *Bálint* began his career as a pick-and-shovel-man, worked later as a farm worker on the state farm, and became disabled at a relatively young age. His wife *Emma* still works in the cowsheds of the state farm.

*Benedek* was a pick-and-shovel man employed by the water management company all his life. To supplement his family income he worked on his household plot, raising pigs and cows. His wife *Éva* was a farm worker on the state farm. She remained a housewife for several years after the birth of the children, and is at present a cleaning woman in the offices of the water management company in a near-by town.

*Eszter* worked as a seasonal farm worker, and later as an unskilled worker in a building enterprise in the near-by town. She had two marriages. From her first marriage with *Bertalan*, who was a policeman but lost this job and became an unskilled worker, she had three children. She divorced and met her second husband *Béla* at her working place in the building enterprise. Béla was the son of a well-to-do peasant; he had studied at a secondary school for the building industry and was a building works foreman. Through this second marriage Eszter achieved an important upward mobility. At the age of 45 she gave birth to a daughter. Her housing and living conditions in the town of Szolnok are clearly the best and the most urbanized of all among the children of András.

*Eliz* married a fire officer, *Bence*. She too migrated with her husband to the nearby town of Szolnok, and this improved her living conditions. But her husband was drinking, and lost his job as fire officer. He now works as an unskilled worker.

*Emese*, the youngest child, married *Botond*, who worked as a milkman for the local state farm. She is a shop assistant in the local shop. By very hard work and a very frugal life-style they were able to build themselves a modern house, give their children a good education, and help them build their own houses. In spite of the fact that neither Botond nor Emese are skilled workers, their living conditions are the next best after Eszter among the nine brothers and sisters.

It is therefore plain that although the living conditions and especially the housing of all the nine children and their spouses have improved in recent decades, in terms of social mobility most of them remained at the bottom of Hungarian society.

Among the twenty grandchildren of András, and among their spouses, there are more persons who have been upwardly mobile. None of them however has got a higher education, and none is a professional; only one of them, *Márta*, the spouse of grandson *Gáspár*, is a clerk; she works in the statistical office of the district of Szolnok. There are fourteen skilled workers among them, but only one, *Lukács*, spouse of granddaughter *Mária*, belongs to an élite skilled group: he is a car mechanic. All the others belong to the lower manual skills: among the men there is a supervisor of canals, a machine operator, two masons, a carpenter who works as a truck driver, a baker, a cabinet-maker, and a hunter; among the spouses of granddaughters, a plumber, and a turner. The two granddaughters are a dressmaker and a shop assistant; while two of the spouses of the grandsons are dressmakers.

All the other grandchildren and their spouses, altogether numbering seventeen, belong to the lower social strata, working as waged peasants, and unskilled or semi-skilled workers.

Many of the women have only temporary employment and work in the tiny household plots given by the agricultural co-operative and the state farm to their members and workers. All the families living in Besenyszög have such a plot and supplement their incomes by small-scale agricultural production, mostly for the consumption of the household but partly for selling in the private markets. Hence their working hours in both the job and the household plot are very long.

Thus nearly half of the third generation of the Hawk family was able to achieve one step up the social ladder by becoming a skilled worker. It might be expected that some of their children will be able to get higher education and thus escape from the lower half of Hungarian society. Nevertheless the main hypothesis that could be derived from this case history is that in a state socialist system, it has not been easier for the members of the bottom strata of the society to enter the higher strata than it has been in advanced capitalist societies. If for those who were born at the bottom of society, the chances of upward mobility became better in the post-1945 era than in the inter-war period, it may be due to the higher rate of economic growth and thus of structural occupational changes in the society, rather than the equalization of chances due to the advent of a socialist system. As the number of peasants or farm workers declined and the number of industrial workers, including skilled workers, increased, the opportunities for moving from the peasant class to the skilled stratum grew by comparison with the pre-1945 period. Thus the Ossowski thesis seems to be confirmed: rather than socialist policies, it is the more rapid industrialization of Hungary in the post-1945 socialist period that produced, for some of the members of the lowest strata, a higher rate of upward mobility than during the stagnant capitalist inter-war period (Ossowski 1957).

As for identifying individual factors that would influence chances of upward mobility, the history of the Hawk family points to four such factors.

First, as in the cases of Bódog and Bence, heavy drinking is a factor strongly hindering the improvement of the conditions not only of the individual, but of the whole nuclear family.

Secondly, marriage to a higher status person, as with Béla and Márta, helps the mobility of the spouse and also of the children, and the general improvement of the living conditions and life-style of the family.

Thirdly, higher education was certainly helpful in achieving upward mobility. The changeover from six-year to eight-year primary education, introduced nationally in 1984, did not help the escape of those in the lowest positions in the social structure. But studying in a three-year school for skilled workers after the eight-year primary education, in most cases resulted in entry to the skilled stratum, and thus an improvement when compared with the peasant and non-skilled strata.

Lastly, those who like Eszter and Eliz migrated to a town and those who like Gáspár commuted daily to an urban working-place also had better opportunities to achieve a modest upward mobility. But although some migrated to nearby villages, few members of the Hawk family migrated to towns. This was due to the very great difficulties in getting housing in urban areas. New state-owned urban dwellings were usually allocated to higher status employees of urban enterprises and institutions, not to their manual workers. Therefore the usual pattern of industrialization and urbanization implied commuting daily between rural residence and urban working-place. In the case of the village of Besenyszög, however, the possibilities for commuting were rather scarce, because Szolnok, the nearest town, is not a major industrial centre, and so offered relatively few employment possibilities in industry. In addition public transport by bus between Besenyszög and Szolnok takes almost one hour and with four buses a day is relatively infrequent, while only a few of the families had their own car, although rather more of them had a motor-bike. Hence commuting to Szolnok was a rather time-consuming and unpleasant way of life. These difficulties in migrating to towns thus restricted the villagers' chances of upward mobility as well as their access to urban services, like health care, educational and other cultural institutions, and specialized shops. By comparison with the Hawk family, the Smith and Chester families were much more migrant. The second generation of the Smith family made great efforts to send its children to student hostels, while in the Chester family one of the grandfathers was already able to migrate to a village on the outskirts of Budapest before the end of the Second World War.

## CONCLUSIONS

We can certainly draw a methodological conclusion from our examination of these four case studies; that family histories do add important new information to the knowledge gained from social mobility surveys. As Daniel Bertaux stated (1987 and 1995), a methodological pluralism is especially desirable in the study of social mobility processes. This statement should be read both ways: not only are survey data poorer without illustrative examples from case histories, but single life histories or case histories can be misleading without the support of the knowledge gained from statistical surveys.

In the Hungarian case, because of the wealth of available survey data, we can affirm that the mobility patterns of these four families are not exceptional. The processes illustrated by the Tiller family were also active in the histories of the descendants of many families or generations of the old bourgeois and professional class. The same holds for rich and middle peasants as with the Smith family, for skilled workers as in the Chester family and for the landless agricultural workers of the Hawk family. These four case histories can be read as typical of mobility patterns in post-1945 Hungary, and indeed this is precisely the reason we have selected them for presentation here.

The most important substantive hypothesis that comes out of the analysis of these case histories is that, in spite of the drastic attempts of the two successive totalitarian regimes to reshape the processes of social mobility, the overall tendencies determined by the structural factors did eventually prevail. In that sense the Ossowski thesis seems to be confirmed. The life trajectories of the people and families exposed to expropriation and political repression sooner or later returned to the path which the structural changes in the Hungarian society implied for their cultural backgrounds. Thus the descendants of families which were at the top of the social hierarchy in the 1930s, like the Tiller family, returned to the top. The descendants of the Smith and Chester families, who were in the lower middle part of the hierarchy, moved somewhat upward, and some were able to enter the top strata, filling the empty places caused by the growth of these strata and by the low demographic reproduction of the families belonging traditionally to the top. The descendants of the Hawk family remained in the lower positions of the social hierarchy, although their living circumstances and their working conditions improved in parallel with the structural changes due to the industrialization of Hungary. Thus the 'iron laws' of social mobility or—to use a more appropriate term—of social distribution (Bertaux 1977) prevailed in Hungary, irrespective of the socialist character of the system. 'Socialist' mobility was not essentially different from the pattern observed in other industrializing societies. Therefore it is not surprising that the social distribution of Hungary in the past fifty or sixty years shows many similarities to social distribution patterns in other advanced societies, including west European capitalist societies.

The history of the Tiller family indicates how important the cultural resources (or cultural capital) of the traditional bourgeoisie and professional class were in their struggle to restore their formerly high position in the social hierarchy.

The histories of the Smith and Chester families seem on the other hand to prove that upward mobility of the descendants of peasants and workers was much more conditioned by education than by political loyalty to the ruling party. If party membership played a role at all in reaching a professional status, it was paradoxically more important in the case of the Tiller family, which formerly belonged to the bourgeoisie and the traditional professional class; party membership may have helped them to remain in the professional class. The members of the Smith and Chester families who achieved entry into the professional stratum were not party members.

This does not mean of course that in order to enter the top power élite, it was not necessary or at least very advantageous to be a member of the Hungarian Communist Party. But such a phenomenon would require a study in itself. It ought to be added that the correlation of party membership with professional status was far from identical in the different sub-periods of the socialist system in Hungary, and might have been very different between one socialist society and another.

While in the first classical period of socialism in Hungary, party membership was an important precondition for having a top job and certainly an asset for upward mobility, in parallel with the economic reforms introduced in 1968 party membership became less and less a necessary condition to achieve a professional career. Thus alongside the party channel of upward mobility, the educational channel became more and more widely open for non-party-members. Among all the professional members of the third generation of the four families only Hedvig Tiller, the oldest member of the third generation, was a party member. None of the younger professionals considered it necessary or desirable to enter the party.

The history of the Hawk family shows how difficult the disadvantages resulting from a low class position are to surmount. The process of emerging from the bottom of the society is very slow. In most cases, even making the most of scarce resources, it requires several generations of effort; and what is perceived individually as upward mobility, the betterment of the level of living, and occupational change, appears from the macrosociological point of view simply the result of the upward shift of the whole society as a consequence of industrialization, higher productivity, and urbanization. Those whose grandparents were at the bottom of society in the inter-war period are still at the bottom today, although this bottom has shifted upwards in terms of education, skills, income, and living conditions. Occupational change and economic mobility are clearly there; but to speak of social mobility, an expression that should be reserved for changes in the relative positions of the social hierarchy, might be an impropriety for such cases.

Thus the life chances of the descendants of all classes—both old professionals and kulaks who were discriminated against, and also skilled workers and poor farm workers who were in principle privileged by the socialist system—were determined in the long run by structural and cultural factors. At least in Hungary, it is only for short periods that political events disturbed the life courses of the members of these different classes.

On the level of human experience, however, one should not underestimate the hardships and sufferings caused by political events such as war, revolution, deportation, concentration camps, expulsion from the native country, from the parental farm or from the family home. It is indeed one of the features of the life stories and family histories that they give us strong insights into these dramatic events and their human consequences.

## NOTES

1. In two respects there were important general differences between the Hungarian and the west European mobility patterns. First, the mobility chances of the children of peasants were closer to those of the children of unskilled workers than in west European societies. Secondly, the mobility chances of the children of the self-employed artisans and merchants were essentially identical to those of the children of skilled workers in Hungary, while they were much more advantageous in Western European societies.

2. One way in which to analyse occupational life histories is to construct three-way mobility tables of father's position, first job, and the present job of the respondent. This analysis revealed a great amount of intragenerational mobility from first to present job. Thus in 1973 half of the workers of peasant origin were peasants at the time of the first job and had moved into the working class in mid-career. One-third of the professionals born in families of professionals had begun their career in non-professional jobs.

   This type of statistical analysis, however, could not reveal, for example, the temporary losses of status in mid-career, when professionals lost their job for political reasons, worked for some time in a manual job, and later returned to the professional stratum.

   Another type of analysis I tried to use was to prepare tables of the occupational distribution of the offspring of fathers belonging to different strata, such as the sons of peasants, at the age of 20, 30, 40, etc. by cohorts. These tables showed the gradual change in the social composition of the same cohort through ageing, and in different historical periods; but individual occupational life histories were lost within the averages. For instance, it could be seen that in the 1950s some of the sons of professionals, who had begun their career as professionals, temporarily lost their privileged position and worked in manual jobs; but later the percentage of professionals of such cohorts recovered to the pre-1950s level.

   Technical difficulties prevented me from applying to the data either path models including more positions between the first and the present job of the respondent, or event-history analysis.

3. The exact number of persons of Jewish background who were killed in the war or in concentration camps remains unknown. It is known however that in 1941, 401,000 Hungarians of Jewish religion lived within the borders of the present territory of Hungary; only 134,000 remained in 1949. Hungarians of Jewish background—either of Jewish religion, or Christianized but coming from a Jewish background—were over-represented in the higher strata, and under-represented in the lower classes (Karady 1984).

4. As for the aristocracy, in pre-war Hungary it was fully part of the top social élite. In the 1930s there were 349 aristocratic families in Hungary. In 1975, 281 of these aristocratic families had male descendants all over the world; in 1989, only 125 of them had descendants living in Hungary. Thus most aristocrats emigrated from Hungary (Gudenus and Szentirmay 1989), so that the mobility fate of their descendants escaped surveys.

5. The recording of the case history of the Hawk family has followed a different logic from the previous three case histories. In the earlier cases

the reference person was a member of the younger generation who happened to be a student of sociology at our university. For the Hawk family the point of entry is not a student, but András the grandfather, a farm worker. As this case history includes the life histories of all his descendants, there is no maternal branch in this case study.

## REFERENCES

Alestalo, M., Andorka, R., and Harcsa, I. (1987), *Agricultural Population and Structural Change: A Comparison of Finland and Hungary* (Research Group for Comparative Sociology, University of Helsinki Research Reports, 34).

Andorka, R. (1968), 'Az intragenerációs mobilitás vizsgálatának nékány kérdése' (Some Questions on the Investigation of Intragenerational Mobility), in *Korszerü statisztikai törekvések Magyarországon* (Budapest), 493–501.

—— (1972), 'Mobilité sociale, développement économique et transformations socio-professionelles de la population active en Hongrie. Vue d'ensemble, 1930–1970', *Revue française de sociologie*, 13, 607–29.

—— (1976), 'Social Mobility and Economic Development in Hungary', in B. L. Faber (ed.), *The Social Structure of Eastern Europe* (New York), 51–70.

—— (1980), 'The Analysis of Social Mobility Life Histories', paper to the Oslo Life History workshop of the International Sociological Association Research Committee on Social Stratification.

—— (1982), *A Társadalmi Mobilitás Változásai Magyarországon* (Changes in Social Mobility in Hungary) (Budapest).

—— (1983), 'Age, Cohort and Historical Factors Influencing the Inter- and Intragenerational Social Mobility of Men and Women in Hungary', in D. J. Treiman and R. V. Robinson (eds), *Research in Social Stratification and Mobility: A Research Annual* (Greenwich), 197–248.

—— and Zagórski, K. (1980), *Socio-occupational Mobility in Hungary and Poland* (Warsaw).

Bertaux, D. (1977), *Destins personnels et structure de classe* (Paris).

—— (1981), 'Introduction', Bertaux (ed.), *Biography and Society* (London).

—— (1987), 'Du monopole au pluralisme méthodologique dans la sociologie de la mobilité sociale', *Annales de Vaucresson*, 26, 305–19.

—— (1995), 'Social Genealogies, Commented and Compared: An Instrument for Studying Social Mobility Processes in the "Longue Durée"',

*Current Sociology*, 43 (2), special issue, 'The Biographical Method', 70–88.

Erikson, R., and Goldthorpe, J. H. (1987a), 'Commonality and Variation in Social Fluidity in Industrial Nations. Part One: A Model for Evaluating the "FJH Hypothesis"', *European Sociological Review*, 3, 54–77.

—— (1987b), 'Commonality and Variation in Social Fluidity in Industrial Nations. Part Two: The Model of Core Social Fluidity Applied', *European Sociological Review*, 3, 145–66.

—— (1992), *The Constant Flux* (Oxford).

Girod, R. (1971), *Mobilité sociale. Faits établis et problèmes ouverts* (Geneva).

Gudenus, J., and Szentirmay, L. (1989), *Összetört cimerek: A magyar arisztokrácia sorsa és az 1945 utáni megpróbáltatások* (Broken Coats of Arms: The Fate and Tribulations of the Hungarian aristocracy after 1945) (Budapest).

Harcsa, I. (1990), interview, *Replika*, 1.

Karady, V. (1984), 'Szociológiai kisérlet magyar zsidóság 1945 és 1956 közötti helyzetének elemzésére' (A Sociological Attempt to Analyse the Situation of the Hungarian Jews between 1945 and 1956), in *Zsidóság az 1945 utáni Magyarorzágon* (The Jews in Hungary after 1945) (Paris), 37–180.

Kovács, M. M., and Örkény, A. (1986), 'Promoted Cadres and Professionals in Post-war Hungary', in R. Andorka and L. Bertalan (eds), *Economy and Society in Hungary* (Budapest), 139–52.

Ossowski, S. (1957), 'Social Mobility Brought about by Social Revolutions', Fourth Working Conference on Social Stratification and Social Mobility, Geneva.

Örkény, A. (1990), 'Féluton. Megjegyzések a társadalmi mobilitás magyarországi kutatásának elmult két évtizedéről' (Midway: Observations on the Past Two Decades of Social Mobility Research in Hungary), *Replika*, 1.

Simó, T. (1984), 'Gondolatok a társadalmi struktura vizsgálatáról' (Remarks on the Investigation of Social Structure), *Statisztikai Szemle*, 62, 1254–7.

Szelényi, I., with Manchin, R., Juhász, P., Magyar, B., and Martin, B. (1988), *Socialist Entrepreneurs: Embourgeoisement in Rural Hungary* (Madison).

# 10

# Social Mobility and the Survey Method: A Critical Analysis

MIKE SAVAGE

It goes without saying that the study of social mobility is fundamental to the study of social structures and relationships. The processes which inhibit and facilitate social mobility play a vital role in constructing and transmitting social inequalities (e.g. Blau and Duncan 1967; Goldthorpe *et al.* 1980; Parkin 1979). And, the factors which affect an individual's life chances include virtually every aspect of social life—including labour market processes, the family, education, locale, social networks, gender, ethnicity, and race. Finally, people's experience of mobility through social space is encoded in their life-styles, attitudes and actions, both individual and collective (e.g. Bourdieu 1984; Giddens 1973). In short, the study of social mobility is central to any social scientific analysis. However, in the years since 1945 its study has become a highly specialized branch of sociological inquiry detached from the concerns of most historians and many sociologists, and it can be argued that much work in the field no longer realizes the promise of its subject-matter.

The reason for this situation is not hard to spot. As the study of social mobility has become increasingly organized around the highly specialized statistical manipulation of survey data, the results of such work have become less intelligible to the non-specialist. It will however be clear to readers that the papers in this volume represent a rather different tradition of social research. The authors do not use surveys. They adopt a wider range of sampling strategies than the random sampling championed by most survey approaches, and they use hermeneutic, ethnographic, and historical techniques of analysis rather than quantitative ones. One of the general questions raised by these papers therefore is the extent to which they offer a remedy to possible defects evident in quantitative research, and it is to this topic that this paper is devoted. The editors commissioned me to write this paper as someone who was both interested in, but also critical of, quantitative approaches to social stratification (see e.g. Savage *et al.* 1992, esp. Appendix 1). My aim in this paper is to evaluate some of the leading quantitative approaches to social mobility in order to identify the sorts of weaknesses and blind spots which qualitative research might be able to remedy.

This is a formidable task because of the variety of quantitative approaches and techniques currently used. Criticisms valid against some perspectives do not apply to others. Nor do I have any interest in launching a 'total' critique of quantitative research *per se*. Such a critique would not only be rather *passé*, but it would also be counterproductive to the overall aim of developing a dialogue between different research traditions in order to enrich our understanding of social mobility. As I shall illustrate below quantitative approaches do have real strengths which cannot be ignored. None the less the main point of this paper will be that no one method can supply all the answers to a topic as diffuse and wide-ranging as that of social mobility, and that it is therefore vital to recognize that whilst quantitative techniques have made major advances in some fields, this has only been by bracketing some relevant issues from view. It is therefore vital to encourage a flexible and open interest in social mobility in which a number of different methods and approaches can be used together in a catholic way (see also Bertaux 1991).

This paper falls into five parts. The first offers a brief introduction to some of the main trends in quantitative social mobility research since 1945. The main analytical point of this section is that the dismissal of all quantitative research as 'positivist' *per se* is to reify what is actually a more flexible, creative, and dynamic body of work. Critics of survey-based research should be aware that they are aiming at a moving target! The rest of the paper offers a series of comments on the techniques and theoretical frameworks evident in the varying perspectives laid out in the first section. The second, brief, section considers the problem of studying atypical or unusual groups within survey research. The third section examines the differing conceptions of causality implicit in different quantitative approaches and argues that researchers face the choice either of examining many variables superficially or a few variables in depth. The fourth section considers the conceptions of temporality and historicity implicit in survey research, whilst the last section discusses how subjectivity and the complex relationship between structure and agency is handled.

## SURVEYS AND SOCIAL MOBILITY

It is generally recognized (e.g. Brieger 1990*b*) that from the early 1960s the work of the American sociologist Duncan and his colleagues (e.g. Duncan 1961; Blau and Duncan 1967; Duncan, Featherman, and Duncan 1972) helped establish a new quantitative paradigm in social mobility research. Social mobility research before this date tended to be loosely descriptive. It frequently combined quantitative and qualitative methods, and also tended to integrate the study of individual and collective mobility. Thus Glass's (1954) survey-based study of individual social mobility in Britain was linked to Lockwood's (1958) study of clerical workers as well as Kelsall's (1954) archival study of civil-service careers. Comparable American research could be found within the community studies tradition of Lloyd Warner and his associates (e.g. Warner and Lunt 1942).

Duncan's key innovation lay in his conceptualization of mobility as movement up or down a hierarchy of occupations, each occupation being assigned to its appropriate level according to its socio-economic standing. By distinguishing seventeen hierarchical levels, ranging from professionals at the top to farm labourers at the bottom, it was possible to use multivariate techniques, such as path analysis, multiple regression, and correlation co-efficents, to study how an individual's movement (or lack of movement) from one level to another could be correlated with other variables. By the early 1970s a sophisticated set of research studies had explored the impact of variables such as father's occupation, father's educational level, and the education, intelligence, aspirations, sex, and race of the respondent on their movements along the occupational hierarchy (see e.g. Blau and Duncan 1967; Duncan, Featherman, and Duncan 1972). The relative importance of different variables on the respondent's socio-economic position could be quantitatively gauged using path analysis, and this approach therefore appeared to offer a new precision in assessing the causes of an individual's mobility.

It can be argued that more recent quantitative approaches to social mobility still fall under the shadow of this 'status attainment' approach, since they were couched either as critiques of, or developments from, Blau and Duncan's pioneering work. None the less, it is important to recognize that since the 1960s survey researchers have moved away from many of the assumptions of the 'status attainment' paradigm. Two criticisms are particularly relevant here. First, it was difficult to use these new techniques to show the significance of structural forces inhibiting or facilitating social mobility (see Breiger 1990*b*). This is because attention was directed at the factors which allowed *individuals* to be socially mobile. It was not, however, possible to examine the overall, aggregate, proportions of certain social groups who were upwardly or downwardly mobile. The study of collective social mobility, or of how social inequalities were implicated in mobility processes were thus obscured from view.

Secondly, status attainment research committed the positivist fallacy of conflating correlation with explanation. Regression techniques saw causality in terms of the 'explanation of variance' (see Lieberson 1985 for a review). These researchers felt that people's mobility could be explained if the range of its variation could be correlated to the variation of other variables. One implication of this was that the success of the technique depended on being able to split variables into as long a numerical range as possible, in order that their variation could then be correlated with that of other variables. It was precisely for this reason that the ranking exercise was so important. It is much easier to explain variation if the variables being explained ranged from one to seventeen than if they ranged from one to three. Researchers needed to differentiate social phenomena as much as possible even though there might be little or no analytical warrant for this. In this way the hierarchical language of numbers, where 2 is more than 1 and so forth, is projected onto the social field, leading to the necessary ranking of supposed occupational classes (see generally Sayer 1984).

Inherent to the status attainment approach therefore was the transformation of elements of the social world into a numerical hierarchy (treating variables as 'ordinal' variables, to use quantitative language). And this, it has often been claimed by critics of positivism, is the root of the trouble. Numbers came to stand in as proxies for a wide variety of complex social processes and inevitably simplify and distort them. In place of the causal chains and connections which might be identified by careful qualitative investigation, quantitative analysts seem to impose a uniform and insensitive language of numbers onto their objects of investigation. Sayer's (1984) argument that the language of mathematics is not able to explore causal processes, but can only establish equivalences (A = B) or hierarchies (2 is twice 1) has obvious relevance here.

The problems with status attainment research are, therefore, tangible and well known. However, it would be quite erroneous to assume that the methods and techniques pioneered by Blau and Duncan are the only ones possible for survey researchers. Contemporary quantitative research should not be judged through spectacles which were originally put in place thirty years ago. In Europe the most prominent alternative to 'status attainment' research is the 'class structural' approach to social mobility associated with the more recent work of John Goldthorpe and his colleagues. Pioneered in the analysis of the Nuffield Social Mobility Study reported in *Social Mobility and Class Structure in Modern Britain* (Goldthorpe *et al.* 1980), it has recently led to a major study of comparative social mobility (Erikson and Goldthorpe 1992). This approach has had relatively little impact on American research, although even in the USA there has been a growing interest in using class rather than (or as well as) ranked occupational hierarchies as the basis of analysis (see Wright 1979, 1985; Kalleberg and Griffin 1980), as well as widespread adoption of the log linear modelling techniques championed by its proponents.

The 'class structural' approach abandons the idea that occupations can be ranked into a hierarchy. Rather, occupations are grouped into a small number of classes according to certain defining features. This might seem a minor modification but it has major ramifications. It changes occupational class from being an 'ordinal' variable to a 'nominal' variable. What this means in practice is that although Goldthorpe distinguishes seven classes, he does not claim that, for instance, class three ranks higher than class four. Rather, they are distinguished by including people in qualitatively different social relationships. The numbers are simply *conventions*—symbols could be used rather than figures—and do not involve any attempt to project a mathematical language onto the analysis of social class.

The quantitative procedures used within this approach are also rather different from those used in the status attainment tradition. As Pawson (1993) summarizes, Goldthorpe's starting-point is the intergenerational 'mobility table' which lays out the proportions of sons mobile to or from various class categories compared to their fathers. These mobility tables provide basic descriptive information on the patterns of mobility between classes in the population. Building on this table does not entail adding extra variables and seeing if they correlate with mobility (as in the status attainment approach), but in using log linear modelling techniques to consider what sorts of mobility outcomes would be expected using certain assumptions about the significance of specific social processes affecting members of some classes but not others, and seeing if these expected patterns match the actual patterns revealed by the data. Or, as Pawson puts it, they 'take a pattern of data . . . and regard it, not as the end of the research process, but as a configuration to be explained. The explanation takes the form of postulating theories about the underlying causal mechanisms which have produced the regularity' (Pawson 1993: 31). The important point here is that the conception of causality no longer rests upon correlation measures. Indeed Erikson and Goldthorpe endorse Lieberson's (1985) critique of positivist conceptions of causality. Taking the example of gravity, Lieberson suggests that some powerful forces are a constant and goes on to argue that 'it is premature to think about the variability in an event before knowledge is developed about the fundamental cause of the event itself. Explanation of a variable's variation should not be confused with an explanation of the event or process itself' (1985: 232). Erikson and Goldthorpe draw upon this notion to examine the extent to which particular social classes either have strong or weak 'pulling power' to retain their offspring.

One of the striking things about this approach to social mobility is that it appears to be much closer to the aims and objectives of the qualitative 'life history' tradition manifested by various papers in this book. Both have a common interest in delineating the processes which govern different types of 'mobility regime'. Bertaux's call for studies of 'anthroponomic distribution' (which refers to the 'overall process, some constraining societal process, by which members of a society, whether they like it or not, are directed, sorted, distributed and assigned to different jobs as they are defined by a socially constructed state of the division of labour' (Bertaux 1991: 75)) is very similar to Erikson and Goldthorpe's emphasis on the need to explore 'the constraints that operate ... (which) serve to impose restrictions, on the aggregate level, on the outcomes of individual mobility trajectories from class origins to destinations' (Erikson and Goldthorpe 1992: 307).

It appears, therefore, that the class structural approach to social mobility is in many ways at odds with status attainment approaches and may avoid some of its pitfalls. I suggest in succeeding sections that it is not quite as simple as that, and there are some losses, as well as gains, associated with it. However, before passing on to discuss this further, it should be emphasized that there are many other quantitative approaches to social mobility apart from these two. From the end of the 1970s, American mobility research has fragmented into a number of different approaches, none of which has attained the dominance previously enjoyed by the status attainment school. Four perspectives are worth mentioning here, and some of them I will take up further below. White (1970) has attempted to remedy the neglect of structure within status attainment research by considering how vacancies within organizations (i.e. structural factors) lead to enforced mobility as people are recruited to fill the vacant positions (see also Abbott 1990*a*). A second perspective, associated especially with the work of Granovetter (1974), is to link social mobility to the study of social networks, by exploring how an individual's mobility is embedded within the networks they belong to (see also Lin 1990). Clear links with the contextual approach of life historians are evident here also. A third approach is the inductive perspective of Levine (1990) which does not conceptualize mobility between pre-defined categories (whether ranked or based on a class schema) but groups people according to the similarity of their mobility profiles. Finally, another emphasis has been to unpack the nature of mobility itself by moving away from the sole focus on intergenerational (father–son) mobility, towards more dynamic approaches more attentive to the complex twists and turns an individual can experience in their lives. Abbott and Hrycak (1990) have championed optimal matching techniques as a means of describing such patterns. Others have paid greater attention to the intersection between labour market processes and social mobility (e.g. Althauser and Kalleberg 1981; Diprete 1993). One interesting by-product is a return to the older practice of linking quantitative and qualitative research in the study of specific labour markets, a trend found in DiPrete's (1989) study of the Federal Civil Service, for instance, or in Abbott's (1988) study of professions as well as individual careers.

This brief discussion should be enough to indicate the variety of quantitative social mobility research. Having laid out these main trends I now want to take a more analytical focus and examine how some critical issues are handled within survey research.

## SURVEYS, REPRESENTATIVENESS, AND ATYPICALITY

Blau and Duncan championed the need for a national representative sample survey, and this stress has rarely been challenged. Indeed, recent developments in mobility research using log linear models actually accentuate long-standing restrictions of survey methods in dealing with unusual or atypical groups who are not well represented in random samples. Most importantly, there is the problem of numbers and statistical significance. Log linear modelling (as well as most other quantitative techniques including multiple regression) only produce acceptable results when the researcher can be confident that the results produced are statistically significant, that is to say that they are unlikely to be the product of sampling error. All standard statistical packages now readily compute whether acceptable levels of statistical significance are indeed reached, but there is considerable difficulty in achieving such levels when the researcher examines atypical groups.

The use of log linear methods in the 'class structural' approach carries with it specific problems. Goldthorpe's chosen technique of log linear modelling depends on having acceptable numbers of respondents in the 'cells' of its mobility table. The 'odds ratios' computed to measure the relative chances that members of various social groups reach certain destinations rather than others are very sensitive to small changes in absolute numbers when only a few cases exist in a particular category (see Kelley 1990). If we can be sure that these differences are real, that is to say that they are not due to sampling error, then this is not such a problem since the odds ratio will correctly map the real patterns. However, in the absence of massive surveys which would be prohibitively expensive to carry out, we can rarely be confident that very small shifts in absolute numbers for small categories are not due to sampling error. Therefore odds ratios in such cases are always vulnerable.

One way round this problem is to ensure that the class categories used in analysis are likely to contain enough people for this not to be an overriding problem. What this means in practice is ensuring that all the chosen categories are likely to be composed of a reasonable proportion of the population. It is striking that the smallest social class distinguished within the influential Nuffield class schema had as many as 9.2 per cent of all respondents within it (Goldthorpe *et al.* 1987). Interestingly, Blau and Duncan, who were not constrained by this problem, were able to distinguish a group of retail salesmen, who only composed 1.7 per cent of their sample (Blau and Duncan 1967: Table J2.1). This issue has already led to stormy debate in the context of the Nuffield class schema. Goldthorpe refused to distinguish a property-owning capitalist (or upper) class, despite the abundance of theoretical and empirical research which suggests its distinctiveness (Penn 1981; Scott 1982). The reason, of course, is that this group is just too thin on the ground to show up in a random sample survey.

There are therefore real problems in studying unusual or atypical groups—such as the migrants to Canada studied by Elliott, or members of specific occupations such as the bakers studied by Bertaux, or the members of particular Italian villages studied by Contini in this volume. Fine-grained detail is lost in the need to retain levels of statistical significance. However, it is important to note that this limitation is not inherent in quantitative analysis. In recent years some quantitative researchers have become more interested in finding ways to analyse data where only a small number of actual cases exist and consequently where usual techniques demanding tests of statistical significance are inappropriate. The Booleian methods of comparative analysis championed by Ragin (1987) and the optimal matching techniques developed by Abbott and Hrycak (1990), for instance, offer alternatives. The latter use algorithms to classify sequences of events for a small number of cases. These allow the degree of difference to be distinguished and typologies of event sequences to be built up. This is a very promising approach to the study of some processes, but it cannot be used to assess the *commonality* of particular patterns unless researchers are confident they have an exhaustive sample—for instance every major revolution, or every particular event in a given place in a given time period.

Another problem is that log linear techniques use random sampling as their main sampling strategy. Log linear techniques compare the chances of groups in relation to others. All groups therefore need to be represented in representative proportions, and it is therefore out of the question to oversample particular groups, since the resulting odds ratios will be distorted to the point of meaninglessness. The result is to rule out sampling strategies (such as stratified sampling) which attempt to compensate for atypicality by oversampling members of specific groups.

Perhaps, therefore, life-history techniques offer a more flexible 'middle way' between either the desire of large-scale survey researchers to reach acceptable levels of significance, or the concern of the narrative and Boolean quantifiers to by-pass the problem of sampling error altogether. Life historians may use a greater range of sampling strategies. Snowball sampling may generate enough cases of a theoretically relevant target population whilst researchers can examine whether enough cases have been sampled by considering whether further interviews appear to offer fresh or unanticipated insights (see Strauss 1987).

## VARIABLE ANALYSIS: BREADTH OR DEPTH?

All forms of quantitative research distinguish variables in order to be able to assess their interrelationship through different forms of statistical analysis. Usually research proceeds by distinguishing a dependent variable which is to be explained by other, explanatory or 'independent' variables. In the status attainment tradition the dependent variable was usually the respondent's location on the hierarchical occupational scale, whilst a large number of independent variables were introduced as possible factors leading to (causing) the individual to occupy that place. In class structural approaches the dependent variable is not the individual's social location but is rather the cells of the mobility table. In other words it is the proportions of sons mobile or immobile which is to be explained in terms of the independent variables, seen here as the causal properties of various social classes which are used to model the data.

## Social Mobility and the Survey Method

The delineation of dependent from independent variables is a very useful discipline for all researchers, for the specification of a dependent variable is closely related to defining a specific research question. However what concerns me here is how the possible explanatory variables are handled. For here there appears to be a crucial choice to be made. One strategy, found within status attainment approaches, involves examining the impact of a great number of possible independent variables on the dependent variable so that the relative importance of different causal factors can be evaluated in aggregate. This may sound attractive, but it runs into conceptual difficulties. In the positivist tradition causality is conflated with correlation and therefore cannot vary by context. If a son's socio-economic standing is indeed largely caused by their father's own standing, this must always be true. The result is that it is not possible to qualify the results according to the particular social context involved. It is not (for instance) possible to say that the relationship between father and son's class is closer at the top of the class structure than at the bottom. One has to be satisfied with an overall aggregate statistic that is not sensitive to variation within the social field.

The class structural approach has the completely opposite approach. To all intents and purposes there are only two variables: origin and destination class. This may sound to be very restrictive, but in fact proves highly illuminating. Since the relationship between father's class and son's class can be expected to vary according to the origin class concerned, class structural researchers are less concerned with establishing general rules about the relationship between parental position and that of respondents than with assessing how members of differing classes have different propensities to pass on their position to their offspring. In reply to Blau and Duncan's (1967: 170) basic model which suggests that there is a direct correlation of only .115 between father's class and respondent's class (though since father's class affects the respondent's education which in turn affects the respondents occupation, there are stronger indirect effects), class structural writers object that this figure is a meaningless average, since it conflates some classes where there is a very high degree of correlation and others where there might be a low one. Erikson and Goldthorpe's work shows that across a range of industrial countries around 59 per cent of men from professional and managerial families followed their fathers into these occupations themselves, compared to 13 per cent of sons from white-collar families who themselves took on white-collar jobs (Erikson and Goldthorpe 1992: Table 6.9). Class structural researchers focus on exploring the processes which allow members of specific social classes to be mobile rather than concern themselves with the spurious averages of an entire population. They are much more concerned with social specificity and context.

However, the cost of this approach is to radically limit what can be said about other sorts of variables, even those which appear to be pertinent to the analysis. The treatment of the family—one of the main emphases in life-history approaches to social mobility, as the article by Thompson in this volume suggests—offers an interesting example of this point. Family factors are a possible cause of individual variation in social mobility (families with certain types of resources or behaviours may be able to place their offspring in certain sorts of destinations), and families are also themselves the product of particular types of mobility processes. They are both medium and outcome of social action (Giddens 1984).

Researchers within the 'status attainment' tradition examined the impact of family variables on an individual's social location. They put family variables (along with many others) into their analyses as possible causes of an individual's social location. Many interesting, if problematic, findings resulted. Thus Blau and Duncan (1967) were able to confirm that those from smaller families tended to move higher up the social scale, that middle children appeared disadvantaged compared to the first and last born and so on.

Compare this discussion of family influences with that found within the class structural approach where the family is treated in a more *ad hoc* and rudimentary way. The social location of the family is measured entirely by the employment position of its leading wage-earner. In earlier formulations Goldthorpe explicitly stated that it was the husband and father who was the chief earner—a view which led to disputes with feminist researchers (Standworth 1984; Dex 1990; Marshall *et al.* 1988). He has now relaxed this rather stringent requirement, and accepts that women may be placed in a higher class position should they occupy a higher class position than their partners (an interesting concession to the hierarchical principles of the status attainment approach!).

Even with this qualification, it can be argued that to assume that the family's social location is simply measured by one of its members is too restrictive. It may neglect the financial contribution of other family members to the overall standing of the family (Britten and Heath 1983); it ignores the cultural and reputational place which the family enjoys as a result of the practices of all, or many of its members; and it offers no purchase on the internal dynamics and tensions which may exist within the household. Again a point of contrast with status attainment researchers is revealing. However problematic the findings may be (given that they are averages of the population as a whole) it is none the less of some interest to note that according to Duncan, Featherman, and Duncan (1972: ch. 7) there is quite a strong correlation (.361) between a wife's education and her husband's occupational status, and even a small correlation (.077) between the 'wife's desire to get ahead' and her husband's status! These are all interesting correlations which however cannot be investigated within class structural approaches.

Erikson and Goldthorpe's strategy for exploring the impact of the family on mobility outcomes is to consider how specific social classes may be differentially affected by family factors. Many of the factors specified by Erikson and Goldthorpe (1992) in their topographical model of comparative mobility rates are precisely designed to explore family influences—for instance the way that the inheritance of property or cultural resources advantage some sort of children over others. However, there remains doubt as to whether their approach is entirely adequate here. The technique involves devising a model of what mobility would look like if certain assumptions were made and then testing whether the resulting model 'fits' the observed data. The assumptions include that some social classes (for instance, self-employed proprietors) find it easier to pass on property than do other social classes. Whilst this may appear to be a reasonable assumption it is not one which is derived from the research itself and is therefore gratuitous. Erikson and Goldthorpe would perhaps argue that if the resulting models offer a good fit that is proof enough that the assumptions are indeed accurate. However, it may be that the fit produced is testimony to another unacknowledged or unobserved process; and at the very least it would appear important to be able to ground the existence of these assumptions in micro-based research which actually demonstrates their existence (a fact which Erikson and Goldthorpe appear to recognize (1992: 397)). Once again a possible rapprochement with the techniques of life historians seems highly desirable.

Furthermore, it should be pointed out that Erikson and Goldthorpe's strategy only allows them to deal with the significance of family forces in so far as they are class specific. However, many family influences might not be expected to vary by class (see for instance Thompson et al.'s (1983) study of the sharply varying family dynamics concerning child-rearing and gender relationships amongst different British fishing communities). So, whilst it would be wrong to say that the class structural approach to social mobility is not interested in families, the range of questions it can address are still limited.

One response to this might be to say that no research can tackle everything and that it is best to treat one variable (social class, in the case of Erikson and Goldthorpe) thoroughly rather than lots superficially. This is a view which has much sense to it. None the less, it can still be argued that there is much about social class which may remain elusive. The formation of social classes as collective groups depends upon more than social mobility (a point Goldthorpe readily concedes, see also Marshall et al. 1988). As Grusky and Van Rompaney (1992: 1723) have recently suggested, 'we would certainly question the assumption that mobility tables index the most salient social networks. Unless we believe that parent–child ties are the only "social glue" holding classes together, there is no reason to give precedence to the relationships in a mobility table relative to those represented in tables of assortitive mating, residential segregation, and the like.'

In summary, survey research offers the choice of investigating the explanatory powers of lots of variables but without attention to context, or of investigating the causal powers of one variable in a more contextual way which is attentive to the specificity of that variable's causal powers. The first route allows lots of different variables to be correlated but can only offer an aggregate summary of their relative importance which is therefore inattentive to context and specificity. The latter allows the specific properties of particular social classes to be examined but does so by excluding, at least heuristically, other relevant variables from view. The choice appears to be either to investigate one variable in depth or many in breadth. One obvious response is to say that what we need is the study of many variables in depth in specific contexts, and it is precisely this which the in-depth qualitative papers found in this book will allow!

Before concluding this discussion I need to add one rider. As I have suggested earlier in this paper it is unhelpful to reify quantitative research. Some recent developments in modelling techniques may make it possible to explore the role of contextual variables and there by allow researchers to combine the strength of class structural approaches with the catholicity of status attainment perspectives. Of particular interest here is the technique known as multi-level modelling (Goldstein 1987) which is designed to examine whether patterns of variation are affected by contextual variables.

## HISTORY AND TEMPORALITY

I now turn to deepen and develop this discussion by moving to consider the question of history. This has always been a central issue in mobility research, since mobility takes place over time (as well as in space). Our understanding of social mobility is therefore critically dependent on being able to specify correctly how time is measured and conceptualized.

This is an area where survey-based research appears well placed because of its attention to how historical time affects mobility rates. By splitting samples into cohorts according to their year of birth it is possible to compare the mobility of different generations in order to assess general trends (e.g. Hauser and Featherman 1977; Goldthorpe *et al*. 1987). It is possible to distinguish those trends in mobility due to historical shifts in the occupational structure (for instance, the decline of agricultural employment and the rise of professional and managerial employment) from those trends due to greater openness or 'fluidity' in the social structure.

Goldthorpe (1980) and Erikson and Goldthorpe (1992) claim that it is one of the virtues of the class structural approach that 'absolute' and 'relative' mobility can be distinguished. The former refers to the proportion of sons in different social groups compared to their fathers. This is bound to be affected by changes to the occupational structure; if handloom weaving is declining, for instance, then there will be fewer sons than fathers who are handloom weavers. Relative chances, however, will not be affected, since the chances of a handloom weaver's son rather than a doctor's son becoming a handloom weaver rather than a doctor will not itself be affected by the overall decline in the numbers of handloom weavers—since this background factor is constraining for both of them. Changes in relative odds are therefore not due to changing occupational structure but to the changing social fluidity and processes of social closure.

This is not the place to discuss some of the specific findings of this research. Suffice it to say that there is general agreement that the rise of middle-class employment has led to a marked predominance of upward over downward mobility measured in absolute terms. The main disagreement is whether there is a historical trend towards greater openness in relative rates, or whether there is 'trendless fluctuation' (Erikson and Goldthorpe 1992).

This is a very important issue. However, it by no means exhausts the significance of time. Griffin (1990) and Abbott (1990*b*) have recently pointed to other ways in which historicity and temporality might be significant in social research. Griffin (1990) points out that much historical sociology views time simply as a context in which things happen, but he points out that it is also necessary to explore how events themselves are sequenced. Time is not simply a background in which mobility takes place, but is also integral to the mobility process itself. Thus it is necessary to analyse the temporality of an individual's (or family's) actual mobility as well as the temporality of the structures within which mobility takes place. These considerations suggest a picture of kaleidoscopic complexity in which all the social processes of interest are historically mutable and changing, with the result that it is difficult to establish secure foundations on which any inquiry can take place.

What is apparent here is that few survey researchers have shown much interest in the precise 'sequencing' of an individual's mobility. Many studies determine whether an individual is mobile largely by focusing on just two temporal points—the time of the respondent at the survey compared to the time of his or her parent at a given period before (usually when the respondent was around 14–16 years old). This is as true for Erikson and Goldthorpe (1992) as for Blau and Duncan (1967). Although both sets of authors then seek to modify this by considering other time points (for instance occupation when respondents first entered the labour market), these are largely included to see if the basic analysis, based on a two-time snapshot, needs reworking.

The problems of relying on a simple two-point analysis of mobility have been well rehearsed by mobility researchers and are now generally accepted within the field (e.g. Erikson and Goldthorpe 1992: ch. 8). Sorenson (1986) argues that the focus upon intergenerational mobility leads to artificial results, since this freezes the class of both parent and child at one moment in time. However, given that people generally experience considerable mobility within their lives, the result is that intergenerational tables are rather misleading, since the 'one moment in time' classification of both parents and children is actually a radical simplification of the more complex trajectories their lives are likely to follow.

The problem of how the dynamism of people's life courses can be analysed using quantitative techniques has become one of the central concerns of social mobility research in recent years. But no satisfactory method of analysing individual life courses has been devised. The basic problem can be stated quite simply. Such is the enormous variety of the possible trajectories an individual can follow that no one method (currently) seems able to handle such complexity. Simplifications need to be made. I briefly review the main alternative methods of analysis.

Perhaps the most frequent method used to analyse change over time is event history analysis. This is a method which examines how long it takes particular transitions (for instance from unemployment to employment) to occur and then explores the factors which might account for varying speeds of transition using multiple regression techniques. The advantage of this method is a much greater sensitivity to the precise timing of particular events. Indeed it is the timing of given transitions which becomes the main object of explanation (dependent variable). The limitations are, however, equally striking. The dependent variable becomes a given transition, not an individual, with the result that it is difficult to examine a number of transitions of any one individual. Thus an individual who has experienced the same transition three times may appear in the analysis three times, alongside those who have only experienced one such transition. In short, the individual trajectory is lost.

A second way to deal with individual trajectories is to examine patterns of mobility within given simplifying parameters. A common approach is to examine occupational mobility within one employing firm, often a large bureaucracy (DiPrete 1989; Rosenbaum 1984; Gaertner 1980; Althauser and Kalleberg 1990). By this assumption the analytical task becomes easier since only particular sorts of job movements (those within one firm) are analyzed. Even this approach needs to simplify to proceed, however. Jobs generally are grouped into clusters (see the discussion in Althauser and Kalleberg 1990), whilst it is common not to examine every job shift but only those within a certain time period (as in Rosenbaum's 1984 tournament model which examines mobility within seven-year periods). Other researchers (Spenner, Otto, and Call 1982) only examine transitions which a significant number of people undertake, so ignoring atypical patterns. The problem with all these studies is that the degree of simplification is bound to lose context and detail and may be totally unsuitable for large numbers of people (for instance those who do not spend most of their lives working for one employer).

Finally, perhaps the most promising is that of optimal matching (Abbott and Hrycak 1990). This technique is designed to overcome some of the problems discussed above and attempts to explore how events are sequenced. By comparing types of transitions which people undertake it is possible to generate typologies of sequences. This approach is more attuned to specific trajectories made by individuals. It could quite profitably be applied, for instance, to patterns revealed by qualitative research such as autobiographies or oral histories. However, it too is not without its limitations. It is difficult to handle events which are not strictly sequenced but which are co-incident, and it therefore depends strongly on assumptions of linear time: an assumption which may not be suitable or appropriate for many sorts of social processes (see Lash and Urry 1994). Furthermore, optimal matching depends on being able to specify temporally fixed substitution costs in order to measure sequences at all.

In short, whilst the study of temporality has become central to inquiries into social mobility, and whilst there is now considerable awareness of problems with existing approaches, it cannot be claimed that an entirely satisfactory technique has been developed to analyse it within the quantitative tradition.

## SUBJECTIVITY AND SOCIAL MOBILITY

One of the most long-standing criticisms of survey research is its alleged inability adequately to measure attitudes, values, and identity (e.g. Sayer 1984). I have no intention of taking up this controversial topic at a general level, but here I consider this issue in relation to social mobility research. Conventionally, subjectivity has been studied by social mobility researchers in terms of the impact which mobility has on identities, beliefs, and practices (e.g. Erikson and Goldthorpe 1992: 2). This is clearly of great importance but I will discuss this only after considering an even more fundamental question: what part do people's strategies and values play in the processes which generate social mobility itself? I raise this, since to talk about subjectivity only as an 'effect'—a dependent variable—is to ignore the way in which subjective processes are tied up with the strategies and actions which produce mobility itself. Since structural processes do not happen behind people's backs, it is vital to examine how people plan, strategize, and reflect on their situation (cf. Giddens 1984).

Status attainment researchers were able to provide a subjective rationale to their accounts. It was a central claim of the status attainment approach that they correctly reflected the way most people envisaged social mobility—as movement through ranked hierarchy based on the socio-economic standings of occupations (Blau and Duncan 1967: ch. 4; Hauser and Featherman 1977: ch. 1; and see also Goldthorpe and Hope 1974). The extent to which this view is valid remains a bone of contention (see Jencks 1990). Lockwood (1966) claimed that this was only one of the possible ways people might imagine society. Pawson (1989) suggests that Goldthorpe and Hope's (1974) study suggests less than perfect agreement about rankings amongst respondents. He also makes the more important point that since interviews are 'social occasions' respondents may have provided answers which had little personal significance for them. Pawson claims that standardized interviews make it difficult to distinguish whether respondents are giving their own views or the views which they feel they are supposed to give.

In any event it is interesting that the class structural approach to social mobility abandoned the attempt to assess whether the categories used by the researchers accurately reflected people's own views. Goldthorpe's class schema was devised according to 'objective' criteria which he, as researcher, thought were relevant and without reference to the findings of ranking research. Initially this may seem to be a step backwards, away from any attempt to take other people's subjectivity and consciousness seriously. But it can be argued that the reverse is true. For one thing Goldthorpe managed to avoid being dependent upon the problematic results of attitude surveys. Furthermore, he argued that the construction of a class schema was not to be confused with social class itself. Unlike status attainment researchers there is no claim that the occupational or class schema necessarily has any significance to anyone: whether it does or not becomes a matter for empirical inquiry. Goldthorpe argues that there is a radical distinction between class formation—the development of social classes as collectivities which includes subjective awareness of class—and the delineation of a 'class schema'. The class schema in and of itself tells us nothing about whether social class is a salient social process, but is devised simply as a tool to help researchers investigate whether it is.

However, this formulation raises a host of problematic issues. First, it installs a strong analytical distinction between social mobility processes and what people themselves actually think about mobility. The implication is that mobility processes can be analysed without consideration of how people reflect on or think about mobility, a fairly rigid structuralist position which might appear to be at odds with Goldthorpe's avowal of an 'action perspective' (cf. Johnson 1990). In so far as Goldthorpe deals with this problem he does so by endorsing the claims of rational choice theory (Goldthorpe 1990: 420) that individuals will tend to maximize their interests, and that for the purpose of analysis this self-interested behaviour can be taken as a constant. This is rather ironic, since it would appear that rational choice theory is better disposed to explain mobility in a ranked hierarchy (since there are good rational reasons for wanting to move up a hierarchy) than through a non-ranked class schema (what rational reasons are there for people to want to move from one class to another if they have roughly similar socio-economic conditions?). Recognizing this point Erikson and Goldthorpe (1992) build their topographical models by considering the sorts of resources or constraints open to particular classes (with the exception of hierarchical effects), and therefore largely exclude the role of subjectivity from mobility processes.

However, it is actually very difficult to exclude lay beliefs from a consideration of the definition of mobility. A notable example occurs in the insistence of Erikson and Goldthorpe that women should be allocated to their husband's class position rather than their own, since survey evidence suggests that women tend to identify their own class according to their husband's occupation. While this may be true, it is a strange case of double standards, since men are allocated to classes on the basis, not of their own, but of Erikson and Goldthorpe's reasoning. Why should women be treated differently?

Apart from inconsistencies such as this, Erikson and Goldthorpe do have one powerful defence to draw upon. This is the line of argument, indebted to Simmel and Weber, that since it is not possible to find out what is going on in anyone else's head, all we can ever do is construct models of what people might be thinking and then seeing if this construction seems valid, at least within its own terms. In other words the option of finding out people's 'genuine', 'authentic' identity does not exist, so why make any effort to obtain the unattainable?

However, even if this argument is accepted (and the dispute amongst oral historians between those who believe that their accounts are constructions compared to those who believe that they represent some sort of authentic account is a hot one, see Samuel and Thompson 1990; CCS 1982), it should be pointed out that the available evidence suggests two ways in which people appear to think about mobility in very different ways from that envisaged within the class structural approach. First, evidence indicates that to an individual, their own work-life mobility is of more importance than their intergenerational mobility. Whilst survey researchers have emphasized intergenerational mobility, people themselves are more interested (for quite obvious reasons) in their own lives. Thus Goldthorpe's own study of life histories, reported in *Class Structure and Social Mobility in Modern Britain* indicates that the respondent's family backgrounds are actually not very significant in affecting current patterns of kinship and sociability. Goldthorpe's main target here is those writers who have seem mobility as disruptive, causing 'status' tensions. He shows that mobile men are no more likely to be alienated or isolated than anyone else. Against the view that the socially mobile are detached from social norms and values he shows that they are often well adjusted and content. And rather than the upwardly mobile being most ambitious and careerist, he shows that it is the second-generation professionals and managers who are more concerned to get on (for instance to better their father). The upwardly mobile are more content to reach a secure middle-class destination and to put their family welfare before further career progress.

This is an interesting critique of the 'status attainment' views of social mobility. However, it also undercuts his own class formation approach. If the mobile are little different from the non-mobile, how can intergenerational mobility affect class formation? This point is particularly pertinent, since Goldthorpe shows that men upwardly mobile into the middle classes tend to have patterns of sociability similar to the established middle classes. In other words the class to which people move seems to affect their sociability much more than the class they move from. This simple point has the potential to undercut the entire class formation project—for why bother to look at people's origins if their actions and views are more dependent upon their present social location?

This point is true also in terms of people's beliefs about mobility. Respondents who in Goldthorpe's terms were not socially mobile, that is to say that they were in the same class as their fathers, frequently thought that they were socially mobile in some form or another. Goldthorpe's caution on this point is instructive. 'where we have characterized our respondents as intergenerationally stable . . . we have *probably not, in the main, seriously contradicted* the sense of their own experience' (Goldthorpe *et al.* 1987: 227, my emphasis). Goldthorpe's triple qualification is evidence of considerable hesitancy here. A further point might also be added. Since respondents were not informed of Goldthorpe's class schema, they were not really given the opportunity to contradict him! There are many forms of subjective awareness of mobility, ranging from feelings of general social improvement particularly important amongst the working class, to the awareness of career mobility amongst the service class, which are simply not captured by Goldthorpe's class analysis.

A second area in which lay perceptions differ considerably from those of survey researchers is the role of the family. The work of Fraser (1984), Steedman (1985), and others indicates that early family relationships are of critical importance in affecting people's own perceptions of mobility, and indeed their identity more generally. Steedman's account of how her own identity was related to the particular nature of her upbringing by a single mother working in the textile industry is a moving testament to this. The danger inherent within the class structural approach is that it gives no purchase on the other social processes which might be as important, or indeed more important, in affecting people's *sense* of mobility.

## CONCLUSIONS

Life historians can learn much from the work discussed in this chapter, whilst survey researchers should also recognize the relevance of qualitative study to their work. As I have indicated at various points there are many points of contact between (some) quantitative and qualitative approaches. The interest in process, and the concern with how specific social groups pass on their advantages is an obvious overlap with class structural perspectives. The interest in the range of different factors implicated in mobility offers the potential for dialogue with status attainment researchers. Life historians can do much to tease out the complex interplay between people's strategies, values, and their mobility, a set of connections which has been rather elusive within virtually all survey-based approaches to the subject. They can help establish whether the sorts of factors which the topographical models of Erikson and Goldthorpe suggest to be significant forces behind social mobility can be found to be operative at a micro level.

It might also be argued that qualitative work offers a way of combining the relative strengths and weaknesses of different types of survey research. Status attainment research is able to give aggregate outlines of the possible role of many variables in affecting mobility. Class structural research is able to provide a comprehensive account of the mobility chances of different social classes. However both measure mobility in a predefined way (either in terms of a ranked hierarchy, or of a class schema) which is of uncertain relevance to people themselves. Status attainment researchers can only offer an aggregate picture of the average effect which particular variables might have. They are less sensitive to variety and context within the social world. Class structural researchers, by contrast are highly sensitive to (class) specificity but are forced to exclude many non-class processes from view. Qualitative research might be able to combine both these sorts of strengths (breadth against depth) in specific micro-settings.

However, this is not to say that survey research does not have real advantages over qualitative research. The study of social mobility involves the study of relative chances. In order to accurately assess the relative advantages of one group over another it is vital to have all social groups represented fully in the inquiry and representative sampling seems a vital precondition for this (cf. Layder 1993 on the combination of micro and macro research). In the end the only way an effective dialogue will take place is if differing research traditions respectfully acknowledge their own limitations as well as their strengths.

ACKNOWLEDGEMENTS

I would like to thank Daniel Bertaux, John Goldthorpe, Helen Hills, Derek Layder, Geoff Payne, and Paul Thompson for comments on an earlier draft of this paper.

REFERENCES

Abbott, A. (1988), *The System of Professions*, Berkeley, University of California.
—— (1990a), 'Vacancy Models for Historical Data', in Breiger (1990a).
—— (1990b), 'From Causes to Events', *Sociological Methods and Research*, 20 (4), 428—55.
—— and Hrycak, A. (1990), 'Measuring Resemblances in Sequential Data: An Optimal Matching Analysis of Musicians Careers', *American Journal of Sociology*, 96 (1), 144–85.
Althauser, R. P., and Kalleberg, A. (1981), 'Firms, Occupations and the Structure of Labor Markets: A Conceptual Analysis', in I. Berg (ed.), *Sociological Perspectives on Labor Markets*, Orlando, Fla., Academic.
—— (1990), 'Identifying Career Lines and Internal Labour Markets Within Firms: A Study of the Interrelationships of Theory and Methods', in Breiger (1990a).
Beck, U. (1992), *The Risk Society*, London, Sage.
Bertaux, D. (1991), 'From Methodological Monopoly to Pluralism in the Sociology of Social Mobility', in S. Dex (ed.), *Life and Work History Analyses*, London, Routledge.
Blau, P. M., and Duncan, O. D. (1967), *The American Occupational Structure*, New York, Wiley.
Bourdieu, P. (1984), *Distinction*, London, Routledge.

Breiger, R. (ed.) (1990a), *Social Mobility and Social Structure*, Cambridge, Cambridge UP.
—— (1990b), 'Introduction: On the Structural Analysis of Social Mobility', in Breiger (1990a).
Britten, N., and Heath, A. (1983), 'Women, Men and Social Class', in E. Gamarnikow (ed.), *Gender, Class and Work*, London, Heinemann.
CCS (Centre for Contemporary Cultural Studies) (1982), *Making Histories*, London, Hutchinson.
Clark, J., Modgil, C., and Modgil, S. (eds), (1990), *John H Goldthorpe: Consensus and Controversy*, London, Falmer.
Crompton, R. (1993), *Class and Stratification*, Oxford, Polity.
Dex, S. (1990), 'Goldthorpe on Class and Gender: The Case Against', in Clark *et al.* (1990).
DiPrete, T. (1989), *The Bureaucratic Labour Market*, New York, Plenum.
—— (1993), 'Industrial Restructuring and the Mobility Response of American Workers in the 1980s', *American Sociological Review*, 58 (1), 74–96.
Duncan, O. D. (1961), 'A Socio-Economic Index for all Occupations', in A. R. Reiss (ed.), *Occupations and Social Status*, New York, Free Press.
—— Featherman, D. L., and Duncan, B. (1972), *Socioeconomic Background and Achievement*, New York, Seminar.
Erikson, R., and Goldthorpe, J. H. (1992), *The Constant Flux*, Oxford, Clarendon.
Featherman, D. L., and Hauser, R. M. (1978), *Opportunity and Change*, New York, Academic.
Fraser, R. (1984), *In Search of a Past*, London, Verso.
Gaertner, K. (1980), 'The Structure of Organizational Careers', in Breiger (1990a).
Giddens, A. (1973), *The Class Structure of the Advanced Societies*, London, Heinemann.
—— (1984), *The Constitution of Society*, Oxford, Polity.
Glass, D. V. (1954), *Social Mobility in Britain*, London, Routledge.
Goldstein, H. (1987), *Multi-level Models in Educational and Social Research*, Oxford University Press.
Goldthorpe, J. H. (1990), 'A Response', in Clark *et al.* (1990).
—— (with C. Llewellyn and C. Payne) (1980), *Social Mobility and the Class Structure in Modern Britain*, Oxford, Clarendon.
—— (with C. Llewellyn and C. Payne) (1987), 2nd edn. of Goldthorpe *et al.* (1980).
—— and Hope, K. (1974), *The Social Grading of Occupations: A New Approach and Scale*, Oxford, Clarendon.
Granovetter, M. (1974), *Getting a Job: A Study of Contacts and Careers*, Cambridge, Mass., Harvard UP.

Griffin, L. J. (1990), 'Temporality, Events and Explanation in Historical Sociology', *Sociological Methods and Research*, 403–27.

Grusky, D., and Van Rompaney, E. (1992), 'Comments and Reflections on Scaling Occupations', *American Journal of Sociology*, 97 (6), 1712–18.

Hauser, R. M., and Featherman, D. L. (1977), *The Process of Stratification*, New York, Academic.

Jencks, C. (1990), 'What is the True Rate of Social Mobility?', in Breiger (1990a).

Johnson, T. (1990), 'Ideology and Action in the Work of John Goldthorpe', in Clark *et al.* (1990).

Kalleberg, A., and Griffin, L. (1980), 'Class, Occupation and Inequality in Job Rewards', *American Journal of Sociology*, 85, 731–68.

Kelley, J. (1990), 'The Failure of a Paradigm: Log Linear Models of Social Mobility', in Clark *et al.* (1990).

Kelsall, R. K. (1954), *Higher Civil Servants in Britain*, London, Routledge and Kegan Paul.

Lash, S., and Urry, J. (1994), *Economies of Signs and Spaces*, London, Sage.

Layder, D. (1993), *New Strategies in Social Research: An Introduction and Guide*, Oxford, Polity.

Levine, J. (1990), 'Measuring Occupational Stratification Using Log-Linear Distance Models', in Breiger (1990a).

Lieberson, S. (1985), *Making it Count*, Berkeley, University of California.

Lin, N. (1990), 'Social Resources and Social Mobility: A Structural Theory of Status Attainment', in Breiger (1990a).

Lockwood, D. (1958), *The Blackcoated Worker*, London, Allen and Unwin.

——(1966), 'Sources of Variation in Working Class Images of Society', *Sociological Review*, 14, 249–67.

Marshall, G., Newby, H., Rose, D., Vogler, C. (1988), *Social Class in Modern Britain*, London, Unwin Hyman.

Parkin, F. (1979), *Marxism and Class Theory: A Bourgeois Critique*, London, Tavistock.

Pawson, R. A. (1989), *A Measure for Measures*, London, Routledge.

——(1993), 'Social Mobility', in D. Morgan and E. Stanley (eds), *Debates in Sociology*, Manchester, Manchester UP.

Penn, R. (1981), 'The Nuffield Class Categorization', *Sociology*, 15, 265–71.

Ragin, C. (1987), *The Comparative Method*, Berkeley, University of California Press.

Rosenbaum, J. E. (1984), *Career Mobility in a Corporate Hierarchy*, New York, Academic.

Samuel, Raphael, and Thompson, Paul (1990) (eds), *The Myths We Live By*, London, Routledge.
Savage, M., Barlow, J., Dickens, P., and Fielding, A. J. (1992), *Property, Bureaucracy and Culture: Middle Class Formation in Contemporary Britain*, London, Routledge.
Sayer, A. (1984), *Method in Social Science: A Realist Approach*, London, Methuen.
Scott, J. (1982), *The Upper Classes: Property and Privilege in Britain*, Basingstoke, MacMillan.
Sorenson, A. B. (1986), 'Theory and Methodology in Social Stratification', in U. Himmelstrand (ed.), *Sociology from Crisis to Science*, London, Sage.
Spenner, K., Otto, L., Call, V. R. A. (1982), *Career Lines and Careers*, Lexington, Mass., Heath.
Stanworth, M. (1984), 'Women and Class Analysis: A Reply to John Goldthorpe', *Sociology*, 18.
Steedman, C. (1985), *Landscape for the Good Woman*, London, Virago.
Strauss, A. (1987), *Qualitative Analysis for Social Scientists*, Cambridge, Cambridge UP.
Thompson, P. (with T. Wailey and T. Lummis) (1983), *Living the Fishing*, London, Routledge.
—— (1988), *The Voice of the Past*, Oxford, Oxford UP (2nd edn.).
Warner, L., and Lunt, P. (1942), *The Status System of a Modern Community*, New Haven, Yale University Press.
White, H. C. (1970), *Chains of Opportunity*, Cambridge, Mass., Harvard UP.
Wright, E. O. (1979), *Class, Crisis and the State*, London, Verso.
—— (1985), *Classes*, London, Verso.

# INDEX

Abbadia San Salvatore 183–4
  development 188–90
  local identity 193–7
Abbott, A. 305, 306, 314
  and Hrycak, A. 305, 307, 316
absolute mobility 313
accents 218, 223
action perspective 318
actionalism 62–3, 67, 80–2
affiliation: relations of 252–3, 258 n.
agricultural communities:
  restrictions on occupations 101–2
  women in 101–2
alcoholism 50, 291
Alestalo, M., Andorka, R., and
  Harcsa, I. 259
Alexander, J. 63
alienation and mobility 319
allotments 143
Althauser, R. P., and Kalleberg, A.
  305, 315–16
America: openness of society 3, 4
Anderson, M., and Morse, D. J. 203
Andorka, R. 259, 261, 278
  and Zagorski, K. 259
Andrews, A. 203
Angus family 223–4
Anheier, H., Gerhards, J., and
  Romo, F. 211, 222
anthroponomic production 19–20,
  304–5
apprenticeship 42
  for women 104
aristocracy 3
  attachment to houses 131–3, 134–40
  Hungary 296 n.
army families: geographical
  mobility 158
attachment to housing 131–2
  country houses and chateaux 131–3,
    134–40
  defensive 154–5
  peasantry and land 140–4
  second homes 145–52, 168
  urban 152–6
autobiography 99, 120 n.
  role of family home 135

Balfour Act (1902) 110
barriers to mobility 67
  family closeness 47–50, 52–3
Bath, Marquess of 135
Beaulieu, François 167–8
Beck, U., Giddens, A., and Lash, S.
  198
Bedford, Duke of: *A Silver-Plated
  Spoon* 135
Bertaux, D. 200–1, 262, 269, 292, 293,
  300, 304–5
Bertaux, D., and Bertaux-Wiame, I.
  200–1, 219
birth control 111
Blandford, Marquess of 137–8
Blau, P., and Duncan, O. D. 299, 301,
  301–2, 306, 307, 309, 310, 314, 317
  *The American Occupational
  Structure* 200
Blenheim Palace 137–8
Bloch, F., and Buisson, M. 21
blocked mobility 198–9, 204–5
Bossard, J., and Boll, E. 44
Boudon 62, 63
Boulay, Robert and Claudine 167
Bourdieu, P. 19, 20, 62, 63, 207, 299
  on cultural capital 44, 130, 216
  on 'habitus' 43
  on social capital 211, 212–13
  *The Logic of Practice* 63
Boyd, M., Goyder, J., Jones, F.,
  McRoberts, H., and Porter, J. 200
Brabant, Beatrice 142
Bradgate, Ben 47
Brander, M. 202
Brasilia Teimosa 165
Breiger, R. 301, 302
Bridges, Ted 38, 40
Britten, N., and Heath, A. 311
Brown, R. 213
Bruce, Mrs 206
Bumsted, J. 203, 208
Butler Act (1944) 116

Cage, R. 203
Canada: Scottish migrants in 25–6,
  198–226

328  Index

capital:
  collective 208–9
  convertibility of 217
  cultural, *see* cultural capital
  economic 19
  material 208–9, 210–11
  social, *see* social capital
  transformation of 211
Caradog family 137, 157
case histories:
  benefits of 12
  comparative analysis 66–7
  sociological significance 67, 76
  *see also* life-stories
Castel, R. 252–3
Castells, M. 130
catastrophe theory 231, 244
causality: complexity of 18, 302, 309
Causse, Albert and Brigitte 162–3
censuses 259
Chartists 128
Chester family 263, 280–5, 292–4
churches 42
civil service:
  studies of 305–6
  surveys of 301
civil service occupations 81–2, 97
class:
  and family forces 311–12
  and housing tenure 129, 131
  property-owning 307
  sizes distinguished in surveys 307
class structural approach 303–5, 309–10, 317–21
Coleman, J. S. 211
collective capital 208–9
collective effort:
  and mobility 199
  for selected siblings 219–20
colonialism and rootlessness 157
Communist Party:
  Hungary 281, 286, 294
  Italy 186, 189–90, 194–6
  Russia 240–1, 242–3, 248–9
Comte, A. 63, 87
Comte, Roger and Alice 162
consumption patterns: changes in 78
Cookson, Catherine: *Hannah Massey* 128
co-operatives 188
counter-mobility 261, 269
country houses and chateaux 131–3, 134–40
  attachment to 131–3, 134–40
  opening to public 135, 138–9
  and personal position 154
Creese, G., Guppy, N., and Meissner, M. 215
Crozier, M. 62
cultural capital 19, 44, 130, 208, 216–20, 251–2
  convertibility of 217, 220–4
  and national 'disposition' 224–5
  plurality of 216–17
  recognition of qualifications 221–2
cultural deprivation 218–19
cultural structuralism 223

de Lauwre, C. 131
de Meyrac, Pierre 139–40
demographic reproduction 269–70
deprivation: cultural 218–19
determination 86–7
Dex, S. 310
DiPrete, T. 305–6, 315
divorce:
  family patterns 53
  and housing 172–5, 181 n.
  and social mobility 53
  stigma of 207
dressmaking 104
Duncan, O. D. 301
  Featherman, D. L., and Duncan, B. 301, 311
Durkheim, E. 3, 63, 87
Durrell, L.: *The Alexandria Quartet* 90–1

education:
  compulsory 101
  family belief in 54–6, 116, 279
  and first job 65
  and immigration 51–2
  institutions 42
  legislation 110, 116
  limited by poverty 110–12
  retraining courses 279
  and Russian Revolution (1917) 240–1, 242–3
  shortage of funds 274, 277, 281
  and social capital 211–12
  and socialism 169
  unfulfilled aspirations 110, 112
élites, theory of 3
Elliott, B. 208
emigration, *see* migration
emotional attitudes to housing, *see* attachment

emotional and moral bonds of families 20–1
employment:
   co-ethnic 209, 210, 213–14
   informal sources of 107, 122 n., 209
   and provision of housing 128
Engels, F. 87
enjoyment of occupations 105–6, 121 n.
   and advancement 106
entrepreneurs:
   enjoyment of occupations 106
   in France 52
   *see also* family businesses
Erikson, E. 44
Erikson, R., and Goldthorpe, J. H. 200, 259, 303, 304–5, 309–10, 311–12, 313, 314, 315, 317, 318–19
ethnic identity and social capital 215–16
ethnic networks and mobility 199, 208–10
event history analysis 315
exclusions 252–3

families:
   and access to employment 107
   anthroponomic perspective 19–20
   case studies and 18–20
   class-specific forces 311–12
   commitment to 21
   conservative influence of 47–50, 52–3, 108–9, 217
   definitions of 43
   emotional and moral bonds 20–1
   father–child relationships 258 n.
   as launching-pad for individual change 2
   need for differentiation between generations 44–5
   research methods and, *see* research methods
   response to downward mobility 217–20
   and social status 7, 20, 64–5
   and social values 43
'Families and Social Mobility' project 22–3, 56–9, 125, 201
family businesses:
   cutlery 186–8
   and marriage 88–92
   metamorphoses 84, 85, 86, 90
   power over descendents 83–7
'Family Life and Work before 1918' project 22, 100, 120 n.

family 'scripts' 21
family strategies 43
family systems perspective 21, 44–5, 60 n.
feminist research 310
Field, Edward 46–7
Fields, Gracie 127
Fine, Rudi 136
Fisher Act (1918) 116
food, attitudes to 125
Fraser, R. 320

Gaertner, K. 315
Garnett family 149–52, 179 n.
Geertz, C. 95
gender issues:
   differences in occupational careers 34–42
   in structure of surveys 7–8, 32–3, 310, 318–19
geographical mobility:
   and attitudes to housing 125
   and family closeness 49–50, 51
   rootless, *see* rootlessness; working class 154–6
Germain, Henri 146
Giddens, A. 13, 299, 310, 317
   theory of structuration 63
gift: intergenerational 21
Girod, R. 261, 269
Girouard, M.: *Life in the English Country House* 131
Glass, D. V. 301
Goldstein, H. 313
Goldthorpe, J. 32, 310, 313, 317–19
   and Erikson, R.: *The Constant Flux* 6
   and Hope, K. 317
   Llewellyn, C., and Payne, C.: *Social Mobility & Class Structure* 200, 299, 303–4, 307, 313, 319–20
grandparents, influence of 46
Granovetter, M. 213, 305
   and Tilly, C. 209
Griffin, L. J. 314
Grusky, D., and Van Rompaney, E. 312
Gudenus, J., and Szentirmay, L. 296 n.
gypsies 156

'habitus' (Bourdieu) 43
Halbwachs, M. 44
Hall, J. 223
Hand family 169–70

# Index

Harcsa, I. 261
Hardie, Keir 128
Hareven, Tamara: *Family Time and Industrial Time* 10
Hauser, R. M., and Featherman, D. L. 313, 317
Hawk family 263, 286–92, 293, 296–7 n.
Hirschman, Albert 244
Hobsbawn, E., and Ranger, T. 133, 226
holocaust survivors 11
home ownership:
  attitudes to 129–30, 155–6, 168–9
  *see also* attachment to housing
Horsley family 50
houseboats 160
housing 24–5
  attachment to, *see* attachment to housing
  building by residents 164–5
  and class 129, 131
  collective ownership 175
  and divorce 172–5, 181 n.
  as dream 174–5
  emotional attitudes to 128
  and family identity 125, 139–40, 141, 152
  and family life-cycle 162
  growth of home ownership 129–30
  help by parents 175, 182 n.
  and independence 168
  inter-generational households 142–3
  as investment 153
  as life-story museum 126–7
  as material base 125–6
  and migration 160–1, 205
  protective function 133, 173
  provision by employers 128, 186
  public 148, 154, 165–6, 169
  rented 129, 165–6
  role of parlour 127
  Russian Revolution (1917) and 245–6
  second homes 144–52
  significance of 124–5
  and social status 124
  sociological studies 130–1
  step-by-step mobility 166–72
  as stronger focus than occupation 163, 170–1
  timing of moves 163–72
  of upper classes 25
  and upward mobility 125
  urban attachments 152–6
housing projects 161–3
'huddling up' 126–7
Hungary 26
  aristocracy 296 n.
  degree of openness 260
  differences from West European mobility 295 n.
  Jewish citizens 296 n.
  surveys of social mobility 259–62
  treatment of kulak families 272–3, 274, 279

identity, suppression of 240, 247–8
illiteracy 101, 192
immigration, *see* migration
individualism, and upward mobility 3
inequality: construction and transmission 299
inheritance patterns:
  Britain 133
  France 133–4
interviews:
  in-depth 13
  use of closed question 9
  *see also* qualitative research; quantitative research; research methods
Italy:
  classification of occupations 97 n.
  peasant gardens in Turin 143
  *see also* Abbadia San Salvatore; Santa Croce sull'Arno; Scarperia

Jackson, B., and Marsden, D. 53
Jencks, C. 317
Jewish migration 161
Johnston, Robert 221–2
Jordan family 168–9

Kaeble, H. 10
Kalleberg, A. and Griffin, L. 303
Karady, V. 296 n.
Kay, Jack 205–6
Kedleston, Geoffrey 160
Keeler, Sue 39–40
Kelley, J. 306
Kelsall, R. K. 301
Kovacs, M. M., and Orkeny, A. 261
kulaks (rich peasants) 271, 272–3, 274, 279

# Index

labour markets, entry into 14–16
Lamont, M. 216–17
language, and social status 218, 223
Lash, S., and Urry, J. 316
Layder, D. 322
Leger, Nicholas and Suzanne 163
leisure: and fulfillment 144–5
leisure classes, and Russian Revolution (1917) 244–5
Lévi-Strauss, C. 63
Levine, J. 305
Lewis, O.: *The Children of Sanchez* 257 n.
LeWita, Beatrix 126
Lieberson, S. 302, 304
life-stories 201, 308
  class structural approach 304–5
  interview techniques 66
  material on motivations and emotions 42
  as myth 34, 59 n.
  as oral history 34, 120 n.
  questionnaires 13, 16–17
  role of chance 17
  and subjective perceptions 7
  as transgenerational transmission 33–4
  uses of 13–14
Lin, N. 305
Lindsay, Mrs 218
Lockwood, D. 301, 317
Lofgren, O. 127–8
log linear analysis 98
London, Jack: *The Iron Heel* 189, 197 n.
Longleat 135
Lucas, R. 202
Luhmann 63

Mackay family 203, 219–20
Malsy, chateau of 139
Mann, Thomas: *Buddenbrooks* 243–4
Manning, Jenny 38–9
Marchessaux, Marquis de 138–9
marriage:
  accepted behaviour in 43
  and development of family businesses 88–92
  and dual lineage 88, 91–2
  effect on women's social mobility 36–42
  as girls' future occupations 108
  'outsiders' in 88–92
  and upward mobility 24, 291
  and women's career paths 23
marriage registers 98
Marshall, G., Newby, H., Rose, D., and Vogler, C. 310, 312
Marx, K. 63
  on social conflict 4
Massie family 158–9
material capital 208–9, 210–11
Mauleon, Yves 141
Mauss, M. 21
Mead, M. 63
memory:
  as social phenomenon 44
  subjective nature of 99
Meuse, Alain 164
migration:
  chain 213, 218, 220
  and cultural deprivation 218–19
  and downward mobility 217–20
  and education 51–2
  from countryside 292
  and housing 126–7, 160–1
  Irish 203, 207–8
  Jewish 161
  long-distance 51–2
  motives for 204–7
  and reflexivity 198–9
  and risk 198–9
  role of cultural associations 212, 213–14, 223–4
  of Scots in Canada 25–6, 198–226
  social and cultural capital for 208, 211–16
  and threat of downward mobility 198–9, 205–7
Miller, S. M. 199, 200
mining 47, 101, 105
  in Abbadia San Salvatore 188–90, 193–7
  and home ownership 128
mobile homes 160
mobility, origins of 1–2
moral commitments 17–18
Morin, E. 62, 63
Morton, J. 203
motherhood:
  cultural influence of mothers 53
  effect on women's social mobility 36–42
Muthesius, S.: *The English Terraced House* 131

National Trust 158, 179 n.
neo-positivism 87
networks:
  and cultural capital 222–3
  ethnic 214
  professional 213
  social 212–16
  women's role in 214–15
Nicole-Drancourt, C. 14–16
Nilaiev family 235–8, 254, 255–6 n.
Normand, Cecile 145
Nuffield Social Mobility Study 303, 307
nursing 104, 121 n., 213

occupation:
  and rootlessness 157–61
  surveys based on 8
occupational deprivation 103
occupational transmission, and emotional relationships 46
O'Hara family 50, 155
Orkeny, A. 261
Ossowski, S. 260, 291

parents:
  attitudes to occupations 81–2
  expectations of children 205
  help with housing 175, 182 n.
  influence on children's aspirations 107–9, 219–20
  and shadow careers 119
Pareto, V. 3
Parker, Roderick 38, 45–6
Parkin, F. 299
Parsons, T. 4, 18, 63
Pascoe, Mont 47–8
Pawson, R. A. 304, 317
peasantry:
  attachment to land 140–4
  urban migration 140, 143–4
Peel, Kathleen 166
Peel, Sally 168
peer groups 42
  and career aspirations 109–10
Penn, R. 307
Percy, Leah 40–2, 46, 156
personal choice: and changes to social structure 2
political activism: transmission of 248–50
Portocarero, L. 215
positivism 309
Poulton family 149–52

pregnancy: as escape from family 50–1
Prigojine, I.: chaos theory 18
property: transmissibility of 93–4
Protestantism and social mobility 4–5
public housing 148, 154, 165–6, 169
Purcell, May 158

qualitative research 95–6, 98–100, 321–2
  linking with quantitative research 305–6
quantitative research 98–9, 117, 200, 301–8
  advantages 321–2
  class structural approach 303–5, 309–10, 317–21
  comparative analysis 307
  correlation and causality 309
  event history analysis 315
  inductive perspective 305
  on labour market and mobility 305–6
  linking with qualitative research 305–6
  log linear techniques 308
  multi-level modelling 313
  optimal matching techniques 305, 316
  path analysis 301
  representativeness and atypicality 306–8
  on small size groups 307–8
  social networks 305
  status attainment 302–3, 310–11
  strengths 300
  using language of numbers 302–3
  using simplifying parameters 315–16
  variable analysis 308–13
  variety of approaches 300

Ragin, C. 307
railwaymen 106, 121 n.
recruitment, informal 107, 122 n., 209
reflexivity: and migration 198–9
Reid, W. S. 203
relational capital 251–2
relative mobility 313–14
Renault, Maurice 153–4
research methods:
  case studies 11–31
  controlled experiments 12
  correlation and causation 302, 309
  event history analysis 315

## Index

family histories 262
feminist 310
ISA paradigm 259–60
life-stories 201
qualitative, *see* qualitative research
quantitative, *see* quantitative research
questionnaires 251
random sampling 299
social genealogies 255 n., 263
surveys 5–11, 27
variable analysis 308–13
retirement 145
revolutions 26–7
  and civil wars 234
  destruction of social order 230–1
  historical significance 230
  Russian 231–58
Rex, J. 130
Ridings family 171–2
risk: and migration 198–9
Roberts, Cledwyn 54–6
role theory 44
rootlessness 125, 131–2, 156–61
  army families 158
  Jewish 161
Rosenbaum, J. E. 315, 316
Russia 26–7
  1917 revolution, *see* Russian Revolution (1917)
Russian Revolution (1917):
  and civil war 234
  and concealment of identity 240, 247–8
  and education 240–1, 242–3
  fluctuations in social mobility 231–3
  and housing 245–6
  inappropriateness of Western-style analysis 253–4
  inversion of values 253–4
  and leisure classes 244–5
  and market economy 253
  population drop 241–2

Sackville-West, Vita 135
Salviac, Pierre 146–7
Samuel, R., and Thompson, P. 319
Santa Croce sull'Arno 183–4
  development 184–6
  local world-view 190–3
Saunders, P. 131
Savage, M., Barlow, J., Dickens, P., and Fielding, A. J. 300

Sayer, A. 302, 303, 316–17
Scarperia 183–4
  development 186–8
  local world-view 190–3
Scott, J. 307
Segalen, M. 131
self-employment: attitudes to 81–2, 97
Selkirk, Lorna 166
selling: and relationships with customers 77–80
sequencing of mobility 314–15
service: work in 160
shadow careers 24, 98–123
  increasing reflection on 112–17
  irrational 104–5
  modesty of aspirations 102–5
  and parents 119
  and peer groups 109–10
  resignation 117–19
  sense of loss 102, 111–12, 118–19
  women 116–17
shantytowns 165
Simbal family 51
Simmel, G. *Philosophy of Money* 5, 63
Simo, T. 261
Sims family 48–9, 155
single-industry economies 101–2
'situs' mobility 278
Smith, Betty 46
Smith, G. 201
Smith family (Hungary) 263, 270–9, 285, 292–4
social achievement 201
social capital 19, 26, 79, 208, 211–16
  and education 211–12
  and ethnic identity 215–16
  of women 214–15
social status:
  in class society 64
  and families 64–5
  and housing 124
  and occupation 32–3
socialism:
  and education 169
  effect on mobility 260–1, 290–1, 293–4; *see also* Russian Revolution (1917)
  family belief in 54
  opposition to 206
socialization processes 65–6
  and appropriation of grandchildren 91–2
Sorenson, A. B. 315

Sorokin, P.:
  on Russian Revolution 231–3, 241–2, 247
  *Social Mobility* 3, 11, 26, 200
Sparkbrook, Birmingham 161
Spenner, K., Otto, L., and Call, V. R. A. 316
Standworth, M. 310
Steedman, C. 320
Steel family 136–7, 169, 170–1
Strauss, Anselm 200, 308
structuralism 62–3, 67, 76–87
  cultural 223
structure versus agency 62–4, 67, 94–5
  and shadow careers 100
subjective perceptions: influence on life-decisions 15–16, 17
subjectivity of memory 34
subjectivity and social mobility 316–21
Summerhayes family 157
surveys:
  questionnaires 34
  and research methods 5–6
  strengths and weaknesses 6–11, 27
Szelenyi, I. 279

teachers: and aspirations of children 110
teaching: as career for women 102, 104–5, 121 n.
teleological reconstructions of past 190–3
Terrenoire family 67–96
Thompson, David 204–5
Thompson, P. 21, 201, 217, 310, 312
Tiller family 263, 264–70, 293, 294
Tilly, C., and Brown, C. H. 213
time: historical concept of 313–16
Tiverton, Dick 136
Tocqueville, A. de:
  *Democracy in America* 3
  on 'habits of the heart' 43
Touraine, A. 62, 63
Trace, Michel 141–2
tradition: invention of 196, 226
transmissibility 93–4
transmission:
  of equivalents 93
  'in extreme situations' 230–54
  and metamorphosis 93
  of political activism 248–50
  and praxis 94–5
  social context 238, 251–3

and transmissibility 93–4
Turner, R. 44
Tuscany 25
  variations between communes 183
  *see also* Abbadia San Salvatore; Santa Croce sull'Arno; Scarperia

unemployment 14–15
  and downward mobility 35
unions: in Italy 186
urban anthropology 131
urban attachments to housing 152–6
urban migration 140, 143–4

Veblen, T.: *Theory of the Leisure Class* 127
Villneuve, Antoine 147–8
violence in families 50, 185, 189
voluntarism 94–5
  *see also* structure versus agency

Ward, Colin 164–5
Warner, L., and Lunt, P. 301
Weber, M. 63
  *The Protestant Ethic and the Spirit of Capitalism* 4–5, 12
Weir, J. S. 209
White, H. C. 305
White, J.: *Rothschild Buildings* 131
Wilson, Harold 206
Woburn Abbey 135
women:
  in agricultural communities 101–2
  broken career paths 32
  class positioning of 32–3, 310, 318–19
  enjoyment of occupations 106
  knowledge of family members 22
  shadow careers 24, 103–5, 116–17
  social capital 214–15
  and transgenerational family influences 33
  transmission of occupations 22
  violence against 185, 189
Woolf, V.: *Orlando* 135
work histories 8–9
working class: urban attachment 154–6
World War One: unsettling effects 113–14
Wright, E. O. 303

Zemlianin family 238–43, 255 n., 256–7 n.